"I worked with Sam in Ben-Hur. He was a wonderful actor. He gave a wonderful performance. He was a gentle and marvelous man."

Charlton Heston, Actor, Academy Award Winner

Sam Jaffe was "a marvelous man who knew his craft and had great expertise in the theater. He gave me so many pointers; little pieces of technique and advice that helped my career. I owe him a debt of gratitude."

Milton Berle, Comedian, Emmy Award Winner

"I first met Sam as a child watching him in films like Gunga Din which were absolutely embedded on my mind. The performance will live forever. It had everything it should have, courage and humility. Whatever came from Sam was so good, so pure ... You see the humanity, the kindness, the craft. You see the greatness of being an actor. Actors do reflect civilization's humanity. Sam reflected all those wonderful things about living, in every part he ever did. "

Julie Harris, Actor, Tony and Emmy Award Winner

"When you look into Sam's face, there's something going on there all the time. That's a great actor. There's something in the eyes that holds you ... a mysterious quality."

Ray Bradbury, 20th Century Writer, Pulitzer Prize Winner

*for my dear Patricia,
a shining light in
my sphere, a master in
the Theatre of Life, and a
joy (in general :))*

Sam Jaffe

An Actor of
Character

*I Love you,
Aeleen Lomance
March 2014*

Other Books by Arleen Lorrance

Facing Cancer Without Fear

The Theatre of Life

The Love Principles

The Two

Images

India Through Eyes of Love

Born of Love

The Love Project Way
(with Diane Kennedy Pike)

Why Me? How to Heal What's Hurting You

Musings for Meditation

Buddha From Brooklyn

Channeling Love Energy
(with Diane Kennedy Pike)

The Love Project

Sam Jaffe
An Actor of
Character

By Arleen Lorrance

A Teleos Imprint Book
LP Publications ~ Scottsdale, AZ

 *A Teleos Imprint Book*

Published by LP Publications
7439 E Beryl Avenue
Scottsdale, AZ 85258-1020

The Teleos Institute World Wide Web site address is
http://www.teleosinstitute.com

Library of Congress Cataloguing-in-Publication Data

Lorrance, Arleen, 1939-
  Sam Jaffe : an actor of character / by Arleen Lorrance.
    -- First edition.
      pages cm
  "A Teleos Imprint Book" -- T.P. verso.
  ISBN 978-0-916192-57-0 (alk. paper)
1. Jaffe, Sam, 1891-1984. 2. Actors--United States --
Biography. I. Title.
  PN2287.J2853L67 2013
  791.4302'8092--dc23
  [B]

                                    2013040913

First edition: December, 2013
Printed in the United States of America

Cover photograph by William Gottlieb, used with his permission.
All other photographs are from Bettye Jaffe's private collection.
Book and cover design by Diane Kennedy Pike.

I dedicate this book to

Bettye Ackerman Jaffe

without whose support I could not have written it. Bettye introduced me to Sam's many friends, helped set up interviews, gave me access to photographs, and proofread the manuscript. My only regret is that she is not alive to see this published book.

Contents

A Tribute by John Huston

At the age of 17, I was given a part in *Ruint* at the Provincetown Playhouse in Greenwich Village. The play, by Hatcher Hughes, was about mountain people and called for deep southern accents of which I had none. I decided at the first rehearsal to imitate the one actor who was the real thing. He was a rather skinny young man with reddish hair that stood away from his head like a dandelion's in fall. It was absolutely the right choice even though it turned out that he was born on the lower east side of New York and was named

Sam Jaffe.

We quickly became friends and remained so through a lifetime — or should I say our two lifetimes. He was older than I but we had a number of interests in common. I hadn't known any others who had read the Russian novelists, could discuss the origin of species, admired H. L. Mencken, and loved prize fighting. I went on to discover he composed music, was an accomplished pianist of concert ability, a mathematician, and a strict vegetarian. He was also, I believed, a virgin.

There is some danger, I realize, of my making a little tin God of him. Well, there's nothing I can do about that. I can only add to the risk by declaring him to be one of the wittiest men I've ever listened to; wit that flashed and shimmered, and changed accents mid-sentence like quicksilver. Only once did I hear it turned against anyone, an anti-Semite who made the mistake of not knowing the man to whom he was speaking was a Jew. Sam, in rapid strokes, reduced him to mute ignominy. I am sure that thereafter he never had a clear opinion on any subject. There would always be an accompanying doubt. But except for that single instance, Sam's humor was for the delight of his friends such as gathered in the Village at Lou and Emily Paley's. Their place became a haven for the likes of George and Ira Gershwin.

Sam had a great influence on my life. Much of what I became is traceable to Sam. A young woman I knew had a marionette show. Her audiences were children and she put on fairy tales. As she wasn't doing very well, I suggested her taking a new tack: a show for grown-ups. I volunteered to write it. I was working on a playlet, *Frankie and Johnnie*, modeling the heads of the characters and painting miniature sets. It had a first night at the Paley's. It was surprisingly moving. It evoked the shedding of tears. Sam, who had attended several rehearsals, played his original music on the piano. George Gershwin was present and went about putting on a dinner party at his new penthouse on Riverside Drive as a showing for *Frankie and Johnnie*. George improvised this time and I heard Sam's theme again in George's variations.

In attendance was Frank Adams and he gave the performance his entire famous column in the *New York Times*, devoting the piece to the puppets. Before the week was out, the show was booked solidly for a month and I had signed a contract for the publication of a *Frankie and Johnnie* book. Today the book is a collector's item. It was my first tentative success at anything other than a few four-round bouts and it was all thanks to Sam. He'd started the ball rolling.

This was also true of my coming to Hollywood. Herman Shumlin was producing the New York theater production of *Grand Hotel*. Shumlin was trying to choose a director and Sam, without telling me, had me meet him. Sam had me read the manuscript and then repeat some thoughts I'd had on it. Sam was to play a role in the show.

I made a few suggestions — none really earthshaking. He repeated them to Shumlin who asked that I come to his office. The meeting was eventful. Shumlin unfolded his plans for the production. It was apparent that he'd assembled a brilliant cast. He was going to have a hit on his hands. All that was lacking was the director. I asked him why he didn't take that on himself and after a long searching look at Sam and me he said he'd take it under consideration. When I left Herman's office, we were on first name terms. Sam told me his idea was for me to direct the play and that in recommending Herman to himself I had foiled his secret intention. Sam thought something might click between Shumlin and me and he offered me the chance. I'd done nothing whatever besides putting on a marionette show to support Sam's idea.

Eventually, Sam too came to Hollywood. He prospered with *Gunga Din*. My own life went on the rocks. I made many mistakes and found myself divorced. Sam did everything in his power to get me floating again, arranging meetings with moguls without my knowing it.

Although I am not of any accredited religion, I do believe in luck. I was in a streak of bad luck. It could well be argued I'd brought it on myself, but looking back from my present view, my mistakes hardly warranted the series of destructive incidents that followed. Life suddenly turned vengeful. It's a canon of the gambler's faith that there is no getting around bad luck. You have simply to hang on, trying to survive until it passes. I chose to leave the scene of my disasters and go to Europe. Sure enough, misfortune dogged me there for well over a year. At the end I was penniless, sleeping on the embankment and singing country songs on Kings Row for what people in windows would throw down to me. Then my luck changed.

It took me two years to get back to Hollywood and this time I couldn't put a foot wrong. What I wrote gained instant appreciation. Presently, I became a director and at long last I had Sam in a film, *The Asphalt Jungle*, for which he received the prestigious Cannes Film Award. Nothing has ever given me greater satisfaction. In the history of our friendship, it was the first time I'd ever done Sam a service, a fact, I can assure you, which never occurred to him.

Not long after, I went to live in Europe. Except for occasional visits, I was away for 20 years. Sam was blacklisted during this most costly time, but the accusations didn't stand up. I doubt if Sam ever did his accusers the honor of denying the charge.

He was the most truly virtuous man I ever knew. I cannot imagine him committing an evil act, even unconsciously. On the other hand, his good deeds, acts of generosity, kindness, nobility, courage, and sacrifices were an unremitting flow.

I've met with a number of so-called living legends in my time. I don't know of any who holds a candle to Sam.

[This was written just before John Huston's death. It is presented in its unfinished state.]

Introduction

Ours is not an age in which idealism thrives. Violence and abuse overshadow compassion and caring. Thus it is easy for us to become cynical, to suffer a loss of faith. When good persons appear in our midst, we tend toward one of two responses. Either we make them into heroes and saints who are beyond the potential of the rest of us or we question their sincerity and look for skeletons in their closets. If we praise them, we revere them and hold them beyond reproach, thus dehumanizing them. If we doubt them, we hunger to know their tragic flaws. We demand the exposure of the dark side of any sweet nature because when we reduce a person's character to its lowest common denominator, we feel more comfortable. It is easier to look great people in the eye when they are on their knees.

Sam Jaffe was revered. When he was just eight years old, he made a commitment to being and doing "good." He devoted his life to that commitment. Perhaps that is why his close friend Zero Mostel called Jaffe "Saint Sam." I conducted over one hundred fifty interviews with family, friends, and prominent theatrical personalities. The frequency with which individuals, in their glowing recollection of Sam Jaffe, spontaneously used the word saint, or great rabbi, or seer, was startling. One even called him a national treasure.

Jack Lemmon had the pleasure of working with Sam Jaffe in the play *Idiot's Delight* in Los Angeles. He affirmed what many said, that Sam was the same in life as he appeared in screen roles. All the best qualities in his intelligent, endearing, and spiritual roles were equally present in the man in his daily interactions with human beings. The discovery did not, in Lemmon's experience, represent the norm among actors. While Lemmon's observation was generally true, it was not always true. All of Jaffe's best qualities were not always present. Therein rests the difference between a saint and a person aspiring to goodness.

Sam Jaffe was no saint. He was a very earthy man who alternated between the high lama and an immovable object! He was unforgiving toward some members of his family who disappointed him, and he shut them out of his life. He was stubborn and impatient. He could be sharp of tongue and even rude. Yet people tended to see only the good when they were with him. Was it that they didn't want to see his dark side? Was it that Jaffe, himself, revealed only what would correspond to the image that was held of him? Or was it that because Jaffe continued his quest for goodness, that was the side of him that was most communicated to others? Certainly, the reverse is true. When individuals are known as "bad," that is what predominates in their personalities. If they do something good, it is seen as an anomaly, if it is acknowledged at all.

Sam Jaffe was an instantly recognizable personality. He had a memorable face, a kindly essence, and penetrating eyes. His brow held creases of wisdom; his mouth curved to express compassion. His wiry, silver hair adorned his head like a halo. For movie and television buffs, his unique countenance would immediately call to mind the ages and stages of man that he had created and embodied. He was recognized as Gunga Din and Dr. Zorba, the master criminal in *The Asphalt Jungle* and the timeless, unforgettable high lama in *Lost Horizon*.

Jaffe's fans had the feeling that they knew the man personally, as if as a friend or relative. So true was this that people would approach him on his solitary walks around Beverly Hills and pour out their troubles, seeking the words of advice and kindness that were always forthcoming. They left having made a friend, rather than being in awe of a screen star. There was something about this man that set him apart from the ordinary, yet made us all feel that he belonged to each of us.

Sam Jaffe was simultaneously an intellectual and a jokester. Zero Mostel remembered when he was a house guest of Jaffe: "Sam is very fastidious. I love to read in the bathtub. One day, after I had been in the tub for an hour, Sam came in and said, `Zero, that water must be ice cold.' So I got out, went to his closet, put on his overcoat and got back in the tub. Sam was delighted. He got me a hat and muffler."

Jaffe was a witty man who thought quickly on his feet. There was evidence of this the day he and his wife, Bettye, went to an early showing of the film *Séance on a Wet Afternoon*. As they stood at the box office waiting for it to open at 6:00 p.m., a man rushed up and said nervously, "Let me in ahead please. I have a compulsion to be first in line." Sam stood his ground. Then, out of his vast experience with unusual behavior gained on the Ben Casey TV series, he said, softly, "Strange as it may seem, I have the same compulsion."

One of Jaffe's weak points was that, except for his wife and his sisters, he could not and would not receive anything from anyone. He depended on Bettye almost exclusively to satisfy his needs. Though she never experienced it this way, those close to Bettye felt that Sam used her, that he made excessive demands on her and that he focused primarily on his own needs. Sam admitted that he was a burden to Bettye, and she confessed that her greatest sin was that she worshipped him. Most people who knew them proclaimed that they had the perfect Hollywood marriage, but there are questions about co-dependence and inequity which will be explored as the story of their love unfolds.

Sam wouldn't let others pay dinner bills or carry his bags. He occupied the seat of generosity and he sometimes carried it to extremes. During a rehearsal of a Broadway show, a company member spied a hobo rummaging through the belongings of the cast. After chasing him away, he informed the rest of the company so that they could check to make sure nothing was missing. Sam Jaffe noted that his coat had blood on it. Rather than be concerned about the stain or that something else might be missing, Sam was immediately concerned about the hobo. He rushed out into the cold in search of the man, found him, and gave him his coat and some money, urging him to see a doctor. Back at the theater, the other cast members remained concerned about their personal belongings.

Sam Jaffe was a man whose honor superseded his need for success. He never tried to save his own skin during the pressured times of the McCarthy era. Though many innuendoes were shot from the bows of unscrupulous accusers, he came away unscarred. He bristled in the face of self-serving betrayal and turned his back on those who practiced it.

Multilingual and conversant in widely varied fields, he was a mathematician and a musician. He read avidly, daily. In his late eighties he studied fresh subjects as if preparing for whatever new career might appear when he turned 100! He remained keen of heart, spirit and mind until the day he died. Two days before his demise, he responded to his nurse's proclamation that he was fantastic with a self-assessment that was congruent with the long life he had lived. "Yes," he said. "Fantastic. Elastic. Iconoclastic."

Sam Jaffe led a commendable, committed life, filled with integrity. Repeatedly throughout his 93 years, he stood with virtue, honesty, and dignity in the face of adverse worldly conditions. He was more than a character actor; he was an actor of character. His life is important because he proved it was possible to embody wisdom and hold fast to principles under any circumstances. By example, he illustrates that one can be pure of motive and survive in the harshest world. His life gave hope that earth could become the Shangri-La of the movies.

When I was a 15-year-old drama student at the High School of Performing Arts, I sat in a hushed auditorium watching the movie *Lost Horizon*, made two years before I was born. I was awe-struck. Something stirred deep in my cosmic memory. The characters endured a fierce blizzard until they found a minuscule passageway in the mountains. They passed into a land of eternal peace where fire had at last been harnessed to benefit humanity.

Shangri-La exists, I believe, not as an actual place hidden in shadowy Himalayan peaks, but in finer frequencies of consciousness. These heights call to each of us as we evolve from raw survival, through ensuing greed, to simple gratitude, and on to living saintliness. The high lama of *Lost Horizon*, nearly transparent in his purity of soul, embodied this spiritual journey in his very being, emitting a translucent light to warm his world. He had merged himself with goodness.

Was he only a fictional character? Is such a world possible for all of us? Can we struggle through the blinding snow storms of our own illusions to find that small opening to consciousness? Can we allow ourselves to take our place in the line of light bearers? How do we make the passage from the Hades of our daily world of hunger, strife and war-mongering? How do we live out within ourselves, and thus collectively establish on earth, God's will, Shangri-La?

The high lama became my symbol, a symbol of the voice with which I called myself beyond ego to world service.

As an adolescent, not yet disillusioned with human nature, I believed the high lama to be real and that we all had the potential to be as he was. When Ronald Coleman's character made his trek back through blinding snow and blustery wind to take his place on the seat of embodied wisdom, I wept with an inner knowing. All of us would one day turn from the dense magnetic pull of personality distractions and move to the heights of self where the music of the spheres sounds continuously.

By the next day, entangled in teenage desires, caught in ego traps, I again shut down in self-protection. But the symbol of the high lama remained. During the next decade, I wondered what it was like for actor Sam Jaffe to create a character for the screen of such magnitude as the high lama. What did he tap in himself? Did he believe that such a man could exist? He must have, else how could he have affected me so profoundly with his portrayal?

At age 33, I met Sam Jaffe. He and his lovely wife Bettye entered the living room I shared with Diane Kennedy Pike, and the four of us became fast friends in an instant. He was, at once, delicate and powerful, pixyish and wise, simple and brilliant, stubborn and probing. He said hello, and I loved him. Over the next twelve years, until his death on March 24, 1984, there were many meetings combining camaraderie with commiseration over world events.

Not long before his death at age 93, Jaffe was asked what life had taught him. "A very simple and yet profound lesson," he said. "I'm just a grain of sand on the beach of the universe. So it would be foolish for me to take myself too seriously. There are many aims I have failed to achieve, but there's one thing in my life in which I can take pride: the friends I have made."

Sam Jaffe made important contributions with his life, but when I asked if I could write a book about him, he declined. He waved the suggestion away with his graceful hand, saying, "Write about someone important."

Sam Jaffe's life was important. He improved the lot of actors through his work on the Council of Actors' Equity Association and he created the Equity Library Theatre which launched countless stars. Jaffe was a model of how to stand up for convictions. He was a man who kept reaching beyond his grasp. In that sense he was a great man. He alluded to many failures in his life. Perhaps his greatest struggle was in maintaining his commitment to goodness. His weaknesses got in his way and yet he persisted. He was a compassionate man who cared. His story, his struggle, is well worth telling.

Whether we revere him or reduce him to his knees, the truth about Sam Jaffe was reflected in his deeds and actions. These were consistently worthy of mention. Perhaps that is why everyone who knew Jaffe well said of this unimposing man who played the title role in the film by the same name, "You're a better man than I am, Gunga Din."

— *Arleen Lorrance*
Scottsdale, AZ

Sam Jaffe

An Actor of Character

****

"On July 5, 1977, between the Award to the Best Actress and Actor and the Award to the Best Play, a special Tony Award was presented to the Equity Library Theatre.

"In keeping with the evening's theme of 'survival' of theater, E.L.T. was recognized for its 34 years of service to our art and industry. Presenter Jane Alexander noted that 'Since 1943, E.L.T. has produced over 600 plays and performed before more than 750,000 people. They create new audiences for the professional theater by developing a love of our art among those who cannot afford to pay regular admission prices. And the reason it is appropriate in this spot? This showcase has been a major incubator of creative talent — over 11,000 theater artists have gotten their start at Equity Library Theatre and many have gone forward to success as actors, directors, and designers.'"

— Equity Magazine, July 1977

****

It was Sam Jaffe who co-founded the Equity Library Theatre in 1943. Of all his accomplishments, he regarded this as his greatest. To honor this fine artistic institution and to show gratitude to Sam Jaffe as its initiator, each chapter of this book will begin with quotations from actors and directors who benefited from E.L.T.

****

RICHARD KILEY

The Trojan Women, 1947, *The Corn is Green,* 1953

"The first thing I ever did on the stage in New York was Poseidon in The Trojan Women. *Poseidon has one marvelous speech, one scene, and then he's not seen again, but it was a good moment. I was not a member of Equity but the great thing was that they did allow a certain percentage of non-Equity people to get a shot at these roles. In that first production, my agent, Steven Draper, who was my agent for 38 years, saw me and I never changed agents until he died.*

"I remember the working conditions in E.L.T. vividly. I was fresh from Chicago and from the Navy. I had about $600 and came to New York on speculation. It was very scary. Finally I landed this thing at Equity Library Theatre, the Hudson Street branch. The little auditorium was in the basement and I think we dressed in the coal bin or

near it. A scanty sheet strung up on a string separated the dressing room of the men and women. It would occasionally whisk open and I would get views of ladies in various stages of disarray. It made it very nerve-racking for me to keep my mind on what the hell I was trying to accomplish on stage. It was primitive. Let's put it that way.

"As to costume and make-up, I was supposed to be God of the Sea. It ended up I came out in a pair of green jockey shorts with sea weed sewn on them and my body painted some God damn gold or something. And that was the extent of my costume. I think I supplied my own athletic supporter because I was a little nervous.

"I remember years later when Sam and I did a Night Gallery together for Rod Serling. The pilot for it was in three parts. I was in one. Joan Crawford was in another. By the way, that was the debut of Steven Spielberg as a director. The third one was Roddy McDowall and Ossie Davis. I played a reprehensible character, a kind of Nazi on the run in South America somewhere. Sam played a lovely, sweet guy who knew who I was, who recognized me as being a beast. We had a scene in an alley where I remember he came out and threatened me and I grabbed him and strangled him. I remember saying, 'It's too hard for me to do this, Sam, because I owe so much to you and I've admired you so much throughout the years.' He was a dear man. I'm so glad I got to work with him finally, even under such bizarre circumstances.

"E.L.T. was a marvelously conceived and appropriate tool for the actor. I remember seeing Sam. He came to every production, at least then. We were thrilled whenever he would come. It was a marvelously unselfish thing. He was, even then, a pretty damn big Hollywood star, a very big name. He was of that group, that bunch of actors that came out of the depression and had that wonderful kind of camaraderie. That was the wonderful thing about him and about that theater and that era. It was the time of the Group [Theatre], wonderfully homogenized people who worked superbly well together and thought of other people. Now we find ourselves worrying about billing and all that crap. In those days, Sam and others were considerate and enthusiastic. Equity Library Theatre was a wonderful contribution."

****

Fame and Fortune

The year was 1961. It represented a major turning point for Sam Jaffe and his beautiful young wife, Bettye Ackerman. Hired to play Dr. Zorba and Dr. Maggie Graham on the *Ben Casey* series, the two became regular guests in thousands of living rooms across the United States. The show's popularity was unequaled then, and Sam Jaffe and Bettye Ackerman suddenly became television stars.

The Ben Casey series represented the beginning of Sam Jaffe's second big career as an actor. He had been unable to work for almost seven years due to the 1950's blacklist. Then, thanks to the great effort of his friend, director Fielder Cook, Sam had won a role in a *Playhouse 90* television show with Lee Strasberg and Eddie Albert. As a result, a new field of expression suddenly promised him a future.

Sam had worried about being fired throughout the filming of the *Playhouse 90* show because the blacklist still hung over his head. There was so much fear present in his artistic life; it is a wonder Sam was able to mobilize his creativity. The blacklist had battered him physically, mentally and emotionally.

Sam had been inching his way to a comeback for several years. During the last two of those years, James Moser, a superb writer, craftsman and technician with some 43 years of experience in radio, television and movies, had been preparing a new television series. He had begun his television career writing 232 episodes of *Dragnet*. He had wearied of the negativity, the downbeat nature, of crime dramas and gravitated toward the field of medicine because it offered hope and promise. When doctors help patients to end their pain, new life follows.

Sam Jaffe's life had been an illustration of that theme. He had suffered great pain when his father deserted his family and then had found new life when he went to live with his Aunt Ray. When his suffering over the loss of his young wife Lillian began to diminish, profound new love emerged with Bettye Ackerman. As the tragedy of the McCarthy era ended, opportunities opened again for Sam as a creative artist. It almost seemed Jaffe's personal history destined him to play a part in the *Ben Casey* series in which Moser intended to highlight hope.

Jim Moser's highly successful show, *Medic*, through Bing Crosby Enterprises, had earned him an ironclad contract with ABC. He had a guarantee of over $125,000 to shoot the pilot of his new venture, to be called *Medicine Men*. Moser also received the latitude to cast anyone he wanted in the new series.

During the two years he was developing the show, Moser did research in a major hospital to study the medical field the series would spotlight. One day, in a neurosurgical lab, he heard a resident taking an intern to task. He knew he had found his prototype for the central character whose name became the revised title — a hardnosed, idealistic young doctor, Ben Casey. The prototype, Dr. Allan Warner, was hired as technical adviser for the show. Warner was so insistent on authenticity that when they built the set, they put in an operating room equipped for actual operations. It contained $25,000 worth of instruments.

By a stroke of good luck for Sam Jaffe's career, Moser took his script to director Fielder Cook, the very man who had helped Jaffe re-enter the ranks of working actors. Although Cook had done some live television, a film for United Artists and a play on Broadway, he had never done a television pilot. But he, like Sam, needed to make some money. The beautifully written script drew his attention and he agreed to direct the pilot.

Even though Jaffe desperately needed to raise his career from the dead, it may surprise readers to learn that he did not readily jump at the opportunity to star in a television series. It took indefatigable coaxing by Howard Koch, Hollywood producer and director for over 50 years and a co-writer of *Casablanca*. He headed Paramount Studios in the 1960's, and became President of the Motion Picture Academy in the 1970's. At the time Jim Moser was developing his new series, Koch was working as Frank Sinatra's production man. When Koch consented to producing the *Ben Casey* pilot, Sam Jaffe kept going through his head. Koch had worked as assistant director on the film *Asphalt Jungle*.

From Koch's viewpoint, Jaffe was the only one for the role of the older doctor, and he persuaded Moser to let him try to get him. Koch was told that Jaffe would never go for the idea because he was a died-in-the-wool New Yorker. Koch was not deterred. He called Sam at home, told him who he was, and announced that he was going to change his life.

Howard Koch lured Jaffe with visions of being able to buy a house in Beverly Hills with a swimming pool. He told him if he played this part he would surely have a long-run TV show. If Koch had been talking to just about any other actor, especially one whose career had been shattered by the blacklist, the enticements might have served to dazzle him. However, Sam Jaffe was not easily seduced. His reply was that he didn't like doing pilots or television unless it had some kind of meat to it. Koch rushed to confirm that this was definitely a show that Sam could get his teeth into. He appealed to the mentor side of Sam telling him how Zorba brings this young doctor along to become a great doctor. Then Koch threw in the one proclamation that did indeed turn out to be true. He told Jaffe that he would be identified as Dr. Zorba for the rest of his life!

Interestingly enough, the original name of the

character was Rosenthal, not Zorba. ABC demanded the name change because of their concern that the series would be too Jewish in its tone. Ironically, it didn't seem to matter to ABC that Sam Jaffe was being considered for the role, even though he was one of the most Semitic actors in the country.

In spite of everything Koch said, Jaffe turned *Ben Casey* down several times. He truly needed the work. He needed the career boost after the long blacklist layoff. But he didn't want to do a television series for fear of being reduced to playing one part.

For a week, Howard Koch called Sam Jaffe every night and sent a wire every morning. Finally Sam said, "I'll do the pilot. You charmed me into it." Then he said to Bettye, "Well, I've just put the bars up." He did not anticipate that television would lead to anything but an artistic dead end.

Strongly influencing Sam's decision to do the series was his need to earn a weekly pay check. He felt that an actor had to go where the work was. Though it wasn't his preference, he could see television was beginning to surpass theater and even film as a work medium.

Bettye, like Sam, felt that Sam was not the type of actor to do a TV series and she discouraged him. She thought it would be better for him to do parts of a different kind — movies and television, but not a continuing role. Moreover, she was studying with Stella Adler at the time and didn't want to leave the class to go to California with Sam to do the pilot. At the last minute, she decided to accompany him because, as she put it, she didn't want to risk his finding out that he could do without her.

During Jaffe's acceptance phone conversation with Koch, Sam asked if there was any part his wife could play. He told Koch all about Bettye. Koch told him there was a nurse, and that he could probably get out of the deal they had made with another actress. He told Sam that he would talk the director into accepting her. However as it turned out, Bettye won the leading role through an audition.

Jim Moser saw Jaffe as one of the heavyweights among actors, for he remembered Sam's superb portrayals in *Gunga Din* and *Lost Horizon*. He was not disappointed. During the pilot, Moser had written a long, page-and-a-half speech for Zorba. He wondered how Sam was going to get through that. Sam took the speech and did what he had done often throughout his career. He executed it perfectly on the very first take. When he finished, the crew applauded. That is a rare occurrence. It was a tough speech, but Jaffe was solid. Moser could count on him. He could throw anything at Sam and know that he was professional enough to field it in an instant.

Moser had taken it upon himself to cast the lead because Fielder Cook was busy working on a play. He chose Vince Edwards, a 30-year-old veteran of both live and filmed TV. He had appeared in practically every live drama telecast from New York in the previous decade. Born in Brooklyn, New York, he was a former college swimming star at Ohio State who, in the early 1950's, had studied at New York's American Academy of Dramatic Arts. Moser wanted Edwards because he thought he *was* the character.

Besides Edwards, Moser had cast the female anesthesiologist. He hired a sexy, busty woman to spice up a rather stringent show. Others remember that she wasn't much of an actress. She gave an abominable first reading. She wore a short skirt, doubled her knees up under her, lit up a cigarette, and blew the smoke all around without asking people if they minded.

Cook immediately saw that the casting of the woman would never work, and he had only four days to find another. He had to find someone who would agree to do a series for five years. This was not easy.

Koch agreed with Cook about recasting the woman but told him that the shooting had to start. He could have the replacement if he could find her.

With Sam in place, Cook began reading every actress he thought could possibly play it. In the midst of racing around in the casting process, Cook was working with Jaffe to develop Dr. Zorba into an elegant man. Cook had flown in his tailor from London to make Zorba's clothes. Sam was having his suit fitted, and he asked Cook to come and see it.

The next part of the story plays out like every cliché tale of being discovered in Hollywood. If it weren't true, it would seem trumped up.

As Sam's "chauffeur," Bettye had driven him to the costumer. Sam waited for Fielder Cook for more than an hour. The wait angered him and he was preparing to leave when Cook bounded in the door.

Cook had been frantically involved in trying to cast the anesthetist. That was why he was late. He finally arrived with the garment cutter. When Fielder looked at Bettye, his eyes lit up like an electric sign.

Cook had met her before. He had seen her work in a Swedish movie and knew her to be a fine actress and a beautiful person. Seeing her sitting there reading, he was absolutely stunned. He got a copy of the script and told Bettye to go with him because he wanted to try something.

Bettye was more than willing, wondering what he had in mind. She honestly thought he wanted her to run an errand because that day she was being the chauffeur. He said, "I want you to read for the part of Maggie Graham."

She protested that she wasn't dressed. And she wasn't. She was wearing slacks and a sloppy shirt and had on no make-up. Cook didn't care. He grabbed her by one hand. The cutter grabbed her by the other. Leaving Sam in his BVD's, they rushed over to the office.

Sam lost no time in putting on his pants and hurrying off to join them. He paced like an expectant father while he waited outside the office.

Fielder handed Bettye a script and told her to take 20 minutes to review the text. He wanted her to do a cold reading for Howard Koch. His encouragement, that she not have a heart attack and that she not panic, couldn't have been very comforting. But the unexpected request might have helped to effectively charge Bettye with enough adrenalin to win Koch's heart. Fielder assured Bettye that she could play the role and that he couldn't imagine anyone saying no to her.

Bettye read through the scene quickly. Fielder Cook did the reading with her for Moser and Koch. When Bettye finished reading with Fielder, Jim Moser jumped up, and said, "Providence sent you." Then he kissed her.

They wanted to know what film work she had done. She told them that she had just finished *Face of Fire*, a film in Sweden. She left her number, but with the wrong secretary, so they weren't able to contact her that afternoon.

Jim Moser felt that Fielder Cook hit the jackpot when he found Bettye Ackerman. He agreed that they had to hire her and fire the other actress. The firing was awkward, because the actress had had the part for fourteen hours. But as soon as he had seen Bettye, he knew that she was right. Howard Koch agreed.

When Bettye got back to the hotel that night, she discovered that they had been calling all day. She returned the call and spoke with Mr. Koch. He told her, "We love you and we want you for the series."

What Bettye said next to Howard Koch revealed the sense of fairness with which Bettye lived her life. It was so atypical of a Hollywood response that Koch has never forgotten it. "I've been thinking about it," she said, "and I have decided not to take the part because I don't want somebody else's job. I don't want to take a part away from somebody."

All hell broke loose. Koch told Bettye it was none of her business. She was perfect for the part. The agreement with the other actress had nothing to do with her.

That was the end of Bettye's objections. She accepted the part and began her research at the Los Angeles County Hospital. Fielder Cook offered Bettye the mock threat that if she changed anything from that initial reading with him, he would kill her!

Work began on the pilot with the completion of casting. Almost immediately, the publication called *Red Star Over Hollywood* tried to get rid of Sam. Fortunately the producer, Matthew Rapf, had a blacklisted brother. The first day Sam worked, *Red Star* put their paper on Matt's desk. They had underscored Jaffe's name. Instead of being influenced to fire Jaffe, Matt simply turned it over to Sam so that he could know of the effort, and that it was of no avail. The power of red-hunters was fading.

The show sold to the ABC network on the last day of the season.

Two medical shows debuted during the fall television season of 1961. Cecil Smith compared the two in a column in the *Los Angeles Times*, Nov. 20, 1961: *Dr. Kildare* "... is pure and simple fictional entertainment — nothing more. ... *Casey*, however, has the very stench of a hospital woven in the celluloid." Smith talked of Casey as a portrait of a scowling, efficient, dedicated man of healing. The show was much more substantive than *Kildare* because it contained the dark, frenzied throb of hospital life. Ben Casey could be nastier than an open wound.

Smith was little drawn to the indulgent guide that Gillespie was to Kildare. He preferred the counterbalance between Casey, the contemporary man of medicine, and Zorba, jabbing and prodding the younger hothead.

It was by no accident that the show had such a feeling of authenticity. The care that went into its devel-

opment served as a model for all those who were preparing scripts or programs for television. Authenticity
and accuracy were the mainstays. While they sometimes
put the production behind schedule, Moser would never
sacrifice medical standards or methods to budget demands.

Appropriately, this was also true of how Sam Jaffe
lived the whole of his life.

Ben Casey was primarily a series of credible adult
stories about people in medicine. The stories dealt with
principal characters and their problems, both personal
and professional. It focused on their patients, and their
day-to-day living, in a 4,000-bed medical arena packed
with emotion, action, laughter and tragedy. It focused on
important human problems.

Moser wanted to take a fair but scrupulously honest look at men of medicine in training: at the older
professional men who had gone before them, and the
younger men who would soon follow in their stead.

The audience could identify with the characters
and could embrace them as real people in their own lives.
This was how Sam Jaffe became "a doctor" to thousands
of viewers who watched him week after week. There was
an examination of the characters on the show for their
faults and their virtues, their loves and hates, skills and
ambitions, strengths and weaknesses.

Ben Casey was the first series for Vince Edwards
and for Sam Jaffe. Although Sam had resisted doing a
television series initially, he did find one advantage it had
over a long-run play: "You're doing the same character
in each one, but the situations are different — you're not
chewing the same cud week in and week out." There was
a chance for the character to develop without the constant repetition of lines as happens during the long run
of a play.

Although he was partial to the stage, the differences in technique required by TV intrigued Sam. "Just as a painter needs to be familiar with charcoal and watercolors, an actor should be familiar with the various mediums. They should be part of his stock in trade," he commented.

For television close-ups, Sam learned that gestures had to be very small, with no exaggeration. He had to learn economy of delivery.

In truth, some critics did criticize Jaffe for overacting. Sam also had to be careful while enacting precise details of surgical procedure. They couldn't afford to have the American Medical Association condemn something as incorrect. Sam said, "Our slogan is: The AMA can say anything it wants to about socialized medicine, but not about *Ben Casey.*"

Howard Koch had told Sam Jaffe the truth. The Jaffes got their Beverly Hills home and their swimming pool. It was only long after the show was a success from every point of view, including jump-starting many careers, among them the careers of Telly Savalas and Robert Redford, that Koch admitted he had given Jaffe a sales pitch. He had believed the pitch, but he hadn't been sure just how much he believed it.

The pilot for *Ben Casey* had been one of the first ever done. The cost had been $150,000. Today it would be $2.5 million.

Koch was right about the series in every way. It continued for five years, just as he had predicted. And he was very right about Jaffe. Sam used to be called Gunga Din when he went out in public. As a result of *Ben Casey*, he became Dr. Zorba. Koch said, "Doing Zorba changed Sam's life. He became known throughout the world. It's still playing all over the world. Actors and actresses never die. You look up at the screen and they are still alive."

In the beginning, the role was a challenge to Sam. It required considerable preparation. He had to learn the medical phrases and how to handle the instruments. Dr. Allan Warner taught him the techniques.

So carefully did Sam prepare for his role that Dr. Warner joked that they wouldn't need him on the show in three months because Jaffe would know all the answers by then. Others thought Jaffe would probably be operating at the County Hospital before long.

Sam's work on his role included recalling all the good doctors he had known. He remembered that the first thing they did was to put the patient at ease before getting on with the examination.

Next, he asked questions of his role. For example, what was his relationship to Ben Casey in this series? He saw it as fatherly, and he worked with embodying that image. He described this work as a conscious process. The unconscious work came next, and then the application of technique to convey the creation.

The major element missing for Sam in television acting was having the satisfaction of performing before an audience. He also experienced too little real character development. There was no chance, as there is on stage, to build on past performances because the material kept changing. While this had been stimulating at the beginning, Sam later missed having the opportunity to expand on the deeper meaning of a stable script.

As a television actor, his tasks were more technical than artistic. For example, he needed to remember precisely how he played a line when the camera was full on him. He would need to repeat the exact delivery, down to the last twitch, when the camera included him from another angle and focused on the other actors in the scene. The film and sound snatches had to fit together as if played live. This aspect of the work was never as interesting to Sam as the development of a stage role.

Ben Casey became an instant and enormous success. Among other reasons, Sam thought it was because "it's a rebellion against the bang-bang. It's a reaction against TV's supposed wasteland. The feeling is it is educational." This is an interesting observation because it was Jim Moser's reason for bringing a medical show in to balance the focus of his *Dragnet* years.

Hailed by reviewers and the public, *Ben Casey* became the new season's number one hit show. In the Home Testing Institute's TVQ survey, *Ben Casey* scored first place over all network shows. The Nielsen Service scored *Ben Casey* with the highest rating of all Monday night programs.

Many well-known directors got their start on the *Ben Casey* show. A case in point is Leo Penn. Inadvertently, Sam Jaffe was partially responsible for the fact that Penn became a director.

Penn had known Jaffe in New York. They were mutual friends of actor and union leader Philip Loeb. After the blacklist period, Penn returned to California to try to work again. He decided he didn't want to be an actor any longer. He called a friend who was directing a *Ben Casey* episode and got permission to come on the set.

It was the first day of shooting and Penn walked in on a tirade in progress. It was from a very unlikely source, Sam Jaffe. Not given to tirades, Sam was shouting about the fact that nobody could possibly say the lines he was to read. "These lines are not human," Sam roared. "I defy you to find me an actor in the world who can say these lines. The scene makes no sense."

Medical shows deal with excessive technical terminology. There was conflict in the scene in question but it wasn't human conflict. It was very cerebral. There was no way a lay audience could understand the language that couched the scene. The writers had fallen in love with their new-found knowledge and they wanted to expose it. The only problem was, it made no sense, and Sam said so clearly.

Penn hadn't seen the script but once he did read

it, he saw that Sam was absolutely right. It was not play-
able. With no knowledge of what was going on, or what
went on before the particular scene in the script or after
it, Penn rewrote the scene and brought it to his friend
who was directing. He said, "I don't know if this helps,
but I do think Sam was right."

The director, Alex March, knew that Sam was right,
but he didn't know what to do about the scene. He liked
what Penn had written and read it to the producer who
told them immediately to shoot it.

In Penn's attempt to help his old friend Sam, he
ended up writing another scene, and rewriting a whole
script before the day was out. Penn had done previous
writing under another name during the blacklist.

The serendipity continued when they asked Penn
if he wanted to direct an episode. Giving due credit to
friendship and fate, Penn said, "If it hadn't been for Sam's
tirade, forget it." From then on, he saw much of Sam. He
directed 26 episodes of *Ben Casey.*

Leo Penn loved working with Sam. But the guest
stars received the best parts in the show. Sam didn't
have much opportunity for human exploration through
his character. He was there to dispense medical terms.

One particular show was written as a love story. For
a change, Jaffe wasn't dealing with the image of the elder
statesman of a hospital. He was dealing with moment to
moment behavior with another human being who was
not a patient. He was wonderful. As Penn watched Jaffe's
performance, he wondered why they couldn't write that
way for Sam all the time.

Leo Penn saw Jaffe as an actor of consummate
delight because of the clarity of his intelligence and his
whole demeanor as a human being: "He was an original.
I didn't know anybody else like him."

Working on a television series was a strenuous en-
deavor. The shooting occupied five days a week, from

eight in the morning until as late as 7:30 at night.

During breaks, Sam and Bettye returned to the dressing room they shared. Jaffe practiced discipline during these precious moments. He took the time to rest quietly, to read, to continue his study of languages. He had an insatiable appetite for knowledge. He would constantly use his time in a productive way. Often on breaks, he would have serious talks with Bettye.

One thing that was apparent to everyone on the set was that Sam and his wife Bettye had a very special relationship despite over 35 years of difference in their ages. They radiated love.

Bettye was Sam's chauffeur except for the days when their schedule was different. Then he would take the bus around 7:00 a.m. for the 18-minute ride to the Desilu Studio. Bettye's choices, both life-shaping and mundane, revolved around her love for Sam. As his chauffeur, she based her choice of car color, blue, on its being a dramatic background for Sam's grand head of hair. As his wife, she often turned down work that would take her away from him. This affected her career. Sam and his career always came first. Sam did not object to the adoration. To the contrary, he encouraged her focus on him. Neither of them turned their attention to the effect of this on Bettye. Instead, they savored working together and being together. In the context of *Ben Casey*, they received payment to do it.

Once it was clear that they had a hit on their hands, Sam and Bettye bought a modest, two-bedroom Beverly Hills house with a lush garden of tropical shrubs. It was at Bettye's insistence that they bought the place. They had looked around for six months. When they walked into the house they bought, they knew immediately that it was what they wanted. It had a swimming pool, just as Howard Koch had promised, and Bettye worked out in it every day.

Karl and Mona Malden had also moved to California in the sixties. He remembered clearly that Sam didn't want a house. New Yorkers lived in apartments! It was a challenge for Jaffe to come to terms with owning property. Once settled in the house, he loved it.

The Maldens and Jaffes saw much of each other. They had moved into different surroundings that no longer reminded them of the blacklist days and they began to have fun again.

When the Jaffes first made the move to California, they kept their apartment in New York for two years. Sam shook his head. "It took me a long time to adjust. It was the feeling that [we were] living on a *Saturday Evening Post* cover, you know? I was accustomed to opening the door and going out and [finding] people [walking in the streets]. [Life in Beverly Hills has] a different feeling. It is a different life entirely. Here everything is dark after dark." He chuckled. "It really is dark!"

He missed having people around him. It was strange for him to have to travel long distances to be with his friends. Compared to New York, he experienced Beverly Hills as a wilderness.

Little by little Sam got used to it, but he and Bettye returned to New York at every excuse, especially each time Zero Mostel was in a new play. It wasn't that Sam didn't like California. He found it truly beautiful. However, Sam was a confirmed city dweller, but real city! He jokingly complained, "I love to go walking. If you walk in Beverly Hills, the cops will pick you up."

Sam loved the movement and action of New York, not to mention that it was the home of theater. On the other hand, Sam didn't consider California the cultural desert other New Yorkers labeled it. The arts that were available pleased him, as did the first-rate restaurants, the art museums, and the great educational institutions such as UCLA, USC and Cal Tech.

By the second year of the Ben Casey series, Sam

and Bettye relinquished their apartment, but New York remained their first love. Sam summed it up this way. "New York is living — activity, élan, movement. Here it's more like retirement. It's beautiful and nice, but it hasn't got go."

Director Sidney Pollack also got a start on *Ben Casey.* Pollack found Sam excellent to work with, humorous and quiet, reserved and very professional. In the seven shows Pollack directed, he couldn't help but be aware that Jaffe "had to swallow something to do it."

Pollack's observation was valid. Sam was swallowing hard because he wasn't happy. After the very first year of the series, Sam tried to get out of his contract. It wasn't the show itself. Sam said, "The writers were good. They had something to say. It was a must for people on Monday because it told them something. It was a good series in that sense. But I didn't like the repetition of the same thing. When you do a role too long it puts calluses on your brain."

****

TOM BOSLEY

Within the Gates, 1952

"I had been in New York only two years. That E.L.T. show was actually the first thing I did. There was quite a large cast, about sixty actors. The only two who got a job as a result of it were Fritz Weaver and I. It was a beginning. When you finally crack that one little thing, it gives you a little more confidence.

"E.L.T., with its small budget, was run a lot like the old stock companies. We made our own costumes, got our own props and people donated things. That's how it functioned.

"An awful lot of actors owe a lot to Sam for starting E.L.T. In those days, E.L.T. was off-Broadway. There was no other place to showcase.

"I worked with Sam once on a Ben Casey. *I always had great respect for him. God, everybody loved Sam. He had eight million friends in this business."*

****

Too Much of a Good Thing

The impact of the *Ben Casey* series was extraordinary. It was so popular that often people would cancel engagements because Monday night was the sacred night for *Ben Casey*. ABC had very few outlets compared to the other two networks, and it was a sensation even with small exposure.

The interviews of Sam and Bettye during the *Ben Casey* years were too numerous to count. There were newspaper and magazine cover stories throughout the United States. They were very popular television personalities. One reviewer praised Sam's performance in the series as "impressively out of place."

Interviews often contain material designed to sell a show to an adoring public. Fans want to know as much as they can about their favorite stars. Many of those who worked on the *Ben Casey* set reported difficulties between Jaffe and Edwards. Yet, in interviews given during the run, Bettye and Sam seemed to go out of their way to say only complimentary things about Edwards.

In one interview in the *Chicago Daily News*, Bettye remarked, "In many respects, despite the difference in age, I see great similarities between Sam and Vince. Perhaps it's why they are so fond of each other and hold each other in such high esteem. It may also explain my own fondness for the frowning young rebel of our make-believe hospital." Today, we might call this a promotional sound-bite.

Bettye went even further, saying that Vince reminded her of Sam, not in any physical resemblance, but with regard to character and emotional depth: "I asked my husband about the friendship that's grown between Vince and himself. He smiled and said, 'He's the young man I once wanted to be.' When I put the same question to Vince, he sounded as though he'd been eavesdropping. He said, 'I like Sam because I see in him the man I'd like to become.'"

Bettye spoke of how Sam and Vince had similar backgrounds. Vince hailed from the Brownsville section of Brooklyn and Sam from Manhattan's Lower East Side. Both their families were hard-pressed to make ends meet. Both worked their way through school, and both had an urgent desire for education.

"Sam and Vince are also alike in being very masculine men, strong-willed, serious in work, idealistic in their defense of the underdog, and in their frank and generous attitudes" Bettye continued.

"They have another trait in common. I'm afraid both are easy marks for a touch, and are sometimes taken advantage of. Since his success on *Ben Casey*, Vince has naturally been approached for help by pals of the old tough days. And, in his generous way, he has tried to steer these struggling actors to jobs and has often made substantial loans. Sam — who has suffered some unfortunate experiences with making loans of this kind — warned Vince to hand out money with discretion, lest he lose rather than hold such friends.

"Shortly after, an old acquaintance came by and asked Vince for a loan. Still mulling over Sam's warning, Vince decided to cut his loan to the minimum and gave the man a ten. So what happened? In a huff, the man approached Sam and sang his song of woe. Sam's heart was promptly touched and it ended with him giving a sizable loan. Whereupon we heard a Zorba type roar from Vince: 'So! So, doctor, this you call medical ethics — to make a diagnosis of my condition, and then practice the exact opposite? Such a schnook!' For once, Sam had nothing to answer. He shrugged and looked like the kid with his hand caught in the cookie jar."

Bettye stated that she and Sam were extremely

happy in their work. She described them as two who enjoyed life and nature, two who liked to make their small contributions to enrich the lives of others. She went on to say that from what she had seen of Edwards, she believed that he was cut of the same cloth: "At the moment it is difficult for him to achieve the tranquil pleasures that Sam and I glory in. Someone recently said to Sam, 'Your boy, Vince, is all nerves. Is he trying to play the angry young man in real life, too?'

"Sam looked this man squarely in the eye and said quietly, 'Have you any conception of what it means to learn the equivalent of three-fifths of a Broadway play every single week? That's what Vince has to do, to carry the burden of this show. Just picture the strain on him. Why, there isn't an actor alive who could keep on doing this and not show the tension.'

"Sam is right, of course. Absolutely. Vince is in three-fifths of each segment of the series. It's a wonder he hasn't lost all his sense of humor. He has a very keen one . . . The other morning, I told him that *TV Radio Mirror* had asked me to write my impressions of Sam and of him. 'Any comment, doctor?' I teased. Vince stared thoughtfully at me until I felt he wasn't to going answer. Finally, he said, 'Bettye, don't sprinkle perfume over me. Just tell the unvarnished, down-to-earth truth as you see things around here.'"

Sam Jaffe and Bettye Ackerman did not spend their time giving interviews in which they complained about the behavior of Vince Edwards. It was not *de rigueur.*

In interviews Jaffe indicated that he thought of the *Casey* Company as a happy family that got along beautifully together. However, he did admit that he had no social relationship with Edwards. He said it was often true in television and in theater as well, that after work, each one goes his own way. "And that's good," Jaffe said.

"Otherwise it becomes a little too ingrown. Off the set, we all have our own private relationships and companions, and when we meet at work it's all very friendly and nice."

Sam publicly affirmed Vince's demand for $7,500 a week in salary because the years of a young leading man were short. He dismissed any suggestion that Vince Edwards was a man of bad character. He said that that characteristic would show up on the screen if it were true. Grinning, Jaffe reported, "You know, Jane Wyatt, who used to be in *Father Knows Best* — and with whom I worked in *Lost Horizon* — once said something I've never forgotten. She said that when you're acting, if you think horse and say cow, then horse comes out on the screen. An actor carries his own biography in his face."

In truth Edwards had a scowling, troubled face that revealed his up-bringing. Script supervisor Betty Fancher spoke of that history. Edwards had a twin and a very difficult childhood in a mixed marriage of an Italian father and a Jewish mother. His was a big family and his father was ill and not working. When Vince was born, his mother said they didn't need another mouth to feed, especially twins. Fancher asserted that his mother was afraid of him when he was a baby in his cradle. She said his mother went back to work in a school cafeteria as soon as she could, and Vince's older brother stayed home and took care of the new babies.

Edwards' early life was one of hardship that trailed him into his adult years. His older brother died of leukemia due to starvation and his high school girlfriend died of breast cancer. He had wanted to send his first *Casey* check home to his father as a surprise, but the night before they started the first day's shooting on the series, his father died of a heart attack. Life was constantly pulling the rug out from under him.

In talks with Bettye years later, when the show

was history and she was not doing promotional press interviews, she revealed that while Vince Edwards was the hottest thing on the globe during *Ben Casey*, his behavior was sometimes not the best, except with the two of them. She described a night they were running late. Edwards hadn't even read the scene they were working on. With the cameras rolling at his order, he learned the lines through 13 takes. He finally got the scene right and called a halt to the shooting. The take didn't satisfy Bettye and she insisted they repeat it until it pleased her as well. While Edwards consented without objection, his bodyguard confronted Bettye during the break, telling her she should be careful or she would lose her job. It was not easy to push Bettye around. She spoke with enough volume for everyone on the set to hear. "Bennie," she mocked. "You can get me out of this series? I think you're wonderful." She barely took a breath as she praised him, all too loudly, proclaiming how she wouldn't have to come to work on Monday. Everyone on the set got very quiet as they watched Bennie shrivel to nothing. While Bettye felt sorry for him, she knew he deserved it. When he slumped out, everybody applauded. He never went near Bettye again.

When I tracked Vince Edwards down for an interview, he was most cordial. He remembered Sam Jaffe as very professional and as a sweet and generous person. He thought him wise, like the wise man he played, with a little mischief about him. Sam's deep convictions and honesty impressed him. Edwards confirmed that they were not social friends. He remembered that Sam had a great sense of humor, telling jokes with double meanings, and using Yiddish humor as well.

There was a surprise element in Jaffe's humor. One simply didn't expect the kind of jokes Jaffe told to originate in the mouth of such a spiritual countenance. For example, he would tell the story of the woman whose parrot kept saying, "Shit, shit, shit." She told the parrot that if it said shit one more time, she was going to have to punish it. The parrot said, "Shit, shit, shit." She admonished it, saying, "One more time and you are really going to get it." The parrot said "Shit, shit, shit." The woman took the parrot and put it in the refrigerator. Once inside, the parrot spied a stuffed turkey and commented, "He must have said fuck!"

Jaffe and Edwards didn't converse much, but Harry Landers, the other regular on the show, sat with Sam Jaffe and talked by the hour. Landers marveled at how quick and bright Jaffe was, and at his ability to go from subject to subject. Landers effused about Sam as a man of the people who was totally principled. He said that Jaffe didn't have one petty little bone in his body.

For Landers and others, Jaffe's effect on people was residual and rippling. Landers said, "It was strictly a one-on-one relationship when he spoke to you. He gave all of himself to everyone."

Landers saw Jaffe as so concerned with people and the world that he often wondered if acting was just an occupation for Sam. While he acknowledged that Jaffe acted easily and beautifully, he didn't think that acting was something Jaffe really loved. It was Landers' view that Jaffe used acting as a way to influence. "I think acting was secondary to his ideas and philosophies."

Sam Jaffe deeply touched the lives of people in the profession and inspired them. It is easy to see why Harry Landers would think he played the role of an actor to bring his goodness to the profession.

It was the uniqueness of Jaffe that enchanted Landers: "It's spooky how you never hear anyone say anything negative about Sam; never once." This author confirms that. No amount of probing brought forth critical comments about Jaffe. Even to demand balanced responses from interviewees was futile. Perhaps it was that, while there were faults, there was nothing wicked in the man, nothing evil. Perhaps it was because Sam didn't show his dark side to his acquaintances and they didn't look for it.

Landers proclaimed, "Words fail me to describe Sam. He was a thrilling man. Sam was a Godfather in the truest sense of the word. God and Father, a Godfather of man."

When Sam Jaffe walked through the studio on his way to the sound stage, every person he passed, from carpenters to electricians to property men, greeted him in the warmest possible way. They obviously had tremendous affection for him. Jaffe dedicated himself to being considerate, caring, and helpful. He knew, for example, that Betty Fancher collected snuff boxes and he bought some for her. When he found out someone needed or wanted something, he would go right out to get it. This kind of behavior further exaggerates the impression of "the good guy."

When Jaffe didn't approve of something, even if he didn't say much, the expression on his face would broadcast his feelings. He rarely volunteered his disapproval, but if asked his opinion, he didn't hold back. The *Casey* Company could tell in the mornings when Sam and Bettye had had a disagreement on their way to work by their set faces. The distance between them on such occasions was in sharp contrast to the closeness they usually enjoyed that caused people to think of them as turtle doves.

Women would frequently recognize Jaffe because of his hairdo. They would charge up to him and embrace him, professing that they adored him. In such scenes, Bettye would always chime in loudly, "So do I."

The popularity of the *Ben Casey* show changed the lives of its three leading players. They became household names and faces. In the first year of the show, Bettye and Sam had to hide when they walked down the streets of New York. One day, a city bus went by and stopped as it passed them. People got off and started to chase them. Bettye went one way, Sam the other.

Often interviewers asked Sam how he felt while handsome, virile Vince Edwards embraced his wife.

"I suffer through it," he said joking. "Our people suffered 2,000 years, so I suffer a little more."

Because the show's development rested on a solid foundation of research, it was able to sustain the initial overnight success and flourish for many years.

It was amazing how many people thought Sam was a real doctor. He and Bettye would go to parties and people would stop him to ask his advice about an ailment. When he saw they weren't kidding, he would advise them to take an aspirin and call their doctors.

One afternoon Sam was having a chocolate soda at the Los Angeles Farmer's Market with his New York friend, industrial designer Freda Diamond. A middle-aged lady came over to Sam and addressed him as Dr. Zorba. She wanted to know about something that was ailing her. It amazed Freda that with the straightest face he said, "I think what you're saying is very interesting. Do you have a family physician? I think you should go and get a closer opinion." When she walked away, Diamond asked Sam how he could do that with a straight face. He said, "People ask me those things. They think I'm Dr. Zorba." What impressed Diamond was that Jaffe didn't make the woman feel like a fool. He treated her with great kindness, addressing and answering her question. He gave her advice just like a professional and he ex-uded sincerity. The woman didn't realize she was talking to an actor. As far as she was concerned, she was talking to the doctor.

This caring aspect of Sam Jaffe was apparent to everyone. On the set, Sam related very warmly to other actors. Like Dr. Zorba, Sam Jaffe reached out to life. He emanated loving gentleness. This was no doubt one of the chosen expressions of his early commitment to being good.

This behavior on the set impressed renowned director Leo Penn. However, Jaffe's response to children struck him even more. Even if they had never seen Sam before, Penn reported, within a few minutes they would want to sit on his lap. There was a kind of magic about Jaffe. Penn said that the only other person he had ever seen with that particular kind of magic was Sugar Ray Robinson. Robinson emanated sweetness.

Erudite as he was, Sam could always bridge the gap between himself as an adult and any children with whom he came in contact. Sam would visit the Penns' small children [one is the actor, Sean Penn, and the other, pop performer Michael Penn] for their birthdays. His magic tricks enchanted them. The children always asked whether Sam was coming. Leo Penn remarked that children see right through to the core of sweetness, whereas: "Adults find it more difficult because they have their own cover-ups."

Jaffe touched children with love wherever he found them. When actor Ezra Stone's son, Joe, was two years old, Sam observed him playing with miniature cars and trucks in his room. Upon leaving, he sent little Joe a very large toy truck. It was the biggest Joe ever had. Today, almost forty years later, the Stone farm grounds are a parking lot for trucks of every size, age and shape. The collection started, Ezra Stone purports, with Sam's love gift.

Besides sweetness and rapport with children, Sam Jaffe had consistency. Hollywood did not change him. The theater did not change him. Even the blacklist did not cause him to waver. He had a reputation for being his own person, and he never gave in to any malaise of the moment.

Toughness in Jaffe enabled him to maintain his integrity and to survive. Sam was singularly lacking in self-pity. Yet, as Leo Penn observed, Sam was wildly compassionate about friends going through horrific times. He was a mensch, a responsible person.

Rather than waste his energy on complaining, Jaffe championed justice. He sometimes did this by responding negatively to individuals and their actions. It was his way of taking a stand. He was immovable in what he believed and stood for.

Sam Jaffe realized the value of life and the shortness of time. He often reminded himself that he was already in his sixties and there were still things that he wanted to see and do. Being in the *Ben Casey* series tied him down.

As part of the promotion for *Ben Casey*, there was an obligation for Sam Jaffe to attend, and even address, medical gatherings. Bettye accompanied Sam, as was their custom. It was often tedious work, but on occasion provided them with a bounty of humor. A case in point was the evening of their invitation to a fund raiser at a very large Bel Air house, attended mostly by doctors and scientists. Bettye grew weary of trying to sustain interesting conversation and went to find Sam. He had obviously just finished telling a long story. As Bettye came in, a woman was informing Sam that she had no idea actors could be so bright. Without skipping a beat, Bettye replied, "I had no idea that doctors could be so dull." The woman's husband, a doctor, jumped up and kissed Bettye.

Making personal appearances wasn't the only unattractive feature of television series work. There was also the typecasting that Jaffe had feared before signing the contract. Less than a year into the series, for example, Jaffe was invited to guest-star as a doctor in an episode of *The Defenders*, adding to the people on the street who sought his diagnostic expertise.

The main element that disturbed Jaffe about being in the *Ben Casey* series was that his part was not enough to hold his attention. It never put his talent to full use. Instead he was always either rescuing or rebuking the young, bullheaded Ben Casey. Charles Witbeck, a critic for *The Citizen Register*, Ossining, NY was sharp enough to pick this up and report on it: ". . . Jaffe shouldn't be made to yell, for he can be far more effective with his own gentle approach."

The quality of the Dr. Zorba role caused Sam discontent, but the producers told him there was no way out of his contract. For this reason he hung in, but he hoped for further character development. An interview with Cynthia Lowry in Indianapolis, Indiana stressed this. "To those in the viewing audience who know Sam Jaffe's acting abilities, his part seemed a waste of talent this past season."

Moser had promised Jaffe that he would have stronger roles in the new season. While Jaffe expressed confidence in interviews that things would get better, it is hard to believe this represented Sam's true sentiments. Most who knew Sam at the time knew that he wanted out of the series after the first year. He lamented, "Doing the *Ben Casey* series was interesting but it was monotonous. I'd plead with them, 'Let me do something else. Give me something instead of just being the brains. Give me something else for a change. Or get the brains into another sort of area.' But it was the same thing. I'd slap him on the wrist.

"How often could you do the same thing? That wasn't the reason I became an actor; I didn't [do it] to have a swimming pool. I became an actor really to feel, to do something inspirational. Shakespeare was what inspired me. After all, it was telling people something, getting them to know something about themselves.

"At one time theater was like church. You went

to learn something about your society. But just to make money is not the function, although all of them do. I don't do commercials . . . and I've turned down many a role for that reason."

As time passed, rather than resigning himself to the ongoing role, he grew increasingly restive about getting out. Writer friend Lou Garfinkle heard Sam speak often about how much he hated playing Dr. Zorba: "It seemed like pabulum to him. He wouldn't talk against it, but it wasn't on the same level that he was used to. It didn't have the subtleties. However, he did have a positive attitude toward dealing with medicine on television and wanting it to be right. He'd discuss Zorba in a deprecating way because Zorba was a pillow." The role was too easy for Sam; it wasn't a challenge.

Garfinkle believed that the Jaffes had a positive and lasting effect on Vince Edwards. He said that Edwards mellowed, became a man, and that people became very fond of him. He thought that Sam may have been a template for Vince.

Sam was a good friend to Garfinkle, and a supporter of his writing talent. When Garfinkle would get discouraged, it was Sam who would remind him of how good he was, and he would be able to write again. [Garfinkle later won an Academy Award of his screenplay *The Deer Hunter*.]

Jim Moser echoed Lou Garfinkle, saying that Sam gave him deep faith in himself. This wasn't Moser's first series, but he was never fully sure of himself: "[Sam] gave me a hell of a boost. It's an overall impression. He'd read the lines the way [I] wrote them, with the same intent as when [I] wrote them, and that was rare. That was an affirmation of my being able to write what I wanted to say. Sam was exciting and he stimulated me. He was contagious and miraculous. He'd go right to the heart of the material. Other actors would give interpretations, putting their own stuff in it, but Sam always caught what was written."

It was no wonder that Sam was nominated for a Primetime Emmy for Best Actor in a Supporting Role.

At the end of the second year of the series, Sam went to Jim Moser to ask that he be given more to do than just upbraid Casey. Moser was a sensitive man and understood Sam's plight. He told him he would put a rider on his contract stating that if the first thirteen shows weren't to his liking, he could have his release. According to attorneys, Moser didn't have the authority to make such an agreement.

The third season, as far as Sam was concerned, held no more challenges for him than the first two. "My parts were so short," he quipped, "I could have written them on prescription blanks. I called them pistol parts — one shot and they were over."

In 1963, in the third year of the series, the success was so great that there was a *Ben Casey* comic strip by Neal Adams. However, tired of the Dr. Zorba role, Sam complained that it was as monotonous as an eternal embrace.

By September of that year, in a column by Ward Morehouse for the Springfield MA *News,* Sam was longing for theater: "'I want to do another play. That's always the dream that keeps you alive. I didn't know what I was getting into with *Ben Casey.*'

"'We're going into our third season with *Ben Casey,*' he said. 'It almost didn't get on the air. The head of ABC said they would put it on if only a minute's advertising time could be sold. On our first program there were fourteen free promotions spots for the network, but the show caught fire within three or four weeks and here we are.'"

After the third year they picked up his option again. They apologized and explained that he would only have to do five shows out of every thirteen, but that he would get paid for ten shows. Sam confessed that all season he felt as if he were holding up a bank.

While Sam's focus was mainly on getting out of the series, there were other aspects of the work that were good and nourishing, especially to Bettye. The relations with fellow cast members were friendly; they were as one big family. Bettye and Sam made it a point to watch the show, not only to observe themselves but to watch their friends who appeared.

Bettye regretted that she and Sam didn't have many scenes together, but when she wasn't working, she would go to the set to have lunch with him. If she had a late call, Sam would stay and have dinner with her. Neither of them had to work on the weekend. They used Saturday and Sunday to visit with friends and entertain.

Bettye stated openly that she too wished she had more to do in the series. There were five regulars, which made it difficult for all of them to have continually meaty roles. In addition, it wasn't easy to provide exciting stories for an anesthesiologist.

Many on the writing staff didn't quite grasp Sam's part and sometimes it was difficult to work him in. Every fourth show, they made it a point to give Sam a major role. Every one of those shows stood up beautifully over time.

Sam had modeled Zorba after a New York dermatologist he once knew: a brilliant man who looked and acted the way he thought a great doctor should. It was important for Sam to hold an image that would enable him to make Dr. Zorba into a human being of great quality.

Jim Moser tried his best for Sam. He was sad that in many of the episodes there wasn't that much for Sam to do. It was just the way it happened. He tried to keep Sam up front because he was a big asset to the show. Moser was also aware of Jaffe's unhappiness that Edwards was very undisciplined and rude.

Moser reported on Jaffe's strong feelings: "Sam

couldn't understand the non-professional behavior. Mostly Sam would make jokes, but you knew what he was saying.

"I remember once they came over for dinner when we lived in the valley. I had pictures of the whole cast on one wall. Sam walked in and saw this big picture of Vince and said, 'What is this, a dagger I see before me?' That's how he got his ideas over."

It was very irritating to Sam that Edwards would leave in the middle of a take to call his bookies. Here was life imitating fiction, or was it the other way round? As Dr. Zorba constantly needed to discipline Ben Casey, so too, Sam Jaffe found himself caught in the unacceptable behavior of a younger actor who functioned irresponsibly.

Jaffe was impatient with lazy actors who played by rote, read their lines and got their checks. There was much of that in television. Moser and Jaffe discussed how much energy and attention an actor gives to a script. Jaffe told Moser, "It's obvious, Jim, that you've put a great deal into these scripts. Research. The least you can expect from an actor is that they give as much energy as they can to match what you put into it." That statement endeared Jaffe to Moser forever. Moser sang Jaffe's praises. "He never walked through a part. He'd get terribly mad at Vince and I could sympathize.

"His only complaint was that there wasn't enough to do. That's why he asked to be let go."

In those days, Norman Lloyd was producing Hitchcock at Universal. Sam met him there for lunch. Lloyd recalled that when he walked with Sam across the lot to go to the dining room, he had never seen such an adoring reaction to an actor in his life.

Lloyd was one of the friends to whom Sam complained about the limitations of the Dr. Zorba role. Lloyd reported, "Sam's character captured the imagination, but Sam didn't like it because he felt that he was repeating himself. He felt he was doing the same thing all the time, slapping the knuckles of Ben Casey, and there was no opportunity for him to express himself freely."

Jaffe lamented that all he had to do was "wash up, look sterile and make wise remarks in the operating room."

After the fourth year, Bettye noticed that the studio was a day late in picking up Sam's option. Bettye kept track of everything when they worked. She knew precisely when they had to pick up the option. This was Sam's opportunity for release. She called the secretary at Matt Rapf's office and asked what was the last day that Sam had worked, just to make certain her calculations were correct. They were. Obviously, someone had goofed.

Bettye felt victorious. "Well!" she later related with triumph, "they must have come by helicopter. The contract was on the front door within hours and I knew they were in trouble. It was here so fast. And then all hell broke loose because they realized that Sam could get out."

Bettye and their business manager, Marvin Friedman, were the only two who wanted Sam to get out because they realized that he had had enough. Sam had told her that remaining on the show was cramping him.

Bettye called a lawyer who told her Sam could get out on a technicality. To keep Jaffe, the producers tried everything. They offered to double and triple his salary, but he didn't see his function as an actor as accumulating money. They offered him script approval and Sam told them that if they did, they would never get anything on the air.

Sam held firm as the tempting offers came in, but if for one moment Bettye would have wavered, he told her he would have continued in the series. Bettye was staunch and stayed on Sam's side. What Sam didn't do was to offer to stay for Bettye's sake. He did not reflect on how his departure might hurt the show and therefore affect Bettye's career.

Years later, Bettye told Sam: "I wanted what was right for you. Of course it was terrible for me to go back to work and not have you there. That was sad. And they were angry with me for a while."

Bettye admitted that the series was not the same without him. But rather than stress that, she focused on praising him for the powerful impact of his characterization in spite of the brevity of his role: "You had no idea of the importance of what you had done, of what you brought to it. It was a nothing part. You were starred in it and what you did was extraordinary."

Sam's quiet response was, "Thank you, my sweet." What he didn't add was an equal affirmation of Bettye's work in the series. It was another example of how both of them focused on Sam.

The producers couldn't believe Sam had simply wanted out of the show. They were sure he had been holding out for a renegotiation of his contract. What Sam truly wanted was freedom. He wanted to start acting again on the stage, in the movies, just about anywhere where he could again gain recognition as an actor. He hoped he hadn't forgotten how.

Bettye was grateful for the series because it got them their house, which they called Ben Casa. The money enabled them to do many things. Sam spoke more pointedly. "We weren't working for the money, but if they didn't give us the money we wouldn't be working." Sam had taken the job because of a need for money. He quit because he needed and wanted to use his talent in another way. But he also quit because he had amassed enough money by that time.

The series was imprisoning to him. *Ben Casey*

was too much of a good thing. One swimming pool was enough. He agreed with his friend Luther Adler that some people, for ideals, will go to Siberia, but for money they go to Hollywood! Sam had enough: enough money, enough of the show.

The fifth season opened without Sam Jaffe. They wrote Dr. Zorba out of *Ben Casey* by saying he had been given a medical grant from the government. The review in *Variety* indicated, "*Ben Casey* may not survive the operation." Format changes produced so many characters and subplots that *Variety* suggested a scorecard would be helpful.

Franchot Tone replaced Jaffe. True to all of Sam's complaints, the new senior doctor had very little to do in the first segment.

Bettye knew something was missing with Sam's departure, but she attributed it to a lack of chemistry between the characters. It was difficult to determine exactly what the chemistry was, but when it was there, it was very obvious. She attested to the extraordinary chemistry between Vince and Sam: "It was the most unlikely casting, but it worked."

Given the various difficulties that went with being an actor, and with doing a series, especially over a period of years, there were rewards not to be underrated. Bettye and Sam Jaffe held an elevated place in the public's attention. *TV Guide* had done a major cover story on *Ben Casey* entitled "The Courtship of Sam Jaffe," by Dwight Whitney. The show had won the *TV Guide* Award for Favorite New Series and a nomination for Favorite Series. Hundreds of thousands of TV viewers had voted. The Jaffes had built a sound financial base and had opened the world of television to themselves.

Sam may not have been very happy with his role, but it did little to damage his reputation as an actor or as a person. Glen Graham wrote in the Petaluma *Argus-Courier*, September 9, 1962: "... I'm going to remember that while Sam Jaffe makes a very good Dr. Zorba, he's even better at being Sam Jaffe."

Agents play a key role in any actor's life. During the time the Jaffes were the rage of television with *Ben Casey*, Hollywood agent Paul Kohner represented the two of them. To their chagrin, they discovered he mishandled them. The Jaffes wanted to know of job offers coming their way while engaged in the series, but Paul Kohner neglected to tell them. Bettye happened to run into director Walter Grauman who told her that he had been trying to get her for months but Bettye had no knowledge of it. When she confronted Kohner, he was very slick about it, taking her to dinner and giving her lovely gifts. Because Bettye was working constantly, she didn't have the luxury of switching agents then.

The ultimate blow occurred after *Ben Casey*. Bettye was offered the lead in another series but she and Sam decided it was important for them to have six weeks in Mexico together. When they returned, Bettye wanted to do a play in New York and asked Kohner to get her a reading for the lead role in *Cactus Flower*. For two weeks she called Kohner every day and he told her what was transpiring between him and the producer and how hard he was working. There was one obstacle after another, until he finally told her that her name wasn't big enough. She let go the effort feeling she had at least tried.

Months later, when the Jaffes were in New York, she discovered that the producer of *Cactus Flower* knew nothing of Bettye's desires. She felt a cold fury and shortly thereafter she and Sam left Kohner. He never told her why he hadn't pursued the role for her, but friends thought it was because he wanted her to do more television for the financial benefits. Television was better for her. "After all," Bettye said with disgust, "because I was an actor he thought I was merely a child and only knew about childish things."

The Jaffes went on to agent Sue Golden Arnold where they had a mutually satisfying relationship. When Sue first met Sam, it was as if he had always been there, as if she had known him all her life. "He was that kind of person," she remarked. "Having them come to me was one of the nicest things that ever happened to me in my life. Knowing both of them gave me the courage to marry again after 19 years of being divorced. They would come to my office and sit on the couch and hold hands. And they had strikes against them: age, Jew with Southern belle WASP, and yet this is one of the ideal marriages of all time. I figured if they can do it, so can I."

The Ben Casey *years: On left, Bettye Ackerman, Vince Edwards and Sam Jaffe. Above, Bettye Ackerman and Sam Jaffe in their series characters.*

****

CHARLTON HESTON, *The Millionairess*, 1948

[*Before appearing in* The Millionairess] *"I had made my Broadway debut and ran for about a year in Katherine Cornell's production of* Anthony and Cleopatra. *I had begun to do live television.*

"Having E.L.T. available was an enormous performance opportunity. The problem with acting as a career is you don't get to do it unless someone says 'here's a part and here's a stage, go do it.' E.L.T. provided that.

"I honestly wasn't aware of Jaffe's contact with E.L.T."*

"I worked with Sam, of course, in Ben-Hur. *He was a wonderful actor. He gave a wonderful performance. He was a gentle and marvelous man."*

*[Very few knew of Jaffe's involvement because he remained in the background and never appeared in an *E.L.T.* show or drew attention to himself.]

****

Building Blocks

Sam Jaffe was good at being at Sam Jaffe, and that was no small accomplishment. Long-time friends such as Rebecca Reis were sure that, "he didn't develop into something. He was born that way. He was complete at every stage I knew him and everywhere I knew him."

Often, during interviews, friends indicated their desire to know of Sam Jaffe's roots and early influences. They had interest in seeing what factors contributed to his being such an exemplary person. I, too, was very curious about this. Jaffe's early life experiences and youthful decisions deeply affected how his life unfolded.

Sam's mother, Ada Epstein Jaffe, came from Bialystok, Russia. Her family was not composed of ordinary peasant people; they were accomplished musicians, actors and artists. Sam clearly inherited a predisposition for the arts and cultural awareness through his bloodline. His was a continental family, a family accustomed to speaking more than one language. As a boy in New York, Sam was exposed to these roots, not only through his mother, but through her sister, Rachel, and relatives, Jacob and Sarah Epstein. They were an older couple who came to the United States by way of South America, and Sam was very fond of them. Jacob was a professional social worker, and he and Sam would sip tea while discussing philosophy. It may have been through the Epsteins that Sam was exposed to the premise that seldom does someone do something on his own. Sam said often throughout his life, "We follow masters. No one thinks for himself, really." This philosophical view was one of many adopted in those formative years.

Ada married Bernard Jaffe and moved with him to

Odessa in Southern Russia. Her mother continued to live in Bialystok, marrying a widower named Kahn when she was almost fifty years of age. The link between the Jaffes and Kahns was a lasting one, and one that influenced Sam's life.

The Kahns were religious people. Ada's new step-father never worked. He just sat and debated the Talmud with other elders. His religious pursuits didn't rub off on the rest of the family, however.

Both had grown children. They never expected to have a child. However, shortly after their union, Ada's mother gave birth to a son, Saul Kahn, who was later to have direct influence on Sam. Shortly after Saul's birth, Ada had her first child, Sophie. Ada's mother went to be with her, leaving her husband and her son, Saul, with a wet nurse in Bialystok. The act of leaving her own infant to go to the aid of her daughter is a thread of support and unity that characterizes the history of Sam Jaffe's family.

In the middle of the 19th century there was quite a large immigration of Jews from Russia to the United States. The news of America as the land of liberty was a promise of deliverance from the denials, persecutions, and pogroms in Russia. Many of the immigrants kissed the ground on arrival. Bernard and Ada Jaffe, with their three children, Sophie, Abraham and Annie [in Russian: Sonja, Sasha, and Nunje], left Odessa and came to the golden land of America in 1890. Ada's sister Rachel, Morris Levy's wife, came with them. Sam didn't know exactly how they made the journey. He was sure it wasn't by steerage because, as Sam colorfully stated, "I know my father, the son-of-a-bitch, had a seltzer factory." The implication was that he had enough money to pay for their passage.

In 1890 all the people from Europe who had sons

hid them from the census-taker. They still had the fear of their sons being drafted as they had been in Europe. Sam Jaffe was born on March 10, 1891. His actual name was Sholom Yaffe, which translates as "Beautiful Peace." The name would have been on his hospital tag, but a midwife delivered him at home. Home had been 32 Orchard Street on the Lower East Side of New York City. [The building nearby is now a Lower East Side Tenement Museum.] However, there is no official record of that birth, due to the custom of hiding sons.

Bernard Jaffe, also known as Barnett Jaffe, was called Barney. His name appears in the census of 1900. Ada's name was Ida, or Chia, the Jewish equivalent. She called herself Ada. The census listed her as Heidi. This mixing up of names, as well as the changing of names, was not unusual during that period. Officials shortened hard-to-pronounce names, or substituted another name. Also, immigrants sought to Americanize their own names. The 1900 census has no record of any of the Jaffe children. Relatives were caring for them at the time.

Sam often used the occasion of interviews to joke about his birth date since there was a dispute as to which of three dates was the actual one. His typical response was that he didn't agree with any of them!

There was also confusion about where Sam had been born. Many press pieces about him proclaimed that he was from Ireland. His birth certificate clearly indicated that he was born in New York City. It seems Sam himself was the source of the Irish rumor. At one point there was a Jaffe who was a mayor of Belfast. Sam joked that the mayor was his uncle. The story grew and before long, many thought Sam had been born there and that his father, Bernard, had been Irish rather than Russian. Sam got many laughs out of how the fib expanded and spread widely. Part of Sam's pixyish nature was that he didn't correct interviewers who wrote stories about him and claimed that he was a son of the old sod.

Sam's half-uncle Saul Kahn also came to the United States where he and his wife had four children, including Irving, Lee, Happy, and Peter.

The four Jaffe children were, of course, first cousins to Saul's children. They were the same age and were always very close to each other. They were so close that Saul's son, Irving, experienced Sam more as an older brother than a first cousin. "Sam used our home as a second home," Irving remembered. "We were always in and out of each other's house. I was about nine years old then. Sam was very fond of me. He had no younger brothers."

Sam's childhood was one of many illnesses. "As an infant," he said, "I seemed to have had every disease available at that time. Once I had been given up as dead because a feather poked up into my nose got no response. But my mother's sister, Rachel Levy, placed me on her shoulder and started massaging my back, calling out Semele, Semele, the diminutive of Samuel. I sneezed, freeing my nose of the stuff that prevented me from breathing, and I was back again among the living, thanks to her."

When Sam was a young man, he had his first physical examination. The doctor discovered that one leg was shorter than the other. The boys on his block had called him Gimpy, and Sam had never known why. The doctor informed him that he must have had polio as a child, as one of many youthful diseases.

When Bernard, Sam's father, first came to the United States, he did spike work. Later he became a jewelry maker. When his family responsibilities became too much for him, he deserted the family; Sam was almost five years old at the time. This was why Sam always referred to his father as a son-of-a-bitch.

Bernard took off for Pittsburgh. Saul Kahn went

there to try to get him to come back and reunite with his family. He was unsuccessful. In those days, there were many cases of husbands disappearing from immigrant families.

After Bernard left, no one ever talked about him. It was as if he never existed. Sam had no memory of his father and had nothing good to say about him.

After sending no word in the interim, his father appeared eight years later at his mother's door with a pound of tea. She completely rejected him saying, "We drink coffee now."

During that visit, Sam and his brother Abe hid with rocks when they heard their father was coming. They were going to stone him. They didn't, but they had wanted to. Sam said that when his father came, he left a $5 check: "There was a question whether we should take it. The answer was, for the human pig even a hair is a blessing. So we would take the $5. That's my great father."

His father's desertion of the family left an imprint on Sam that would last long into his life. He never opened his heart to him, nor did he ever express any interest in Bernard's side of the story.

From Orchard Street, after Bernard's departure, the family moved to 411 Grand Street to join other relatives who lived next door. Sam recalled, "they were cold-water flats with an oven. They had no bathtubs. You would wash in the washtub. They were truncated little things with two sides, for cold water and for hot water. You'd use a wash basin to wash your hair and if ever the soap got in your eyes, you'd yell bloody murder. And when insects got into your hair, lice, you'd have to use kerosene.

"They had quarter meters. The gas would be good for 25 cents and the minute it went out you had to put another quarter in. You had to have a supply of quarters to keep the heat going. Of course, the heat you got was from a stove, a coal stove.

"A dumb waiter opened into the flat for deliveries as well as for the disposal of garbage."

The apartments were all walkups. Elevators didn't make their appearance in apartment houses until much later. When they did, there were two kinds: one for the tenants and one for service. Sam regretted that in his time Blacks could use only the service elevator. He believed that restriction continued in New York City until 1935.

Sam Jaffe grew up near Grand Street, and a grand street it was, with a high class restaurant named Malbins and three fancy department stores, Lord and Taylor, Ridley's, and Kurzons. While Grand Street represented elegance, the Lower East Side was a mixture of everything. Sam lived two blocks from Hester Street where pushcarts containing wares of every size, smell, and color enticed street shoppers from all over the city. The peddlers were characters who had their own unique style of selling. An example was the man who sold herring by rolling up his sleeve, reaching down into the big barrel, pulling up a herring, wrapping it in newspaper, and handing it to the customer.

Even though the Lower East Side was heavily populated by Jews, Christian missionaries abounded in trucks with bands and loud speakers. Sam never forgot the Catholic mission for Jews on the northwest corner of Grand and Attorney Streets. It impressed him that they held services in their store front.

Jaffe painted a vivid picture of the neighborhood in which he grew up. "In the summertime people on the East side would sleep on the fire escapes," he said. "And on hot days you'd be up on the roof and have some cold lemonade. It was a totally Yiddish-speaking culture. We always spoke Yiddish in our house.

In those days, it was very important to the immigrants that they learn to speak English and that they become assimilated. Their own children discouraged their speaking Yiddish at home. They focused on becoming Americanized and ridding themselves of babushkas and other articles of clothing that classified them as foreigners. Sam's extended family did all they could in this regard. They availed themselves of educational and cultural opportunities. They went to concerts and bought standing room at the opera.

Sam reminisced: "Cars were first drawn by horses, and later by storage batteries, as were trucks. When the first Ford autos appeared, cries of 'Get a horse' met them. The Second Avenue elevated [train] in my day was powered by a locomotive. Before the change to electric power, the storage battery street cars gave way to the Third Avenue Trolley Line. It received its power from a third rail several feet below the car. In Brooklyn, the trolley's power line was several feet above the car. There were a great number of trolleys in that borough, and the people had to take great care to avoid accidents. Brooklyn residents were therefore called the artful dodgers, hence the name of the Brooklyn Ball Team, The Dodgers."

An early memory of Sam's was that the great Yiddish writer Sholem Aleichem was a neighbor of his in Grand Street: "I believe he lived at 420 Grand. I would see him from time to time standing outside taking in this part of the new world."

I was fascinated by Sam's mention of this connection because my English teacher at the High School of Performing Arts was Bel Kaufman who wrote *Up the Down Staircase*. Bel was the granddaughter of Sholem Aleichem. She had a big influence on my creative life. She taught her students to carry a small pad and pencil so that we would never miss a bright idea or phrase. I have done that ever since. Bel is still alive and writing at almost 102.

Sam always talked of his mother with extreme affection and sympathy. Even though he had a dreadfully unhappy childhood, he developed a significant trait of turning a negative into a positive. He focused on how very caring his mother was, and how difficult her life was.

His mother Ada, needing a way to support her children and herself with her husband gone, took in borders. They got the bedrooms. The children slept wherever they could in the apartment. Sam reported, "My mother became our sole support. She wondered how she was going to take care of the four children. It was too much. Fortunately, she had a beautiful soprano voice and was accepted in the Jewish Theatrical Chorus Union. She was engaged as a member of the chorus in the Thalia Theater on the Bowery."

A handsome woman with fair skin, freckles, and curly medium-brown hair, Ada had a flair for acting. Many of her borders were actors in the Yiddish theater. This enticed her to pursue her own career. As time passed, Ada was to become successful. This brought the needed financial resources, but it also meant that Ada had to farm out her children. She spent much of her time at the theater and on the road.

Some two decades later she revealed to her niece, Lee Reichart, what parting with her children had meant in her life. She watched Lee bathe her baby and said sadly, "I never had this in my whole life. I had to work. I had to be out. I didn't have the pleasure of raising and suckling a baby like this. I never had this." Ada had been an affectionate person; however, she wasn't around to display it.

Others in the family had the pleasure of raising Ada's young. "To relieve my mother of some of her burden," Sam reported, "her uncle, the Rev. Morris Epstein, and his wife, Leah, who lived in Brownsville, Brooklyn, volunteered to take my brother with them. Brownsville was, then, a little grass-covered, country town where nanny goats roamed freely. After being with them for some time, my brother felt that he was being used too often as an errand boy. So one fine day, he decided to quit and he walked all the way home. He was only ten. He then began writing poetry. Hearst's newspaper, The *Evening Journal*, published several of his poems. He left school at eleven to help my mother. Armed with a recommendation from the *Journal's* editor, he got a job as a runner in the Stock Market for a brokerage on Wall Street. By 16, he familiarized himself with the market and his recommendations to friends proved profitable. In a little time, he acquired enough money not only to turn over his weekly salary to my mother, but he was also able to buy her a pair of diamond earrings for Christmas."

Sam didn't have a very close relationship with his brother because they farmed Abe out at such an early age. Given Sam's lack of a father figure, it would no doubt have served him well had he been able to benefit from more bonding with his older brother. Though his mother turned from family and domestic matters to concerns of support, Sam's sister Sophie sustained the influence of the matriarchy on Sam. Ada put her in charge. She did the cooking and cleaning, and functioned as head of the family. At every stage of his childhood and youth, Sam was influenced by nurturing women, but he lacked satisfactory male role models in his formative years, and it is possible this delayed his maturation.

Later, Sam's Aunt Ray (Rachel) was dominant in his child rearing. She and her husband Morris further eased Ada's burden of responsibility by adopting Sam. While it was not a legal adoption, Sam was nevertheless enrolled as Samuel Levy at Public School 92 on Broome and Clinton Streets. Lee Reichart, Sam's first cousin, believed that Sam was Ray's child. He not only had their name but one could tell that he "belonged to them," she remembered. The Levy's lived at 414 Grand Street.

Morris Levy's mother, Grandma Tobias, was not happy that Sam began to carry the Levy name. She had inherited several Lower East Side tenement houses from her second husband, and the properties gave her power in the family. Morris took care of them for her. She had a daughter, Fania Cass, who had a young son, Chauncey. Fearing that Sam would be the Levy heir instead of Chauncey, she went to the school to have Sam's name changed from Levy to Jaffe. She made quite a fuss about it, but she didn't succeed. Sam retained the name Levy until he graduated from C.C.N.Y. In the end, Sam changed his name back to Jaffe to bring peace to Grandma Tobias. His giving up the Levy name settled all arguments. However, Sam did remark, "I should have left it. Jaffe was a lousy name for me because my father deserted." The statement revealed how, even in later life, Sam held on to his hard feelings. They were so strong that he wished no association with the Jaffe name.

Not one to be defeated by the schools, and wanting to fully protect her interests, Grandma Tobias prevailed upon Morris to give up having Sam in his care. First, Sam's own father had abandoned him. Having adjusted to living with his aunt and uncle, and having taken Rachel into his heart as his mother, he was again tossed from a secure home base.

Sam had no place to go. He went to live with his Uncle Saul (Sol) Kahn, his mother's half-brother, who had one little room in a house in which he was boarding at 413 Grand Street. His uncle took care of him for several months. At one point, Sam's brother Abe lived with them in the cramped space. Sam said it would have made a great Dostoevsky novel: "Abe and I always made fun of Uncle Saul. We called him Solomon the Wise. It's not that he wasn't smart. He was convinced of his own wisdom. [Sam didn't want this next bit of data told.]

Uncle Sol slept with his mouth open and we would catch flies and throw them in his mouth. We didn't like him. We slept in the same bed with him."

Sam Jaffe allowed for prankish behavior in his life, but he backed away from the nasty. Putting flies in his uncle's mouth could be considered a prank, but perhaps the reason Sam didn't want it reported was that it expressed his active dislike of his uncle, and that caused the prank to border on the nasty.

While Sam and Abe stayed with their Uncle Sol, Sam's aunt Rachel continued to care for and about him. She loved him as a son. Sam reported softly, "Every afternoon when school ended, my aunt would be waiting for me on the stoop of 411 Grand St. with a warm sweet potato. She felt terrible that I'd been ousted. Then one day, thanks to her, I was back with my Aunt and Uncle Levy."

Rachel used to fix Sam's breakfast every morning. Years later, when he went to college, she would prepare his lunch. She fed him on many different levels, giving him a sense of security in the midst of his unstable early years. Sam thought of her as a rare person.

In the late 1970's, Sam and Bettye appeared in *Lovers or Liars*, a television series pilot about famous couples. It starred the Jaffes, Steve Allen and Jane Meadows, and Patty Duke and John Austin. A famous guest would ask either husband or wife a question and the other would say whether it was a lie or the truth. They asked Sam if he had the chance to spend one hour with anybody who has ever lived, whom he would choose. He promptly said his aunt.

Tears filled Bettye's eyes as she recounted the story: "They turned to me and I said, 'Of course, that's true.' Later I said to Sam, 'I didn't know you felt that way.' He said, 'I'd give anything in the world to be able to tell her how much I loved her.'"

Morris Levy had leased 414 Grand St. It had formerly been a Democratic Club known as the Seminole Club. He turned it into a hall for weddings, parties, meetings and social events. Although Sam was only in primary school, he worked nights at the affairs. He would participate in the weddings in many different ways and was a very resourceful child.

At age nine, Sam was in charge of renting the hall for weddings and meetings. If a large number of people attended, the Levys provided the hall free of charge and threw in a quarter keg of beer. The hall made its money by charging to check hats: 25 cents for a man and 15 cents for a lady. One couldn't go in until checking the clothing.

Sam's memory of the time was surprisingly clear: "My uncle's mother was the recipient of the hat check fees. One day I was asked to count the passes. She came down and let me have it because I was checking up on her. They asked me to.

"When I worked for my aunt and uncle I used to be able to carry fifteen glasses of beer. They were schooners with handles. I'd be able to carry seven in each hand and one in the middle, holding them together. I waited on the tables with soft drinks and beer. And we had protection from the station house. We gave them a certain amount of money and they permitted us to sell liquor. When a detective would come, they would ring at the front door and notify us, so all the liquor bottles would go under the bar. We had no license. A license was very expensive."

Sam loved the weddings. He especially enjoyed the rhymester who would let tears fall down his face when he discovered that the bride's mother was in Europe and had to miss the great event. The rhymester made his living making people sad, and they loved being sad at a happy occasion.

Sam's Uncle Morris went around twirling his cane and his mustache while his Aunt Ray did all the work for their various business endeavors. With the few pennies she would get, Ray would make things and Sam would go around selling them around the neighborhood. Sam called it her "pin money." He remembered: "With the little money she had, she would buy some candy. I would carry the candy around on a tray and sell it to the people in the dancing halls at weddings. I'd practically push it in people's faces to get them to buy. This was her pocket money."

Sam avoided talking about his uncle. He didn't want to go into details. Again, he refrained from speaking negatively about another person. What was clear was that his Uncle Morris did not fill the gap Sam suffered for a fine male role model. His own father had abandoned his mother, and his uncle took advantage of his aunt. Sam said, "I don't care to say anything against my uncle. It would be more for a novel. He dressed well, had his nails manicured and was a bon vivant. My aunt worked very hard, doing all the cooking. She would do the catering for the weddings for maybe 120 people. She worked herself to death, dying when she was about 60 years of age."

As far as Sam was concerned, Uncle Morris had made a 'slave' of his Aunt Ray. There were obviously strong feelings in Sam for his aunt and about his uncle's treatment of her. Instead of expressing them he went on to talk of some of the things his Uncle Morris did: "After my aunt died, he married somebody. This is not flattering to him so I don't want to go into detail, I shouldn't. [Here again the push-pull.] He married somebody. It wasn't for long. When he died, he asked that they bury him next to my aunt. He was very bright, but in Russia he used to make false passports for people to leave. I imagine when a person does that, that kind of falsity is through his life too. You can see it tinges and colors his life."

Sam said that Morris accepted him but that there was no particular love between them: "I had no father and my mother was my aunt."

Sam touched into his memory bank: "I really didn't know my mother. She would visit. She would come once in a while. Ray was my mother," Sam said firmly. "She really took care of me. My mother was completely away. When I went back to my mother, she was in a play in Brooklyn in the Jewish Theater. I could see her coming home after the matinee to make dinner for the family. She'd have her pantaloons on and cook, and with a hat on sometimes because she was always ready to leave."

It must have meant a lot to Ray to have Sam to love and care for. She and Morris had no children of their own. As Sam saw her as his mother, surely she saw him as her son. Bettye reflected that Sam's Aunt Rachel "must have been an angel. She had raised two half-brothers of Stella and Luther Adler. The wife of the great Jacob P. Adler had had two boys by her first husband. Sam's aunt brought them up. The two became a lawyer and doctor. Then Sam came along and she showered love on him."

"As children," Sam reflected, "we used to do little plays, our own, and we would charge a penny a piece. I never knew that I would be an actor. As a matter of fact, when I went through college, my main subjects were math and physics. I was going to go into engineering or science. But somehow or other there is a parallelism that runs through one's life and it manifests itself."

As it turned out Sam was the first one the family to have higher education, higher ambitions, and higher interests. He had always exhibited intellectual curiosity.

There was an old square piano at 414 Grand Street. Sometimes Sam would sit down at the keyboard. As mentioned earlier, he came from a long line of musicians and he, himself, had a natural ear for music. Later on, his sister Sophie, who was a master piano teacher, took Sam under her musical wing.

Sophie had been profoundly influenced by an uncle who had come to New York from Paris following the loss of his wife and daughter. He brought with him medals that his daughter had won in musical competitions, and he urged Sophie to quit school in favor of studying the piano exclusively. Sam had been very distressed that Sophie had dropped her academic education and blamed his Parisian uncle for interfering in Sophie's life.

Although Sophie quit high school, as did her brother Abe, she continued in evening school because she loved learning. She was very industrious, exceptionally bright, and her music was very important to her. She owned a beautiful grand piano and taught privately. She saved her money in order to travel to Paris in the summers, to study with Nadia Boulanger at Fontainebleau. Boulanger was probably the greatest music teacher of the 20th century. Her students included Aaron Copland. While Boulanger trained her students to be serious about their music, she also taught them to relate to what they played with a great, affectionate joy.

It was Sophie who taught Sam how to play the piano and encouraged his musical ability, which included composition. He would play what was then modern music by Satie and Debussy. As a teenager, Sam was very serious about the piano and considered becoming a concert pianist.

At that point, however, at about age 12, he would just fool around when everyone was out. He would try to play something he had heard. Eventually, he played for the dancing school for beginners, named scholars of the dance. Sam imitated what he had heard so often when they would announce 'scholars, dance for scholars only, one two three, one two three, one two, one two, one two three.' Popular at the time were square dances, polkas and waltzes, and ethnic dances.

As Sam was growing up, he got a good dose of

Jewish theater. He remembered it as the happy place where people went to have a good cry! He called the Thalia "A four walls wailing spot." He remembered crying during a play in which they kidnapped young Jewish boys during the reign of Alexander II to convert them. He couldn't forget the ignorant and prejudiced peasants who persecuted the Jewish people in the Russian villages, and the vicious priests who incited pogroms in the plays he attended.

"The arch villain was usually [played by] Maurice Moskovitch," Sam recounted. "He knew how to twist the knife, to draw tears. And I can never forget the great Jewish actors. They were giants: Kessler, Morris Morrison, Mme Kalish, and Rudolph Schildkraut who came much later. I saw Maurice Schwartz, too, but he was a sort of Johnny-come-lately to the Yiddish stage. His talent didn't come up to that of Jacob Adler, or Kessler."

As early as the age of four or five, Sam had heard a socialist make a speech. He learned it all by memory and performed it on the stage of the Thalia Theater. One of the lines of the speech was: "The rich man's wives, they wear diamonds. Our wives wear coals." Upon hearing this, Bettye remarked, "That was the beginning of the blacklist for you; you started it when you were four." It was certainly true that Sam's sense of fairness began early. He seemed to have an innate knowing of agape.

"I think I said the speech first in Yiddish," Sam said, "and then later in English. The memory of a child until seven is terrific. Anything you hear, you can reproduce. A whole story read to a child will be remembered and repeated. The socialists would have meetings in our hall. There were also meetings of the Bundists. They were nihilists. They had in their watch case a little vial of poison and they went to Russia to assassinate the Czar."

Sam's practice of imitating continued throughout his life. When he was 14, he sat in on a meeting of the

Havarah (a group of friends from the town). After the lecture ended, Jaffe stood at the lectern and mimicked the speaker in Yiddish. He took on all the posturing of the man as he harangued the audience to welcome the people who came from their town. Sam used the meeting hall as if it was his own theater.

Jaffe had an excellent memory, even until the end of his life. In his later years, he could recall and perform songs that he and other Lower East Side kids sang. He wasn't shy either. He would take a breath and belt out lyrics such as: "I stayed seven years in State prison and seven more years must I stay, for killing a man in the alley and taking off his golden watch and chain; sad, sad and lonely, sitting in the cell all alone, all alone, thinking of the days that go by me and the fact that I did wrong."

It goes on: "I once had a father and a mother. I wonder if they ever think of me. I once had a sister and a brother. I wonder if they ever think of me; sad, sad and lonely, sitting in the prison all alone, all alone," etc.

Another was about Arabella who kissed the fella ten times down the cellar. Sam remembered how the boys would follow a girl who they thought "gave it freely." They knew them as "schemios," which meant tricky. The boys would follow them and call them Arabella.

In reviewing his childhood, Sam had no memory of any girl who might have been the first one he kissed. He said, "I don't think I was for girls. We suspected them of being schemios. I didn't kiss anyone. I didn't have any relationships with any girls. My friends were boyfriends." It was quite a while before Sam had any interest in the other sex.

The young Jaffe was very much one of the guys, enjoying the wonder of boyish pranks. When fellows in the neighborhood would call him, "Sam, Sam the butcher man, takes a knife and kills his wife," Sam would chase them. "Once I chased them," he remembered with pride, "and fell and got a terrible gash in my knee cap. I still have the scar. I had 15 stitches. We went to the doctor immediately.

"They used to call me spunky because I wasn't afraid of anything," Sam went on. "There was a big store on Grand Street, a drug store. We would play 'follow the master.' I would be the master. You'd open the door and yell and run. Crazy. They'd follow you and do the same yelling."

He continued, "We would steal sweet potatoes. The grocery stores had them outside. We were fast. My aunt didn't know we did that. She'd punish us if she did. Being good came later. We'd get wood and empty boxes and save them in the cellar and then we brought them out and made a big fire. When it came down a little bit, we'd put the sweet potatoes in."

As Jaffe told stories, he would re-enter his boyhood, capturing the essence of what he described both in his voice and his animation: "We'd also steal watermelons. We went up on the roof. We didn't like the man who had a stand, an open stand. So we would eat the watermelon and throw the rind down on him. There were many bad things that we did."

During Sam's live-in time with the Levys, he used to work until late into the night. "My bed, during weddings, was used by babies and a woman watched them," he said. "When it came time for me to sleep it was too damn wet. So I slept in my clothes on the floor. All I had to do in the morning was wash my face and go to school."

The wall in Sam's little coatroom, used for a bedroom, didn't go to the ceiling. Sam used to have nightmares of people coming in because of the transom. During his marriage to Bettye, he would fight in his sleep and wake up yelling. The nightmares always had to do with someone coming over the wall. They evoked great fear in him and he would wake up soaking wet. Once, he even socked Bettye from within his sleep-fear, as if fighting someone off.

As a child he would put his blanket over his head when he would go to sleep. He always felt it was a wonder that he didn't suffocate himself. His nightmares continued into the 1970's. Then, all of a sudden, the dream left and never came back.

As early as eight years of age, Sam Jaffe had already seen the seamiest side of life. He knew just about everything because his work involved making deliveries to private rooms. However, no matter what he saw, he always felt enormous respect for the people involved. He constantly reminded himself that being good was the most important thing in the world. Whereas many who knew him thought that Sam was innately exemplary, Sam's need to remind himself to be good shows that such a commitment requires work and constant vigilance.

Sam had been born into a non-religious family. He knew that he was Jewish and was proud of being Jewish by heritage and tradition, but he didn't like any religious trappings. Long into his life, he remembered how strong and religious the Orthodox Jews in his neighborhood were. He told of Jewish people who sat in front of the synagogue on East Broadway on Yom Kippur and ate food in defiance of those inside. The Orthodox stoned them for their lack of respect.

Sam's grand uncle, Morris Epstein, prepared him for his Bar Mitzvah. It was at the Beth Midrash Hagadol on Norfolk Street that he said his portion of the Torah. Throughout his life, Jaffe had little interest in any type of religious expression and he did not attend services, even on the High Holy Days. It was only in his later years that he bought himself a Hebrew grammar and taught himself the language. Learning and studying, especially language, were very important to him. He got to a point where he could read and speak Hebrew fairly well.

Sam Jaffe was a Jew in his sense of social responsibility and commitment, his generosity and his caring. He had great identity with Jews as an ethnic group and he became a strong supporter of Israel. As he grew older, Jaffe felt more Jewish than in his early years. He very much appreciated the courage the Jews had through two-thousand years of persecution. They held fast to their ethical teachings.

Jaffe used to tell the story of the Persian who asked to be taught the Jewish Bible while he stood on one foot. Shammai, who was a contemporary of Hillel, drove him out. The Persian went to Hillel and asked the same thing. Hillel replied, "Don't do to your enemy what you wouldn't do to yourself." The Persian asked if that was all. Hillel said yes, that all the rest was commentary. The Persian responded that if that was the case, then he wished to learn the Jewish bible. Hillel's philosophy was a pillar in Jaffe's life.

Jaffe was also always mindful of the vast contribution made by Jews throughout history: Marx, Freud, Einstein and many others.

Although Jews had much to offer, they suffered discrimination in job hiring and other areas. Sam recalled many instances of Jews being locked out or held back during his youth: "They didn't employ any Jews in the telephone company or the electric company. At Harvard you had to send a photograph with your application for enrollment. They had quotas."

After P. S. 120, Sam went to P. S. 160 on Suffolk and Rivington Streets. In the American Jewish Committee Oral Memoir, Sam reflected on his neighborhood and what it was like to grow up Jewish: "On Jackson Street, about ten blocks away from where I lived, there were public baths to which we would go. Jackson Street was an Irish neighborhood. We were a Jewish neighborhood around Clinton, Ridge and Attorney Streets. The Italian neighborhood was on Chrystie Street. When [we] went to the Jackson Street baths, the Irish would see us nude [circumcised] in the baths and they'd beat us up. We called the Irish 'Mickey bottles' because of their uncut penises."

Sam went on: "When they came to St. Mary's Church on Ridge St., a few blocks from where I lived, we'd wait for them to come down out of church and we'd get our revenge by beating them. There were even fights among different blocks. Suffolk Street would come and fight us. They would search [us] and it was, 'Put up your hands.' They'd go through [our] pockets and say, 'What streeter are you?' If we said the wrong street, then they would jump us. We would fight. I fought too.

"There were the boilers. They were used for boiling clothes. They had an oval shape and a big top with a handle. That top was used as a shield. We would take them from the house and use them to fend off a bottle or a stone. The battle cry was, 'Go on there! Go on there!' And whoever won would clear the block of the opponent, and the opponents would then go up on the roofs and they would throw bricks down on us as we were clearing the block.

"There were tough guys at school, too, who would demand a couple of pennies from us or give us a sock in the nose."

As Jaffe related his memories, the scents, sounds, and colorfulness of the crowded Lower East Side of the turn of the century became palpable. It was easy to walk with him through a potpourri of people.

"Our relations with the Italians were peaceful," he recalled. "Their pushcarts were laden with fruits of all kinds which we bought. The Italians ate a lot of vegetables, so we called them gruz-eaters, grass eaters. They were always nice. The Italian neighborhood on Chrystie Street was about eight blocks west of my street. A few blocks south of the Bowery was Chinatown where for five cents you'd get a large hunk of sugar cane as well as litchi nuts.

"But I must tell you an interesting thing with respect to the Jews and how we got even. If a bearded Jew passed a Christian neighborhood, they'd pull his beard. In like manner, if a Chinese passed a Jewish or Christian neighborhood, we pulled his braid."

Sam went on to tell how the Chinese wrote laundry tickets in Chinese and tore them in half. "You brought back the half to pick up the laundry. We'd always run into their laundries yelling and playing follow the master. They'd be ironing shirts and dunking them in a tub of water and all steam would come out and we would run away. If we were nice when we got our laundry, they'd give us a couple of litchi nuts. They kept their tea in a basket, to keep it warm, I suppose. They slept on boards: an upper and lower like on Pullmans. They slept right on the board."

The Chinese weren't the only ones who lived and worked in the same place. In those days on the Lower East Side, before the unions, it was common practice. Sam recalled how people worked at home making cigarettes: "They would fill them. They'd get the gillehs, which was just the empty paper, the munshtik, that's the mouth piece, and then the little piece where you put the tobacco in. They'd push it through, get it all together, cut the ends down and put it in a box. They were paid so much per box."

The coming into being of the Amalgamated Clothing Union changed the work-at-home situation. Sam got to know organizer Sidney Hillman very well: "They beat him when he tried to unionize the people working in the tenements." Sam grimaced as he recalled the strikes and fires in 1907 and 1908. The worst was the Triangle Fire on 23rd Street. It was a catastrophe because all the windows and exit doors were closed. The women workers were burned alive because they couldn't get out. It was one of the terrible disasters in New York's history. The unions were the first ones to demand decent working conditions and wages, and the elimination of sweat shops.

When Sam was in high school, the whole family moved again. The Kahns moved to a brand new building at 810 East 108th Street. The Jaffes moved to number 1012. Where the Kahns moved, the Jaffes relocated. The two families were always together and there was great affection between them. It was an environment in which generosity was modeled. No one had very much but everything they did have was shared.

Sam was a universal man. He had the feeling that he belonged to people who were always one for all and all for one. His whole family was like that. The family gathered to celebrate events. They were Jews who were humanitarian rather than religious. Whoever was in need was helped.

****

JACK KLUGMAN, *Bury the Dead*, 1949

"I'd been doing off-Broadway and summer stock, but a lot of producers came to the Equity Library Theatre. Out of that I got an audition for the road company of Mr. Roberts with Henry Fonda. That started me working. It was a wonderful showcase.

"When I was cast I felt like I always felt when I was cast, elated. It was a fine place to work and wonderful actors to work with. Those were the days of Rod Steiger and Lee Marvin. Everyone was around. It was fun.

"I was a very young and raw actor then. I was going with the woman who became my wife. She came to see the play. I was playing the sergeant and I bellowed every line. I loved the drama of it. She came backstage and we talked about it. She said, 'Why don't you go over it and see how many lines you can say without shouting.' I worked all night because we opened the next night and I realized as I went through the lines there was not one that needed to be shouted. It was an experience that for the next 35 years stood me in good stead.

"Equity Library Theatre had a good reputation and big agents came religiously. I know a lot of people who got jobs as a result."

****

Family Influences

As Sam Jaffe entered adolescence, he remained separated from his mother and siblings. Ada had become even more involved with Jewish theater and could not participate in the raising of her youngest son. Rachel and Morris Levy continued to bear responsibility for Sam. In spite of his transient living arrangements, Jaffe excelled in school and earned the honor of acceptance to the Townsend Harris Preparatory High School. Townsend Harris exposed students to great learning, including the study of Greek and Latin. The two brightest students from each school in New York City were selected for admission. The honor enabled Sam to complete high school in three years, and then to attend City College tuition-free.

At first, the location of Townsend Harris was 23rd Street and Lexington Avenue. Sam was able to walk to classes with his equally bright friend, Adolph Noschkes. They would hold stimulating discussions about current events as they walked uptown. Throughout Sam's life this practice with friends continued and was very important to him.

Before long, Townsend Harris moved to 137th Street and Amsterdam Avenue, into a building of Gothic architecture woven into the City College campus. Then Jaffe and Noschkes would meet to take the subway from Spring St. to 137th Street.

In those days a subway ticket was only five cents. That five cent fare took passengers far and wide, from upper Manhattan to Coney Island. To make the point about how much transportation one got for his money, Sam told of the service offered by the Jewish newspaper, *The Forward*. It ran a page with pictures of husbands who had disappeared and invited the deserted wives to come there for counseling. They asked one woman where she thought her husband might have gone this time. Her answer was, "Who knows, perhaps a great, great distance, at least for fifteen cents carfare."

After they graduated, Noschkes ran the Educational Alliance Roof Garden and he put his friend Sam in charge of the gym. Sam was muscular, lean, and very strong. It was one of many varied jobs he had before starting his life career.

Sam never forgot his days at Townsend Harris, nor did they forget him. In December 1962, at the 82nd Alumni Dinner held at the Grand Ballroom of the Hotel Astor, Sam Jaffe won the Townsend Harris Medal for distinguished post-graduate achievement. They listed him as an actor of stage, screen and radio and television "who has distinguished himself in a long series of outstanding character roles."

Sam Jaffe had also been President of the Student Body at City College. [By coincidence, his future wife Bettye was President of her student body when she attended Columbia College.] Jaffe graduated from City College of New York in 1912, with a Bachelors in Science degree.

Although Sam didn't live with his mother and sisters, they all helped support him while he was in college. His Aunt Ray, with whom he did live, had seen him through elementary school, high school, and college. Ray died not long after Sam graduated from C.C.N.Y.

Rachel and Morris went to live on a farm in Thompsonville, New York, between Fallsburg and Monticello, just before her death. The Levys didn't farm but ran a summer boarding house so that he could make a living. Mothers and children would come for a few weeks' vacation, or for the summer, and the fathers would come on weekends. The building had three bedrooms upstairs, a living room, dining room, kitchen downstairs, and an outhouse. Morris put in plumbing, built on little cottages, and advertised for summer boarders.

Sam's Uncle Saul gave Morris Levy his start. It was another case of the Kahn branch of the family supporting the Jaffes. Morris needed money to buy supplies, such as flour, sugar, and coffee. Saul gave him a lump sum for the summer and sent his own children up there. His help was in the form of rent. Family people always got the worst rooms and the paying guests would think the families were charity cases, even though they were the prepaid people.

When the Levys moved to the farm, Sam moved in with his mother because he needed a place to live in the city. He was 21 years old and it was the first time he had lived with her since he was a small boy. He brought his salary home to her, such as it was, to help with the support of his sisters. He had taken a job teaching English to foreigners in evening school for about $20 a week. Following his sister Sophie's lead, he also taught piano during the day. He would make his students sing and try to find the melody on the piano, thus familiarizing them with the instrument.

Before long, some friends of Sam's started The Bronx Cultural Institute to ready students for college entrance. Sam became Dean of the Mathematics Department and prepared people for the Regents. Although the title sounds impressive, Jaffe had still not chosen a life's work.

His uncle, Saul Kahn, took him to task for this because he thought Sam wasn't ambitious. Kahn would ask him when he was going to get a real job or settle down to a career. He wanted Sam to promote himself and get recognized for his talents. Sam was content to study, to read or to play the piano.

It was during this time of living with Ada that Sam

started playing the piano more seriously. He hoped that eventually he would find himself. Rather than having ambition, Sam let his life unfold. He didn't actively pursue much of anything, not even women. There is no indication from anyone who knew him that he dated or sought the company of women even into his late twenties. It wasn't that he didn't like women; rather, he had more interest in fostering intellectually nurturing friendships with male peers. His need for male bonding was great because of the lack of it in his early life.

Here Sam was, a college graduate in his early twenties, holding odd jobs to earn money, and living with his mother rather than setting up his own apartment. It would seem that Sam was still in the process of maturing during that time. He hadn't settled on a career, hadn't found full-time day employment, and wasn't dating. His ties to his family were very important. It may have been an act of completion for Sam to move in with his mother after more than 15 years of being farmed out. Perhaps it was Sam's way of giving his 'inner child' what it had missed.

Until about 1916, when he was 25, Sam spent every summer at Levy's Cottages. He served as the social director. He would run the Saturday night shows and everyone praised his talent. He wrote and performed parodies, and conducted amateur nights.

Sam not only spent summers at the farm belonging to his Uncle Morris, he stayed on after the season was over, and went up during the winter. Irving Kahn recalled "going when I was twelve and Sam taking me sleigh riding. He was a tall guy. He'd put me on a sled and I could ride on his legs. There were a lot of hills. We had some very nice Christmas holidays up there."

Irving looked up to Sam as someone who had great patience with people, and who took time to answer questions. He saw him as an inherently good teacher and said that having a relative like Sam was an extraordinary experience.

Important changes occurred in Sam's life as a result of his experiences out of the city. It was on the farm that Sam became a vegetarian. He had witnessed the birth of a calf. It was a very exciting event, but to his horror, after a few weeks, the calf was taken from the cow and sent to the slaughter house. "It killed me," he lamented. "The poor cow mourned for a long time." The cow had wailed so profoundly that the sound haunted Sam long into his life. What was even worse for him was that "people were each demanding certain portions of the calf when they brought it back from the slaughter house. It was horrible. So I stopped eating meat." This story underscores Jaffe's sensitivity.

Jaffe also stopped eating chickens when he witnessed their slaughter. He noted with dismay: "The Christians cut the head off. The Jewish way is that you cut the jugular vein and let the blood run out. The chicken walks a couple of steps and then falls down. So I stopped eating chicken. On Passover they served me the head of a fish with the eye popping out. So I stopped eating fish. In my day, the eggs used to be candled. You could open an egg and be greeted by a chick. So I stopped eating eggs. I became a complete vegetarian."

He was very picky about what he ate. He lived on nuts, fruit, and vegetables for a long time.

Years later, while working in a play in New York, he contracted a rare tropical fever and was in the hospital. Everyone begged him to come back or the show would close. He did return, only to suffer a terrible relapse that left him near death. His doctor insisted that he add fish and eggs to his diet. Jaffe wouldn't eat eggs in an omelet or scrambled, but he consented to having them in cake or bread. He also began to eat fish, and he learned to enjoy it, but he remained a non-meat eater to the end of his life.

Sam had a sweet tooth while never claiming one. While guests were visiting them in their Beverly Hills home, years later, Bettye served tea and cheese cake. After Sam had eaten the cake, he reported to his guests that he never ate sweets. Bettye did a double-take, but waited until they left to confront him. She reminded him that although it was three o'clock in the afternoon, he had already had three desserts. His response was very childlike. "I don't put sugar in my coffee," he replied. Sam never understood why that was so amusing to Bettye. It was simply the way it was for him. He wasn't attempting to be funny. If he didn't take sugar directly, as far as he was concerned he wasn't eating sweets.

During the time Sam lived with Ada, she was appearing in the chorus in a Brooklyn Jewish theater company. These shows were scripted and the actors also improvised. The actors performed so many shows on any given day that they were not expected to memorize their lines, relying instead on prompters when they got lost in improvisation. Sam further wet his theatrical feet by filling in as a prompter.

Sam remembered, "In the big cities like Chicago and Philadelphia, even Montreal, there were always Jewish immigrants. They were eager for Jewish companies to come and perform. To take along a prompter was rather expensive. They'd have to pay his fare. So they'd pick up some Jewish person to be the prompter. You heard a Jewish play twice, first from the prompter and then from the actor. (He laughed.) I learned how to prompt that way, you know, just a little ahead of time. And they got one prompter who, so my mother tells me, opened the book and didn't hear anything from the actor. So he said, 'Nu, let's hear a word?' He didn't understand that he was to feed them their lines.

"The later Jewish theater was divided — half Yiddish and a little English. When a man comes to a new country he wants to speak the language as best he can. That was the time when there were the famous English-Jewish plays about Jews in the clothing business; Montague Glass plays. They were very successful. He came from England. And then I think it was the B'nai B'rith who was opposed to any caricaturing of the Jews, so they stopped, although the plays were very amusing. But they felt it gave a wrong image of the Jews. This must have been in the middle '30's. The Yiddish theater was of course very active from the 1900's through the '20's."

Spending time with his mother in and around Jewish theater awakened Sam's interest in acting. Her lifestyle affected the whole family. Sam's nephew, Merwin Dembling, spoke of how his grandmother, Ada, played at the Regent Theater vaudeville house on 116th Street. Merwin would go up there during his lunch time and she would warm up some soup over her mascara heater. He described her as a wonderful, warm woman who was always telling him to "Vatch your diction, damn it." She was a seasoned trooper. She had made a home for herself in a small studio apartment, a satisfactory place on Mt. Morris Park, with tiffany lamp shades she later passed on to Merwin. He didn't get to see her very much because she was always on the road.

Sam was to follow his mother's lead. His eventual career took him on the road as well. Merwin remembered a long corridor outside Ada's apartment. Residents would have to sidle through because there would be six big wardrobe trunks: Ada Jaffe Hotel, Ada Jaffe Theater, Sam Jaffe Hotel, Sam Jaffe Theater, Lillian Taiz Hotel, and Lillian Taiz Theater. [Lillian Taiz was Sam's first wife.]

Sam always retained a close connection with his immediate family, feeling a bond with them even when he lived with the Levys. When his sister Sophie moved into her own apartment on 8th Street, she ran it the way her mother did, as a stopping over place. If people were broke or in-between jobs, they could come up and sleep and eat at Sophie's. There would always be other people there. It was a live-wire crowd, very happy people, full of jokes and eccentricities.

Sophie was a unique personality. According to her nephew Merwin Dembling, his aunt never voted and never paid any income tax. She paid cash for all her purchases. As far as he knew, she never had a bank account. She went to Europe every summer, and was a typical spinster.

Sam had great respect for Sophie because she took care of herself. He valued that quality highly. His sister Annie wasn't as ambitious and needed more support from her brothers. Family members spoke of Annie as a good-looking woman with a fine singing voice, the kind you would read about who would sit and eat bon-bons, and do nothing. Annie's husband was a pharmacist named Dembling who had a store on 8th Street. Their son, Merwin, lived in New York and was a writer for technical publications. The family did not fare well financially.

Annie wasn't an intellectual like her brother Sam but she was someone who was very caring toward people who were in trouble and needed help. She was good, the way Sam was good.

There was a strong value in the immediate and extended family on helping people in need. They had helped and cared for Sam, and he observed, repeatedly, how his relatives extended that hand even to strangers. Although the Jaffes didn't have great material wealth, they were very cultured people. In their humble little apartment on 108th Street, they had first class oil paintings because they had befriended unrecognized painters and shared their food and money with them. The Jaffes didn't have much money because they earned little and they shared what they had.

Annie (left) Dembling and
Sophie Jaffe, Sam's sisters.

Sam Jaffe as a young man.

Later on, when Sam was appearing on stage, his sister Annie used to say that Sam's friends would line up at the stage door on pay day and that he would give all his money away. Although Sam would occasionally help a friend, he called Annie's comment an exaggeration.

The resilience of the Jaffe family impressed Irving Kahn very much: "Sam was a remarkable man. He was very cheerful, loved a good laugh and a good joke. The Jaffes were all that way. Abe and Sophie would get you laughing until the tears rolled down." It impressed the Kahn family that the Jaffes were very happy people even though they had endured the disappearance of their father and their mother had very limited income as an actress. Sam wasn't a particularly good money-maker either in those early years. It was thanks to his brother Abe and his Uncle Sol that the family got financial aid. Sophie's piano teaching also helped.

Sam Jaffe had a particular and special place in his family from the time he was very young. Similar to Abe and Sophie, he had a fantastic sense of humor and he used it to great advantage. But he went a step farther. Cousin Lee Reichart marveled: "He could take any situation where people were very tied up in knots and find a way to unravel the knots by saying the right phrase. Whatever it was, he could solve a problem, not by solving the problem but by taking the anxiety out of the problem."

It was hard to describe how Sam accomplished this. He would gesture like a mime, even when he was very young. He used his body to form the question, "In the end how is it going to matter?"

When word came to the family that someone died, everyone would worry about what the widow was going to do. Sam would break through the worry asking, "Who ran the household before?" He would do it in a light-hearted, gay way so that everyone would accept it. No one else in the family did this and it served to change the prevailing mood. He could somehow make light of a tragic situation without making a mockery of it.

Reichart spoke of Sam's many friends: "Remarkably, there was always enough food for whoever came into the house. Sometimes Soph would make a meal on Friday hoping it would do for Saturday. By Saturday afternoon Sam's friends had eaten it all up already. So she'd come up to my house. By the way, we never called ourselves by just a name. Cousin so and so is the way we addressed others, or uncle, or aunt. It always preceded our name; it was a way of life.

"We all had endearing personalities. We'd see each other and half an hour later we'd see each other again and we'd kiss, we'd hug. We were a very affectionate family, always. Demonstrative, but we didn't put on shows for each other or pretend. We never boasted. We were poor people. We didn't have things to show off."

Sam began teaching and turning his money over to the family. His mother gave it to his brother, Abe, who had a candy factory. She felt everyone needed to support him. When Sam's father died, he left $8,000 to the family. That money also went into the candy factory. No one had any objections. Everyone was committed to supporting Abe, with both their money and their time.

Sam described working there: "We used to cook. We'd whip up dry eggs from China, add water and whip it up. We had two large copper bowls and boiled the glucose in those and then poured it into a huge tank in which we put the eggs and mixed it up. We poured it out into the little sizes of the nugget. We'd cut it in a big slice and the workers put the paper [actually, a sugar coating] over it, cut it to size, wrapped it. I gave it the name Snowflake, melts in your mouth. But the people didn't know that the candy melts. So his candy was not successful. My brother advertised on the elevated stations but it didn't go."

The failure must have been a terrible disappointment, especially considering the investments made on every level by the whole family.

Abe had always been very supportive of the family, and that continued after the collapse of the factory. When he was in his thirties he married a redheaded gentile German girl named Dorothy. This was while Ada was on the road in *Abie's Irish Rose*. Dorothy was afraid when her mother-in-law said she was coming to visit. She went to a Jewish neighborhood to find out how to make gefilte fish and chicken soup. She wanted to make a very Jewish meal for Ada.

Dorothy eventually died in an automobile accident in San Francisco. According to June Jaffe, Abe's daughter-in-law, Dorothy died as a result of alcoholism: "She ran out of the house after an argument with Abe. She was in her nightgown with no identification and was hit by a bus. She was a Jane Doe for days in the morgue until someone came down and identified her. It wasn't exactly an auto accident."

True auto accident or not, a motor vehicle killed more than one person in the Jaffe family. An auto accident took the lives of Ada and Morris as they traveled to his place in the country. This was just before she went to New York to be screen tested for the film version of *Abie's Irish Rose*. The accident occurred in Tuxedo, New York. The year was 1927, the year of Sam's 35th birthday and the year of his first marriage.

As was true of Abe's wife and Sam's mother, an auto accident killed Sophie in New Rochelle, New York. Sam said, "She was run down by an automobile that had no windshield wipers. They took his license away from him. After about two years he came to me asking what he could do to get back his license. I felt two years was enough punishment so I went and spoke for him so he could get his license again. Sophie didn't die right away. She had damage and was in the hospital. She had a brain concussion. It was exactly the year that I was in *Gunga Din*, 1938."

Most who knew him thought of Abe as a wonderful gentleman and a very hard worker. Later on, he became an executive for Peter Paul Mounds. Irving Kahn reported, "Abe got some stock in the company and was the only one in the whole damn family that had any money." While the factory hadn't been a success, the candy business was where Abe made his fortune. He remained generous to his family following his success.

Abe was an entirely different personality from Sam in that he was an extrovert and a very successful businessman. He adored Sam because Sam was the intellectual and the artist. Like Sam, he was a very generous person and a genial man who seemed always in good humor. He was taller and more robust than Sam, with a round face, and a love of drink, dress, and fine restaurants. He was a bon vivant.

Abe and Dorothy had a son whom they named

Sam Adason Jaffe. Young Sam was a news correspondent for ABC. Before that, he had written feature stories for the New York *Herald Tribune*. Once his byline started to appear in the drama section, his Uncle Sam, the actor, began receiving call after call asking him when he had taken up writing.

When Sam Jaffe the newsman was with CBS News, his uncle was on the payroll as a frequent *Playhouse 90* performer. The network auditors always managed to send each the other's tax forms and withholding statements.

Charges that he was a double agent between the CIA and the Soviet Union eventually destroyed young Sam's career. Though he fiercely denied all charges against him, like his uncle before him (albeit for other false charges), he was blacklisted.

ABC brought Jaffe back from Hong Kong in 1969 and never told him why, although he demanded to know and was sure the CIA had ordered his return. Jaffe also charged that when he was in Vietnam, network newsmen "went out into the field and did what we felt were constructive stories to inform the American people. Time and time again they were shelved. The network chiefs, the news chiefs, were not interested." He said this was because of government pressure.

Sam supported his nephew during his blacklisting difficulties, no doubt remembering his own. The good relations did not last long, however.

The early family influences of generosity, support, and mutual caring played a big role in the development of Sam Jaffe's personality and in his choosing of values by which to live. These values became convictions. While they were admirable, Jaffe would later slip over an edge, overlaying his convictions on others in his family, namely his nephews. This led to great unhappiness, as well as to painful rifts. Jaffe had always been a healer and able to see a larger picture, but his entrapment in his own values caused him suffering and held him bound in a limited perspective in his family relations.

Shortly before Abe's death, he talked with Sam about wanting to leave him money in his will. Sam said he didn't want anything from him. He hadn't helped Abe in the candy factory for subsequent reward. Because Sam rejected his offer, Abe said instead that he would see to Annie's support. Relieving Sam of any such obligation was Abe's way of repaying his brother.

The two brothers truly loved one another. When Abe died, Sam didn't talk about it. He stored his inner grief and kept it to himself.

It was following Abe's death that the tremendous rift developed between Sam Jaffe and his nephew, Sam A. Jaffe. The elder Sam documented his grievance:

"My brother left his son about a quarter of a million in Peter Paul stock, besides some other stock, with the request that his son continue to take care of his mother's brother Charlie, and of our sister, Annie, as Abe had done; that is, by sending Annie two hundred dollars a month. I don't know the specific amount assigned for Charlie. Sammy honored the request for Annie for just one month. I doubt that he ever sent a cent to Charlie."

Annie had told Sam that she got only one or two checks. Sam became furious with his nephew. Bettye remembered that young Sam's wife, June Jaffe, wrote the most scathing letter in which she said that Annie was lying. She claimed she went into the attic and had listed the checks that they had sent to Annie. Bettye was livid about this response because June never sent actual cashed checks as proof, and because she had accused Annie of lying.

After Abe's death, Sam sent Annie a hundred dollars a month. He wrote to his nephew, admonishing him for his failure to honor Abe's request. What happened next led to the complete dissolution of relations between the two. Sam was beside himself in reporting, "Instead of writing me — he was too guilt-laden — he called our dear friend Mona Malden, asking whether I was senile. Mona told him that she wished everyone was as lucid as I am. It's a strange and sad turnabout when an ignoramus dares to pass judgment about his intellectual superior."

Aube Tzerko, one of Sam's most intimate friends said Sam recoiled at the mention of Sammy's name. He would wave the name away. Sam never forgave him.

Tzerko reported: "If Sam turned negative toward someone, he'd totally eclipse this character, wipe him out of his life. Sam had some dramatic hates. The war period, the extermination of Jews, the inhumanity of any situation, these deeply affected him. He would voice it. It wasn't just an individual thing. It had to do with injustice. He had a sense of justice, of right from wrong, and it regulated his life."

This report from Tzerko speaks volumes of just how outraged Sam was about his nephew. Practically everyone who knew Sam spoke of him as did his first cousin, Irving Kahn: "He was a soft-spoken cultured man. He didn't have a temper. He was the kind of guy who, if you spit in his eye, he'd probably take out his handkerchief, wipe his eye, and continue the conversation. He might be angry in principle, about injustices. He wasn't vituperative in any way. He was too bright a man. He was philosophical. He knew it didn't do any good to start screaming. He was an exemplary man. He knew it was better, as they say, to light a candle than curse the darkness. He attracted friends and kept them for years. He always helped people. He didn't expect any rewards for doing the right thing."

Jaffe would remind a friend like Aube Tzerko to temper his critical opinion of another by saying, "Why do you want only to look at these bad things or these negatives?" Then he would immediately juxtapose a positive.

But Jaffe didn't do that when it came to family.

Annie was his sister. Even when he hadn't seen her in a long time, she was always in the back of his mind. Sammy was his blood, and that seemed to make all the difference. He felt his nephews had an obligation to live the exemplary lives that he had led. If they didn't embody his standards, it was a reflection on him and he couldn't stand it. It was as bad as if he had done the bad deed himself and, therefore, it was unforgivable.

There is a clear example of this. After Abe died, young Sam came with his wife, June, and their baby, to stay with Sam and Bettye for a few days. According to Sam and Bettye, the visit dragged into weeks, with Sammy and June imposing themselves. After they left, Sam and Bettye collapsed in fatigue. However, neither of them had asked Sammy and June to leave.

When spoken to about the visit, June Jaffe expressed puzzlement: "For someone they didn't like, they would always invite us to dinner parties and out with friends. I don't know what triggered that unless the underlying thing was money, unless they thought we were sitting here on millions." June said that during the visit Sam was always pleasant to her and that she bought gifts to say thank you. "It wasn't a one-sided thing," she stated.

Bettye was closest to Sam during this period of family tribulation and had a full dose of his feelings and thoughts on the subject. She made no bones about the fact that neither she nor Sam cared very much for either of his nephews, Sammy and Merwin. "Sam was crazy about his brother. So was I. If Sammy wanted something, Sam would say I'm not doing it for Sammy, I'm doing it for Abe."

The issue of money was a sensitive area for Sam Jaffe. When he gave it, he gave it freely, not as a loan but as a gift. He refused anything in return. An example of this was the money he gave to his friend Philip Loeb toward the care of his son. When the son died, Philip had stipulated that some money should go to Sam amongst other people. Philip's executor, Ezra Stone, invited Sam and Bettye to his house for dinner and gave Sam a check from Philip Loeb. Sam refused it saying, "I do not want to benefit from anybody's death and certainly not Phil's." Ezra gave it to the Academy of Dramatic Arts instead.

Merwin Dembling had another side of the story to tell: "Sam was always the very center of the family. I think he skewed the entire family. There was no appeal from his dicta. He was adored by all."

June Jaffe had heard the same assessment from her husband, Sammy. His aunts Sophie and Annie lived together as "a really odd couple in their little studio apartment on Waverly Place. They had a grand piano and a hot plate to cook on. The place was full of clippings from Ada, Sophie, Sam and young Sam. They lived in this past. They watched movies and went out to eat most of the time."

June went on, "They idolized their brother. Sam, Sam, Sam . . . a lama in everyday life, all the time. He could do no wrong. First Annie idolized him and then Bettye. I'm sure he wasn't that perfect," she mused. "I don't think he was conscious that he used his money as control within the family. He had control anyhow because my mother and her sister and his brother Abe all adored him and deferred to him right and left. He was the first one to go to college. Abe was always the steady one, the business man type and he lit out early for the west and did very well."

Merwin wouldn't say that Sam was controlling; it was rather that everyone else allowed him to be. Merwin had gotten several thousand dollars in presents for his bar mitzvah that he never saw. When his grandmother Ada died, he was the beneficiary of a life insurance policy on her life from the National Vaudeville Artists. He thought it was $10,000. "Sam wouldn't let us take the money. He said it was blood money," Merwin reported in response to being told of Sam's upset that he had borrowed $2,000 from his mother and never paid it back. Merwin's retort spoke of his deserving reimbursement for his losses as a boy or for what he never received. As to the life insurance, Sam was against benefiting from someone's death, and he made that decision for Merwin despite what Merwin's feelings might have been.

Sam seemed unable to make room for Merwin's actions toward Annie and held his nephew in an unfavorable light. Yet, Sam had a similar event in his own background. Though he had no desire ever to speak of or see his father, he recounted one story about an exchange with his father: "I was with the Washington Square Players, playing in Pittsburgh. One day there wasn't enough money in the till, so I borrowed $300 from my father to get out of Pittsburgh." His father was working there at the time, selling old gold. According to Sam his father never got the money back, and he never got over it. The action on Sam's part might well have been a son taking from his father a small symbolic piece of what was his birthright.

Merwin continued his lament: "My father was not exactly the strongest personality in the world and whatever my uncle said was the law, graven in granite, for my mother. I had nobody to stick up for me at that point. I might have felt rebellious. I got the hell out of there and went to Europe."

Again Merwin made excuses for Sam's behavior: "It wasn't Sam who was dominating the family. It was their attitude toward him. It was not his attitude in general that I objected to. It was them in relation to him. I don't think anybody can ask to be adored and then be adored. His sister [Sophie] never married because she said she could never find anybody who was as good as Sam. I couldn't stomach the adoration."

As Merwin continued, his childhood story took on

additional similarities to his uncle's: "I never really had a home. I lived from relative to relative. My mother kept saying she didn't like housework and she didn't do any. I never had a room of my own. I had a folding bed that I used to make up every night and sleep in the living room.

"When Lillian [Sam's first wife] died, my mother spent every day in Sam's apartment, cooking, cleaning, and doing everything. That really pissed me off. She did that for him but she wouldn't do that for me."

Annie told Merwin that his birth had been very difficult; he was born Caesarean. She told him, "Samele said if I have another baby he'll never talk to me again. So I never did."

Merwin said that Sophie had the same kind of relationship with Sam: "He was a saint to all his relatives and friends. There are things I would have changed in Sam but then he wouldn't have been Sam. He wouldn't have been the same person.

"I would have changed his attitude toward me a little bit. I'm a very poor retainer. I can be a friend but I can't be a retainer in the Shakespearean sense: A person serving another, an adherent. I think he had mainly retainers. I think Karl [Malden] was a retainer. Zero [Mostel] was a friend and yet also there was this admiration or adoration. He surrounded himself with family and friends like that. He didn't have friends who were not achievers. I don't know whether he discouraged them or what. I wonder if mine isn't the standard poor relation's perspective."

Merwin also felt misjudged by Bettye: "When we were living in London, she was over there and she got some crazy idea that I was talking about her. It wasn't true. I don't know anybody that I could talk about her to."

There was never a healing of the rift between

Sam and his two nephews. He wanted nothing to do with them, nor did he have any interest in changing his point of view. He was either tenacious or unforgiving.

****

JAMES EARL JONES, *Dark of the Moon*, 1959, *Mr. Johnson*, 1963

"*At the time of* Dark of the Moon *I had just been into my career for two years. I had finished the American Theatre Wing in 1957. I got my first off-Broadway job at that time in commercial theater where I got paid $30 a week.*

"*I reflected on* Dark of the Moon *later on when I did Genet's* The Blacks. *That was the beginning of a gathering of what were called 'mummers' in those days, actors of color. The choice that Vinnette Carroll made was to do it with a predominantly black cast. She flip-flopped the ethnic composition. I think there was one Caucasian lady in it. The same way you'd ordinarily have one black person in a Caucasian cast. Vinnette Carroll gathered all the actors who were prominent, and are still prominent in the theater, and to some extent, in motion picture and television today.*

"*Roscoe Lee Brown headed the cast as the preacher. I have never seen him more wonderful. The event of being on stage with him was one of the most electrifying, exciting things I can remember about my career, my time in the theater. Roscoe who is known as a poetic, drama performer, who to a great extent has a great use of language, was playing a down home, backwoods country preacher. He used all the same power he's known for in his poetic work in that dialogue.*

"*The atmosphere there was high because we were all excited to work with each other. It wasn't anything that anybody had to whip into shape. So often in those days, even today to some extent, when you got a group of black actors together, they all brought with them the frustrations of not having been cast when they could have been, should have been, because of the social and political conditions of the country and the theater. Eventually the frustrations would outweigh the talent and come crashing down on the whole experience.*

"*In that case it didn't happen because we were all young, and it was a non-commercial event. The critics were not looming over us. Our agents were not looming over us. None of those bad pressures were brought to bear on the* production. We were all there to delight in each other. It was good, basic, raw, and always healthy, human energy applied to characters. The positive energy overruled any negative.

"I got good experience out of the shows at E.L.T. It attracted the best of us and usually the best from us."

****

A Natural Thespian

Sam Jaffe became interested in acting during backstage visits to his mother at the Thalia Theater. She was appearing on the Bowery in the chorus of Jewish theater, a prominent genre of that era.

The original Jewish theater relocated in New York from Romania. The troupe included Mogolefsky, the great comedian, and Bertha Kalish, who later appeared in Hollywood movies. By the time Sam's mother began working, three Jewish theater companies responded to the needs of the large immigration from Russia. Each of them revolved around a key actor. The Thalia had Kessler; the Windsor, Thomashefsky; and the People's Theater, Jacob Adler. In the early years most of the presentations dealt with the persecutions of the Jews.

Jewish theater productions were imitative of many of the classics. For example, Jacob P. Gordin was a playwright who wrote a version of a Faust play that he called *God, Man and Devil* (Gott, Mensch and Teifel.) There were Jewish theater versions of Shakespeare as well. Later, folk plays became prominent.

Ada Jaffe graduated from the chorus to acting. Later in her career, she married a wonderful Russian actor named Myerson. There is no indication that Sam ever had any relationship with Myerson or that the marriage met his need for a father. His mother and her new husband went on tour with their own company, called Ada Jaffe and Company. At the time, Sam was living with his Aunt and Uncle Levy. Myerson eventually went back to Russia. He wanted Ada to go with him, but she declined. She chose to remain in the States because of her children. Her loyalty no doubt meant a lot to Sam.

Jaffe's mother was a very charming, fairly good-looking woman, and a talented performer. She had an aggressive personality but never pushed her children in any career direction. During those early years, it didn't occur to Sam that he might have a career in the theater, nor did Ada influence him in that direction. He did delight in the great actors, and he often entertained friends and family with impersonations and pantomimes. In addition, he had an early ability to speak in dialects. The stage was set for Sam Jaffe to have a career, but he hadn't yet stepped onto it.

Ada left the Second Avenue stages to go on a vaudeville tour with James B. Carson in a sketch called *To Be or Not To Be*. After one season, Carson sold the sketch to her and she began touring with her own company. When they were in Colorado, she had a juvenile in the act who was mad for baseball. Every time they would come to a fresh town, he would look up the bush league team and play with them. Ada worried that he was going to get hurt.

One day she came backstage prepared to go on and she saw somebody going through her hamper where the costumes and the props were kept. When she asked what he was doing, he told her that he had just bought the act. Incredulous, she demanded to know what he was talking about since it was her act. He pointed to the juvenile and told her that he had sold it to him. Ada hit the ceiling. Apparently the young actor had been gambling on baseball. He needed $700 badly and quickly, so he sold the act. Ada paid the man his $700 and kept the juvenile on staff until he worked off the debt. Then she fired him. In the meantime, she had wired to New York to Milton Hockey, her agent, to find her someone else. She replaced Joe E. Brown with Jimmy Cagney!

Cagney, in his autobiography, mentions that he appeared in vaudeville with Sam Jaffe's mother. In going over some of his old papers many years later, Sam came across a crumpled telegram sent from the vaudeville booking office, saying: "Pay Jimmy Cagney fifteen dollars for half week in Buffalo." He mailed it to Cagney to keep as a memento.

Sam, at age 18, had the opportunity to direct his mother in her act. He also played his mother's husband in Philadelphia. This was the first of many 'beard,' or old men, roles Sam would play in his fledgling theatrical attempts. An amusing incident occurred during the run of the show. Sam went out to do some skating and had removed his beard. When he returned to the theater, the stage doorman wouldn't let him in for a while because he didn't recognize him. Sam was a very young eighteen, making it no small wonder that the stage doorman challenged his proclamation that he played there as Ada's husband.

Sam's main focus during those years was on completing his college education. He didn't study acting, but having been exposed to it through his mother he developed the belief that one couldn't become an actor

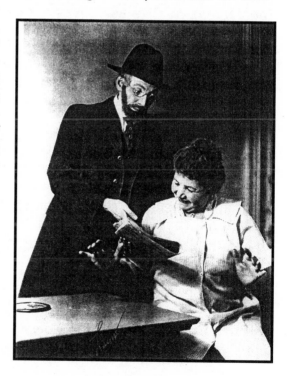

Sam Jaffe as an eighteen-year-old man playing an older man (hence the beard) in a play in Philadelphia with his mother, Ada Jaffe, seated.

unless he had studied something! "I studied people," he said. He also read novels to inform himself on character development.

Sam's friend and classmate at C.C.N.Y., Milton Hockenberg, felt Sam had talent for the theater. Jaffe remembered, "He had seen the potential when we were classmates. When we had meetings of the boys, I would either recite or do something. He wrote two acts for me. One was the *Grocery Store* which I did in vaudeville, in English. I got booked through Lewis and Gordon who booked most of the acts.

"Vaudeville acts were in English, unless we went down to the special Jewish night club that Thomashefsky had on the Lower East Side." As Sam talked of this, he made one of his typical asides. He said, "Today, his grandson is quite a marvelous young conductor, Michael Tilson Thomas. Thomas [the name] is the circumcision of Thomashefsky." The aside was Sam's way of expressing his dismay, albeit indirectly, that a Jew would shorten his name so as not to be identified with his people.

Sam did a vaudeville playlet which Harry Green had done very successfully, *The Cherry Tree*. Jaffe, however, eventually chose theater over vaudeville.

Though Jaffe had dabbled in acting during his undergraduate years, he had remained focused on civil engineering and his strong inclinations all his life to build bridges. Columbia accepted Jaffe in their engineering program. However, a vague restlessness gradually overtook Sam. That inquietude, plus the fact that his aunt and uncle did not have the money to enable him to remain in the program, caused him to leave after his first term. He relegated the bridge he had intended to build to the file of previously worthy ideas. It was at that point that Sam became Dean of the Mathematics Department at Bronx Cultural Institute in New York.

Although Sam enjoyed teaching mathematics, his

destiny began luring him in the direction of the stage. He described how circumstances led to his acting career: "While teaching, we wanted to raise money for our Institute, so we thought we'd have a dramatic soiree. We got the Washington Irving High School and put on some plays. The first was the Shaw one-act play *How He Lied to Her Husband* in which I played the poet. And then I did a protean playlet: a play in which I impersonated several characters. Milton Hochenberg had written it for me."

As previously mentioned, one of the first signs of Sam's theatrical talent had been his ability to imitate a number of the famous actors of the day. His work in the protean playlet made him think there were possibilities for him in theater. It was such a rich experience for him that he seriously wondered whether that was the path he should take. Sam was fortunate because, unlike most aspiring actors, things fell into place easily for him.

During that time, Sam had the privilege of meeting a wonderful woman named Grace Griswold who had been an actress. He remembered her vividly: "She was very imposing looking, an amazing continence, gray hair, looking like one of the Daughters of the American Revolution." She gave him recommendations to all the big producers on Broadway, but he didn't use them. More important to him than advancing his acting career was to become a great friend of her family. To this young man displaced from his birth family, a sense of belonging was the highest priority.

Sam did several plays with Griswold. She starred Jaffe in a full-length play attended by Edward Goodman who had also seen him in the protean playlet at Washington Irving. Goodman was the head of Washington Square Players. Very impressed with Jaffe, he invited him to join the company. Sam responded without question by quitting his job as dean and going with Goodman. The year was 1916. Jaffe's career began in earnest at age 25.

The Washington Square Players was a perfect company for a young actor. They ran a Players School of the Theater and had as their purpose the stimulation and development of new and artistic methods of acting, producing and writing for the American stage.

Jaffe began by understudying at the Washington Square Players. "That was my first real whiff of theater and my separation from teaching," he remembered. "It was the golden era of one-act plays. There was even a *One-Act* magazine."

Eventually he played the role of the old man in *The Clod*. It was his debut on the professional stage. At 18 he had played his mother's husband. Now in his twenties, he was again cast much beyond his years.

He went on the road with the Washington Square Players and truly enjoyed touring with them. "It was for sure my first opportunity to travel," he enthused. "We played in a number of cities like Washington and Chicago."

In the road company, there had been an actor named George Sommes who, with the actress Elizabeth Herndon Kearns, engaged Sam to do several roles in a Shakespearean company that they sponsored and in which they played the leads. Sam had strong memories of the adventure: "Sidney Blackmer was in that company. We did an interesting tour through the south, and north in the Dakotas."

"In Milwaukee," Sam continued, "I asked a man in English where to go for lodging. He didn't speak English. He could only speak German. It was a German town."

"Very often you had to shoulder your valise and hunt for lodging," Sam recalled. "All I got was $20 a week. There was no Actors' Equity and therefore no floor yet on wages. I sent $5 a week home. Fortunately the dollar could buy much more than today. I could manage on $15. I would save money by sleeping in the same berth with another actor while we toured. We ate in cafeterias when we had extra money."

Sam elaborated, "They had subscriptions then. The Drama Leagues would guarantee company performances in the various cities.

"One of the leading actors left in a huff after the night show of *Much Ado about Nothing* and I inherited his roles. We were in a place called Ozona, Texas, which is just a few miles from the Mexican border. They hadn't seen a troupe for a long time. I learned two parts over night because they wanted a milkman's matinee. The electric lights used to go off at midnight. So I studied for the role by the light of candles — and played it the next day," Sam said with a reminiscent grin. "I had the scenes all written out and I'd go over them before I went on. Shakespeare is so great. His writing is so economical and logical that it's easy to memorize. When you're younger, your memory is so much better."

Sam interjected with one of his quips: "They used to say that garlic helps memory, at least Mrs. Roosevelt said so. She said she took her garlic tablets for memory, if she could remember to take them. She was a great lady."

After the tour Jaffe returned to New York. By this time the Washington Square Players were producing full-length plays. He had a regular part in *Youth* and then they cast him as the Reverend Samuel Warren in George Bernard Shaw's *Mrs. Warren's Profession*. This was Sam's first appearance of consequence. It was also the initial presentation of the play in New York.

Jaffe revered Shaw even though he never met him. "George Bernard Shaw," he proclaimed, "was one of the biggest influences in my life, in every way: his liberal thinking and his support of a political movement for women. He was, in a sense, omniscient. There isn't anything he didn't write about. I have almost a complete library of his work. He was a musician; he conducted. He could read any score right off. He was a vegetarian who wouldn't wear leather shoes. His plays were an education for me. His criticisms were marvelous. He ran for office. He was courageous in his thinking. When he married his wife, he specifically said, 'No sex.'"

Bettye Jaffe jumped in quickly after hearing this remark and blurted: "Well, that didn't influence you!"

She told Sam that he, like Shaw, had a reddish beard and a pixie quality. Sam closed any comparison with, "That's where it ends. He was an amazing person."

In the regular company of the Washington Square Players at the time were Glenn Hunter, Helen Westley, Roland Young and Frank Conroy. Those who ran the Players later organized The Theatre Guild, which, in its day, was the theater.

"With Theatre Guild," Sam reflected, "I did *The Death of a Rat* and a very important English actor [John Gielgud] came backstage afterwards to praise me."

A somewhat frightening incident on opening night exemplified Jaffe's professionalism, even that early in his career. Jaffe was seated on a couch with a young woman character to whom he was declaring his love. The audience became restless and began murmuring as they observed smoke rising from the wire of a floor lamp standing next to the couch where they were sitting. Sam was delivering devoted dialog when the wire began crackling and sparking. By that time, the audience was very nervous. Jaffe's friend Sam Raeburn was in the house that night and gave a first-hand report of how Jaffe handled the potential crisis.

"Sam got up while continuing to speak," Raeburn marveled. "Without missing a beat, he began to stamp on the wire while proclaiming his love. If you listened to that with your eyes closed, you wouldn't know that anything was going on. Sam was wearing a sparse, handsome beard in the play. Parts of the beard began to hang loose and give, as he stamped on the wire. I can't describe how he did it because it was awesome."

Without interrupting his dialog, Sam crossed to the French window looking out on a garden. He stood looking out, talking to the young woman over his shoulder while fixing his beard. For those in attendance, it looked as if Jaffe had expected the whole thing to happen. He had the smoothness of a very experienced actor.

World War I interfered with Jaffe's career. He enlisted. Because he was a pacifist, they assigned him to a munitions factory in Montreal. Following his honorable discharge, January 23, 1919, Jaffe joined the Provincetown Players. It was another innovative company that produced many of Eugene O'Neill's plays.

In his early theater days Jaffe felt as if he could conquer the world. What made him happiest was being in a company because it meant becoming part of a family. That was more important to him than performing. After a play, he kept up the relationships. Perhaps there was a way in which theater, more than anything else, represented family for Sam because that was where his mother went when she left Sam and his siblings behind to support them. If home is where the mother is, theater was home and family for Sam.

At the Provincetown Playhouse, Jaffe appeared in *Ruint* by Hatcher Hughes, a play about South Carolina. Sam played a backwoodsman, and for the role he developed a drawl. John Huston, then 17 years old, appeared in the production. Once he and Jaffe met, they remained friends for life.

On July 15, 1986, the author met with John Huston to talk of this lasting friendship. Huston had been in the hospital with emphysema and was still hooked up to an oxygen tank. It was very difficult for him to speak.

However, his love for Sam Jaffe was so great that he wanted to participate anyway.

"You'll permit if I swerve away from the inspirational questions," he began, in response to a query about how Jaffe influenced him. "It would start off taxing me emotionally. I'd much rather approach it from a more pedestrian angle and talk of the first time I met Sam."

He spoke of *Ruint*: "It was about Southern Mountain people. I decided to fix on someone who was the real article [he chuckled] and imitate him. I had no southern accent. There was one voice that seemed to be absolutely valid, so I picked up his tones and copied it. It turned out to be Sam Jaffe from Cherry Street on the Lower East Side of New York!"

When Huston reflected on the friendship they developed, he remembered Jaffe as being his peer. Oddly, Sam was a crucial twelve years older, given that John was 17 and Sam was 29. There was an ageless, as well as a youthful, quality to Jaffe that lasted long into his life. It was that same agelessness that made him appear very young in person, but believable while playing old men on the stage.

By this time, Sam was living with his mother in the Bronx. Huston would visit there and delight in Sam's very Jewish mother.

Huston's father, Walter, was making the transition from vaudeville to the theater. When Jaffe and the elder Huston met, they also became friends with mutual interests in literature and music.

Huston spoke of his Aunt Margaret who had been an important figure in the musical scene in New York. She had married into money and she helped support English-speaking operas. Sam knew her and there was one occasion when they didn't agree. Huston called it a nasty instance: "She attempted to lord something over Sam and he called her on it, bringing her down very quickly. Sam was quite capable of it."

In his autobiography, *An Open Book*, Huston recalled how he and Sam hit it off immediately. He spoke of him as a rare combination of pianist, composer, philosopher, and boxer: "I've known Sam Jaffe for over fifty years now, and it is hard to describe him without making a panegyric of it. He is a devout vegetarian who doesn't smoke or drink, but never tries to win you over to his views. He is marvelously quick of wit, with a rare talent for the comeback. He went on, of course, to become one of the finest actors on the American stage. He worked with me on two films, *The Asphalt Jungle* and *The Barbarian and the Geisha*."

Jean Hagen and Sam Jaffe in The Asphalt Jungle, *directed by John Huston.*

In those days of Jaffe's budding acting career, a young boy named Milton Berle impressed Ada Jaffe with his talent. Berle and a little girl partner performed scenes from *Romeo and Juliet* and Sam Jaffe coached them. Berle commented with deep affection: "Sam taught us and staged the act. He was a very big help to my career." The girl didn't continue, which led to Berle striking out on his own at age 14.

Milton Berle also became very fast friends with Jaffe. He described Jaffe as "a marvelous man who knew his craft and had great expertise in the theater. He gave me so many pointers; little pieces of technique and advice." What Jaffe passed on to Berle all those years ago, still stands as good advice.

"Be it comedic or dramatic," Jaffe insisted, "in your playing of the material, you must be very honest, sincere, and truthful."

Jaffe knew about setting up a joke, the "suck-in." He told Berle that there must be so much truthfulness and reality in the voice that the audience believes what you are telling them is the truth. Then, you hit the shock punch line. That was very important to Berle and he never forgot it.

Milton Berle studied with Jaffe in 1921 and found him to be such a sweet man that he simply fell in love with him.

Berle talked of his unfolding career and the role Sam played in it: "When I started to work by myself in 1924, I did the first standup without a partner. It takes a lot of chutzpah for a young kid of 14. I grew up and I got very lanky so I couldn't be doing a kiddy act any longer. Sam used to catch me doing my standup. I didn't have too much material because I couldn't afford it in those days. My mother traveled around with me. What material I had I got out of magazines and *Captain Billy's Wiz Bang*, all those magazines with little one-liners. Sam would say, 'That's funny. That isn't. It isn't sharp enough. I think you can do better than that.' He gave me a lot of advice. His tips really helped my career and I owe him a debt of gratitude. I miss him terribly."

When Sam did *Gunga Din* at RKO, Milton Berle was under contract there and they struck up their friendship again. In conversation on the lot, Berle praised Jaffe highly, but Sam wasn't much for receiving accolades. He thanked Berle but reminded him that if he weren't able to do it, it wouldn't have helped. Berle remarked, "He played it cool and down. He had a low profile. That's the way he wanted it."

Jaffe had a profound and lasting effect on Berle in another regard. Committed from an early age to being good, Jaffe passed this way of being on to anyone who was of like mind. Berle described himself as having the very brash, aggressive, flippant, and comedic style of wise guy in his younger days. "Sam taught me values of simpatico and feeling toward other people," Berle said, "and it showed up in my work. Instead of punching and throwing put-down lines at people, Sam said, 'There's another way of doing that, with a little bit of charm. You don't have to be that brash and flippant. You know, with the insult style.'

"He said, 'Whatever the line is, you can do it and take the curse off it by saying, I was just kidding, sir. I notice you're bald. You shave pretty high, don't you? But it's going to happen to me too.' He said, 'There's a way of throwing out a line at someone else's expense and putting them down, but not roughly. You have a lovely suit sir, who shined it for you?' Then he would tell me to take off the embarrassment by adding a line like, 'I'm only kidding, I've got a whole closet full of those.' He told me to make yourself part of the joke after you've done it. That's different than the put-down comics like Rickles and all those people who just say it and let it lie. They don't clean their own acts up."

Berle continued with his reminiscence: "I played vaudeville, and the Loew's and Orpheum circuits. Times change with each era; today it's a different style. There's a looseness of censorship, saying four-letter words, going into very deep verbal pornography, using curse words that are not necessary. When I was in vaudeville, they had signs backstage in the '20's and '30's. If you said hell or damn in your act to the audience, you would immediately be canceled. It's a whole new show business, the comedy stores. The school that I went to was the school of hard knocks. It took us many years in the minors before you hit the Palace and two-a-day, sometimes eight to ten years with a lot of work on the act. [Jack] Benny and [George] Burns and [Bob] Hope and myself, guys who played vaudeville, we had to be as clean as a whistle."

Berle was repelled by the plethora of foul language used by comics in this modern day. He had always been opposed to censorship but he was starting to change his mind because the obscenities are unnecessary. He grumbled, "They use it to hype a joke. You take a standard joke, put the 'f' word in it and they think it's gonna help the joke."

What disgusted Berle most about the practice was that the comics use vulgarities for their own purposes, to free themselves. He complained, "I think that they get their own jollies by saying these words."

The saddest part for Berle was that there is a big audience for the smuts because the audiences speak that way too. As for Berle, he never used such language and he wouldn't dare do it. Without being self-righteous, he remarked, "I don't think some of our legendary performers have ever done it. We don't need it."

Throughout his life, Sam Jaffe also had very strong objections to appearing in any production that used foul language, even if it wasn't in his specific role.

In addition to John Huston and Milton Berle, Sam Jaffe made deep connections with other like-minded people and linked his life with them as if they were relatives. One such person in Jaffe's life was Edward G. Robinson. They met at Townsend Harris High School. Robinson had quit in his junior year to become an actor. He had gotten a scholarship at the American Academy.

Sam reminisced about Eddie that he knew Hebrew and had come from Romania where his grandmother had been very religious: "At first he was going to be a rabbi. Then he thought he'd become a lawyer to defend the poor. It's not much of a step from a lawyer to actor because of the dramatics. He made a big hit at the Academy and a big hit in his first appearance on Broadway. He wasn't an influence on me [to become an actor]. We were just friends. He was a generous and wonderful person."

While Jaffe was working at the Provincetown Playhouse, he ran into Robinson on the street one afternoon and Eddie told him to go up and see Arthur Hopkins because he was casting. "He told me that Hopkins sees people," Sam said. Then he digressed: "It wasn't as easy to arrange an appointment with others, such as [David] Belasco [famed producer], for instance. There was a spiral staircase. You'd go up to the top and the secretary would have you go down unless you had an appointment. Once, there was a woman who had an appointment. She climbed, and slipped, and fell on all fours. She looked up at Belasco and said, 'Oh, Master, Master.' She got the job. He was the great producer."

The tip from Robinson turned out to be a boon. It resulted in Jaffe's first Broadway appearance, for Arthur Hopkins, in *Samson and Delilah*, with Jacob Ben-Ami, Pauline Lord and Edward G. Robinson. Jaffe played a prompter. It was one of Sam's first opportunities to shine. "That was my entrance into the legitimate theater," Sam said.

A Hopkins convention of the time was to have the actors play with their backs to the audience. Jaffe remembers sitting at a table facing the scenery throughout the length of the play. When not called upon to speak, he leaned over the table, presumably pondering. What he was really doing was engaging himself in a marathon tic-tac-toe contest.

"We were all very much on the alert." Jaffe recalled. "If an actor stumbled over even a single word everyone waited to jump into the breach to cover up. One night Ben-Ami was late for an entrance. Eddie Robinson, Robert Harrison and I were on the stage. Feeling like little heroes, we all started to ad lib at once. `I wonder . . .' we began and then the three of us would stop. There would be a dead pause and then we rushed in again. We started and stopped three times creating much more confusion than if we had just waited for the stage manager to get Ben-Ami. Mercifully he came on before we could start again."

Jaffe's next appearance was in Sholom Asch's *The God of Vengeance*, starring Rudolph Schildkraut. Morris Carnovsky was also in the cast. Sam thought the world of Schildkraut: "He was a tremendous actor. He could really shake the rafters. He was Romanian and didn't know a word of English, but he could manage. He could understand. He knew the entire play. If anybody ever went up on their lines, he could prompt them; an amazing man."

Much as Sam raved about Schildkraut, his own performance was attracting attention. In a column called "We Predict," Jaffe was singled out as a comedy lead: "His character portrayal has attracted considerable notice. Some years ago he did character parts with the original Washington Square Players. He is still a very young man. Watch this career."

The God of Vengeance was a boon to Jaffe's career and to his personal life as well. It was in this ill-fated show that he was to fall in love for the first time.

****

ROSEMARY MURPHY, *Amphitryon '38* in 1951, *Detective Story*, 1953

"It was almost as hard, in those days, to get into an Equity Library Theatre show as it was to get into a Broadway play.

"I had just arrived in New York and I met a lot of people because of E.L.T. People do see you in things like that. There wasn't any other kind of showcase in those days. I was very excited to be cast in E.L.T., to do something in New York. When you're just beginning, anything you got was very exciting. They did good productions.

"James Costigan told me that I was cast years later in Eleanor and Franklin, for which I won an Emmy, because I'd been nice to him during Amphitryon. I helped them with the readings after I got through with my little one-line part.

"It's primarily about being a working actor. It doesn't matter if you're not getting paid. You hold your head higher. You go to appointments knowing you're working.

"E.L.T. was a great idea."

****

A Great Love

As a boy, Sam Jaffe treasured his friendships with male peers. He had no interest in girls. The non-interest continued into adolescence as well as through his college years. It was not until he was in his early thirties, appearing in *The God of Vengeance*, that he "met someone." Lillian Taiz, a fellow cast member, was a young woman just approaching twenty. Sam saw her as very gifted and talented. She was slim and small, with an expressive face. It was a face that had soul. For Sam Jaffe it was love at first sight.

While the show at hand had her showing off her dramatic skills, Lillian, born Leah, was primarily a singer. She grew up in South Philadelphia on South Alder Street, a narrow alley more suited to pushcarts than motor vehicles. Her father ran a meager candy and stationery store. In the evenings, he worked on inventions in hopes of achieving wealth. Her mother, Lydia Lewovina Scynnyskia, taught her Russian folk songs at a very early age. Dutch folk songs came later, and then French. Eventually she sang in five languages and contributed to the family's small income. Lydia hoped her daughter would have the career she never had. Lil-

Lillian Taiz.

lian, or Leahska, her name at home, was a very bright child. She entered high school at the age of 11.

The woman most responsible for getting Lillian's career started was Dr. Lucy Langdon Wilson, the warm and sympathetic principal of the South Philadelphia High School. Throughout her career, she interested herself in two students primarily. One was Marian Anderson; the other, Lillian Taiz. When Lillian was eleven years old, Wilson took her to Leopold Stokowski, conductor of the Philadelphia Symphony Orchestra. When he heard her sing, he told her to drop the lessons she was taking and give up struggling with singing arias. He encouraged her to study multiple foreign languages and to continue singing what her mother was teaching her.

Lillian was again pushed toward arias during her marriage to Sam. He wanted very much to have her become an opera star. This may have been an incorrect urging on Jaffe's part because Lillian was a natural for musical comedy. Her voice was a cut above most performers in the genre.

When Lillian was 13 years old, Wilson entered her in the Music School Settlement competition in South Philadelphia. From behind a screen, 300 contestants sang. Stokowski was one of the judges and awarded her first honors.

Soon Lillian gave recitals in Philadelphia. Her first newspaper notices there said that she "might rightly be regarded as a find. The audience recalled her from the wings after her first number. She was always an enlivening figure and her lines were delivered in tones of fluency and were well controlled." Wilson arranged for Taiz to be in the cast of the Civic Opera Company. She made her debut as the soubrette in *The Queen's Lace Handkerchief*, and appeared at intervals thereafter with the company at the Academy of Music.

Lillian graduated from high school at the age of 14. If this was any indication of how bright she was, it is easy to see how one as intelligent as Sam Jaffe was drawn to her.

She led a very protected, small-neighborhood life, running errands along the docks accompanied by her dog. Soon, she got a job and began saving money so that she could go to New York to help support the family.

It was Wilson who helped her achieve this goal. She set Lillian up with an emergency fund in a bank in New York, depositing $500 of her own money. It was this fateful move that put Lillian in position to meet the love of her life, fellow actor Sam Jaffe. Wilson arranged a job for her at the Provincetown Playhouse where she appeared in *Crowns* at the age of 18. This was her debut in professional theater in a small part as a flower girl.

God of Vengeance was her second production of Players Company and her second role in professional theater. She called this beginner's luck. It was a thrill for Lillian to work with the great Rudolph Schildkraut. He, in turn, had a high regard for Lillian. He often spoke of a scene at the end of the second act when her delivery was so fine that she perfectly prepared the way for his heart-rending exit.

Percy Hammond, in the New York *Tribune* on December 20, 1922, said of Lillian, "Her acting was better than her lines."

God of Vengeance moved to the Greenwich Village Theater and became a hit. It was Lillian's first experience of success. Later, the production moved uptown to the Apollo to meet the growing ticket demand. It became so popular that orthodox Jews complained and the authorities shut it down for presenting "indecent material." The irony was that before leaving Philadelphia, Lillian's parents had admonished her to get a clean theatrical job. Instead she was receiving notoriety for being indicted, convicted and fined.

The attack on the play left Jaffe nonplused: "Judge

Resolsky shut it down saying that actors appeared nude. They had policemen make phony complaints. The judge felt it wasn't right to show a Jewish brothel keeper. Parts of the script were never used, for example, where two lesbians meet. But they swore they heard it and so they closed the play and arrested us. We had some of the best men in the country testify for us, and theologians even appeared for us. But they closed it down because of a holier-than-thou attitude. This was in the '20's."

The legal uproar left Schildkraut bewildered. The play had been a modern classic that he had performed all over central Europe.

"Sadly," Sam lamented, "it closed. Unfortunately, there was a line from it: 'I'll cut your bowels out!' and *Variety* quoted it as 'I'll cut your balls out.' When we were down in the Village it was nothing, but it was so successful they moved it uptown on 42nd Street. I had a very good part. I was a matchmaker. It was a great opportunity to be with a great man; one of the great actors of our time." Later they appealed the case and won, but it was too late.

As a result of the raid on the company, a patrol wagon carted the cast off to the station house. Story has it that on the way, Sam Jaffe and Lillian Taiz teased each other. He said, "Miss Taiz, I'm ashamed of you." She scolded him for being an old jailbird. In the time they had to kill behind bars, Sam chose to woo Lillian. He wasted no time on preliminaries and simply asked her to marry him. She didn't say yes immediately. The offer was slightly abrupt for her and she suggested that they become engaged instead; the engagement lasted over two years.

Typical of the actor's life, the inevitable search for the next job began with the closing of the last one. In Sam's case, he had no agent. He described his dilemma: "You would meet on 45th Street and Broadway in front of the drug store and your actor friends would give you leads. 'Hey, they want such and such a character at so and so's office.'

"There was a play, *On and Off the Lot,* with five Jewish uncle parts and someone on 45th St. said, 'Why don't you try for that?' I had bearded pictures from the playlet with my mother when I played her husband. I was interviewed for the part speaking with a Jewish accent. They hired me. Then, during the rehearsal they heard me speak and they felt I had deceived them. I was not the real article."

Unfortunately it didn't occur to the producers that Jaffe was quite an actor and dialectician!

In this period of the '20's, immigration had slowed down. The Jewish theater, in order to make a go of it, had moved uptown to 44th St., to Shubert's theater, and with the move came higher prices. Jaffe laughed as he told an "I knew you when" story: "A man would put down fifty cents and say, 'Give me a ticket,' and they would say, 'It's $2.50.' He would reply, 'Look, I know you from downtown yet.'"

Jaffe's performance in *The God of Vengeance* led to a one-line pantomimic part in *The Idle Inn.* As a result of this role, S. Jay Kaufman picked Jaffe as a comer.

As for Lillian, after *God of Vengeance*, in November 1923, her reputation as a singer of folk songs had grown so that she was an attraction at the largest theater in Philadelphia. Her next job was as the general understudy in *The Clinging Vine.* Peggy Wood starred and had her own understudy, Irene Dunne. Lillian was in good company.

As Sam continued with his career, Lillian accumulated her own credits. She worked next in *Going Up* at the Arlington Square Theater in Boston, in March 1924. Her reviews were excellent. The press called her a real flapper who played her part with admirable lightness and daintiness.

In October 1925 she appeared in *Stolen Fruit*. From there she played in a vaudeville review through arrangement with Hockey and Green. No doubt Sam had a role in securing that engagement since he knew them well.

Through May Burland, Lillian met Moss Hart who was casting director at the Augustus Pitow office. He had seen her in *God of Vengeance* and *Clinging Vine* and chose her as the ingénue in May Robson's *Something Tells Me*. It ran for 44 weeks. Her career escalated much more quickly than Sam's.

After the show closed, Lillian returned to Philadelphia. To quote Sam: "In the period of about two years, she had made appearances on Broadway, in musical stock, and in vaudeville. She had trouped, been stranded, and gone through a season of one-night stands; a history of theater in capsule form."

In a scrapbook covering Lillian's career [prepared as a memorial after her death for the Theatre Collection of the New York Public Library at their request] Sam described, in detail, what it was like in those days to be an actor on tour. His memorial is important theater history, especially because of his first-hand experience of it:

"For the player, there were many hardships. [There was] the business of unpacking and packing before or immediately after the show; running for the train, or very often waiting up for it till the early hours of the morning; poor accommodations — if you can call them accommodations at all — in the smaller towns; bad dressing rooms. It may not be as bad as having to stand on one's trunk to keep dry in a flooded room, or to throw one's shoes at the rats from that height, but it can be and often is very terrible. The actor's convenience, you learn, is an afterthought in the theater.

"Any kind of room is better than none. This fact is brought home with all its terrors when you enter a small town in the Northwest where a regional festival is going on and people from the neighboring states have literally taken over. This is quite unlike the convention that comes into the big city and takes possession of the large hotels. Here practically every private dwelling is swarming with visitors. Your advance man has sent on word about this, and when you arrive you accompany the manager straight to the police station, where a list of every home and its accommodations is kept for this emergency. The fear of being roofless is resolved only after a long and anxious session.

"For those starting on their first tour, these inconveniences and hardships are absorbed in the romance of the trip. You just put up with them; that's all. You have not yet learned that there are agencies such as your own Actors' Equity Association to demand decent dressing room conditions for you, or perhaps you just accept all these discomforts, along with living in your trunk, as indigenous to this kind of existence. What matters most for you is that the road affords opportunity.

"The company becomes more of a unit on tour. You get to know each other at rehearsals. Now you travel together almost daily. Usually a train car is given over to the troupe. You read and discuss the notices from the last town, you make your plans for the next; you sing and carry on to your heart's content and endure the annoyance of the older members and the company crew — the stage carpenter, electrician, and property man. But what of it? You're having a good time and you have the run of the car, and you'll run it for all it's worth. At those times when the star is present the behavior is more restrained. But more often she occupies a drawing room, thank God, as becomes her position.

"One of the most exciting things in these one and two night stands is bringing theater to people who are really thirsting for it. The long line waiting for the doors to open at the balcony windows where one price prevails and the seats are not reserved but sold on a first come

first served basis, is a heartening sight. Here is real theater appetite. Such queues were the regular thing before
the movie days. We found it still true of as great a city as
London [Ontario] on our visit there in 1936, and in some
of our own cities like Columbus when Lillian accompanied
me on a tour of *A Doll's House* in 1937.

"Where there are so many distractions as on tour,
the problem of the daily repetition of one's part doesn't
seem to exist. There are fresh notices praising your work
which act as a pat on the back; an occasional discern-
ing criticism helping you perfect your role; and even the
knowledge that there are critics out front in every town
is a stimulant.

"What fills out one's time is visiting the points of
interest in each town and occasional excursions into the
country. What if you only enter a town in the morning
and leave at night; there is plenty of pleasure in prowling
about and getting the feel of the place. And what a relief
from the day before which was divided between train and
theater.

"The Coast, and particularly San Francisco, added
a new type of adventure — an adventure in food. Here
were large settlements of Spanish and Portuguese, with
restaurants catering to their native palates. Now these
foreign dishes have become commonplace, but in the
early 1920's they were purely local delicacies.

"There were receptions for the star and the rest
of the cast was also entertained. There are no bounds
to the hospitality shown visiting players. People will extend themselves and outdo one another in their efforts
to show the actors a good time."

Sam wrote of the special circumstances of touring in Canada. "Crossing the border into Canada for the
first time is a real adventure. First the company manager
has you fill out a Canadian Government blank. Then he
collects your trunk key for the baggage car inspection.
After that comes the personal visit of the customs of-

ficers, who go poking through your belongings, upsetting everything you so carefully packed for the trip. As if you had any other purpose but bringing entertainment into the country. With the exception of the Canadian currency and, yes, scones for breakfast, you feel perfectly at home. There is a chance to buy English woolens and Irish tweeds tax free up to $100, but that is out of the question on your salary.

"You manage the Canadian money easily, it is so much like our own, but the excitement occurs when you leave and have to get rid of it in a hurry. Since the payment is made dollar for dollar in Canadian currency, and the exchange favors our own as high as ten percent, you are forced to take that much less back with you. The Actors' Equity Association has halted this practice and obtained payment for actors in American dollars or its equivalent for salaries up to $200.

"There is, of course, a much better chance to get to know a town when you are booked for a week or two. At such times the publicity man usually arranges for the company to be present at a tea or social function of the leading club or literary society. Where there is a formal program, the player who can sing or perform on his own usually takes part in it."

While Lillian was on the road and Sam was in New York, he would telephone her in various cities where she was. In those days it was not as easy as picking up the phone at home. They had appointed hours and he would have to go down to the Grand Central Station with all his nickels and quarters to phone her. It was important to both of them to keep in touch.

When Lillian returned to New York, she joined the Chorus Equity classes in soft shoe and tap dancing. These classes were very popular with actors, and, more particularly, with singers to whom musical comedy was an outlet. She later studied with Jack Blue and then Ned Wayburn to round out her dance routines.

A little more than two years from the time he had asked her to marry him, Lillian said yes. When she did commit to marrying Sam, she did it with complete devotion to him. They married in 1926. Sam was then 35 years old, Lillian, 20.

The wedding took place in Horace Kallen's apartment on 23rd Street, at the rear of The New School for Social Research. Kallen was one of the founders, and an American philosopher and psychologist. He was also the literary executor for William James, a psychologist who wrote like a novelist. At Harvard Kallen had been the assistant to Josiah Royce and George Santayana.

Sam met Kallen through Lillian and the two men became great friends. In almost all cases through his life, Sam Jaffe associated with persons of quality, intelligence and goodness. Kallen was one. Sidney Hillman, Secretary of Labor under Roosevelt, and economist Leo Wollman were two others. Jaffe marveled at how Hillman would come up with a creative addition to any idea presented to him.

Although Jaffe had many meetings of the mind with peers of great prominence, according to John Huston who was then his confidant, Sam, at the time of his marriage to Lillian, "was still virgo intactus. I don't think Sam looked forward to the conjugal arrangements with any great eagerness. Marriage was a hell of a big step for Sam to take."

When Sam married, he rented a room just below Huston's on MacDougal Street in the Village. It was an alcove in a building next door to the Provincetown Theater. Huston reflected that Sam wanted to be in his building because he didn't want to be too far away from a friend. The tone of this observation implied that Sam Jaffe, even at the age of 35, lacked something in his sense of security. Perhaps his early unstable childhood was still an influence. His need for proximity to Huston may have represented the nurturing he had missed, especially from a male. Even though Huston was a dozen years his junior, Jaffe relied on him, needed him, as an anchor.

The choice of home, as described by Huston, was not the best: "Sam was on the floor below me. It was a disreputable neighborhood. I remember I was robbed twice before I ever got into the place. While we were moving, a typewriter was stolen. I drove a big spike into the door to hold it shut. To get in and out, I would enter through Sam's place and climb up the fire escape to my outside window.

"The ramshackle building was certainly a dubious place to bring a new bride. On the first floor was the 1920's version of a discotheque, where somebody played the piano while customers downed bootleg liquor." A liquor retailer approached Huston and Jaffe on their block and asked to hide merchandise in case the police came. This was during prohibition. Both refused. Every night, until three in the morning, they heard customers singing, "I want to be happy."

Huston kept Sam busy in their shared neighborhood. He formed a poker club and they played every Saturday night. The members, in turn, gave a dinner the night of the game. The dinners became increasingly elaborate as each member tried to outdo the others. Often, they would invite one of the better New York chefs to prepare his specialty. All the members were good players, and while it wasn't a big game, it wasn't a small game either, as the players could win or lose $1,000.

What Huston next revealed added to the picture of Sam Jaffe as a very young 35-year-old: "After they got the apartment, he continued to live with his mother while he and Lillian proceeded to furnish the place piece by piece. The last thing was to be the bed. As soon as they bought the bed, they would move in and commence their lives as man and wife."

As John Huston related this rather intimate information about Sam Jaffe and his new bride, he chose his words with great care when referring to the event of the consummation of the marriage:

"Sam didn't want to come to terms, physical terms, with his marriage immediately. He wasn't quite ready for it. He talked with me about it. He didn't seek my advice. He let me know what was going on. He wasn't prepared. His virginity was not up for immediate contract. And he looked forward to the day when their marriage would have a communication of the flesh. Presently, that would be overcome and they could go to the more important things in life," John said with a chuckle.

"It all hung, this part of it, on the bed. They decided on a bed, and when it was to be delivered, Sam called and asked them to delay the delivery. He was getting his nerve up. Well then, Rachel (he called Lillian 'Rachel'), would call, and say where is the bed? When is the bed coming? This went on for days. Finally the bed came and Sam's last bridge was burned."

It is certainly not the average male who not only waits until past the age of 35 to engage in intercourse, but delays the consummation with his wife.

A fascinating note is that Jaffe called his beloved Lillian 'Rachel.' His aunt Rachel, the woman he thought of as his mother, was one of the most important people in his life. Bestowing her name on his wife was certainly a gesture of meaning.

Not long after Sam and Lillian's union, his mother Ada died in the auto accident described earlier. Sam had lived with Ada for fifteen years, from his college graduation, at age 21, through to his marriage, at age 35. Again this speaks of Sam's need to restore the missing elements of his childhood. While he held his Aunt Rachel in his heart as the mother who raised him, there is no true substitute for the physical mother.

Sam never had second thoughts about having given-en up teaching to become an actor. He said, "I had known that Plato spoke of life having many doors. You went into one and you'd go a certain way. Each had a world. The door you left was finished. That much of your life was gone. So I figured since theater was the door that finally opened, this was the world I wanted to be in."

The next door to open was a big one. Early in his marriage to Lillian, he was hired to play Judelson in Samson Raphaelson's *The Jazz Singer* with George Jessel. It was a big hit at the Cort Theater, running for two years and then touring for a year.

During this period, Lillian had just completed her 44 week run as the ingénue in *Something Tells Me*. At the time, she met Holland Robinson and Mark Harshberger. Robinson was a gifted composer and Harshberger, a designer and illustrator. They saw her as something fresh in musical entertainment, and they were eager to prepare some material for her. However, Sam was leaving on the tour with *The Jazz Singer*, so Lillian put aside her plans in order to be with him.

On Sam's recommendation, Lillian joined the cast in its second season on tour in a small role. She signed a contract on August 13, 1927, to appear as Mary Dale and understudy at a salary of $150 a week. She eventually replaced Ruth Abbott, playing opposite George Jessel. She continued to play the lead for the remaining two seasons of the run.

While Sam got good reviews for *The Jazz Singer*, it was Lillian's career that was advancing. C. Pannill Mead's review of her work, in the Milwaukee *Sentinel*, was a fair sample of what the critics said: "Lillian Taiz was not only lovely to look at but possessed of a magnetism and a voice that was charming both in speaking and singing."

During the tour, there had been a special interview in the Pittsburgh *Gazette Times*, on February 19, 1927.

In it Lillian reported, "I have found that a splendid bit of philosophy to cull from life is to stock the memory with only pleasant remembrances and thoughts. Unpleasant memories are utterly destructive to ourselves and our associates. It is within us all to be the bearers of constructive, helpful, beautiful thoughts that later will be 'memories.'

"I find, too, that this simple little rule brings its own reward as soon as it is adopted, for with it comes peace and harmony, enabling us to have the gift of understanding, which later develops into memories' garden of fragrant flowers."

That statement by Lillian tells us not only what kind of person she was, but also why Sam chose her for his wife. What Lillian described was certainly a goal of Sam's. He preferred to release unpleasant interactions and never bring them up again. However, as previously indicated, he was not always successful. This was borne out in his clinging to hard feelings about his nephews and refusing to forgive them. Perhaps in Lillian, Sam found someone who could fulfill his life commitment to goodness even better than he, and serve as an inspiration for the renewal of his pledge.

The Jazz Singer had a prominent place in movie history, for it was the first successful talkie [talking movie]. The Warner Vitaphone shorts had indicated the possibilities of the new medium; now they were realized in a full-length drama with song. According to Jaffe, "We played in Detroit when the picture opened against us. Whether it was price or the novelty of this new screen offering is hard to say, but it was impossible to compete with them. We closed almost immediately.

"Jessel and I were to have been in the movie. But Jessel asked for more money, so Jack Warner engaged the great Al Jolson."

Following the tour, Lillian and Sam returned to

New York. Composer Holland Robinson had not forgotten the impression Lillian had made on him. In 1928, he wrote "The Riverside Bus" from *The Ballad of a New York Child* and dedicated it to Lillian. Manager William Harris had wanted Lillian to star in the musical *East Is West*. However, he sold the rights to Ziegfeld who wouldn't risk using an unknown in one of his expensive productions. As it turned out, Lillian's Broadway destiny was fulfilled through another source, her husband.

Whenever Sam was in New York he spent his time with friends who, like himself, were talented, creative, intelligent individuals. He brought his wife into this circle of friends that was the young vanguard of cultural and artistic excellence and included George and Ira Gershwin.

Sam had met George Gershwin through his friends Emily and Lou Paley. Emily's sister Lenore was Ira Gershwin's wife. Emily and Lenore were daughters of the Strunsky family who owned a very fine restaurant on Washington Place called "Three Steps Down." It was a gathering place for the artists and creative people of that era. The family, very active in the Russian-Jewish intelligentsia, also owned the Atlantic Hotel in New Jersey.

Emily's father was a very well-known character in the '20's and '30's in Greenwich Village. He and his brother owned houses on Washington Square. He rented apartments to artists and writers, and he was very indulgent with them. It impressed Sam that "when a tenant couldn't pay his rent, he was moved up to the Bronx. When the tenant couldn't pay his rent in the Bronx, he was moved back into one of his [Strunsky's] houses." Sometimes Strunsky would take a painting in payment, or something out of the ice box.

Emily's husband, Lou Paley, was a school teacher who, along with his brother Herman, wrote songs and had a publishing company. Lou met George Gershwin and the two became great friends. Lou had written lyrics for a number of songwriters and some with George before Ira took over. Lou and Emily Paley's home at 26 West 8th Street functioned as a salon. Gershwin played his preludes there. Persons of budding talent who would later become names of importance, such as George Kaufman, Oscar Levant and Abe Birnbaum, were regulars at the gatherings.

Jaffe delighted in learning about how George Gershwin's musical career began. When George was not quite twelve he came home from school one day and said, "Ira, guess what? I played the Star Spangled Banner on the piano today." Ira said, "I didn't know you could play." George said, "Neither did I."

Gershwin then asked his parents to buy him a piano and, as Sam so aptly put it, "his genius took over. They didn't have a piano in the house. George and Ira's father's work was supplying sandwiches at the Woltin Turkish Baths on Forsythe St. He had the concession there. George told me that once his father was outside the door listening to him play. He heard George struggling over a melody. So he knocked at the door and he came in. Then he whistled and said, 'Will that help you, George?'"

The story tickled Sam and he went on: "Another time he said, 'George, what is that tune you played in that musical? I can't think of it. And George began with the overture and said, 'Is this it?' The father said, 'No.'

"'Is this it?' asked George. 'No,' his father replied. He went through the entire score and the father said, 'No.' George said, 'I've played the entire score.' His father said, 'Play it again.' The first tune George played, his father said, 'That's it.'" Sam laughed heartily.

The Paley's salon was the place where Gershwin first played "Rhapsody in Blue." When he returned from Europe with "American in Paris," he played that there too.

The writer Martin Dibner, who was the founding director of the California State Arts Commission in the 1960's, was part of the erudite grouping that gathered at the Paley's as well as in sessions at the Gershwin's.

Dibner singled Jaffe out of the esteemed grouping. He said, "Meeting Sam was like paradise revisited. I felt a strong bond with Sam. We're both Jews out of a New York background with a union of interests. I always feel that if Sam hadn't been born, Isaac Bashevis Singer (1978 Nobel Prize winner for literature) would have invented him. He's a character for all ages, seasons. When we talked he was always very puckish, warm."

Dibner described the Sunday morning gatherings in the Gershwin's twin penthouses: "George Gershwin would always play what he was writing, even before it was published or heard in public. He was very enthusiastic about playing. The story goes that his producers told him they wanted people to sing his songs after they leave the show not before they come in. He was so generous with his talent."

Someone once asked George to play and he jumped right up, forgetting he had a lovely girl on his lap. She simply fell off because he rushed to comply with the request immediately.

It's not often one can have early memories such as this one of Sam's: "I heard George play *Porgy and Bess* while he was writing it. There was a big party given to him on opening night of *Porgy and Bess*. We were there. It was not a success then. It didn't bother him. George was completely confident. He said that his music was an expression of the American experience."

Emily Paley remembered that Sam had a lovely marriage with Lillian. She recalled how they would walk along the street holding hands. Lillian had light brownish hair and was attractive, but her skin was pockmarked. Emily said, "She was not a great beauty." In comparison,

Emily thought Bettye, Sam's second wife, to be much more beautiful.

Although Emily had the highest regard for Sam, she spoke of what she saw as a pattern in him that was disconcerting to her. "If Sam was composing and if Lillian wanted to go out to do something he said no because he was playing the piano and he didn't want her to go." He didn't want to have to answer the phone if it rang. Perhaps it never occurred to him that he could just let it ring or that he could take it off the hook. He wanted his solitude and privacy but he didn't want to miss calls which might be important to him. He wanted his wife to serve as the household secretary. Lillian curtailed her activities to meet Sam's wishes.

Emily's observation seems to imply that Sam was controlling, that he saw himself as the key figure, and that his wife was there to serve him. Although Emily felt Bettye knew how to handle this behavior in Sam, the pattern was repeated in the marriage with Bettye, who sometimes curtailed her activities in deference to Sam.

Paley thought Jaffe was a rare man; however, she said that she took that for granted because many of their friends then were rare people. As she advanced into her ninth decade, she found it more difficult to find people like Jaffe and Gershwin. She commented, "All our young men then had much more idealism than our young people now."

Through Sam, others were invited to the privileged circle of creative giants. Zero Mostel was one such. Sam met Zero during a broadcast and they formed a spontaneous friendship. Jaffe introduced Zero and John Huston and Eddie Robinson to the Gershwins and Paleys.

Huston remembered: "Sam and George were very close friends. George was a musical talent who had no equal at that time. He was among the most modest of men, too. He had a reputation for being a complete egotist. People didn't realize he gave no thought to his own role in any of this but only the music. And he would play with such generosity of expression. It was just marvelous to be present; a real privilege. Owing to Sam, I was present."

Huston thought of the gatherings as the last word in elegance. Jaffe impressed Huston because he knew every one of the top musicians, writers and theater people in New York. It was through Sam that he met people such as Lillian Hellman and Louis Untermeyer.

That was Jaffe's world: artists, writers, musicians, actors. They were all young people with tremendous potential who were seriously devoted to their chosen art forms. They nurtured each other with their various talents. It would seem that the energy circle they created together served to prepare the individual participants for their future. Each inspired the others and each was lifted to higher accomplishment by the strength of the group. The imprint of the gatherings lingered for decades in the memories of those who were fortunate enough to be present.

Freda Diamond, the New York industrial designer who met Sam after Lillian had died, was a friend of Emily Paley. She too remembered the open house weekends at the salon. It was where Sam Jaffe and the great singer-actor Paul Robeson met. Diamond reflected on how much the two men loved each other in spite of their many disparate points of view. Both men had concern for the underdog. They shared a similar compassion for humanity. Sam was much honored years later when he received the Equity Paul Robeson Award.

Freda Diamond touched on a key element in Jaffe's nature: "Sam didn't say what he was against as much as what he was for. He wasn't a negative person."

This was exemplified often. He was quick to speak of the goodness of the people he knew. He didn't want any bad stories told. For example, he didn't want to expose his views on Emily's mother being a bitch, a vixen, because he didn't want to hurt Emily. It is not that Sam didn't have negative feelings; it is rather that he often would not give them voice.

Much good came out of those shared creative times. Lou Paley wrote songs for Lillian and designed costumes she wore in recitals. He made sure that Gershwin heard Lillian sing. She took the floor and held it for fully an hour! George was very taken with her talent. He showed his enthusiasm by taking her the next day to see Ziegfeld, the same man who didn't want to risk having her in *East Is West*. She sang for him and he offered her Magnolia in the road company of *Show Boat*.

Meanwhile, Aarons and Vinton Freedley who did George's first show were looking for an ingénue for Rogers and Hart's *Spring Is Here*, which starred Glen Hunter and Charles Ruggles. George arranged an audition for Lillian with the producers and writers. She got a $500 a week, run-of-the-play contract. In the show she created "With A Song in My Heart," "He Who Loves Me Dearly," and "Yours Sincerely."

Unfortunately, rehearsals went on for the first seven days without Lillian who was ill. The producers were patient. After another week went by, she was strong enough to work.

Ira and George Gershwin went to the dress rehearsal in Philadelphia. Their confidence in her was well-founded. Reviewers said she displayed a fine sense of humor and a very pleasing personality. Not only did she have a good voice but she could act as well.

The show opened in New York in March 1929. Brooks Atkinson, in the New York i, found Taiz to be "altogether delightful and when she sings in a full and supple voice, Mr. Rodger's music seems very good indeed."

Gilbert W. Gabriel in the *New York American* said of Taiz: "Unusual stock of grace and youthful verve, a voice of velvet and a real knowledge of what to do with it."

This comment by Alison Smith in the *New York World* would certainly please any singer in her first starring role: "Her true and wistful young voice took the curse off the vapid quality of the usual musical-comedy heroine." Many reviewers were so admiring of Taiz, they proclaimed that even a theater as large as the Shubert wouldn't be able to accommodate, at a single sitting, all those who proclaimed to discover the charming prima donna."

Lillian handled her assignment expertly and was able to retain audience sympathy for a character that was petulant. She impressed people with her grace and knowledge of acting. Her singing was considerably above the Broadway average. So good was she that George Gershwin called her his discovery.

Not only was there a significant professional alliance between the Jaffes and George Gershwin, there was a continuing and deepening friendship. This was evidenced by personal meetings and follow-up notes such as this one from George on March 16, 1929:

"Dear Lillian,

"I want to tell you how much I appreciate your and Sam's gifts. They were just made for the skyscraper bookshelves on the wall. I love them.

"Of course, it goes without saying that I was made very happy by the way you performed and 'got over' with the first night audience at the Alvin Theater.

"Please come with Sam to see me soon. And once again, thanks.

Yours, George" [He included a bar of music, which always followed his signature.]

The Jaffes received a wonderful gift from Gershwin: the sheet music of "Rhapsody in Blue" signed "To Lillian and Sam with love, George."

Lillian's career soared. The Color Gravure section of the New York *Sunday World* on May 12, 1929, bestowed this honor alongside a photo: "Lillian Taiz, considered the most promising of the new ingénues."

Gotham Life featured her as one of their "Ladies of the Theatre: Lillian Taiz is the newest enthusiasm of this town's playgoers. Almost unknown she came to Broadway and overnight was famous. She is prima donna of *Spring Is Here* and the way she puts over Rodger's music and Hart's lyrics are just nobody's business. Her name was originally Deutsch and has gone through a series of changes until it became the four-letter word [sic] monosyllable that fits so nicely into an electric sign. It is pronounced "tays" to rhyme with days ..."

She went from *Spring Is Here* (which closed June 8, 1929) to the role of Emmy Lou, the lead in *Great Day* on June 28, 1929, replacing Gladys Baxter. The show didn't make it to Broadway.

With little respite she was hired for *The Duchess of Chicago* that played in Boston, Newark, and Philadelphia. The *Boston Post* on November 16, 1929, remarked "Lillian Taiz, a very pretty girl with charming manners, and a smoothly convincing way of acting. She has a fine feeling for comedy, and can seem romantic without getting silly about it. A very gifted little lady, one would say, on first acquaintance."

Sam would no doubt have agreed with the *Evening American* in Boston that reviewed his wife as "A vivacious bit of femininity, as easy upon the eye as she is lively." Lillian could knock all the melody out of high notes and be charming and sweet at the same time.

In 1930 she appeared in the review *Artists and Models.*

Sam and Lillian had music in common. He loved to compose and she loved to sing. During their marriage, she learned the female roles in 13 operas. As mentioned earlier, Sam urged Lillian in this direction. This was in spite of Leopold Stokowski's recommendation years earlier that Lillian give up struggling with arias. Sam boasted that she could imitate certain opera singers. This was clearly very important to him, and something he wanted for her. It isn't known why he preferred that she pursue this rather than musical comedy when she was clearly destined for musical comedy success.

After *Spring Is Here* and a contract with the Shuberts, Lillian picked up on Stokowski's suggestion to her as a young teenager. She decided to do her own recital work of folk songs and spirituals. She reconnected with Holland Robinson and Mark Harshberger. They wrote songs for her and designed costumes for her recitals which Lillian herself made by hand. She was booked in private homes.

With great pride, Sam remembered, "She had a very active professional career. She was very wonderful. Gershwin was very taken with her."

Earlier in her career Lillian had sung on the radio every week, earning $25 an hour. Besides the *Mediterraneans* and the *Prophylactic Hour*, other radio programs kept her busy. She was one of the entertainers sent by NBC to the National Advertisers Bureau convention in Washington in 1928. Taiz was the soprano and Nelson Eddy was the baritone in the Dutch Masters commercial.

Lillian had been a guest star on several occasions. NBC considered her a find and tried hard to build a program suitable to her talents. The concert manager urged Lillian to sign a contract, stressing that radio was something new and there would be great opportunities in it. While tempting, other possibilities were cooking for Lillian through her special contacts with Gershwin and others. Once Gershwin invited her to be his soprano on the *General Motors Hour*, she had contracts totaling $400 a week for two hours of singing. She was thrown into the arena of coast to coast hookups. Her audience, and therefore her publicity, went national. She held the titles of Miss General Motors and Miss Hudson-Essex.

George Gershwin had been a key figure in Lillian's career, as well as contributing to the Jaffes' quality of life. His devotion to excellence served as an inspiration. Together, Sam and Lillian admired and loved their great friend, and together they endured his death on July 11, 1937. It was a loss of mammoth proportion.

Sam reminisced about the end of Gershwin's life: "George died of a brain tumor which was cancerous. Jestingly, George had told me that he was playing tag as a kid and a horse kicked him and that's how he became a genius. He told Eddie Robinson, when he came to visit him in the hospital, 'You and my chauffeur are my only two friends.' He could have been saved if they knew to operate. He was 38 when he died and he had already done about 27 musicals."

George Gershwin had represented the epitome of youth, enthusiasm and joy. Friends such as Sam and Lillian carried the legacy of his inspiration as they developed their own careers.

****

JANE ALEXANDER, *Royal Gambit,* 1963

"In 1962 I was a standby for Sandy Dennis in A Thousand Clowns *on Broadway. I was in good shape for someone who was twenty-two.*

"I wanted to do Royal Gambit *at E.L.T. because the process of working excited me, and because it was a really interesting piece about Henry the 8th.*

"The conditions were not different from off-Broadway.

"Then, to be in an E.L.T. production was a very good thing. I felt proud that I had been cast and that I was doing it.

"My husband, Ed Sherin, was in an E.L.T. show early on and he always speaks proudly of having appeared.

"I thank Sam for the vision, the status that it gave actors. I remember the sense of pride of being a part of that production. I thank him for that. It was the union theater. That meant a lot to me. It meant that I was part of the company of players."

****

Triumph in the Theater

While Lillian's career was advancing, Sam Jaffe was taking stock and making vital decisions for his future. The role of Judelson in *The Jazz Singer* had been another old-man-with-a-beard part. When the run was finally over, Jaffe only received offers to play 'beards.' He decided he would rather not act at all than be typed in one role.

This is never an easy decision for an actor to make. It takes great courage. Jaffe continued to make decisions like this one throughout his career, even when the stakes were much higher. The best example, decades later, was when he left the lucrative *Ben Casey* series because he was playing a non-stimulating, brainy doctor role that resulted in his again being stereotyped.

Jaffe removed himself from guaranteed work and refused offers. He knew that his range went beyond the casting that came his way, and he had an inner conviction to go for the greater that remained unknown to him. He risked everything to reach for an unseen "more," and he held to his decision.

His determination eventually led to one of the finest roles of his early career, Kringelein in *Grand Hotel*. The creation of that role and the myriad of responses to Jaffe as an actor demand a full chapter of exploration. It provides information about how an actor develops and sustains a role, and on qualities in Jaffe as an artist.

While he was between shows, Sam rarely wasted precious moments. He continued his study of languages. He played the piano and composed. He kept up his interest in art and read extensively. Most importantly, Jaffe sustained his friendships.

Sam's first friend in the theater was Lou Sorin. They appeared in *God of Vengeance* together and as a sideline they wrote a number of blackouts. They sold one of these short comedic skits to the Theatre Guild for the Garrick Gaieties.

In contrast to the "beard-roles" he was offered on-stage, off-stage Jaffe was a very youthful character. For example, he and his friend Lou entertained themselves with practical jokes. They knew that their pal John Huston loved horses. While Huston was living at 434 Lafayette Street, they pulled off a great prank. Sam spoke gleefully about how they "got a nag and we brought him to John's and tried to push him up the stairs. The owner came out and yelled, 'What are you trying to do?' He yelled so much that John's father [Walter Huston] came out. John and his father enjoyed it tremendously as we tried to push the horse upstairs and the owner was telling us we can't do it. The fact is we couldn't have done it; it was impossible to get him up. The nag's back was sagging. The ribs were out. He was an immovable object. The fun was in the trying. It was for John's birthday."

Here was Jaffe, in his late thirties, married to a woman who was starring on Broadway, romping around with his men-friends as if he were still a young boy. He and Huston took in boxing matches together. Earlier in their lives they had both boxed professionally. It was how Sam had lost his two front teeth!

During his self-imposed unemployment, Jaffe kept in touch with directors and producers so that he would remain in the forefront of their consciousness as new roles emerged. One of those persons was Herman Shumlin. He had previously offered Jaffe a 'beard part' for a play subsequently abandoned on the road. Though he had turned down the role, Sam made sure not to break the connection with Shumlin.

At one point, it was Jaffe who gave Shumlin a production opportunity by bringing him a play that a friend had written. Sam said, "He didn't do it, but he remembered me when he looked for someone to play Kringelein in *Grand Hotel*. He was a very warm friend throughout his life. I did a good deed and was done by a good deed. You toss the bread upon the waters and it comes back sponge cake."

The casting came about in a fortuitous manner. Shumlin passed Jaffe on the street, turned around and called to him. Without Jaffe's needing to audition, Shumlin offered him the key role in *Grand Hotel*.

Sam recalled, "He remembered me and entrusted the part to me in spite of the fact that some people were opposed to me. They said I wouldn't be right in it. [In response to their objections] he offered me a run-of-the-play contract. Once he made up his mind, he adhered to his decision.

"I had no idea it would be such a hit," Sam said, exuding enthusiasm. "I liked the role. The applause was so great that we knew it was a great hit. It was tremendous. Later we traveled with it. It was in 1931. Things were pretty bad. We had a panic in our country. I was fortunate in having a job."

Sam Jaffe, who carried his friends around in warm corners of his mind and heart, was always quick to recommend a friend for a job: "Shumlin was looking for a director for *Grand Hotel* and I said, 'I have the man for you, John Huston.' He said, 'What did he do?' I said, 'We appeared in a play together, *Ruint,* by Hatcher Hughes, performed at the Provincetown Playhouse in New York. He played the lead and I was a tobacco chewing Southerner, Lum Crowder, and we formed our friendship then in 1917. John was 17 then.' I told him he wrote a little playlet, *Frankie and Johnnie*, for a girl who was doing marionettes and didn't have any subject. He wrote it and it was so excellent that it was printed. I wrote music for it. Then, when it was performed at George Gershwin's house, George said he would write the music. When it was published, John wanted me to have my music in it but since George was going to have a hand in it I bowed out. Shumlin said, 'I'd like to meet him.' He met him and he gave him the play because I had recommended him so highly. John took it home, read it and didn't like it. He turned it down. It didn't meet his high literary standards. John didn't show him the appreciation that he should have shown."

This recollection of Jaffe's differs slightly from what Huston reported in his tribute at the front of this book. In Huston's memory, he had not been offered the job but had suggested to Shumlin that he direct it himself.

In any case, Huston made an impression on Shumlin and when Shumlin went to Hollywood to do *The Watch on the Rhine*, Sam Goldwyn asked him for some young talents he knew and it was Shumlin who recommended John Huston. That was John Huston's introduction to films. Shumlin recommended him as a writer. "We all didn't want him to leave," Sam remembered. "We felt it was too bad that he was going away to Hollywood."

When Huston didn't work out for the direction of *Grand Hotel,* Jaffe encouraged Shumlin to direct the play himself. Shumlin didn't think he could do it. "It was the first play Shumlin had ever directed," says Jaffe, "and he was very modest and frightened. He planned the jack-knife stages necessary for the quick scene changes and had the entire intricate production ready in two weeks."

With Eugenie Leontovich, Henry Hull, Siegfried Rumann and Hortense Alden in the cast, the play ran for 86 weeks. A theatrical cartoon celebrated Jaffe and Alden appearing in Grand Hotel on the front page of the Sunday, August 9, 1931, New York *Herald Tribune*.

Jaffe could remember only one bad incident in the run. One night in the hotel corridor scene, an exciting moment depending on the quickness of the action, someone accidentally locked a door from the inside. He had to walk slowly across the broad stage and pretend to get the key with which to open it so a stage hand could open it from behind the door.

Grand Hotel, opening on the night of November 13, 1930, changed Jaffe's status in the theater through the role of Kringelein. First-night audiences greeted his performance with unrestrained enthusiasm. They cheered and stamped their feet.

Sam's career had what he called "a peculiar hit and miss kind of destiny." Joan Klein reports in *A Journal of Jewish, Semitic Silhouette: XXIII*, "Herman Shumlin ... recognized immediately something different about the man [Jaffe], an almost eerie kind of beauty, a touch of daft mysticism, perhaps. Instinctively Shumlin knew that he had met not just another character actor, not just a new and competent player of roles, but a new personality, a new individuality, a new man ...

"The play made Jaffe, because Jaffe made the play. A kaleidoscopic view of lives ... was given unity and meaning by Jaffe's Kringelein. Perhaps in the role of poor Kringelein, doomed to die, who wanted to live before he died, we capture a key to Jaffe himself. You can say, if you will, that longing for life is universal, that it has been, always, and will be forever. Yet, in Kringelein's longing to live, there was something mystic, something almost unreal, something more than the natural and universal unwillingness to die. And Jaffe, too, has this desire to catch life, to live it fully, in the same way. In one of those marriages too rare in the theater, part and player were one."

These were key observations about Jaffe. He was more than a character actor. He was an individual who stood out in appearance and manner as very different from most people. He caught the mystical dimension and grounded it in the very character he was in the world.

This unusualness stood out even more because

Jaffe didn't focus on what was different about himself. Instead, he concerned himself with bringing expressions into being through himself and on observing what transpired around him.

Grand Hotel achieved a major accomplishment by being able to draw full houses of attendance even though the film, with its numerous stars, played against it in the same city. The movie of *The Jazz Singer* had put the play out of business, but this was not true of *Grand Hotel*. Jaffe attributed the difference to timing. *The Jazz Singer* had been a novelty because it was the first of its kind. By the time of *Grand Hotel*, each medium had established its own foothold. Jaffe delighted in the play's continuance because it supported his belief that theater would never die.

The reviews on Jaffe's performance as Kringelein were nothing less than unanimous raves.

Kelcey Allen in *Women's Wear Daily* on November 14, 1930, said Jaffe "shows a fine sympathy and understanding of his role and accordingly he gives a superb performance."

In the *Herald Tribune*, Richard Watts Jr. noted that Jaffe achieved "the difficult business of combining gawky comedy with authentic tragedy; he effects the alliance with true humor and honest drama. You will find no finer moment in the current theater than the one in which he defies his employer, because, knowing that he is a dying man, he understands also that at last he is free."

Often, the words "flawless, poignant, disarmingly simple, and frank" described his performance.

Ben Washer turned in a key observation in his article "Actor and His Role Merged by Sam Jaffe's Kringelein." It allows us to traverse time and be present to the Jaffe of decades ago. He reports: "It's not often the theater reveals an actor so thoroughly his character that the audience has little impression of what the actor might be when he is finished with his work. Sam Jaffe, the now renowned Kringelein in *Grand Hotel*, has created one of these *rarae aves*, a character too complete to be separated from its actor.

"Tracked into his dressing lair at the National Theatre, Mr. Jaffe is instantaneously disarming. Here is the head and face of Kringelein. Kringelein, the weak and yet so strong creature, the fearing and yet so brave doomed-to-die man standing before you, robust, happy, sparkling-eyed.

"There's something sad about the disillusionment. You look at the man. Soon you're staring, searching for Kringelein. And a stare brings him to life. He's in Mr. Jaffe's face, in the tender, delicate eyes possessed with a fragile, thin-spun quality. It explains the subtlety of tragedy Mr. Jaffe brings to life on the stage. It explains Kringelein."

What Washer described is very different from the character who becomes the actor. Audiences experience this all too often in the form of actors who are identifiable as themselves no matter what roles they are playing. In Jaffe's case, the character and actor merged so completely, the actor became the character. Yet off-stage, the character "disappeared" and could be found only by identifying certain qualities in Sam Jaffe that enabled him to create the character. Washer felt disillusioned because Jaffe had so imprinted the audience with the character of Kringelein and had used himself so artfully to do it that he seemed to disappear. During Jaffe's long career, he achieved this many times. The marvel is, each time it was with a very different character.

Reviewer Robert Garland described Jaffe as both laughable and moving. He called him "an astute serio-comic personage."

Sam Jaffe (center) as Kringelein in the New York production of Grand Hotel, *1930-31.*

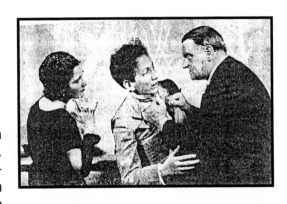

Later, on April 13, 1932, Garland, in comparing Jaffe with Barrymore in the film version, confirmed that Sam Jaffe's acting as Kringelein was unequaled.

Charles Darnton joined in that praise: "Eugenie Leontovich and Sam Jaffe were conspicuously effective. Mr. Jaffe gave an ingeniously appealing performance of the young man, hungry for a taste of life, with death staring him in the face. He had a distinct talent ..." Percy Hammond in the *New York Tribune* hailed him as "a fine actor," recommending his performance "to those who care for intelligent behavior upon the stage."

J. Brooks Atkinson, wrote a splendid review for the *New York Times*: "A free spirit, Kringelein, the doomed clerk, asks for nothing more substantial than giddy sensation — luxury, excitement, interesting companions. Caught willingly in the whirlpool of the *Grand Hotel* he finds life more exhilarating than he had ever imagined it. His guileless character brings him many friends.

"As Kringelein, Sam Jaffe, plays with endearing simplicity and with the headiness of a man tasting the sweets of ambition. These are the two glowing parts in *Grand Hotel*; Miss Leontovich and Mr. Jaffe, conspire with Madame Baum to make them vivid and memorable. ... Sam Jaffe is disarmingly simple, frank and excited."

Grand Hotel was truly the sensation of Broadway. Its author, the German Jewess Vicki Baum, became the most bitterly realistic German writer of her day.

In finding Jaffe for Kringelein, Herman Shumlin found the ideal. Sam was tall and high-shouldered, with a narrow chest. His great crop of bushy hair, his boyish smile, and his high-pitched voice all combined to bring the character to life.

As a result of *Grand Hotel*, Jaffe earned general recognition as the leading character actor on Broadway, and was held in the same esteem as Rudolph Schildkraut and Paul Muni.

Reviewers called Jaffe an utterly appealing figure, remarkable, wistful and pathetic, one who instantly wins the sympathies of an audience.

Frank Aston of the *Cincinnati Post* said, "Sam Jaffe pries his way into one's consciousness to become a haunting, stinging memory."

Reviewers seemed to want to capture their own experience and pass it on to potential audiences.

As one reads of how Jaffe stole the show and touched people deeply, a desire emerges to have been there and lived that piece of theater history. Stage performances of that rare nature remain alive only in the memory of those privileged to attend and in the words of reviewers whose imprint lingers in press archives.

In a single, powerful role, Sam Jaffe established himself as an authentic and powerful actor of the stage.

Harvey Gaul stated on April 12, 1932, in the *Pittsburgh Post-Gazette*: "He gives the part the requisite simplicity, the sort of doddering imbecility. In every way he was the artist ... he made us all feel for that tragic hungry little soul."

As rewarding as the performance was, it was equally testing of the actor's endurance. The character is on the stage about half of the play's three-hour run. During this time he is at high tension. He is at once a sick man on the verge of death, and yet one who is vitally alive, grasping at life's chimeric straws. Jaffe's task was to strike a balanced determination to enjoy life. Had his playing not been so excellent, he might well have been too bright or too full of suffering.

Once cast, Jaffe read the script in the original German to get the nuances. As an actor he was always very thorough in his work.

Sam used little or no make-up for the role. He went beneath the surface to the essence of who Kringelein was and gave the character life before his death. During the very long and successful run, Sam missed only about ten performances. The production played to capacity houses through two bad seasons on Broadway.

There were some wonderful interviews with Jaffe during the run that exemplify how he worked as an actor. They are informative to readers wanting to have a first-hand experience of the craft, and especially to actors or students of acting. For example, interviewed on August 22, 1931, by the *Post*, Jaffe spoke of what it was like to become so profoundly identified with a role that audiences no longer separate the actor from the character.

The article reads: "Certainly the legend of Sam Jaffe being Kringelein was borne out by the first sight of this lean and lanky man, with the eager, kindly face and the large, almost patriarchal head, topped by an unruly shock of hair. The first question, as blunt and as stupid as all such questions are, was: How does it feel to be Kringelein?

"'It feels great. But it has its small disadvantages. I used to go on the street without a hat, but I can't do it anymore. I'm constantly being recognized, not as myself, mind you, but as Kringelein or just plain *Grand Hotel*. It embarrasses me, and without a hat, I'm lost.'"

This phenomenon of being identified with a role happened more than once in Sam Jaffe's career. For years everyone knew him as Gunga Din or as the High Lama. To this day, even after his death, his fans remember him as Dr. Zorba. When this occurs so many times in an actor's career, it says something about how fully the artist bonds with the role. It is rare.

The *Post* article continued, quoting Sam: "'I never played a part like it before and I don't think anybody else ever has. What intrigued me about Kringelein from the time I first read the script was his range. Most underdogs and worms that turn in plays are just funny, but Kringelein is that and many other things as well. He has humorous scenes, pathetic scenes and really tragic ones. He lives a complete lifetime in the 36 hours which the play covers.

"'I belong to a school of actors who believe that they must live a part every time they play it,' Mr. Jaffe confessed frankly. For once you could believe the statement. 'I can't play in a detached manner, but must feel everything I do. For this reason my first lobby scene, in which I am supposed to be very angry, is extremely difficult for me. I am never satisfied with this scene unless I am actually angry and I try to get mad at something, or somebody, before I go on. Sometimes someone really does make me angry and then I feel that I have really played it well. Otherwise, I only get angry with myself because I haven't played it well, but then it is too late. My grill scene with Preysing and my gambling scene are much easier because then I am caught up in the action and can believe that these things are happening to me.

"'I have never known a play which required such concentration on the part of the actors. One second's hesitation and you are lost — the play and the other players have passed you by. Our opening telephone scene, with its lightning tempo and cues that must be picked up like lightning, sets the keynote for the whole play. From this one scene we can tell how each of us is going to be through the entire performance. It is a kind of a contest in which there is the greatest friendly rivalry. With so many short scenes divided among us, each of us must make his point with speedy precision to keep up our end. Like time, *Grand Hotel* waits for no man or no one actor.'"

Jaffe's approach of going from inner feeling to action was in contrast to many other actors of his day who worked from the outside in, following the tradition of posturing. First, Jaffe felt the emotion intensely. Then he thrust the emotion into outward expression. In Cleveland, critic William F. McDermott reflected on this factor: "The effect is one of exceptional sincerity, as if the emotions were real and expressed simply because they were too real and deep not to be expressed."

It is easy to see how a role like Kringelein, which reveals the spiritual aspect of Jaffe's character and characterizations, led to his eventually being cast as the Grand Lama. His earlier playing of one old man after another, even in his twenties, was further preparation for the lines of destiny that were to cross a few years later.

Although Jaffe was not cast in the film version of *Grand Hotel*, reviewers continued to acclaim his performance over Lionel Barrymore's. In the *New York Evening Post*, Thornton Delehanty proclaimed Barrymore miscast: "Though a comparison with the stage version is perhaps irrelevant, one cannot escape the feeling that Lionel Barrymore's Kringelein lacks the pathos of Sam Jaffe's."

Sam made more than an impression in *Grand Hotel*; he also made a great deal of money. He earned $750 a week; $39,000 a year. Significantly, this was in 1931!

Jaffe so made his mark in the role of Kringelein that Lloyd Lewis named him the year's best actor: "To pass over Katharine Cornell's moody perfection in *The Barretts of Wimpole Street* and to ignore Walter Hampden's noble creations, may seem wrong to you. Eloquent nominating speeches can be made for each of them, as well as for Leontovich in *Grand Hotel*, but something of the favor shown both Miss Cornell and Mr. Hampden is a reflection of their careers — their long service.

"No such assistance came to Mr. Jaffe's portrait of the pathetic and desperate wage slave who takes his last fling at life in the *Grand Hotel*. He came on unknown, took his audience in his hands and, no matter how often the staccato scenes of the play forced him to leave the stage, he always came back to grip his auditors with entire authority. The test of great acting, by modern standards, is to give spectators the illusion of reality and at this Mr. Jaffe was, for me, the year's success.

"He did what another actor of more technical skill, Charles Laughton, failed to do; he made me forget he was an actor."

It is an art to achieve such a distinction, to so thoroughly remove the player from the character being played that the character is all that remains visible.

One afternoon, during a run of the show in Philadelphia, Sam settled into a canvas steamer chair to be present to an interviewer. He was tired, he said, because he had had to go to New York that day.

The interviewer suggested that Jaffe could do the weakness of Kringelein realistically that night, because of his weariness.

Jaffe sat forward with interest, his eyes sparkling as an actor's eyes always do when he discusses the theater or his art. He said, "No. That's the funny part of it. You can't. You've got to be feeling right in order to do it. You've got to have all your strength to put the right feeling into it. If you're not well, you can't put yourself into it, you can't feel it. I was sick for a while, and I came back into the play too soon, and at first I couldn't do it right. I hadn't the control. I'd start with my voice too high and get low. People noticed it." His natural voice is several tones lower than the weak, almost falsetto tone of Kringelein.

"It is a strain, this part, but it's a wonderful part. And it's a wonderful play."

Grand Hotel caused Jaffe to become the rage on Broadway. It established him as a leading Broadway actor. His performance in the long run play won him citations from all the major drama critics as the best performance of that season. Reporters and interviewers flocked to reflect on the 'overnight success' story.

Brion, in a piece entitled, "A Timid Soul On Broadway, A Portrait-Interview with Sam Jaffe, Broadway's Latest Find," noted that before *Grand Hotel*, Jaffe had indifferent success: "He was never regarded as a star or even as a potential headliner. Jaffe was just an actor who had to amble along with the handicap of too much intelligence and too little chutzpah. You know what we mean. Jaffe understood his parts perfectly, often even discovered in them shades and nuances which the author had never dreamed of. But his own critical mind bothered him.

"He was too intelligent to live his parts. He was one of those actors who are afflicted with brains and who usually wind up by becoming directors and sometimes playwrights but very seldom stars.

"... Today Jaffe is generally recognized as the outstanding character actor on Broadway ...

"'You don't know what it is,' Jaffe's voice sounds as moving as Kringelein's cry that he wants to live — 'to go from one producer to another, asking, pleading, explaining. One feels so small and futile. After a while one is ashamed of one's self. But there is that insane urge driving you back because you feel that you want to act, that the stage's make-believe is real life and that acting is the only thing that you can do. I have been through it! What a relief when the process is reversed and the producer comes to you. It pays you back for all the anguish, heartburn and humiliation.'"

Jaffe knew the actor's casting struggle, and the insatiable drive to act. This may have been a motivating factor for his bringing the Equity Library Theatre into being so that actors could have venues.

In the midst of the interview with Brion, Sam turned solicitously to Lillian and commented facetiously that it felt great to have newspapermen swarming around. Brion, in observing Jaffe, reported that he could do little to hide his timid, gentle soul and that those qualities felt out of place in the glaring spotlight of Broadway. He also noted that there was an apologetic note in his voice, apologizing to Lillian for his successes.

Jaffe felt that Broadway had been very kind to him because it never asked him to compromise or to distort himself to please.

Brion continued the interview asking if Jaffe felt tempted to return to the Yiddish stage: "Sam Jaffe blushes. With a forced, nonchalant voice, he explains, 'The Yiddish theater is dead. Not sick, dead. There is no more audience; there are no more plays and there are mighty few actors left.'"

Jewish theater began to die in the late 1930's. In February 1942, H.S. Kraft wrote a piece in one of the Yiddish newspapers concerning Jewish theater's demise: "When immigration was at its height, from 1900 up to the outbreak of World War I, the Jews huddled in the East Side and not understanding English, flocked to the Yiddish theaters and supported the star system. They did not, however, exercise much discrimination regarding the plays. All of them had come from the hovels of Poland and Czarist Russia and consequently the sound of Yiddish spoken openly and publicly was a treat for them. But the plays fulfilled not only this particular need; the theaters were also the meeting place where large groups of landsleit could gather and renew acquaintance. The system of benefit performances was inaugurated and the lodges and the brotherhoods were kept alive by the few dollars they made in selling tickets."

The plays in Jewish theater were predictable stories with repeated themes. There was little progressive thought and many of the stars refused to play the villains or common workers. "In the main, however," Kraft continued, "the theater produced tear-jerkers, despite the fine acting of the great names of the Jewish theater. The history of this period is a summary of sacrifice on the part of the actors, skullduggery on the part of the actor-managers, and unequaled exploitation of actors by theater owners, aided and abetted by sharp practices by union officials."

Maurice Schwartz tried to keep Yiddish theater alive, but his plays, which were either classics or set in old Russia, didn't speak with liveliness or relevance to the theatergoers of the day. Production costs were rising and, with diminishing audiences, the genre gave way.

Although Jaffe was wise enough to choose the theater of the future rather than one on the wane, he was observant enough to see the values embraced by Jewish theater and to make those a part of his life as a creative artist.

In conversation with Charles Higham, Sam spoke of something that existed back in those days that can be found only sporadically today. It was total unselfishness on the part of the actors. Higham recalled Sam's description: "It's like an organism. A cast in those days was not just a collection of egos fighting for position on the stage. They were an organism. They were one body. Sam taught me that an actor shines at his best when he is part of such an organism. That each one is not thinking of himself but of the overall result." This is what came out of Yiddish theater. For Jaffe, acting had to be an organic experience. It should never be the display of the personal ego.

Sam had no desire to play in Yiddish, although he

spoke it well. Hebrew tempted him and the Habima, the national theater of Israel, attracted him because it was a theater of the classics. Therein lay his real ambition. He said, "There are so few roles that can stand critical analysis in the modern drama, and one cannot always shut off his intelligence, you know!"

Jaffe had played the role of Kringelein for 80 weeks. He said, "After a long run you feel you have scooped yourself dry; your emotional vitality for that particular part has run out." This statement might describe life itself.

While Kringelein sought one last fling, Jaffe had an altogether different dream. He wished for a little house in the country. During free moments he and Lillian searched Westchester and Connecticut for the perfect place. It had to have a garden and be hidden away from the road. He sought something simple and 'nooky,' but it had to be large enough to accommodate the friends he loved so dearly because of their great minds. Jaffe used to say, "As a man thinketh, that's the only interesting thing in the world!"

Jaffe had a discombobulating experience during the run of *Grand Hotel*. One of his co-stars, Henry Hull, used as his audition for motion pictures, the gambling scene from *Grand Hotel*, and all its characters. When the company saw the film later, Sam Jaffe suffered shattered nerves. Seeing himself on film was a mental shock and for several nights he could hardly go through his part at the theater. It was as though he had died and somehow had seen his own ghost.

The experience was so shocking to Jaffe that he harbored fear of appearing in motion pictures. As often happens, what we fear most is our very next challenge. The success of *Grand Hotel* lifted Jaffe from his well-earned, high perch on the stage, into a career in the very talking pictures he dreaded.

OSSIE DAVIS, *Stevedore, 1949*

"*My career was at the bottom when I did Stevedore. I had married at that time and my wife and I had finished a tour of* Anna Lucasta. *Nothing was happening. Nothing.*

"*The director invited me to read. He was young then and went on to become a resident director for* As the World Turns. *I felt good. I felt included again. Going to* Stevedore *was a lifeline thrown down to me. It made the difference.*

"*Working conditions at E.L.T. were bare bones and minimum all the way around. There was a paucity of things in all cases. There was nothing to recommend it. When we went into rehearsal there was no glory or glamour or anything very exciting except that we were doing it. The people I worked with turned out to be exciting names in the theater, but that was later. All of us were just a symbol of this very quiet director who was dynamite in his effectiveness and the way he got things done. We quietly rehearsed little by little, piece by piece, day after day until finally we had a play.*

"*In the company we had Rod Steiger, Jack Klugman, Roy Hill, and Lloyd Richards.*

"*Being in the production served me artistically. The director, for all his patience and gentleness, really was a man of iron reserve and resolve. I had to learn what acting was. When I came into the theater, acting was about going on the stage and saying lines; saying them loud so people could hear them and have a good time. You were who you were before you went on stage. You were who you were when you got on stage and that was it. This was the first time that I was challenged by the necessity of becoming a character, something other than myself.*

"*We had in those days a word that described the situation of the black actor. There was a style of acting which we described as 'ufta.' 'Ufta' was what you did as a black person to impress the white director that he knew more about being black than you did. You catered to his knowledge of black folks. You might extend the stereotype; include a little head scratching to make him feel comfortable. Dan, the E.L.T. director, helped us get over the bullshit aspects* of the whole thing. He helped us to deal honestly with the piece in front of us as a human being rather than the stereotype. E.L.T. was salutary in getting the taste of 'ufta' out of our mouths. You have to hate yourself for doing that kind of thing. You couldn't feel good about yourself as a human being.

"The second thing was the importance of the piece. Stevedore had achieved something in the theater as an original work so that we felt that what we were involved in was not just another piece of theater, as Anna Lucasta was. Here was a historical piece that still had relevance. It still touched on the kinds of conditions a young black youth might find in the segregated south. Those of us who were in it felt we were making a contribution.

"I was in World War II. Racism had just been so vividly illustrated to the whole of humankind by Hitler. There was a focus in Actors' Equity that these horrors had to be attended to. The first connection between culture and the activist philosophy met me when I got on stage. And in those days, after performance, somebody would always say, 'Hey let's go to this party to raise funds for Willie McGee in Mississippi who's going to be electrocuted.' At the party would be a Paul Robeson or an Orson Wells, a Marlon Brando. The theater took itself rather importantly. Actors' Equity had come up with the rule forcing no performer to play in the National Theatre, Washington, D.C. because they practiced segregation. Artistic and social responsibilities were current in the theater then.

"Stevedore fit into that. It was an art form and it was drama but it was also life, and America facing up to the concept that racism must end. Stevedore was part of that kind of response. It dealt with racism in a visceral way. It gave us a chance to make statements about it, to show who we were and that we weren't going to accept this view of life. Racism was something that had to be driven out of the system. We were proud to be part of it.

"We also took it out on a road tour at various places in the New York area. It had an extended life.

"I remember people coming back stage and agents getting my name and number. I was hired by the director again and also sent on his recommendation to castings.

"About E.L.T. folding, I feel depressed and a bit ashamed because it did do something for me and I never gave back. I always meant to but I never did. I remember, in 1960, when Ruby [Dee, his actress wife] had finished doing the film A Raisin in the Sun *and we went to Mexico. We went to the theater that the actor's union had in Mexico. I said, 'Now that's what E.L.T. has to have: a building, a program.' The Mexican actors were proud of their theater and it was a marvelous thing that they offered to people.*

"We didn't do that with E.L.T. and I'm sorry. What we did with E.L.T. is so typical of how we Americans behave with things. I'm still ashamed of my malfeasance in connection with this thing that was so important in my life.

"It was also an example of how a good thing sometimes encourages us to leave from one place and go to the other without giving us the necessary way to reach back and put back what we took. I'm a product of community theater in Harlem and another little theater out of which Anna Lucasta *had come. With* Anna Lucasta *there was an opening up on Broadway and the black performers from that little theater were welcomed onto Broadway. We all went and we never got back. The doors that we had been pounding on for so long opened. We went through the door and we didn't look back. We didn't preserve the bridge that brought us over. With E.L.T. we did the same kind of thing. I'm sorry about that.*

"The organization itself has an obligation to build in the opportunity for us to reach back and give. Otherwise we convert Broadway and the theater into a transit place; a place where you train while you are really heading to Hollywood or some other place. You get your basic training there but it's not a home. It's a rite of passage and you live not only to shine on Broadway, but you live to use Broadway as a stepping stone to something else. Even now, when there's a dearth of plays on Broadway, when we've converted to musicals, Broadway turned away people like Tennessee Williams and Arthur Miller. Broadway didn't reach out and say these are my glories. Broadway accepted itself as a point of transit through which people went but nobody stayed to repaint the walls and decorate the house. The old American tradition of using the land until it's fallow and then instead of refurbishing it, moving on to another spot. We Americans are great for that. Broadway is a good example of one of the ways we've got to change ourselves. I feel deeply about that."

****

Legendary Roles in Classic Films

Sam Jaffe's film career began as a result of his long-running Broadway success as Kringelein in *Grand Hotel*.

At the end of 1932, Sam did a screen test for the lead role in the film version. He didn't get the part because they chose an all-star cast. Even to this day, top billing on Broadway doesn't necessarily translate to star status in Hollywood. While Jaffe didn't get to play Kringelein on film, director Josef von Sternberg watched Jaffe's test. He was searching for a capable actor to play the zany part of Peter I, the Duke, in *The Scarlet Empress*, starring Marlene Dietrich. The test Jaffe had made for *Grand Hotel* involved a scene of emotional outburst. Since Kringelein had only six months to live, he released all his fire. That test was enough to persuade von Sternberg to use Jaffe in the part of the Duke.

Sam Jaffe as the Duke in The Scarlet Empress, *with Marlene Dietrich.*

Sam Jaffe recalled many idiosyncrasies about Josef von Sternberg as a director. He was a wonderful photographer who used visual symbolism, often phallic, to excite the audience. One of his strokes of genius in *The Scarlet Empress* was having the Duke bore a hole into the room of the Empress so that he could see what she was doing.

Sam marveled that von Sternberg himself was always on the boom. He rode it around as if he were on horseback. Even the cameraman didn't have a chance because he cleared the stage of all crew and wanted to handle everything himself. He would change the writing and even the art work, proclaiming to know more than those hired to do the tasks. During the musical scoring, von Sternberg was searching for a note he had in head but couldn't find. He had the stagehands bring him a small studio piano. He played every note, rejecting all of them. A concert grand was wheeled in and again he struck all the notes. Not finding it there either, he demanded they find a new piano with more keys.

Jaffe reported that the scripts von Sternberg distributed to the actors were completely without punctuation so that all the words flowed into each other. This was how he controlled the interpretation of all the parts.

Jaffe didn't hold back in his complaints about the director. Quoted in the book *Marlene: The Life of Marlene Dietrich*, by Charles Higham, Sam noted: "Directors are to bring the best out of you and what the author has to say ... to make sure that you're in keeping with both those things.

"I hated the son of a gun. His trouble was that he never let you alone. A good director leaves you alone so you bring up whatever goodies you have for him. If a man begins to tell how and what to do, the spontaneity goes out. He tried to act every part himself. That's how he directed. He was a lousy actor. He'd want to fix everything, design everything. He tried to correct everything himself."

Jaffe had several run-ins with the infamous director. He saw him as tyrannical and convinced of his own greatness. Every actor had to bend to his will. However, Sam wouldn't yield. There was a scene Jaffe had to play with Miss Dietrich in which he had to blast her. Among the gems Sam had to deliver was the line: "There you sit with camphor balls on your mouth."

Jaffe reminded von Sternberg that the story took place two hundred years ago and there were no camphor balls then. Von Sternberg ordered Jaffe to say the line anyway. Jaffe followed his direction but he didn't play the scene to the director's satisfaction and he had to repeat it eighty-seven times in succession. After the eighty-seventh time, Jaffe refused to play it again. Nothing could budge him. Von Sternberg had to give in.

Jaffe rebelled against him repeatedly. In the last scene of the film, von Sternberg was again unhappy with the way Sam was playing a moment of pouring out venom. He took it upon himself to give Jaffe a line reading. Jaffe tried it again, and then again, to the dissatisfaction of the fulminating director. Von Sternberg was famous for taking scores of shots and then using the first or second one. Jaffe heard von Sternberg say that he had the scene 'in the can,' but he continued to have Jaffe replay it. After the 27th time, Jaffe quit. Von Sternberg told Jaffe he would never be able to play in movies again. Jaffe told him that he didn't care to work in pictures. He was a stage actor and he just came out to do pictures when he was between engagements. It was a standoff.

The problem was that Jaffe had more scenes to do. Von Sternberg took Jaffe for a walk the whole length of the sound stage. It was one of those old, big studios. He tried to calm him down and gave him a long lecture. He said, "I wonder if you have any idea how important I am. I have seventy million followers in Japan alone!"

Jaffe got the last word with the retort, "That's wonderful. Christ only had twelve!" Finally, von Sternberg agreed to take only one shot of Jaffe for future scenes and Sam became known on the lot as One-Shot Sam.

Jaffe's standing up to von Sternberg was a phenomenon of such earthshaking dimensions in Hollywood that at the end of the picture, the cast, including Miss Dietrich, and the crew signed an enormous testimonial to Sam.

The press got wind of the troubles on the set and gossip began to appear. They said that Sam walked indignantly off the set of *The Scarlet Empress* as a protest against von Sternberg's coaching in the histrionic art. They quoted Sam as hurling these scathing words over his shoulder as he left: "Who taught you drama? Hitler?"

Jaffe wasn't the only one von Sternberg tried to dominate. Sam reported that he wouldn't leave Marlene Dietrich alone. She would speak a line and then he would speak it for her and raise her dress a bit, exposing her marvelous legs. He corrected another of her lines and raised her dress even more. Sam and Lillian began doing a classic satirical mimicry of von Sternberg directing Dietrich. It caused hilarity at Hollywood and New York parties.

Sam said that Marlene Dietrich was darling and that everyone who worked with her adored her. She had done *The Blue Angel* and *Morocco* with von Sternberg and he tried to be her Svengali.

He made her endlessly replay a dinner party scene. He shot it over so many days that the boar's head at the center of the table began to decay and stink horribly. Eventually, Dietrich fainted. Von Sternberg softened but insisted that she must continue. She did.

In another instance, von Sternberg made Louise Dresser, the dowager empress, endlessly repeat a scene of blowing out of candles. He screamed at her, ordering that she emit less breath. She finally walked off the set until he stopped his demands.

Given all of Jaffe's grievances about von Sternberg, the following interview of Jaffe by Leonard Hall seems to contradict what he previously had to say about working with him:

"'One of the most remarkable things about Dietrich,' Jaffe said, 'is her working relationship with von Sternberg. ... His attitude is one of adoration for, and service to, a great artist. I felt, when they were working together on a scene, that he was forever paying her tribute — that there wasn't the slightest whim of hers, that he wouldn't gratify at any cost.

"'As for Dietrich, she trusts his artistic judgment implicitly, almost blindly. That's why they are probably the greatest director-actress team that pictures have ever seen. Most actors, taking direction, listen to the boss with one ear and then do it their own way. Some only pretend to listen. Not Marlene. Believing wholeheartedly in her director's picture wisdom, she will do a tiny scene fifty times to achieve perfection in his eyes. And when the last shot is in the box, the result may not be perfection to the critics and the fans, but it is one-hundred percent perfect to Joe von Sternberg!

"'He directs Dietrich entirely in German, calling her anything that enters his mind which ends with the affectionate German diminutive chen. It may be putschen. Then again, it often sounds like Mutschen or Kutschen. But it is always little something or other.

"'It's a treat to watch him rehearse her. It's all a lot of tender cajolery.

"'Putschen, he'll say, Setzen — so! Jetzt, bitte — augen recht, augen links! Ah, so! Aber, Putschen, mehr, bitte! So! Danke! So they go through it — eyes right, eyes left — until von Sternberg is satisfied. It may be once or twenty times. He checks the sound, the camera, the lights. Then he signals for a 'take' with his own copyrighted word of command: C'MON!

"'And believe me, they all c'mon with everything they've got, when the boss barks like a leather-tongued football coach!'

"' . . And now, Sam, tell me,' I said, breathing heavily, 'Is she really so beautiful?'

"Jaffe's eyes grew misty, and he looked around to see if the Missus was within earshot.

"'Beautiful?' he crooned. 'You should see! Mmmm-mmm! You wouldn't believe!'

"'And those legs, Sam!' I said.

"'Like angels!' said Sam."

Jaffe may have been a novice in Hollywood, but he was experienced in giving interviews and passing on anecdotes appropriate to publicizing a film. Given Jaffe's daily objections to von Sternberg and his tactics, the content of this laudatory interview has Jaffe speaking out of a second side of his mouth. We saw this in earlier chapters when he spoke in defense of Vince Edwards while being critical of him off-press. Because Jaffe was so true to himself and held that as a life value, this behavior in interviews seemed out of character as he sought to promote the project.

The reviews of *The Scarlet Empress* and of Sam were wonderful.

Chicago Daily News, "The New Films," Clark Rodenbach: "... The grand duke, as played by Jaffe, is completely nuts, and a mess to look at, as opposed to Doug Fairbanks' duke, who was a handsome fellow with occasional moments of lucidity ... Sam Jaffe ... turns in an excellent performance."

Los Angeles Times, Edwin Schallert: "... Outstanding in the moments allotted to him is the character actor Sam Jaffe. His strangely expressed childlike disinterest in his wife furnishes an unforgettable episode. The scene is isolated and alone in sheer acting effect. Otherwise he is extraordinary as a personality, belonging in the domain of the grotesque."

Louella O. Parsons proclaimed that no one could

play Catherine's husband better than Sam Jaffe. According to Harrison Carroll in the *Herald Express*, Jaffe stole the picture's acting honors with his memorable portrayal.

Mollie Merrick praised Jaffe's amazing interpretation, saying that he played the secret delight of the maniac to perfection. She added that Sam Jaffe "should be one of the greatest artistic additions to our screen."

Following this performance, Jaffe did *We Live Again* for United Artists in 1934, with Fredric March, Anna Sten, C. Aubrey Smith, but he always returned to New York and to the stage. He called the theater "the mother of us all." But he was clearly destined for more screen roles.

On June 30, 1936, Louella O. Parsons reported: "Sam Jaffe has been elected to play the Grand Lama in *Lost Horizon*." In terms of Jaffe's career, this was a profound accomplishment. It hadn't come easily and it was to leave a lasting impact on his life, and on the world of film.

Casting the role of the high lama had been no small task. It was Charles Laughton who had first called attention to the importance of the role. His enthusiasm soared after reading the story and he wanted more than anything to play it. Columbia Pictures had given *Lost Horizon* to Frank Capra to direct. Capra had had a series of successes including *Broadway Bill, It Happened One Night, The Bitter Tea of General Yen*, and *Mr. Deeds Goes to Town*.

Laughton was under contract to another company but he called Capra, insisting that he be cast in the role. Capra's attention had not been on the Grand Lama at that point. He had been concentrating on the more romantic leads, eventually played by Ronald Colman, Jane Wyatt, Margo and John Howard.

Laughton called Capra's attention to the role and

it was then that Capra began to realize that the entire film did center on this extraordinary character. Laughton persuaded Irving Thalberg to give him a release from Metro-Goldwyn-Mayer so that he could play the part. To his chagrin, Ronald Colman was engaged with another film and would not be available for an entire year. By that time Laughton was working in London, making him unavailable. As a result of Laughton's calling attention to the Grand Lama, Capra felt the role required the services of a fine actor, just the right actor. He despaired that Laughton was unable to do it.

Capra set out on a massive search. First, an actor friend of Ronald Colman's, A. E. Anson was brought in from his home in the desert to take a test. He was quite old, and so very ill that he had to make the trip to Columbia studios in an ambulance. Pleased with him, Capra signed Anson at the largest salary he had ever received. However, two days later Anson passed away in his sleep.

By now, urgency overcame Capra. He sensed that the film's credibility rested on the proper casting of the Grand Lama. He tested almost as many actors as sought the role.

Any actor will tell you of the importance of being in the right place at the right time. This was definitely the case with Sam and the role of the high lama.

Jaffe had been cast as the Adversary in the New York stage play *The Eternal Road* by Franz Werfel. It was to be a stupendous spectacle, eventually costing $463,000, produced and directed by Max Reinhardt, with music by Kurt Weill. The cast included Baruch Lumet, Kurt Kasznar, Roger De Koven, Mildred Dunnock (as a woman of congregation), Dickie Van Patten and Sidney Lumet (as small boys), Olive Deering as the Alien girl, and Lotte Lenya as Miriam.

Herman Shumlin had introduced Jaffe to Max Reinhardt, known as a genius in Europe where he had five theaters. Reinhardt had seen Sam's work in *The God of Vengeance* and he called him for *The Eternal Road*. Sam experienced Reinhardt as a humorous and delightful human being who was a good listener. Before the casting of any actors, Reinhardt had an ability to envision the characters fully. This impressed Sam greatly when he read for him. As if composing music, Reinhardt could hear inside his head the timbre, pitch and tempo of the characters.

He had in front of him an annotated book in which he had scored each speech. He knew how it would be said, what the character would be doing, and where the character would be on stage. He did this for every role so that when the company appeared on stage for the first rehearsal, a framework existed upon which to build. He was open to changes, allowing dimension to emerge.

Although Jaffe preferred working with directors who gave actors freedom to create, he did not feel constrained by Reinhardt's approach because there was room to make Reinhardt's terms his own as he continued with his character development.

Jaffe held Reinhardt in equal esteem with Stanislavski. He saw the former as a man of practical application to balance the latter's genius with theory.

The Eternal Road was one of the greatest pageants New York had ever seen. There was a chorus of 300 people besides the cast. The production was vast in conception and achievement.   Its

Sam Jaffe as the Adversary in Max Reinhardt's The Eternal Road, *1937.*

bulk alone was impressive, as well as its great pictorial beauty. While visually powerful, many critics complained that it lacked defiance. It dealt with persecution of the Jews by the Nazi regime, but rather than fighting the evil, it defined the persecution as a necessary part of the whole. In the role of the Adversary, Jaffe became the heroic figure who denounces the mysticism that would accept oppression as a virtue.

The production had been scheduled to open in early January of 1937 at the Manhattan Opera House. However, it was such a mammoth undertaking that it suffered a series of postponements.

Because of the delays, Sam Jaffe was brought to Hollywood to work with Marlene Dietrich in the film *Hotel Imperial*. As way leads to way, the film was abandoned when Marlene Dietrich quit and her successor, Margaret Sullavan broke an arm the second day of shooting.

Sam prepared to return to New York but was held up by arbitration over a week's salary that he claimed Paramount owed him for *Hotel Imperial*.

Jaffe lost the arbitration, but in the interim made a test for the Grand Lama role thanks to his friends, the vaudeville producers, Hockey and Green. They told Jaffe that everybody was trying for it, and suggested that he have his agent set up a screen test. Sam had nothing to lose and followed through on the advice.

Since Capra continued to test, Jaffe returned to New York in March of 1936. On a hot day in July, he received a wire from his agent, Eddington and Vincent, informing him of the feather in his cap: he had been chosen to do *Lost Horizon*.

Though he was in rehearsal for *The Eternal Road*, he needed to fly the very next day to begin shooting the immortal speech of the Grand Lama. He arrived to find Capra shooting sequences in the 'Ice Box.' It was a big refrigerated studio where the outdoor scenes were made.

Jaffe described having to don fur-lined boots and big overcoats before entering. He recalled, "They had already shot the funeral of the Grand Lama even if they hadn't taken any pictures of him, so my arrival was sort of a resurrection. They were doing the sequence where Colman was leaving Shangri-La for the outer world with the porters. For every remake, they had to fill up the footprints with big cakes of ice ground up and shot through a hose. For the avalanche scene, where all the porters are lost, they had two big rooms full of corn flakes soaked with flour which they dropped on the actors, who took a fifty-foot slide down a hill of ice."

Sam arrived on what was to have been the last day of shooting. The day was devoted to filming the death scene of the Grand Lama and his long speech to Ronald Colman.

This single role and long speech stand as cornerstones in Jaffe's movie career. Beyond that, they live and breathe in the hearts and minds of millions who were profoundly affected by them on the screen. Here was a wisdom figure, over 200 years old. It was as if his face was of glass and the only thing visible through this man was his soul. Sam Jaffe played the ancient quality by letting the audience feel their way through the character into his great mind and his accumulated inner wisdom.

Harrison Forman was the technical expert on *Lost Horizon* and a member of the Explorers Club. He had spent a year in Tibet and was the second white man to interview the Panchen Lama, who would be played by Sam Jaffe. He spent time researching at the Kumbum Lamasary. He was responsible for finding Tibetans in Hollywood for extra parts. Scores of Chinese had been hired, but Chinese were not true Tibetan types. Forman, a perfectionist, found an Indian reservation at Pala, about 125 miles from Los Angeles, the inhabitants of which closely resembled Tibetans. He hired the whole reservation because in feature, stature and temperament these

Indians looked as if they had just stepped off the Tibetan plain. They were high-cheek-boned, copper-colored, and slightly slant-eyed and had the happy-go-lucky temperament natural to the natives of Tibet.

Because of his credentials, when Harrison Forman made observations about Jaffe's excellent work as the Grand Lama, it was a confirmation of the highest order. The powerful speech of the Grand Lama was eloquently described by Forman in a promotional piece, as if to set the scene so that those who weren't present during the shooting could share in the experience:

"An old man speaks slowly, almost painfully, in a voice scarcely above a whisper. His upturned eyes are misty and agleam with fitful highlights from a flickering candle at his side. Simply robed in the classic toga of a Tibetan lama, a huddled figure seated in the dimly lit corner of a room whose walls are lined with floor-to-ceiling bookshelves, he is the focus of attention for half a hundred technicians — cameramen, sound men, props, and grips. No one moves.

"This is the death scene of the High Lama of the mythical lamasery of Shangri-La — a dramatic climax in Columbia's picturization of James Hilton's *Lost Horizon*.

"The minutes tick on ... six, seven, eight ... Extraordinarily long for a single scene."

Soon, Forman continues, "he has half risen. ... His voice tails off to a whisper. Suddenly he drops back; shoulders droop, eyes roll shut, and his head slips limply forward.

"A long minute of silence; then,

"'Cut!'

"Impulsively applauding, Director Frank Capra advances toward the player. "'Good work, Sam,' he says, as he grasps his hand. 'And thanks.'

"There are tears in his eyes as he turns away.

"The appreciation was deservedly earned by Sam Jaffe for his magnificent portrayal of the dying High Lama."

The speech that Jaffe delivered as the High Lama carried universal import. Here it is:

"It came to me in a vision long, long ago. I saw all the nations strengthening, not in wisdom but in the vulgar passions and the will to destroy. I saw their machine power multiplying until a single weaponed man might match a whole army. I foresaw a time when man, exulting in the technique of murder, would rage so hotly over the world that every book, every treasure would be doomed to destruction. This vision was so vivid and so moving that I determined to gather together all the things of beauty and culture that I could and preserve them here against the doom toward which the world is rushing. Look at the world today. Is there anything more pitiful? What madness there is, what blindness, what unintelligent leadership. A scurrying mass of bewildered humanity crashing headlong against each other, compelled by an orgy of greed and brutality. The time must come, my friend, when this orgy will spend itself, when brutality and the lust for power must perish by its own sword. Against that time is why I avoided death and am here, and why you were brought here. For when that day comes the world must begin to look for a new life. And it is our hope that they may find it here. For here we shall be with their books and their music and the way of life based on one simple rule: be kind! When that day comes it is our hope that the brotherly love of Shangri-La will spread throughout the world. Yes, my son, when the strong have devoured each other, the Christian ethic may at last be fulfilled and the meek inherit the earth."

Decades later when told that great numbers of people reported that he changed their lives by the way he played the role of the lama, Sam replied, "If they said so, I'm happy. It certainly had a very moral message. Roosevelt used a paragraph from my speech in his Chicago address ... something about the lamp of democracy burning low."

Sam once performed the speech on the Joey Bishop Show. Even in the midst of an entertainment interview show, the response was complete silence. The audience was spellbound.

In his typical style of calling very little attention to himself, Sam's response to this was, "Well, it was quite a speech."

Not only was it quite a speech, it was quite a long speech. It was so long that a crew member up in the flies fell asleep and began snoring. Capra asked him, "What are you doing? You snored." The man said, "No, I was just sleeping." He said, "You snored. And don't do it again." Jaffe remarked that von Sternberg would have run him through with a sword. He had no doubt about it. Capra was a gentleman. He told the man he could sleep but not snore.

Capra chose, at first, to shoot Jaffe in silhouette, trying to get the essence of the character rather than the corporeal being. He decided he could do better with lights, using certain luminous effects and shadows. He hoped to give the idea of a benign man who shows age without emphasizing too much physical deterioration.

The scene lasted eight minutes with Capra recording the action using six cameras for editing later from every angle. Capra shot the scene in only four takes. In that brief period, they exposed seventeen thousand feet of film. The structure of the film rested on this dialog.

As for the acting performance, Jaffe was told that he had created film history by his recital of long speeches without costly blunders or mistakes which would have necessitated shooting the entire scene over again. In addition, Jaffe had absorbed the character of the old lama completely by the time he reached Hollywood. Everybody present on that day of that first shooting told him he did a great job with it. Smiling disarmingly at the compliment, he joked, "It's just the lama in me."

The Grand Lama had a rich background of worldly culture combined with a dedication to priest-like sincerity, to a life of harmony, peace and infinite understanding. Jaffe's devotion to goodness, the spirit with which he lived his life, and the objective view he constantly sought, all combined to make him into a figure compatible with the role he was to create for the screen.

Jaffe had never visited Tibet, nor had he ever met a lama. He studied the character, mulled over it; dreamed it. "I read Tibetan and Chinese literature, the wise, clipped sayings of the East," he revealed. "All this I brought to my conception of the part."

Sam discussed the complexities of the Grand Lama with Marguerite Tazelaar, in a New York *Herald Tribune* article on August 16, 1936: "'You see, there were many problems in connection with this portrayal, and so many angles to present him from. Mr. Capra and I spent hours conferring over an exact representation,' he said. 'We wanted him to show, not just physical age, but age that expresses itself through wisdom and understanding.'"

Unfortunately, Capra did not achieve his desired effects with the use of the silhouette. He decided they must show more of the character to sustain audience interest. This decision necessitated additional shooting days and complex experiments with altering Jaffe's face. They created a wax mask for him.

Because the human frame shrinks with age, they used a surgical rubber dressing on the mask to simulate a deeply wrinkled, drawn look. To this, they added little pieces of paper fitted together to resemble a small, shrunken skull of head hunters.

For three days, under glaring lights, Jaffe and Colman worked hard to reshoot the scene. During all that time Jaffe's face remained encased in the flexible mask, and he had to sit in a cramped position to represent a one-legged man.

Sam related with a smile, "A minor discomfort means nothing to me since then; I can well understand how a Hindu Fakir can become accustomed to the painful poses he assumes. My amazement at my own capacity for physical discomfort was equaled only by my astonishment at the patience of Frank Capra. Nothing ever ruffled him."

That patience would turn out to be sorely needed before the film was completed.

Sam Jaffe and Charlton Heston in Ben Hur, *1959.*

****

THEONIE V. ALDREDGE, *Arms and the Man*, 1957

The E.L.T. production was one of the first shows Theonie Aldredge designed in New York. It led to her meeting with Joseph Papp and their starting of the New York Shakespeare Festival.

"In those days you just took your portfolio and walked around forever. If nobody gives you a chance to do something, where are they going to see your work? When you get the chance, in the right time and place, then you have to deliver. That chance might not come again.

"The conditions at E.L.T. were very poor. There was no shop to work in and no materials. And this [play] was a period piece. I made every piece of garment because they gave me no money to hire any help. In the end it was a good experience.

"Arthur Laurents saw my work at E.L.T. and when he was doing I Can Get It For You Wholesale, he called and said, 'I'm Arthur Laurents.' I dropped the phone because I thought it was a joke. He called back and said, 'Now, wait a minute, it's really me. It's not a joke. I saw the show and put a circle around your name. I said the first show I do I'm going to use her.' I have worked for Arthur ever since. He's never done anything that I haven't done."

Before the end of her career, Theonie earned more than $200,000 a show.

****

The Grand Lama and Gunga Din

Sam Jaffe's acting career spanned almost seven decades. Because he was born before the turn of the century, he had the distinction of participating in several entertainment mediums as they originated during his long lifetime. Some actors were not able to cross from one discipline to another. Their talents were not eclectic enough. This was not true of Jaffe. He moved easily from one to another, and back again. Although he began on the stage, and that arena remained his true love, he excelled in motion pictures. Given the length of his overall career, he appeared in relatively few films. Yet, several of those films rank as classics and his performances in them remain seared on the memories of moviegoers.

With the successful shooting of *Lost Horizon* under his belt, Jaffe returned to New York to continue rehearsals as the Adversary in *The Eternal Road* at the Manhattan Opera. When the show finally opened, Jaffe received great praise for his performance.

However, before Jaffe could get settled, Capra summoned him back to Hollywood. While *Lost Horizon* had turned out well, the picture ran for five hours because no one, including the director, could bear to cut one minute of it. Even so, they redid scenes. The painful editing shortened the film to two hours and twenty minutes. After Jaffe had re-made all his scenes, he left the eternal *Lost Horizon* to re-enter his role in *The Eternal Road*.

Lack of operational funds forced the extravaganza to close shortly after Jaffe's return. At the invitation of Max Reinhardt, Sam and his wife Lillian sailed for Europe to be guests at his castle in Salzburg. During the visit, Reinhardt gave Jaffe a letter of introduction to the great theater master, Constantin Stanislavski. However, Sam was afraid to go into Russia because of the purge that was occurring. The political climate could be felt all around them. Reinhardt, for example, had had to abandon one of his castle theaters to make room for Hitler. While the Jaffes visited with Reinhardt, swastika flags flew over the former theater structure. Hitler himself lived right across the tracks.

While they were at the castle, the Jaffes attended a rehearsal that Toscanini conducted. They marveled at how the great maestro stopped when the trumpet player didn't have the right music. Toscanini then dictated the melody while the trumpet player put it down. It was evidence of his greatness.

Sam and Lillian returned to New York at the end of September, 1937, and were hit with the news, in a Hollywood column, that the Grand Lama's scenes were being remade with another actor.

Producer Harry Cohn had never wanted to do the film but he yielded to Capra's strong desire. It turned out to be Cohn's most expensive production, having cost $2,000,000 and it was a year in the making. Cohn had objected to the casting of Sam Jaffe, but Capra had insisted.

The reason for the remake was unsatisfactory reviews from the critics. Their greatest complaint had to do with the make-up mask worn by Jaffe. While the actor delivered his lines perfectly, the grotesque and horrible face spoiled the mystic, ethereal portrayal.

Because a redo of the make-up was necessary, Cohn pushed Capra to read Walter Connolly, Cedric Hardwicke and Fritz Leiber for the part of the Grand Lama. The remakes were shot using Connolly, but Capra had worked out a compromise with Cohn in which the preview audiences would decide which actor they preferred.

The press reported that while the director regarded Jaffe's work as flawless, Harry Cohn, Columbia's President, thought his lama was too weird. He preferred Connolly who could exude more benignity and fatherliness.

Jaffe had a slightly different version of the struggle. "Capra hated Harry Cohn because he made him redo it," he said. "They took a vote and the audience chose me. I got it by a democratic vote. So you see, there's nothing wrong with democracy, sometimes. They called me back. They changed the dialogue, and we did it again.

"Apparently, Harry Cohn, who was himself a Jew, didn't want a Jew to play the Grand Lama. [Sam laughed at the irony, but that laughter may have been masking a feeling of outrage given his strong response to those who denied their Jewish heritage.] So he put a beard on Connolly. Connolly was a very excellent actor and when I came back and he saw me he apologized, 'I didn't want to do it, but I was under contract and had to do it.'"

To devalue Harry Cohn, or at least to call his qualifications as a producer into question, Jaffe reported that before Cohn had graduated to his current status, he "had been a conductor on a street car in Brooklyn in the old days. They called them 'nickel snatchers' because they would work for the company and work for themselves. They had spotters to catch the conductors."

Capra didn't discuss the issue of Jewishness raised by Cohn. According to Sam, "Cohn had been extremely good to Capra and probably Capra didn't want to blacken his name." Jaffe cut through the speculation on the matter with the definitive line, "Truth is a sometime thing."

The press had followed the struggle with great interest and was quick to report on the outcome. This blurb appeared in the New York *World Telegram*, Hollywood, December 24, 1936: "Sam Jaffe, the veteran stage actor, will portray the role of the Grand Lama in *Lost Horizon* after all. Director Frank Capra originally used Jaffe for the role, but then remade all the scenes with Walter

Connolly as the Tibetan patriarch. Still not satisfied, Mr. Capra today switched back to Jaffe and started making the scenes again. This time Jaffe will wear a different make-up, giving him a more aged appearance."

The previous experimental make-ups had been torturous. Jaffe had had a beaten egg smeared over his skin. When it hardened, it didn't photograph satisfactorily. Next, they had pasted on little wisps of tissue paper to get the effect of skin cracked with age. This was followed by sharkskin stuck to his face just below his eyes. They had pulled it down tightly and anchored it under his chin. He had required four applications, altogether, at $500 each.

Jack Hawks, make-up man for *The Good Earth*, had developed a new kind of plaster make-up. It represented a highly technical process and Columbia Pictures was eager to try it in the area of simulating age.

After more trial and much error, they experimented with making a mask of Jaffe's own face. They worked it over with wrinkles and shadings and then tested it from every possible photographic angle. Sam had to sit perfectly still with the mold on his face until it had set. He was not allowed to move a muscle of his face. Obviously, he couldn't speak during this horrendous process. If he wanted anything, he had to feel around for a pad and pencil beside him and jot it down.

The extraordinary make-up cost the film company about $2,000 — and that was six months after all his scenes had been 'shot' with the inferior make-up, which had also cost $2,000. Sam Jaffe was up at four every morning, because the make-up man, under contract to another company, had to get in his work and be at his home studio by seven.

Weeks of work with the patented substance went by. The differences in features were then worked out in plastic material and applied to the actor's face. It made a big difference for Sam. The make-up didn't submerge his personality. He was fully able to communicate the character through his voice and eyes.

Although they didn't know this in advance, the make-up innovators had stumbled on a technique that allowed them to make the actor age into his own ancient face. Actor Edward Albert, Jr. confirmed this: "When Sam played the Lama in *Lost Horizon* it was a considerable make-up job to get him to look like that. As he grew older, he looked exactly like the Lama. It was astonishing."

During all the trials with make-up and re-shooting, Lillian was on the set watching her husband go through his struggles. She was very proud of the fact that nothing hindered his delivery even though he had to act under these most trying of circumstances.

The pains endured by Jaffe should certainly diminish what many cling to as the glamour of being a Hollywood movie actor. It took two hours every morning just to apply Sam's make-up. Make-up artists spent forty minutes on his hands alone.

Along with all of this, Jaffe had to work out the interpretation of the Grand Lama, creating a small, thin voice and the trembling, unsteady movements of great age. Next to Kringelein, Jaffe considered the Grand Lama the most interesting character he had created.

His labors did not go without reward. When he appeared on the set for the first time in his new make-up as the Grand Lama, everyone fell into silence. When Jaffe finished speaking his lines, there was a pause rarely witnessed in a studio. Cast member Jane Wyatt confirmed that the message communicated was that Shangri-La is in the heart of every person. This observation was especially important because if the audience didn't believe that Shangri-La could exist, the film would be hokey rather than inspiring.

There were critics who complained about the

dreadful musical score and the highly implausible setting. However, Jaffe's last speech pulled the piece together. The viewer could believe the words of the Grand Lama, and therefore the premise of the entire film.

The new make-up was much more effective. However, the portion of the film in which the lama expounded about Shangri-La was eliminated in order to shorten the film. They not only cut the lama's part to two scenes instead of three, but they also shortened the scenes.

After the re-shooting, Sam wasn't quite sure about the size of the role. "When you see the picture," he said, "all they may have left of me is that much." He snapped his fingers. This was not true, but his role had been significantly reduced.

Jaffe also found a prophetic voice in the Grand Lama's strictures on present-day society. "I realize the Hilton novel is escapist literature," he said, "but there is much that is pertinent and terribly apropos in the aged priest's plea to salvage something of our culture out of the current chaos."

Actor Ronald Colman approaches Sam Jaffe
as the High Lama in the film Lost Horizon.

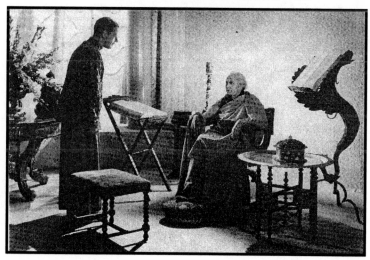

Although most of Jaffe's friends experienced the same high quality in him as in the lama he portrayed, he experienced himself as a more ordinary man. He felt embarrassed by the comparison and maintained that people should not read into a person what they saw him play.

In spite of Jaffe's wishes, many a person held an idealized view of him. Producer Stanley Kallis identified congruity as Sam Jaffe's greatest contribution. "I think he was the role he played. I think he was the high lama, on screen and off." He spoke of Sam as a focused individual with a very powerful personality. He said Jaffe had a magic about him that drew people to him.

To Julie Harris, who worked with Sam on tour with *The Lark,* his legacy was the great parts he played, es-

pecially on film. She said, "You see the humanity, the kindness, the craft. You see the greatness of being an actor. Actors do reflect civilization's humanity. Sam re-

Sam Jaffe as the high lama in the film Lost Horizon.

flected all those wonderful things about living, in every part he ever did. I never saw any faults in him at all. He was always there. He was always supportive. He was ready for the work."

While Sam didn't wish association with the roles he played, they were so powerfully distinctive, the impression they left was lasting.

Was it the role or was it the man? Teacher-director Lenore DeKoven, whom Jaffe influenced strongly in her early years, offered this opinion: "Sam grew into or became the high lama he had played, if he wasn't already that person. He had the predisposition or destiny to be that. He was one of the purest people I've ever known. I don't know if I'll ever meet anyone like him again. You meet one like that once in a lifetime."

Lenore had wanted to abandon college and go directly into a career. A talk with Sam was an important turning point for her. He persuaded her not to leave school. Today, teaching, which she could not have undertaken without her college education, is the most satisfying part of her life.

DeKoven said, "Some people climb mountains in India to meditate with gurus. Sam wasn't like that. He didn't set himself apart as separate or distinct. He was one of the guys, a regular human being who did all the things persons do. That's what made him so unique. When you were with him you were enriched. He was an ordinary person who was exceptional." While DeKoven saw Jaffe as an exceptional yet ordinary person, she proclaimed him synonymous with the high lama. She said that he didn't set himself apart but that she and others did set him apart.

Artist and writer Francoise Gilot met Sam Jaffe and Bettye Ackerman when she came to California in 1969 for her Los Angeles Hatfield Gallery exhibition. The origins of her desire to meet Jaffe dated to *Lost Horizon*, and to hearing President Roosevelt speak of Shangri-La as the ideal of peace. She was seventeen then, a student of Buddhism and a young painter. For ensuing decades, she carried the wish that she would one day see the film.

During the 1969 trip to Los Angeles, she stayed with her friend Eduard Franz and upon discovering that Sam Jaffe was very close to him, she told him of her great desire to meet Sam and to see the film. He told her it was easy to arrange and he set up a showing in the private auditorium of one of the film's stars, Margo. [She was known in her profession by this single name.] In addition, he made sure that the Jaffes were present.

She had waited a long time to meet Sam, and she wasn't disappointed. Gilot and the Jaffes became good friends as a result of the showing and the subsequent discussion.

Gilot and her husband Jonas Salk, whose early fame was that he discovered a polio vaccine, were more focused on Sam Jaffe's spirituality than others who knew him. While Gilot didn't enter into specific discussions of meditation and Eastern wisdom with Jaffe, Gilot knew without question that they were on the same wave length. She conveyed that the spiritual experiences the four of them [Bettye and Sam Jaffe, Jonas Salk, and Gilot] had together were beyond the boundaries of time. "They are ecstasies," she effused, "... of stillness, a state of rapture. They can't be described because if we do, we use words of the linear reality."

Gilot spoke of having little windows of eternity that open on other dimensions that can be experienced but not talked about. Creative art could reveal unspeakable experience, she said. "This is what Sam Jaffe could do in creating a character because he knows the inner world. My husband is the same way in science. We use intuition and deeper experience of the spiritual life, but we don't abandon rationality." In her view, Jaffe was both the master and the instrument. He emanated the spiritual world through the parts he played. *Lost Horizon* was a prime example of this.

According to Gilot, Jaffe was a master because he was able to fill the Zen Buddhist requirement of being able to make any kind of movement in an exquisite manner that is appropriate to the goal. He was able to make a little part of the invisible visible. Each time he came on the screen, he would introduce realness.

These discussions of Sam's spirituality, of windows of eternity that open on other dimensions, are precisely what I referred to in the introduction to this book about Sam. Before I had myself awakened to Cosmic Consciousness, I was "called" at age 15 to this world beyond linear reality by Sam's portrayal of the Grand Lama and by the "concept" of Shangri-La. I knew it existed; I knew it existed in each of us. It was a matter of destiny that I would meet Sam and have this privilege of writing about him, of revealing these deeper dimensions of his being.

Although others called Sam Jaffe a master, he looked for the masterly dimensions in others. He found it in Frank Capra. He was unprepared for the kind of greatness Capra embodied. According to Jaffe, Capra seemed almost not to direct. His genius lay in bringing out the best is in his actors, and letting them play their roles as they thought they should be played. "It is a matter of evocation." Jaffe said. Capra had a quiet, inexplicable way of bringing out abilities of which the actors themselves were not aware.

One of the things Jaffe loved was that after Capra discussed the character with him, he would look him in the eyes to make sure he knew what he was saying. Capra wanted to be sure the actor had the meaning, not just the idea.

To his surprise, Sam found working in films to be

as fascinating as work on the stage. It became a joy to him once he grew accustomed to dealing with scenes out of logical sequence.

In his personal preparations for the role of the Grand Lama, Jaffe had thought through a complete characterization. However, the minute he put on his costume, he looked at himself and discovered that he was a person other than what he had thought. Suddenly multiple possibilities emerged. He allowed those dimensions to come to fruition.

In conversation with comedienne Nanette Fabray, Jaffe revealed how he worked on a role. He said, "I learn my lines and I think about what my character is inside and out. Who I am, what I am, what I'm like, what do I do, what would I do, not just in this script, someplace else. And when I go in, I have a whole character, a whole person, a whole human being. No matter how small a part it is, I know exactly who and what I am." Ideas coming from directors didn't threaten him. He would add them to what he already had and would expand them from there.

Sam's approach to a role was a clear example of Stanislavski's "Method" Acting. He had it all down as if he had studied for a long time with the master. In Sam's case, it appears he came to the same approach on his own, using his inner guidance to create his roles. As a long-time student and applier of Stanislavski's contributions, I can attest to Sam's remarkable application of these techniques.

Sam didn't talk about studying techniques, yet it was clear that he had them and created from within them, albeit intuitively. Similarly, he didn't go to synagogue but was a Jew in the highest sense of the word in that he sought to be the best human being he could be in the world. He had a sense of responsibility and compassion for his fellow human beings. While he didn't talk about technique, he was devoted to living it, to being it, to doing it.

Sam Jaffe received smashing reviews for his work as the Grand Lama. Although some of them are recounted here, what supersedes the reviews, and can't possibly be captured, are the comments from millions of ordinary people who, like Franciose Gilot and me, were so profoundly affected by the lama's inspiration that their lives were changed.

Reviewers spoke of Jaffe's performance as unforgettable, mysterious and compelling. They said he wove a magic spell over the audience. Surely, they surmised, Jaffe had personally observed a lama in Tibet to create such a complete character.

It is no wonder that reviewers were impressed. Sam Jaffe read 35 thousand film feet of dialog before he muffed a single line.

Claude A. La Belle, writing for The *San Francisco News* on March 3, 1937, was floored by Jaffe's ability to create such an incredibly old, visionary and benign lama. He said that "Ronald Colman's scene with the high lama (it took nine and one-half minutes, undoubtedly a screen record) was as careful and telling acting as I've yet seen in celluloid. This goes for both Jaffe and Colman."

Critics agreed that the Grand Lama's speech was one of the longest and most difficult speeches ever recorded on a sound track. While Jaffe's appearance in the picture was brief, the responsibility of bringing credibility to fantasy rested on his shoulders. That he succeeded is what brought him the highest praise. He brought dignity and impressiveness to the role and was able to embody wisdom and sustain incredible age. It was a camera triumph in realism.

Often, Sam Jaffe was referred to as a superb study in abstract and austere serenity as the high lama.

Fine reviews are most welcome to an actor. Surpassing them is the arrival of kudos from fellow players. Ronald Colman sent the following telegram to Sam:

"Saw press preview today *Lost Horizon* stop All critics and I feel you completely stole the picture stop As usual your performance surpasses all others stop. . . . Regards Lillian and you, Ronald."

A wire also came to Sam from film maker Dimitri Tiomkin, sent to his apartment at 313 W. 74th Street on February 21, 1937: "Heartiest Congratulations, your performance is unforgettable."

When *Lost Horizon* opened at the Globe Theater in New York in 1937, it was in good film company. *The Good Earth* with Louise Rainer and Paul Muni was showing at the Astor, *The Last Mrs. Cheyney* with Joan Crawford was at the Capitol, *Man of Affairs* was at the Criterion with George Arliss, the Roxy had *The Woman Alone* with Sylvia Sidney, and the State was billing *The Plainsman* with Gary Cooper and Jean Arthur. As the years have progressed, the longevity of *Lost Horizon* is the most impressive.

Critic Mark Hellinger predicted the film's durability when it first opened. He commented: "In the months to come, you will hear many people say that *Lost Horizon* is the greatest picture they have ever seen. I will not go that strongly, but I will say that it is as fine a film as I ever hope to see. And that is strong praise in these days when great pictures follow one another in rapid order.

"Any film that carries the name of Frank Capra as its director is an assured success from the start. In *Lost Horizon*, however, Capra outdoes himself. He has taken James Hilton's novel and made of it a film of such beauty that it is actually frightening in spots. He has taken Ronald Colman, Jane Wyatt, Margo, H. B. Warner and Sam Jaffe and worked them into performances that each must regard as the peak of his or her career. He has done a glorious job. *Lost Horizon* is the modern film at its very best. It is a triumph for Columbia Pictures, for all of Hollywood, and — greatest of all — for Frank Capra."

In 1973, 35 years after the filming of the black and white classic, film-maker Ross Hunter announced, "Sam Jaffe played the Grand Lama of *Lost Horizon* when he was 37 years old. . . . We would like to offer him the same role in the remake we're doing." The film was re-done as a musical. Sam declined, saying, "I didn't see the new musical version because I didn't want people to ask me how I liked it and what I thought of the man who played the part and so on. I didn't want to give compari-sons, so I didn't see it."

Columnist Jack Smith met Sam Jaffe on June 13, 1973, at a cocktail reception. He recounted:

"'Come meet Sam Jaffe,' someone said, and led me over to a man who looked like a leaner Norman Mail-er, older and more secure, but astonishingly young for the high lama of the original *Lost Horizon*.

"'I saw *Lost Horizon* in Australia in 1937,' I told him, 'and I thought you were dying then.'

"'That's what I always do,' he said, 'I die.'"

Sam Jaffe's performance of the Grand Lama has had a long life since the film's release in 1937. Often, into Sam's ninth decade of life, he was called upon to deliver the famous dying speech. Producer Stan Bass recalled a night in Beverly Hills in 1971, following a showing of *The Telltale Heart*, an American Film Institute short made by Steve Carver, starring Sam Jaffe. "Sam is so endear-ing," Bass stated. "He wasn't feeling well this night but he stayed for hours answering the audience's questions. When you spend time with Sam, you walk away with tears in your eyes. He was such a great human being.

"That night, in response to a question, he went right into the speech he delivered as the High Lama. I closed my eyes and it was all right there."

Writer Lou Garfinkle called Sam's creation of the lama in *Lost Horizon* "the best portrayal of God I've ever seen or anyone has." Garfinkle proclaimed in the next breath that Jaffe's next best portrait was of a corrupt, intelligent man in *Asphalt Jungle*. This was Sam Jaffe's gift. He could capture, enter, and embody characters of diverse nature and convincingly bring them to the screen. He portrayed humanity's polarities.

Jaffe's career was on a roll. In 1938 he happened to be in Hollywood when they were seeing actors for the part of Gunga Din. They had wanted Sabu who played in *Elephant Boy* but after testing him, he didn't meet George Stevens' requirements. Garson Kanin had seen Jaffe as the lead in *The Bride of Teresko* on Broadway and he suggested that Sam be tested. Sam was hired immediately for 12 lucrative weeks of work. The producers even agreed to give Jaffe two weeks to keep a previous commitment. He went to Penn State to star as Shylock for director Benno Schneider.

It was ironic that Jaffe was cast in the title role of *Gunga Din*. Before he had decided on a life as an actor, while studying engineering at C.C.N.Y., Sam tested his wings by auditioning for the drama club. "I failed," he smiled. "I did the Gunga Din speech and they wouldn't take me. I thought I was good. They didn't think I was good enough."

It was clear that Jaffe had an inner connection with the Kipling work. Throughout his life he could recite the whole of the poem "I, Gunga Din" from memory, with full force delivery.

He reflected on the production of the film: "There were 300 extras," he recalled, "and they built the little shacks for them. There was a fire at one time and we were all called to put it out. We had a bucket brigade. The next day, in the newspapers, who was given credit for putting out the fire? The three stars (he laughed). In truth, it was the extras who served as firemen because Stevens wouldn't risk the lives of the stars."

Gunga Din, R.K.O.'s $2,000,000 spectacle, was filmed high up in the Sierras in 108 days. Two and a half months were spent in a sprawling city of tents with temperatures ranging from 36 degrees to 115 degrees. 1,200 members of the company, including the crew, four elephants, four horses and donkeys, devoured 26 tons of food weekly.

The Gunga Din Bugle, Vol. I No.1, Gunga Din, Calif. July 26, 1938: "Watch Your Waistline! We're Eating 14 Tons of Food Every Week:

"... Right now the Anderson Boarding and Supply Co. is feeding 325 of us — there'll be more later on.

"But even now, when we have chicken for dinner it means preparing 450 pounds of chicken or 225 birds, for that meal. Two men spend most of their time peeling and preparing 200 pounds of potatoes daily, and others brew 90 gallons of coffee, 100 gallons of iced tea, prepare 80 gallons of milk and ten gallons of cream each day for us.

"It keeps two bakers busy all day long baking, among other items, 100 pullman loaves, 100 dozen rolls and 60 pies daily. And two more devote their waking hours to the tearful task of peeling 150 pounds of onions every day, squeezing lemons for 80 gallons of lemonade.

"It requires a sack of sugar daily for cooking, sweetening coffee and other drinks. It all totals up to 14 tons of meat, groceries and vegetables each week, trucked in from Los Angeles twice weekly and kept well refrigerated by part of the 2,200 pounds of ice which is brought up from Lone Pine every day.

"All told, there are 37 on the commissary staff: seventeen in the kitchen, 13 waiters, six janitors and one maintenance man — and two unlucky fellows who spend their whole time washing dishes.

"... Oh, yes, the above figures do not include the four bales of hay consumed daily by Anna May and her three elephant friends, who also raise the devil with un-peeled bananas in large groups, carrots by the bunch and other delicacies left around within trunk's reach."

For the battle scenes, 800 pounds of dynamite and 85,000 rounds of ammunition were used, most of it specially prepared because the guns were obsolete and dangerous to use under normal conditions. 27,000 gallons of crude oil were poured over the ground in the British cantonment to change it from its natural gray shade to a nice Eastern Indian black. Highlights of the encampment were a recreation hall, Gunga Din, and the weekly newspaper, *The Gunga Din Bugle*.

Sam vividly remembered what it was like to work on the picture:

"We'd go back to RKO to do some scenes and then back again to Mount Whitney. And it was cold; terribly cold. The snow was on the peaks of the mountain and the minute we did a scene we had to rush back into the automobile.

"In the scene with the elephant, we crossed a very shaky bridge and we wondered whether the whole thing wouldn't topple down. But the great thing of it is the trick camera. We were only 14 feet off the ground. When you saw it in the picture it was about 180 feet from the ground. It's marvelous what they can do in pictures."

A non-byline vignette in the press of the day captures more of what impressed Sam at the time: "Better Men Than Gunga Din, Says He: Sam Jaffe is still rubbing his eyes over the casual miracles he saw tossed off by Hollywood's carpenters. ... Jaffe saw a contingent of them near a Hindu village, a British army cantonment complete with barracks, officers' quarters, stables, elephant stalls and parade grounds, and a Hindu temple. He saw a shipment of lumber turn into glamour before his eyes ... into a simulacrum of India. He knew that barrels of paint, kegs of nails and truckloads of pine had done the whole trick. But there was something so genuinely

Indian in the villages, temples and outposts of the Tibet borderland of the nineties that the more he looked the more the marvel grew.

"'The heat helped the illusion,' says Jaffe.' It was 123 degrees in the shade. On windless days, vast packs of cumuli clouds looked as if they were painted over the mountain scene, and added the final touch of verisimilitude. It was one thing for a fellow like myself to feel he was actually in India. It was another for the Hindu extras — several hundred of them were drummed up — exclaiming that this was just like home. You heard their exclamations in their native tongue. There were oxen, Ghurkas, temple bells and elephants, and so far as I am concerned it was perfect India.'

"Jaffe found that the prop department had enough cloth on hand to start a general store competing for any countryside's business. The cloth was used for flags and costumes. The same department produced dynamite and fuses when Stevens decided to blast a rock big as a room that stood in the way of a new road he wanted built for a column of marching soldiers. Stevens called for flares to light up an improvised bivouac scene, and flares — hundreds of them — were produced.

"'Why, they even had a water bucket for me,' says Jaffe. As the water-boy of *Gunga Din*, which now is being shown at the Music Hall, he needed a bucket."

Sam thought that George Stevens was a great director and a wonderful man. He said, "He had been a cameraman at one time himself, and could sit down and change a scene and just make it right. That was quite a production ...

"The film was a great money maker. To this day the dialogue is still so fresh.

"Stevens really understood. You do the best for him; you bring your nuggets, so to speak. He puts you at your ease. But a tyrannical man just paralyzes everything."

As always, Sam Jaffe stood out in his performance. One reviewer thought it a pity that Gunga Din himself received only fourth billing in his own picture! For all the impression made by the three stars, Cary Grant, Victor McLaglen and Douglas Fairbanks Jr., the observer noted that it was the humble, ascetic, stooped, yet somehow sublime, figure of Sam Jaffe that one remembers: "An for all 'is dirty 'ide, 'e was white, clear white, inside, when 'e went to tend the wounded under fire," said the poet, and the sentiment, Victorian and patronizing as it may be, echoes in the heart. There is infinity, humility, age-old patience and pity, in the way old Din kneels to offer water to the living and the dying. And, though bent under the weight of his perspiring water-skin, his agility in dodging bullets is marvelous to behold. As Sam Jaffe plays him, Gunga Din is not only a better man than any in the cast; he could be a serious contender for the best performance of the year."

This opinion was shared by many other reviewers. Don Freeman, TV-Radio Editor, the *San Diego Union*: "*Gunga Din* is among my all-time favorites — it's the child adventure that's never been captured again. The scene when Gunga Din, played by Sam Jaffe, crawls to the top of the Temple of Gold and blows a warning to the British Troops — it's always overpoweringly moving."

Regina Crewe said in her review: "... The star [Cary Grant] had a lot to say regarding the great portrayal of Sam Jaffe in the title role, and also of the technical care given the production in the interests of authenticity."

Here was a distinguished Jewish gentleman, already well into middle age, putting on a loin cloth and turning himself into a convincing Indian. He did it without upsetting the Indians themselves who hated to see anyone play an Indian on the screen. He became the most likable element in the film because he studied, willed himself, felt his way into about as alien a human being as one could imagine him playing.

Jaffe's performance was excellent, inspiring and lasting. In the *Los Angeles Times*, in 1971, Jack Smith said in his column that he had seen *Gunga Din* five times and that it was Sam Jaffe's finest film. Sam's response was typical vintage Jaffe: "I try to do the best I possibly can do in every film I do."

Like *Lost Horizon*, *Gunga Din* has had continual impact over the years. Jaffe was always able to hold the personal tribute in proper perspective. "Well, it's the hope of mankind. I mean, the ideal state is a general hope of humanity."

In today's world there is more consciousness of the issue of imperialism. The film *Gunga Din* is often criticized because it glorifies the evil. The film probably wouldn't be made now, given heightened sensitivity. The question is whether it is appropriate to condemn a decades-old artistic statement by today's standards. The unfolding course of life events takes us all to new perspectives. "We don't just form history; history forms us," commented Diane Kennedy Pike, author and widow of Bishop James A. Pike, and a good friend of Sam Jaffe in the last 12 years of his life.

Bettye Jaffe remembered when someone gave them a copy of *Gunga Din*: "We had dinner and ran it for the Scotts [Evelyn Scott and Urban Hirsch] and Maldens [Mona and Karl]. Sam said, 'I don't want a captive audience.' I said, 'So when the lights go down, why don't you just go in the bedroom and read and when the lights come up, come back in.'

"We saw the film and when the lights came up a voice in the back said, 'It's a good film.' Everyone looked around and said, 'You never saw it?' He said no. This was in about 1980. He'd never seen it but he'd heard a lot about it. When he was asked why he hadn't seen it, he said, 'Well, there's nothing I could do about it.'"

Sam Jaffe as Gunga Din.

****

EARLE HYMAN, *The Triumph of the Egg*, 1949 and *Mr. Roberts*, 1962, *All God's Chilren Got Wings*, around 1952.

"I had been in England for two years. When I came home, nobody knew me. Everything had changed. Even television had just begun to rear its fantastic head. But Earle Hyman meant absolutely nothing to producers and directors. I had to wait eight months, which I realize now wasn't long at all. I thought I'd never act again, ever, ever, ever, in a million years. And I heard that they were going to do All God's Chilren at the Equity Library Theatre. I read for it and got the part. It was a big success and then came job offers and Earle Hyman was back in New York. That show meant more than anything. I'll never forget that.

"Mr. Roberts *gave me a chance to play comedy, with which people didn't associate me. I was starred in that, my name above the title, in order to help E.L.T. grow. We played it on Riverside Drive and 103rd St. and then toured it around the boroughs. I was no star, really, but they put me there and they thought I would bring people in. And we were paid as a result of touring the boroughs. I was also a member of the board.

"Thank you, Sam, for giving me an opportunity to know within myself that, regardless of the circumstances in terms of the market place, I was an actor, am an actor, still want to be, still trying to become a better actor, and will try to as long as I live. You gave us a place in which to stretch and to grow and make those attempts. And a place to play in fine, fine plays that were simply not, at that time, or even today, viable on the Broadway scene. They were risky.

"At E.L.T. they'd say, 'Oh Earle, you can play this part.' But no one else believed I could. They didn't believe I could play comedy in the Cosby Show. But Bill had seen my work throughout the years. I knew him very slightly for about ten years and it was his idea to come in and read for the director because he didn't know my work at all. [Once hired,] I thought it was just for one episode. [Hyman played Cosby's father for seven years.]

"Sam was a very gentle man and a very special actor. He was totally unforgettable. Sam meant encouragement to me. Keep going. KO KO Keep on keeping on. That's Sam. Standing on that copula in Gunga Din: That was Sam, standing there blowing that trumpet. And he will live forever."
****

The Gentle Warrior

As was his wont, Sam returned to New York after the filming of *Gunga Din*. While it was playing at Radio City Music Hall, he was prominent in the Group Theatre's production of *The Gentle People* by Irwin Shaw. The Group Theatre produced it at the Belasco with an illustrious cast including Elia Kazan, Sylvia Sidney, Franchot Tone, Karl Malden, Lee J. Cobb, and Martin Ritt. Harold Clurman directed it.

This was a critical time in the career of Sam Jaffe. He was starring on Broadway. *Gunga Din* had won acclaim as the best picture of the month, and, in this year of 1939, he was singled out for the Box Office Blue Ribbon Award. The impact of his performance as the Grand Lama lingered in the consciousness of movie-goers. He was known for roles of integrity. His art, in the view of author Charles Higham, "was in ennobling and immortalizing what in other hands could have been merely ordinary characterizations."

Sam played characters who embodied the potential of humankind and lifted people from all walks of life to new levels of hope. Julie Harris said that she first met Sam as a child, "watching him in films like *Gunga Din* which were absolutely embedded on my mind. The performance will live forever. It had everything it should have, courage and humility. Whatever came from Sam was so good, so pure."

Sam Jaffe was more than an actor. He was a man intimately involved with the issues of his time; an activist rather than an observer. He was innovatively radical in his thinking, evolutionary in his vision, and unwaveringly persistent in his follow-through. He lifted injustices from where they lay mired in complaints and carried them into the light of full exposure for confrontation and change. A good political fight stimulated him and he knew how to hold his own in the face of strong opposition.

In his early years he had been a pugilist, even toying with the idea of becoming a professional boxer. He was gentlemanly in the sport. He was also adept, knowing when to throw punches, when to retreat, when to dance around his opponent, when to duck, and when to go for the thrust of the winning blows. Later in his life, he was to transfer this innate ability and timing to his political bouts, especially during his decade-long tenure as councilor for the Actors' Equity Association.

The '30's and '40's were stormy years at Actors' Equity Association (A.E.A.); a rather conservative, entrenched administration was very much on the side of managers and producers, as opposed to the very actors they represented. They were afraid that if they made waves that distressed managers they would jeopardize actors' employment.

A.E.A. was only about 20 years old then, born of the strike of 1919. Before the union, and in its early days, actor-managers shared in the fortunes or misfortunes of the theater companies. The tradition of such theater, as old as theater in the colonies, was still very strong. There was a holdover of actors, the old guard, who had grown up under that system.

The United States had begun with revolution, and that method of bringing about change continued to be favored as the way to overthrow stifling restraints. In *The Revolt of the Actors* (Greenwood Press, Publishers, Westport, Connecticut, 1929), Alfred Harding recalls the development of theater and the conditions that led to the demands for radical change. Throughout the following several pages of history, many facts are drawn from his excellent chronicling.

Sam Jaffe and Philip Loeb, his close friend and fellow actor and unionist, struggled against practices that hung on from the past. Sam and Philip were, in part, serving as a bridge between the outdated ways that were repressing the actor and new ways of working that were untried and involved risk.

The Civil War ended in 1865. A mere 26 years later, Sam Jaffe was born in New York City. In those 26 years tremendous changes occurred in the United States, especially as a result of the development of transportation that made great stretches of country west of the Mississippi accessible. Business boomed in every arena, including theater. So much and so quickly was this the case that there was an immediate and growing need for organization. This led to the birth of booking agencies.

By the time Sam Jaffe was five years old, there emerged in August of 1896 The Theatrical Syndicate, a booking office so comprehensive and influential that it became almost monopolistic. It governed the fate of dramatic and musical comedy theater bookings throughout the country for many years.

The artistic dimension of theater took a back seat to the power of The Syndicate. With money as its authoritative voice, it dominated over what productions, and what actors, would appear when, and on what terms.

It was in 1896 that a significant and influential split occurred. Alfred Harding tells us, "The functions of playing and management, hitherto pretty generally intertwined, became separate and the men who came forward as managers under the new regime were primarily business men, unacquainted with, and without much sympathy for, the traditions of the stage and the privileges enjoyed by the actor under them.

" ... The considerable advantages which accrued to the theater from these changes were all in favor of the manager, and the actor, so long considered the very backbone of the theater, was given least consideration of all the factors concerned in the production of a play."

Even when they were in the right, actors were at the mercy of management. There was an absence of a standard contract of any kind. Actors had no way of knowing in advance what would be required of them. Each manager wrote his own contract that contained legal loopholes enabling him to evade anything and everything.

"And," Harding continues, "... if disputes arose the actor could either accept the manager's ruling or go to law. A lot of good that was likely to do him, for a suit brought for a stranding in Los Angeles might find the actor at work in Chicago, New York, or New Orleans when it was called for trial.

"Even if the actor won and got a judgment, there was the growing tendency of producers and backers of plays to incorporate to avoid individual responsibility."

Actors were the last of creditors paid; there were no limits on free rehearsal periods, which often ran up to ten weeks for drama and eighteen for musicals; salary was for time actually played; there was no two-weeks-notice; half salaries were paid at holiday times; being stranded happened frequently; actors were often required to pay transportation to and from performances as well as supply their own costumes; conditions backstage were bad; and, a Satisfaction Clause left the manager as sole judge of the acceptability of an actor's work and continuance in the job. The last-mentioned clause, while unfair, was legal.

Before the formation of The Theatrical Syndicate, the Actors' Society of America came into being on May 19, 1986. It was a social and business organization designed to discriminate between responsible and irresponsible managers and to assist actors with the securing of contracts. However, the Syndicate became so powerful so quickly that they ignored the regulations and wishes of the Actors' Society because it had little or no power. Its membership dwindled and the Society disbanded in December of 1912.

On the day of its death, men who would not give in because the cause of the actor remained, birthed a new organization that was to become the Actors' Equity Association. The original members of the committee were Albert Bruning, Charles D. Coburn, Frank Gilmore, William Harcourt, Milton Sills and Grant Stewart. That was the year that Sam Jaffe turned 21. Both he and Actors' Equity came of age in 1912. A time of testing began for actors, who had never succeeded before because they weren't strong enough to survive battles with management or even their own internal factional disputes.

The first official meeting of A.E.A. was May 26, 1913, with 112 persons in attendance. The press ignored the event. It viewed actors as supportive of their own egos only.

Harding submits that "... the *New York Review*, organ of the Shubert theatrical interests, commented: "The most recent attempt of actors to unionize themselves ... is likely to go the way of other similar ventures.

"An actors' union ... having actors exclusively for members is doomed to failure because the foundation upon which any such sort of League must stand to be successful is absolute equality.

"It is quite absurd to suppose that any actor would admit that any other actor is his equal. In no other profession or art do egotism and jealousy show themselves more luridly.

"Every actor considers himself the nonpareil in his own line and wants a larger salary than any other competitor. Therefore to regulate pay and form of contract would be an impossibility because on these questions no set of actors will stand together.

"... Where there is jealousy, envy, vanity, and the refusal to admit that one's fellow is one's equal, there can be no union or joint action.'"

Actors could, and would, and did, after a long time of struggle, join together for the greater good. Management, on the other hand, exhibited the very behavior they named, and, as they themselves predicted, fell to eventual defeat.

Sam Jaffe was a prime example of one who upset the apple cart of management assumptions by replacing competition with comradeship, ego with equality, individual vanity with mutual victory. Paradoxically, these are the very values that were labeled "red" ad nauseam during the McCarthy era.

Equity's uphill struggle against the disregard of management was arduous. The Association was more like a beggar at the first negotiations on January 9, 1914. Its 2,000 members were spread across the country, diffusing its strength. Publication of the *Equity Magazine* began in December, 1915, to meet the need for an official means of communication. This was the very year that Sam Jaffe made his professional debut as an actor with the Washington Square Players.

Equity was getting nowhere with its primary focus of securing an equitable standard contract. The Association moved toward alliance with the American Federation of Labor and White Rats Actors' Union of America, largely vaudeville performers, to the dismay of many actors who turned up their noses at unions or at being affiliated with organized labor. Artists wanted to remain artists and not be classified as laborers. This was a major thread of weakness with the Association that served to divide and diminish mutual strength even more than attacks from management. The crisis over whether to be identified as artists or laborers prevented the membership from taking a stand as a unified body.

On March 10, 1915, Jaffe's 24th birthday, a call went out for simultaneous meetings in New York, Boston,

Philadelphia, Chicago, and Los Angeles. Harding tells us of the unfolding drama that was rapidly moving toward a climax: "For several years this association has been 'whereasing' and 'resoluting.' They have asked managers to meet them; they have sent courteous gentlemen and sane and cool-headed men to meet them, to talk it over with them. These men have either been refused a meeting or snubbed; there is no other word to use ..."

Manager William Brady made the truth clear when he told A.E.A. that he believed their contract was fair, but when asked when he would adopt it, he replied, "When you make me."

This is the very reason for the existence of unions. Unions make employers toe the line.

The Association, over 2,500 strong, was gaining confidence and reputation. Persistently it increased its powerfulness as a body and its ability to assert its imprinting force. Patience was necessary. The first standard contract was negotiated with a small group of managers on August 23, 1915, for players in Chicago. Though the managers signed the contract, they didn't get around to sending it to the printers until its final adoption October 2nd. However, it was the first Standard Minimum Contract between A.E.A. and a group of producing managers.

After more than four years of negotiation the actors had won the follow rights: two weeks' employment minimum after rehearsal of four weeks in drama and six weeks in musical; if the show ran longer than four weeks, company must receive one week's notice, or two to individuals; costumes for actresses earning under $150 a week; eight performances a week plus 11 holidays played free according to established custom; transportation, and right to arbitration.

While contracts were made, it was almost as if they were made to be broken, or at least management was pushing to test Equity's true strength. There was deception in the management approach. The Shuberts made agreements and then reneged on what was signed, sealed and delivered. Management listened politely to Equity as it complained of contract violations and then went on to do nothing about them.

Management also resorted to smear tactics. When an Equity representative called a manager, demanding agreed-upon payment for a previously performed matinee and threatening to cancel the day's performance, the manager's bitter retort was, "Bolshevik stuff." Here was communist name-calling by capitalist managers, making agreements seem un-American. Until the breakup of the Soviet Union in the early 1990's, the same tired technique remained in political, economic and social arenas; paste the "C-word" label across the face of any cause and thus dismiss it as invalid without benefit of consideration.

By May, 1919, the Association had over 3,000 members representing between forty- and fifty-percent of actors in the legitimate theater, many of whom were the best, most prosperous and responsible. Harding reports, "If they could agree to stand together and to play only in such companies where all members were Equity members in good standing, the remaining actors would have to come in and stay in. Equity actors were the sort the managers considered the backbone of their companies, and there were not enough such actors outside of Equity to supply the casts of many first class productions.

"And, once Equity had all the actors in the country buttoned up in its uniform the managers would have to issue the standard contracts and keep them, too, in order to stay in business."

As Equity grew stronger through inner alliance and commitment, it moved from its initial hat-in-hand approach to management for basic conditions, to more sophisticated demands such as a closed shop. This made management blood boil. The more complex the Association's demands, the more amenable the managers were to the previous lesser demands.

Equity took its stand on the issue of an eight-performance week and set the showdown for a May 26 meeting.

Management said it was willing to listen but it was unwilling to submit to arbitration. They sought to substitute handshakes for contracts, as if they could be trusted. They tempted actors with jobs and money if they would forget Equity contracts. The fate of the Association depended on the visionary ability of the actors caught in the immediate survival struggle. One had to sacrifice now for later gain which couldn't be guaranteed.

A turning point came when a serious weakness showed up in the Producing Managers' Association. It was the weakness that managers had long projected onto actors saying it was why an actors' association would never work. It was, as Harding points out, "... the inability of its members to sink their divergent interests, forget their feuds and jealousies, and fuse their considerable resources for a common effort. Even in ... crisis they were unable to give entire authority to any one of their number."

A strike loomed.

Management went all out with its temptations, offering small time actors big time roles to defy Equity. The antidote was solidarity.

In August, the Association called a strike, not for more money but for the right to arbitrate. Their effort became theatrical in nature. Members of the cast of *Lightnin* went out with banners proclaiming "Lightnin Has Struck!" In one day, three hundred new members enrolled and membership was at almost four thousand.

Management made a last all-out appeal saying

that actors were destroying their art form and profession. They said that businessmen ran the theaters and would do so only if it paid them a decent profit to continue. If not, they would turn their undisputed abilities into some other businesses. They weren't limited to the theater. They could succeed in anything, taking their capital and their talents into trades presenting fewer hazards.

Management stated clearly that they were in the arts for the money and if there would be no satisfactory profit they would leave and all would crumble behind them.

Managers resorted to every tactic to end the strike, short of meeting the demands. David Belasco and others threatened to abandon the stage to its fate if the actors won.

The tables turned as solidarity took hold. Not only was Equity able to maintain its own ranks but other theatrical unions joined in support of its cause. Support came from the International Alliance of Theatrical Stage Employees, the American Federation of Musicians, and Chorus Equity Association of America. Actors who could rehearse 12 weeks without pay, could as easily strike for 12 weeks without pay.

Actors' Equity Association did not fall; rather, the Producing Managers' Association crumbled. It had become a war machine seeking the destruction of Actors' Equity. Focused on disharmony, they accomplished their own dissolution.

Equity's victory produced the following accomplishments:
1. A standard contract for each class of production;
2. Compulsory arbitration of contract disputes and Equity shop;
3. Limit on rehearsal: four weeks, drama; five weeks, musical;

4. Regular pay on Saturday night;
5. Requirement of managers to post bonds to guarantee two weeks;
6. Return of actors to originating point in case of road closure;
7. Transportation charges;
8. Wardrobe for actresses;
9. Layoffs with salary;
10. No half salaries for holidays;
11. Two weeks' notice;
12. Probationary periods with rehearsal pay;
13. One week's notice of closing to company.
14. Actors' Equity membership jumped from 1,200, on its date of organization, to 10,000.

Over the ensuing years, while the union was growing in number, stature and strength, Sam Jaffe was doing the same as an individual. He was developing himself as a fine actor, working on Broadway in a three-year run in *The Jazz Singer*, and then on to smash success and reviews in *Grand Hotel*. Simultaneously, he was involved in causes, investing his energies in humanitarian efforts and in struggles for the underdog. His penchant for justice led him naturally to activism within Actors' Equity Association and he ran for a seat on the council in 1940.

Because the fear of communism was already alive in U. S. politics, Sam's background of humanitarianism was 'cause' to question his patriotism. In spite of a campaign against his candidacy, Sam Jaffe was elected on April 9, 1940, to serve a five-year term on Council, along with Walter Abel, Matt Briggs, Sam Levene, and Leon Ames. At that time, Bert Lytell was President, Walter Huston, first Vice President: Florence Reed, Second Vice President; Augustin Duncan, Third Vice President; Peggy Wood, Fourth Vice President; John Beal, Recording Secretary; and Paul Dullzell, Treasurer.

Because the Nominating Committee had sought to keep Jaffe out of Council, Philip Loeb took issue with the policy at the October 1940 meeting of Actors' Equity. He expressed his distress over the functioning of the election machinery, saying that the Nominating Committee and its selection of a regular ticket should be replaced by direct nominations. Even though Jaffe had already been elected, the larger issue was at stake: how nominations came into being. Jaffe and Loeb expressed concern for those who were to come later, seeing to it that they had the protection of a just system. Loeb described his friend Sam: "One of the finest, noblest creatures in the theatrical profession, a man of culture and an asset to the profession." He was certainly not someone the Nominating Committee had cause to reject.

Sam Jaffe was one of those rare artists as concerned about his colleagues as he was about himself. Most performers almost compulsively focus on being "working actors." Sam Jaffe devoted himself to the goal of actors working. He put himself on the line, lending his wisdom and life force toward making the working conditions within the profession more nourishing for the creative process.

Many of the old-timers in the union sought to control the membership. They did not think of themselves as dictators. Rather, they saw the younger members as children in need of their direction because they didn't know how to take care of themselves. Actress Sarah Seegar called it innocence in them. She said, "These were nice old people who lived in the theater, lived in another world, and really didn't know what they were doing. It was an insidious thing, yes, but not intentionally destructive."

Although what Seegar states may be true, the old guard sought to stifle progress. The causes that Jaffe and Loeb supported were so just and necessary it is difficult to conceive of the conservatives opposing their proposed benefits.

The objections that surfaced harkened to early Equity days when actors saw themselves as artists and not laborers. The opponents reminded union members that they surely didn't wish comparison with furriers and butchers. However, the major point of disagreement was economic. The conservatives feared that if actors made economic demands on management, thus increasing their risk, management would withhold investment capital and reduce employment opportunities for members.

The arch villain in this regard was Frank Gilmore. He was described as a little Napoleon. As chair, he would rule at meetings and disregard the majority's expressed wishes. Jaffe and Loeb would challenge but he would ignore them.

Although Jaffe was a quiet man, his vocal pitch would rise in volume when Gilmore refused to recognize him even though he was the only one standing and demanding attention. Treatment like this would send Loeb into rages. Sam tended toward irritation or annoyance and would transfer those feelings into a louder and more persistent demand for a hearing. During these times, Jaffe's color would change. He would redden up, his brows would furl and his eyes would get very sharp. However, he was kind rather than pejorative in his delivery. He remained philosophical and issue-oriented. It wasn't just the union that was important. It was the dignity of the human being and the upholding of the aesthetic world.

On one occasion, seeking to adjourn a meeting, Gilmore asked for a voice vote. The nays thundered through the ballroom at the Hotel Astor, and he said, "The yeas have it." Then he adjourned the meeting. Everyone was aghast. Jaffe and Loeb took action. They decided to move the adjourned meeting to the Actor's Church. Philip grabbed the microphone and made the announcement to the membership meeting. Over three hundred of them marched out of Astor Hotel, up Broadway to the church where the rebels met regularly in a rump organization called the Actor's Forum. It was an unauthorized group of actors meeting together to discuss the issues that were vital to all of them. The Forum sought to make Actors' Equity a union for actors rather than a company union. Sam complained that the Council had been a rubber stamp. He said, "They did anything the president wanted. The Forum would suggest things and bring it up to the union." The union decided to declare The Forum an illegitimate branch, dual unionism, and called in the American Federation of Labor.

A power struggle surfaced between the old order and the new. This schism between the liberals and the conservatives was similar to the larger society itself. There were heated fights between those who wanted to move with great speed and those who didn't want to move at all. It was a battle between idealistic progress and the exertion of restraint. It was Jaffe's involvement in the Actor's Forum that would result several years later in his being falsely accused of being a communist.

Actors present during those years described the meetings as fabulous, crazy times. There were always many arguments on the floor. The Equity meetings were high dramas: staged, lighted, costumed, and acted to the hilt by those who assigned themselves roles as leading players. Jaffe and Loeb were as much a part of the overall dynamic as any of the other principals. They had a highly developed technique which might be called the good cop/bad cop routine.

They would carefully plan a strategy about who would seek recognition from the chair. Sometimes Philip would speak first as a councilor from the dais. Sometimes he would lay back and let x number of members speak and then Sam would do a synthesis. It was all calculated with nothing happening by chance. The arguments were well-rehearsed and then delivered as a finished performance. Loeb and Jaffe would carefully work out what the points were, what to avoid, who would stress what, and what the summation would be. They constructed the presentations beautifully and performed them as if they were a good actor's speech. Philip would commit his speech to memory and when he delivered it, it seemed extemporaneous.

Sam's usual seating was in the second row on the right side of the auditorium. He always took a position so that when he rose to speak to the chair, he was profile or full-face to most of the membership. Even in these circumstances he knew not to perform with his back to the main portion of the audience. Adrenalin up, he would be playing to the full house in the union hall, uttering significant stage whispers, taking charge with a few potent phrases augmented by well-chosen gestures. These appearances at meetings were among the most important in actor Jaffe's career. They were performances of self before peers, thus requiring highly polished delivery.

Ezra Stone, actor and director and husband of actress Sarah Seegar, had been a student protégé of Philip Loeb after graduating from the American Academy of Dramatic Arts where Philip had taught. Stone was to become an important component in the Jaffe-Loeb campaigns. He was very youthful and enthusiastic, but he was also very naive. He was certainly no match for the pranks of Jaffe and Loeb.

For example, one day Sam and Phil took him to dinner in Los Angeles. "We went to the cheapest place, which was Phil's main thing," Ezra joked. "Sam cared only about being able to eat vegetarian. Then they took me to Grauman's Chinese [Theater] to see all the footprints. One imprint read LAWD. Sam was right next to me. I said, 'Well, where are the footprints?' Sam told me that Rex Ingraham [who had just completed *Green Pastures*] felt that there shouldn't be footprints for the lord. I believed him. Months, maybe years, later, idiot me, I realized I had been standing in front of a block of cement which was the water connections, Los Angeles Water Department."

Caught up in the romance of being a union rebel, Stone delighted in being appointed to a mission by Sam and Philip. They gave him the name of La Petitionera: that was their parody of La Passionara, a messenger of the Spanish revolt in the same period of the 1930's.

Their lives were like a scene from an intense play. The outcome was always in question; the stakes always high. La Petitionera would wait in Philip's hotel room for the geniuses to achieve the proper wording of a petition that had to be circulated to obtain the number of signatures needed for it to go to the A.E.A. Council. Omnipresent deadlines heightened the drama. Philip would invariably stretch out on the bed while Sam sat in a chair with his feet up and each would have a tablet. Ezra would wait. Whatever was cooking in the two great minds either had to be presented at the next council meeting, or was a critical proposition, or a refutation of the administration's stand on some untenable issue or other. The air was tense with thought and discussion.

Soon, the fever of strategy would break and Philip would peck out the proposal on his little typewriter. With ceremony and flair, La Petitionera, who had stood faithfully at the ready, like Sancho Panza, would be given the vision and sent to gather signatures. On a matinee day they knew that Ezra could guarantee 100 names. Proudly, Ezra Stone recounted his days of triumph: "I had worked out a route for myself of the stage doors and I knew when various shows were breaking and which actors came in early to make up." Having gathered the signatures, he would deliver the petition to Loeb.

Stone spoke of how stimulating the strategy meetings were because he would hear both sides of the issue, the cautions, the skullduggery, the conniving of the opposition. Only a handful of people attended the meetings.

Occasionally they invited reporters from the drama desk of the *New York Times*, like Jack Gould, who could be very useful when they needed news to be leaked. When certain elements of strategy were not to be revealed, the reporters respected that.

"It would be a fascinating group packed into Philip's room. It would get quite vocal," Stone remembered. "Tension would be broken, either by Sam with his very calm and persuasive manner and logical thinking, or by Phil just deciding to be humorous or silly.

"Five or six regulars were there, so-called rebels of the time. Alan Hewitt ... Eugene Frances. And almost always, whoever was Philip's female consort of the period would be there."

Sam's wife Lillian wouldn't attend, but at times they would all go down to the village and meet in Sam's apartment. Then Lillian would serve as hostess to the union rebels.

Philip and Sam dedicated themselves to radical change. They were working on corrective reforms such as pay for rehearsals. In those days actors could be hired and put into rehearsal without a cent, without even subway fare, for four or five weeks.

First, Sam and Philip drafted a reform insisting that management get only five free days for a play, seven days for a musical, for the firing or replacing of actors. It was known as the five-day clause, seven-day clause. After that, management had to give the actor two weeks' notice. Then, Jaffe and Loeb addressed rehearsal pay. It was a long, nasty battle. Later, they fought for minimum salaries. These began with $25 a week for junior members, $40 a week for senior members.

There were many obstacles to progress. Stone spoke of how the union had to cope with accusations of communist dominance and infiltration, made by Congressman Bilbo, and then Lambertson. They sought out communists in all unions, but they knew they would get the most newspaper space by going after the actors. The McCarthy hearings used the same tactic years later.

There were, of course, card-carrying Communist Party members in the union who spoke up for the same issues as Jaffe and Loeb. These communists had their own agenda. For the most part, everyone knew them and Philip would kid about them to their face.

As a team, Jaffe and Loeb were two complementing aspects of one 'Man of La Mancha.' The vision looms of riding a stallion into the dust of dispute. The Philip half of the character, shouting and thrusting his sword, was always very vocal, passionate, theatrical and colorful. The other, the elegant Sam, standing in soft light, whispering words of truth, used a Talmudic approach. He would speak after Philip and would, in his very dulcet tones, say, "I believe that what Mr. Loeb says has some merit for us to examine." It was a perfect juxtaposition. It was as if Jaffe sang a lullaby to lull the members to embrace his thinking through his manner of delivery. The two men were an absolute contrast one with the other.

To illustrate the closeness of their association, during one meeting, Loeb raised his hand to speak. The chair recognized him but called him Mr. Jaffe. Ever the wit, Philip said, "Jaffe is a stage name; at Equity meetings I'm called by another name, Phil Loeb." Bill Ross could easily understand the chair's mistake. "I used to call them the Bobbsey Twins," he said. "They worked together but each had his own life, his own individuality, and they disagreed with each other occasionally. Neither was a rubber stamp." When Ross sat listening to them, he felt he was in the presence of two of the greatest men in the world. "I still think that," he reflected 50 years later.

Jaffe and Loeb were men of great substance and intelligence. They were a pair of compassionate compatriots, standard bearers of Equity's honor, and disturbers of Equity's peaceful complaisance. They directed their combined wealth of inner strength outward in service in the hope of benefiting and elevating the life and dignity of actors. Their joining in mutual effort was one of the keys to their success.

They were the vanguard in their early Equity days, functioning on a frequency band that was just ahead of their time. What they did was to move an entire profession and art form from one mode of functioning to another. In the early years, it was difficult to identify Equity as an actors' union because of its orientation toward management. Actor-Managers had been juggling both ends of the profession at the same time. The shift needed to come so that the artist was recognized for himself as a creative performer, and management needed to separate from that. Jaffe and Loeb helped bring about that change. They were visionaries.

The struggles within Actors' Equity were fierce, requiring Herculean efforts. Jaffe and Loeb were tireless fighters for decent wages and working conditions. They were themselves both artists and workers. They had tremendous pride in their profession and shared equal focus on the mission of the union. Theater needed to be a place where one could devote one's life to the creative process and earn a living at the same time. Jaffe and Loeb were determined to make that a reality.

Sam Jaffe divided his life between union responsibilities, working as an actor, and delighting in his treasured marriage to his wife Lillian.

****

LONNIE CHAPMAN, *Missouri Legend*, 1950

"*My career was just beginning. I'd come back from be-ing on the road for a year in the Chicago company of* Mr. Roberts. *People forget you when you're away. This show gave me exposure. I had been in one flop on Broadway. But after I did* Missouri Legend *I did* Come Back Little She-ba.

"*I felt good being cast in* Missouri Legend *because I liked the part. I was playing Jesse James. It was a very professional setting. There was little money. We rehearsed in several places.*

"*What stands out for me is the people I was working with. Lois Nettleton was in it; John Marley directed it. About 50% of them became successful actors. A couple of them became directors.*

"*E.L.T. has been a marvelous thing for actors.*"

****

Loss

As their careers took off, Sam and Lillian moved from Greenwich Village to a top floor apartment at 325 Riverside Drive, overlooking the Hudson River. Every window had a beautiful view and when the wind blew, the chandeliers would shake. The apartment was warm, relaxed, colorful, theatrical, and with the feeling of a museum because Lillian and Sam were collectors. Every memento had a story of its own.

Their environment was simple rather than grand. Sam filled the space with his personality more than with furniture. The piano was the central piece in the apartment.

The apartment on Riverside Drive was a celebrity hub. Sam's nephew, Merwyn Dembling, recalled that he "met all kinds of people up there: Kurt Weil, Lotte Lenya, Thornton Wilder, Elmer Rice. Sam traveled in very, very good circles." Douglas Fairbanks Jr. once answered the door to receive a delivery and the boy stood there as if struck by lightning.

When George Gershwin came to visit the Jaffes at the Riverside apartment he would sit down and call on Sam to perform his humorous routines. Gershwin knew them all and would ask for them by name. Sam was excruciatingly funny.

Gershwin displayed his admiration of Jaffe's comedic ability in his requests that Sam perform. This was unusual behavior for Gershwin. Whenever he went anywhere else he would immediately sit down at the piano and play. He didn't have a reputation for indulging in conversation. He played for a long time, his own compositions. Sam returned the tribute by never playing the piano when he and Gershwin were together in another's

apartment. Each man deeply respected the other's special gift.

Sam and Lillian entertained often. She was a fine
hostess and an excellent cook. Their friends talked of
Lillian as charming, delightful, good-looking, and humorous as well. She and Sam had a wonderful relationship
and their love for each other was visible to all.

One of their guests was a very young Karl Malden.
In 1938, Sam and Karl met during rehearsals of *The
Gentle People*. Malden had a very small part and he was
quite impressed with the stars and the glamour.

Karl and Mona Malden had gotten married during the rehearsal period. They were beside themselves
when Sam, who was a star, invited them to come to dinner between a matinee and evening performance. They
have never forgotten that invitation. To them it meant
that they were more than just actors, they were part of
the industry.

At the Riverside apartment, paintings by many
of Sam's friends covered the walls. The Maldens were
very much taken by this. Karl and Mona were extremely
young and impressionable and they couldn't relax when
they first entered the apartment. They remembered the
tremendous windows overlooking the river, and the piano, but not much else. There were no servants, and this
impressed them even more. Lillian cooked and served
the dinner herself.

Mona Malden described Lillian as a medium-sized
woman with dark hair: "I remember her as being very
sweet and kind to us because I was terrified. I remember
her as putting us at our ease and being very gentle the
way Sam was."

When Malden and Jaffe became friends, Sam was
48 and Malden was a young 27. Sam always seemed
able to bridge age gaps; indeed, to be ageless. John
Huston had thought him his contemporary when there

had been over a decade separating them. Lillian was 15 years Sam's junior. And in 1956, when Jaffe married Bettye Ackerman, he had 36 years on her! There was a childlike quality in Sam, never childish, but capable of cavorting in ways most adults leave behind as they enter adolescence.

As always, Sam's reviews in *The Gentle People* were splendid. The New York *Herald Tribune* praised Sam as the tortured father: "... The acting of Jaffe and Kazan is dynamic, electric, and infinitely true."

Vogue singled out "Sam Jaffe as an unknowing Aristotelian, outwardly docile, inwardly of steel. Without tricks, Jaffe used all the knowledge that he has absorbed ... all the experience he acquired. ... Most of his parts have been facets of kindness; all were added up for the rounded portrait of a good man pushed too far."

Other reviewers saw his playing as sincere, humorous, and affecting, having extracted the utmost from the part.

In December of 1940, Sam Jaffe participated in what most reviewers called a theatrical disaster, a production of *King Lear*, directed by Irwin Piscator. One of the more kindly assessments was from Richard Watts, Jr. who said of Jaffe, "... I fear that Lear will never be among his favorite roles."

Irwin Piscator, a man who fled Nazi Germany, refused to follow orders or be herded. He had an epic plan to turn theater into a stimulant. While in Berlin through the 1920's, Piscator, as director of several theaters, conducted experimental productions.

Once in the United States he headed up a dramatic workshop at the New School for Social Research. He decided to present a unique version of *King Lear*. The cast included Jack Bittner as Doctor, Herbert Berghof as Fool, Roger DeKoven as Edmund. DeKoven had left a lucrative radio show to work with Sam.

Sam was dumbfounded and delighted when Piscator told him he wanted him to do Lear. Sam had worked on Lear for years and looked forward to this opportunity. Piscator said, "Ve do it. Ve do it. I vill direct. My most exciting production in America."

Sam responded, "This is the ambition of my life coming true. I can't tell you how much this means to me."

Then Piscator told Jaffe he would see to it that he got the script quickly. Sam told him he had and knew the script but Piscator had a surprise for him that should have augured the disaster to come. "No, no, mine boy, no. I have the most wonderful translation."

Sam protested that he had already learned the original. Piscator dismissed the information. "No, no, no. Ve don't pay attention to that," he emoted. "The German is so superior to the original that I have had an excellent translation done."

And that is what they played, a translation from the German rather than the original English version!

The critics did not have a positive response to Piscator's *Lear*. They said the production was filled with mechanical novelties and unusual staging, including actors roaming the audience and speaking inaudibly from backstage. It was raucous, noisy, and distracting.

Piscator had, unhappily, added to the play, and removed some of its great lines. The reviewers came down hard on the non-conventional attempt and on Jaffe's Lear.

John Mason Brown sneered, "... the play becomes an experience which would be laughable, if it were not so dull and dispiriting. Sam Jaffe, often an admirable actor, is completely lost as Lear. His old king lacks other things besides his beard. Passion, greatness, imperiousness, wisdom, tragic power, rage, even pathos — all these are sorrowfully missing."

Sidney B. Whipple announced that "Mr. Jaffe's Lear was a fretful, unsympathetic father, a solemn, unimaginative old man rather than the baffled, pitiful figure that ordinarily comes to mind in the role. Mr. Jaffe is not cut out, I am afraid, to be a Shakespearean tragedian."

In the *New York Times* review, Brooks Atkinson was strong in his objections. "... No matter what stage arrangements a director may be making, the intelligibility of a performance of Shakespeare depends upon the skill of the actors and the skill the director has for molding a design out of their playing. In these two respects this *King Lear* is painfully wanting.

"For Mr. Jaffe lacks talent for Shakespeare. His accent is common, his voice is weak, his articulation imperfect and he has no instinct for the rhythms of Elizabethan verse. None of his associates has much talent for creating a character of the play. Herbert Berghof's ability to make a character out of the Fool is masked behind a heavy foreign accent. Although one can understand the difficulty he has with English speech, the playing of Shakespeare in English presupposes some mastery of the language.

"... There is never a substitute, on any stage, for intelligent acting, honestly directed in the service of the author. Let us not forget that the author of *King Lear* is William Shakespeare, a poet."

Louis Kronenberger was a bit kinder to Jaffe, saying "Most of the acting was wretched; but there is something to be said for Sam Jaffe as Lear. He was never very impressive. He even misread crucial lines and misdelivered crucial speeches. But he revealed so great a sincerity and so genuine a devotion for the role that he somehow seemed divorced from all the brummagem and meretriciousness of the production."

There were even a few "good notices." The *Shakespeare Association Bulletin*, January 1941 Vol. XVI No. 1, called the production: "A Unique *King Lear*: ... a source of unusual pleasure and satisfaction. We came away thrilled and with a new sense of what wonders Shakespeare can contribute to the modern theater if intelligence and artistry are brought into play in producing and interpreting his works.

"... Of Mr. Jaffe's Lear we can say only that in his outbursts of rage and in his mad scenes he was every inch a king and that he often moved his audience to great pity for the sufferings of the outraged father ... "

Arthur Pollock found the production striking. "... Everything moves with an assiduous swiftness, forcing Sam Jaffe, who plays the king, to act faster than, it is likely, he has ever acted in his life and making the play perhaps a little more confusing than it need be. But this is dynamic Shakespeare, sudden and forceful.

"... Sam Jaffe as Lear .... plays always straightforwardly, without stuffy embroideries."

Benson Inge, of the New York *Herald Tribune*, had talked with Jaffe during rehearsals and found him strong on the side of Piscator's experiment.

"'Every player has certain pet parts he sees in a very personal light.' Jaffe said. 'It has been my ambition to present Lear as a human being caught within the very same elements of social strife that confront us today. Dictatorship was a very common failing in Lear's time, just as it is today. And the old King grew into the tyrant through boundless lust for power and more power. That is the pattern for King Lear as I and Mr. Piscator see it. Something removed from the usual hokey and sentimental treatments of family misrule.'"

Sam supported the view that those who degrade others only degrade themselves. Dictatorship ends as a boomerang, in its own overthrow.

Director Ted Post told a different story about Jaffe's position. He said that Sam had a very rough time thinking of Lear as a fascist. Because fascism was so alien to

Jaffe, Post reported, "He was being bent into a pretzel trying to make Piscator's point. He was extremely unhappy doing it."

What was the truth? During Jaffe's career, he made negative statements in private while offering a positive assessment to the press. In this particular case, Jaffe publicly revealed his true position years later.

Post recalled Jaffe's behavior at a memorial for Piscator at the Desilu Studios which was attended by his former students and people who had worked for him. "Tony Curtis, Walter Matthau, Bea Arthur, and many others," Post said. "Everybody got up and gave their feelings about Piscator, speaking in a very complimentary fashion about what a great genius he was in the field of production concept and the kind of things that he innovated at the New School."

Then Sam rose and called Piscator a son of a bitch and a fascist. He said he hated him. Jaffe shocked everybody at the memorial by condemning Piscator's lack of sensitivity in handling him and for trying to make King Lear into something he wasn't. Everyone was so stunned that at the end they just walked out the side doors.

I can't help but wonder why Jaffe hadn't quit if had felt so strongly? I couldn't even find any indication that he spoke up for himself or challenged Piscator at rehearsals. This surprised me because this side of Jaffe is in sharp contrast to other stances he took throughout his life.

Ted Post's reflection of Piscator's *Lear* differed from Jaffe's: "Instead of ingratitude and all the things that Shakespeare had in mind," he critiqued, "Piscator twisted it so that it caused the downfall of his entire family. There was something that was not so far off base. It could have been made very workable. It may be that Sam had been miscast because Sam, as unconventional as he was in many ways, and as original and inventive as he was, may have found this too much of a stretch.

But Piscator had a justified position which might have worked had he cast someone else."

A few years after having played Lear, Sam called it "The most difficult part I ever played. There's such a sweep to it — emotion carried to the nth power, you might say. The actor who plays the mad King has to virtually generate a thunderstorm all by himself, and it isn't very easy." This seems to validate Post's view that Sam was not up to the role whether Piscator's interpretation was appropriate or not. Jaffe's attack on Piscator shocked those present at the memorial. Sam might have addressed his own difficulties with the role but instead he focused on Piscator's interpretation.

The generally devastating reviews and the overall horror of the experience must have been particularly difficult for Jaffe, especially because it was very important to him to play Shakespeare. He often said, "An actor can't call himself one until he has done Shakespeare." In fact, 43 years later, at the age of 92, when asked if there were particular roles he would still like to play, Jaffe said immediately, he would like to do Lear again.

Although *King Lear* was a disaster for Jaffe, he had a place of solace to which to return. It wasn't so much his River-side Drive apartment as it was his wife Lillian. Those who knew Lillian loved her. She was a truly good person with a marvelous voice and a classic face, though

Lillian and Sam Jaffe.

not a great beauty. Lillian and Sam had a beautiful relationship and adored each other. However, beneath the surface of the mutual adoration, there were issues which raised concern in others. Lillian lived for Sam. Whenever he was in a play, she was constantly at his side. He was her whole life. This devotion was not only received by Sam, he seemed to crave it. Some, looking from the outside, felt he demanded it.

Sam's nephew, Merwyn Dembling, loved Lillian. He found her darling, very beautiful, talented and able. Dembling asserted that Lillian always wanted a baby but Sam didn't want one. His assessment of his uncle was that Sam was not too fond of competition in any area. He liked being the center of attention.

Dembling insisted that he knew that Lillian wanted children: "She said it to me and to my mother. When my mother broached the subject to Sam, he said, 'Don't be silly,' and that was the end of the conversation."

Dembling affirmed that Sam and Lillian seemed perfectly mated and matched, having the same interests. He thought Sam was supportive of her career but only up to a point. He revealed, "That point was reached when she wanted to do musical comedy. He kept pushing her toward opera. She was good and charming but she really didn't have the voice for it. She should have been in musical comedy."

Emily Paley confirmed this. She said that Sam always thought of Lillian as an opera singer. He didn't have as much respect for musical comedy as he did for opera. Close friend Rebecca Reis reported that Sam asked Lillian not to pursue her career. "He told me later that he was sorry that he did that," she said. "He was an actor, and he thought one career in a family was quite enough."

Almost everyone who knew Lillian experienced her as gentle. Ezra Stone said that while Lillian didn't seem dominated by Sam, she was recessive in his presence. She was there but she was not prominent in any way.

She was not protective, as Bettye was later in Sam's second marriage, but neither was she a partner involved in his crusades. Sam adored her, but Stone saw in her face a sad look, a Mona Lisa look.

Although Sam and Lillian had what everyone called the perfect union, Lillian sacrificed many of her wishes and needs in favor of devotion to her husband. She gave up her desire for children, she pursued opera rather than musical comedy, and she retreated in their relationship rather than becoming more assertive. Perhaps Lillian gave up too much, and in the end this proved devastating for her.

Sam, himself, was later sorry that he had discouraged his wife from some of what she sought for herself.

The woman Sam Jaffe adored, his beloved wife, became seriously ill with cancer of the uterus in her mid-thirties. Lee Reichart, one of Sam's first cousins, told of Lillian's fastidiousness. When she got sick, she would not allow anyone to do a vaginal examination. Lee's sister Happy was married to a doctor and Philip was the one who had urged her to see a physician. She wouldn't. Lee said, "In those days, cancer was something you hid. Lillian didn't know it was cancer. It had to do with private parts, and you just didn't do that. She died very quickly."

Lillian's illness had come crashing in on the Jaffes at a time when they had everything going for them in their careers. Sam took Lillian to Florida, in the hope that the warm sunshine would help her to recover. He would go out and buy special foods for her. Nothing helped, and they returned to New York. She became desperately ill. The doctors finally operated, but were able to do nothing and closed her up immediately.

Lee's brother, Peter Keane, visited Sam and Lillian in their Riverside Drive apartment not long before she died. Lillian was in bed at the time and in great pain. He recalled that Lillian made Happy's husband Philip swear that he wouldn't tell Sam the enormity of the illness and that it was terminal. According to Peter, Sam later berated Philip for not telling him.

Even in her dying, Lillian was utterly protective of Sam.

Sam recalled the story of the events of Lillian's illness and death quite differently. He said that Lillian went to Philip and complained of her pain but that he called the referral doctor in Florida and told him her condition was mental. Sam lamented, "She died of cancer shortly after. So I didn't see the Reicharts for some time. I didn't care to see him, an idiot. What kind of a doctor, to call the doctor she was going to and say don't pay any attention to her, it's all mental. I never said anything to them anymore. I didn't care to say hello to them. They were an anathema to me."

Lillian's illness and death were impossible for Sam. He had regret about missed opportunities with Lillian. Perhaps the only way he could cope was to have some of the blame rest on Philip. What Sam didn't know was that Lillian would not allow Philip to tell him anything of her condition.

Sam had other hard feelings about the Reichart branch of the family. The family name was Cohen but they changed the name to Kahn. "And later their children called themselves Kane," Sam sneered. "Cohen is not good enough. Morris Raphael Cohen is a world famous philosopher but to them Cohen is no name. I suppose the next generation is going to be McKane. Peter no longer feels he is a Jew. He is an Episcopalian, an Episcopalian Jew. That makes me think of the story of the beggar with a hunchback on the steps of the Episcopalian church and down came Russell Kahn who was a very well-known philanthropist. Of course, he gratified his palm and he said to the beggar, 'What denomination are you?' He said, 'I'm Jewish.' Kahn said, 'I was once Jewish.' And the beggar said, 'I was once a hunchback.'"

Lillian had fallen ill in November of 1940. Within three brief months, in the 15th year of their marriage, on February 28, 1941, Lillian Taiz was dead. [On that very same day the woman who, 15 years later, was to become Jaffe's second wife, was celebrating her 14th birthday.] Lillian's death desolated Sam. He not only loved her, he depended on her.

The funeral and internment took place in the Birdie Black Chapel, Westchester Hills Cemetery of the Stephen Wise Free Synagogue near Armonk, New York. Lee and Peter's parents were interred there, and later, Sam's sister Sophie.

Sam's nephew, Merwyn Dembling, from whom he was estranged years later, attended the funeral. As Merwyn spoke, there was a bit of a sharp edge on his words: "Lillian died two weeks after my father died. It was quite a mess. My father died when he was 48. At Lillian's funeral, Sam cut up something fierce. He was very demonstrative in his grief. We came back to the Riverside Drive apartment and Sam wanted to sleep on the floor. This is some sort of penance that he was doing and we all had to talk him out of it. There was nobody to stay with him but me. My mother went back to open the drug store and I was alone in the apartment with Sam who was half frantic. I was terrified. He was pacing and moaning and doing — I hate to say this — all sorts of theatrical gestures.

"I must have been nineteen. I stayed with him for the better part of a week. He didn't actually sit shiva. He was almost incapacitated. Many people came by."

Letters of condolence arrived in abundance.

John Huston wrote from Warner Brothers Pictures in Burbank:

"Dear Sam,
"I only just heard this terrible news. What is there
to say? Nothing! If only there were something I
could say or do that would mean anything. But
there isn't, I know — there's nothing. John."

Attorney Louis Nizer lamented:

"My dear Sam:
"I know how futile words are. There is a mystery
about the reason for such a tragedy which cannot
be solved. We must rely upon and derive strength
from a fatalistic philosophy that so it was destined
and nothing could prevent it. Fortunately it is one
of the inexorable phenomena that time will reduce
the pain and grief while correspondingly increasing the sweetness of her recollection.
"I will call you in the near future and I hope that
you will be able to spend some time with Mildred
and myself.
"I send you affectionate regards steeped in deepest sympathy.
Sincerely,"

And from S. J. Perleman:

"Dear Sam,
"Any of the formal assurances of sympathy Laura
and I could offer you seem so stilted and inade-
quate. We ourselves have just been through a terrible and trying time, and I believe we understand
completely how one's sadness can be tinged with
resentment and futility at the meaningless pattern
of things.
"It is unnecessary to say that we shall be only
too glad to help in any way we can and that we
would like very much to see you as soon as you
feel able.
"Always,"

A week after Lillian's death the following comments by Richard Watts, Jr. appeared in the New York *Herald Tribune* on March 6, 1941:

> *Miss Taiz was not only an excellent singer of good songs. She was likewise a deft and charming player, with a sure talent for both emotional and lighter scores, and she possessed a combination of romantic appeal and straight-forward naturalness that made her attractive, likable and human on the stage. She was an ideal heroine for a Rodgers and Hart show, and that is a high tribute to pay any performer. I never could understand why she was not more in evidence in the theater; she should have been one of the most distinguished of musical comedy players.*

Here again the question is raised about whether Sam's urging that she turn her attentions to opera had interfered with her career in musical theater. Lillian had yielded to Sam's suggestions. What her career wishes were remains unknown.

Lillian Taiz died of uterine cancer. Sam had told his second wife, Bettye, that Lillian had had an abortion. He always worried that that may have caused the cancer. He said it was Lillian who wanted the abortion.

When someone dies it seems natural that the survivors look for reasons or try to figure out how things might have been different: "if only ..." Could Lillian's cancer have been caused by the abortion? Who knows?

The uterus as an organ of birth is also a symbol for the creative process. Might Lillian's cancer have been stirred by an improper 'carrying' of her talent? Could the tremendous grief Sam felt after her death have had elements of guilt in it because he directed her toward opera rather than musical comedy?

Conjecture, hindsight, and second guessing are all

entertainment for the mind. Alas, they lead to nothing conclusive.

While we don't know if Sam felt guilt, we do know that he felt regret. It was 15 years before Sam Jaffe married again, one year alone for every year he had been married to Lillian.

****

FRITZ WEAVER, *Within the Gates*, 1952

"*The status of my career when I did that play was zero. I was in from the provinces, so to speak, penniless and without much hope of anything. It gave me a huge shot in the arm. On the day I was cast I was walking on air. I felt that I had arrived.*

"*It was odd because there really was no off-Broadway in those days. E.L.T. was a pioneer in that way. There was Broadway and there was unemployment. There were a few hole-in-the-wall places to do plays but you were careful not to do too many of those because you had an amateur status that way. What you hoped for was to be a professional. Being in E.L.T. was to be a professional. You were Equity members.*

"*As to the conditions, to me it was as if I had died and gone to heaven because I didn't expect to be working in New York that quickly. I really hadn't been there too long. Being able to hold my head up with other professionals was a great confidence builder. I was in New York and functioning as an actor.*

"*Tom Bosley and Jimmy Greene were also in that production. We all were playing fairly small parts. They have gone on to wonderful careers, too. They were both playing lowly chair attendants. I was a company guardsman.*

"*I got married that year too, so the whole thing has a golden glow for me.*

"*My own confidence in myself was enriched there. I felt, 'Now I can do it.' I didn't know until that moment. It's what I remember most about it.*"

****

Crushing Grief

As if Lillian's illness wasn't tragic enough, Sam was unaware of the terminal nature of her condition because she had sworn her doctors to secrecy. As Lillian was struggling with impending death, Sam was in the throes of performing *King Lear* to the worst reviews of his career. What an irony that he was playing the despairing king who held his beautiful, young, dead daughter in his arms and lamented over her. Then, in a cruel unfolding of life, two months later he would repeat the wailing with his own beloved wife.

For the first six months following Lillian's untimely death, Sam suffered unbearably. He missed her. He needed her. The grief was profound.

Unable to tolerate living in their Riverside Drive apartment without Lillian, Sam rented it out for over a year. Leaving the spacious, light-filled environment behind, he withdrew from the world, moving into a tiny one-room kitchenette flat in Greenwich Village where he retreated into a monastic life.

Compared to Riverside Drive, Sam's cell was dingy and dark. He chose consciously to put himself in a hole and forget everything, a hole such as the one Lillian went into in death. He took his piano with him but he brought no paintings. This was unusual because he had never been without that form of nourishment. He brought all his photographs of Lillian and took them out of their frames so that he could carry them with him everywhere he went.

Sam so surrounded himself with images of Lillian that it was impossible to turn in any direction without seeing her face. He was as devoted to her in her death as she had been to him in life. He shut out the world and yielded to grief. He was as close to giving up as he ever came in his life.

Friends would come to visit and he would play Lillian's records for them. They would insist that he get out into the world, but Jaffe was too low in his spirits and his energy to partake of life. He would doodle on the piano as if the music brought him closer to his dead wife. He just sat, for what seemed an eternity, in his little apartment with Lillian's face and a stack of her records. He was a prisoner in his own dungeon and his sorrow was very intense for a long period.

During what was to be a relatively short career, Lillian Taiz Jaffe garnered an impressive collection of reviews. After her death, the New York Public Library requested a record of her work for its theater collection as a memorial to her. In spite of the loss of her press books, Sam welcomed the request as an incentive to duplicate them.

He said in the foreword of the scrapbook he completed on August 12, 1942, "We can only estimate what the future ought to have been from what opinions remain. This is as complete a record as I have been able to assemble. In compiling and arranging this material it became clear that more than a record of achievement was here: it was a story of theatre." Certainly this is true even if we limit our consideration to the portions quoted earlier which revealed life on the road in the early '20's.

Roger and Mona DeKoven joined Sam every day for several months to help with the work on Lillian's memorial. The upset over her death was so prevalent in Sam's grief chamber that Mona felt herself suffering Lillian's symptoms. As preoccupied as Sam was he would immediately bring out food when the DeKoven's arrived. They protested saying it wasn't necessary to constantly feed them. Sam insisted. He said, "Mona, you don't have to eat it. But the first thing you do when somebody comes to your house, to show that they are welcome, you offer them some food or drink. You don't have to eat it but I'm going to continue to do it."

The DeKoven's young daughter Lenore accompanied her parents during these visits. She had never been exposed to such grief, nor had she ever known anyone who had the mystical feeling that he was in touch with Lillian. Everyone worried about Sam. The picture engraved on Lenore's memory is of Jaffe at Lillian's grave site. His complexion was ashen and the look on his face was like a Jew in a concentration camp.

The bounty of Sam's love remained unexpended; it was unfinished, prematurely stifled. He was living out the remainder of the energy he had, like finishing a piece of music.

In the hot summer following Lillian's death Aube and Saida Tzerko would take Sam to Jones Beach. They would sit around until four o'clock in the morning watching the electricity in the water when the waves broke. They would sit in the warmth and unbreakable bond of friendship, and cool off in the breeze blowing off the water.

Besides healing time at the ocean, Sam went to visit friends in the country where he loved picking berries. Such journeys reminded him of the Levy farm and of his treasured years with his aunt. During Sam's marriage to Lillian, the two had often gone to the country in the hopes of finding a house to buy.

Aube Tzerko, once head of the Piano Department at UCLA, was one of Sam's closest friends for over 50 years. He and his wife Saida tried to get Sam to move out of the confined quarters. The ambiance was such that you felt Lillian would walk through the door at any moment.

It was eerie. Saida said, "It was as if he was still living with Lillian. That's why he secluded himself. In his inner life, he was still communicating with her. His insides were involved with the relationship."

Aube said that Jaffe never talked of his pain. He would speak only of his happiness with Lillian.

Sam Jaffe kept his personal feelings to himself. He knew how to reach out and be helpful to others, but he found it difficult to open the door of self in the other direction. For almost a year Jaffe rarely went to sleep before dawn; very few of his friends thought that he would ever get over the loss. They were concerned about his making a hermit of himself and that he thought he was communicating with Lillian spiritually.

Arnaud d'Usseau, a well-known playwright and one of Sam's good friends, said he had never known anybody so extremely unhappy. It was d'Usseau who was with Sam when he began having visions of Lillian. Sam would go to the cemetery every day. Then he would come home and play Lillian's records repeatedly. D'Usseau despaired that Jaffe was subject to what he called hallucinations. He said, "Grief can cause a toxic condition. People see ghosts because they just cannot accept that this is going to be a permanent situation."

D'Usseau wanted so much to help Jaffe. It had been Sam who had helped him get his plays on Broadway and obtain screen writing jobs. They met when Sam was in California making *Gunga Din*. After they returned to New York, Jaffe helped d'Usseau secure an agent with whom he stayed for 30 years. It was a kindness d'Usseau never forgot but that was not easy to return. Sam Jaffe was inconsolable.

There may have been one person to whom Jaffe exposed his feelings, Zero Mostel. If it hadn't been for 'Z,' as he was known, Sam's veil of grief might not have been lifted for many years. Karl Malden explained that he and other close friends couldn't be a comfort to Sam. The tragedy of Lillian's death repeated itself when someone close to her visited with Sam. They were a part of Lillian and it was more than Sam could handle.

'Z' hadn't been in Sam's earlier life and therefore they could talk on different terms. Zero Mostel was a naturally funny man who exhibited his great humor everywhere: in the street, on the subway, in a restaurant. Knowing Zero made a big difference for Sam, especially by making him think of other things. Zero did more for Sam than anyone. He visited the cemetery with him and he gave him all his time.

Mostel found a way to make a joke of anything. A clear example occurred later in his life, in the 1950's, during the McCarthy times. Mostel was questioned on television at the hearings. He profusely praised his accusers: "Thank you for putting me on television. I haven't been on in a couple of years. It's a great pleasure to know that somebody wants me on television." He would always make fun of what was very serious. It was such unexpected humor that lifted Sam's spirits.

When Jaffe was with Mostel he became more prankish and pixyish. He was lighter in spirit and more uninhibited. One night Zero and Sam were traveling on the subway. They were talking as quietly as the subway permits when Sam got up and took a leap on one of those white poles, right up to the roof of the car. Then he let himself down slowly, looking around exactly like a benevolent gorilla. This was the Sam who for so long had been morose, who didn't want to live, and who had no interests.

Karl Malden remembered some of the shenanigans that Zero and Sam engaged in during the period of his recovery from grief. Mostel performed in nightclubs at the time. The last show ended at 1:00 a.m. He and Jaffe would walk around after that and then show up at the Maldens for middle-of-the-night breakfast. Karl recalled: "We had an apartment above the Gaiety Delicatessen on 6th Avenue, up four floors. It never failed, at least twice a month, at two or three o'clock in the morning the bell would ring. 'Open up!' It was Zero Mostel and Sam Jaffe.

'Open up! The deli's closed; we need breakfast.' And the two of them would come up and Mona would have to make scrambled eggs and toast and we'd sit there for a couple of hours schmoozing and talking. We've never forgotten it."

Before Lillian's death, Jaffe had been a great clown who liked telling jokes and making people laugh. With Zero he was able to reawaken that side of himself. They both knew how to let their childlike selves out to play. In that, they were made for each other as they performed spontaneous routines.

On one occasion they were to meet in a restaurant. Zero arrived and Sam got up from his chair. Instead of going directly to each other, each went a different way and passed each other. They didn't shake hands until they had each made a complete tour and turn of the restaurant.

Zero Mostel was larger than life and he was a joy to Sam Jaffe, releasing frivolity in him. The difference between them was that Zero was always on and Sam chose when to be silly. Sam would encourage Zero's magnetism. He did that with many people, encouraging them to shine while he took a subdued position. He had a way of making people come forth without his noticeably pulling them out.

While Zero had a serious side, he never let it linger for very long. Long years into their friendship there was an incident in Zero's dressing room that exemplifies this. As he sat looking at himself in the mirror, his shoulders began shaking and he broke into heavy sobs. He revealed that he had gone to a party the night before and he should have left early because he had promised his sons that he would do something with them in the morning. They had been after him forever. Zero had stayed late at the party and overslept that morning. He simply forgot. When the boys tried to wake him, he shouted at them and sent them away. When he awoke hours later, the house was empty and over his bed was a big sign reading: "Here lies Zero the liar." Saying that broke his tears and he burst into laughter about what a hilarious thing that was for the boys to do.

When Sam heard the story he was serious at first, but then he too laughed. Jaffe was very loyal to his friends. However, the incident had little humor for Zero's sons.

When Sam's playful side was alive and well, there was no stopping him. Once, when Zero was working in a play, Sam and Philip Loeb showed up in the front row reading Jewish newspapers and eating behind them whenever Zero was on stage. When they couldn't break his concentration, they began donning and removing false beards.

Zero got his "revenge" on Jaffe during *Cafe Crown*. He walked up on stage and entered a card game that was part of the action. Later, he threw the cards up into the air during the curtain call.

Slowly, painstakingly, Sam began to emerge from total seclusion to tolerable despair. He started the flow of his creative juices in a play called *The King's Maid*, by Ferenc Molnar. The out-of-town tryout opened in November of 1941, nine months after Lillian's death.

The King's Maid was Molnar's answer to Hitler. Its thrust was a familiar one in Jaffe's repertoire of conscious choices: an earnest effort to find a common spiritual meeting ground for Christians and Jews. It was a plea for tolerance, stressing that Christ himself was a Jew. Sam played a mistreated Jewish peddler who exhibited Christ-like qualities.

The production brought together Jaffe, Karl Malden and Margo. She received glowing reviews for an inspired, radiant performance. Originally Sam did the play with Teresa Wright but she was cast in a film and was replaced in Baltimore by Margo, who scored impressively in the stage and screen versions of *Winterset* and in *The World We Make*, at the Guild Theater. She also played Lo-Tsen in *Lost Horizon*. Bettye reported that Sam and Margo had planned to get married during the run of the play but Margo told Bettye that she (Margo) had come along too soon after Lillian's death for Sam to take that step.

Jaffe had turned down a film offer that would have netted him several times the stage salary. He was called well-nigh perfect in the role of Rosenbaum, investing the part of the peddler with commanding eloquence. Molnar wired Sam on Nov. 24, 1941: "Colonel I love you every day more and more."

Karl Malden had a touching memory of Jaffe's emergence during *The King's Maid*: "Photos of Lillian and his grief over her death filled Sam's dressing room. When we came to Philadelphia, we rehearsed in the morning. We broke for lunch and came back to rehearse in the afternoon again before an evening performance. I came back early with Mona who was with me out of town. We went to the front part of the theater and there was Sam playing the piano. We saw him; we looked at each other. 'My God, something's happened. He's beginning to play the piano.' He was beginning to act again. It was a long period from Lillian's death to the opening of that play."

Though Jaffe was just sticking his head above grief, he had not lost his wit. An actor in the company with a long string of credits had a little trouble during dress rehearsal. He was all decked out in an immaculate uniform, with white gloves and an air of authority. He had a long sword at his side and bragged of his ability to carry it with the required dignity. During dress rehearsal, he had to stand up and walk across the stage to Jaffe. Somehow the dangling sword was always getting caught up in his legs, ruining his dignified cross. The director was getting disgusted and the actor very frustrated. Sam broke up the entire cast by suggesting that the actor make good use of the recurring problem. "Why don't you just ride it like a horse and come over here!"

The King's Maid, while a wonderful exploration of religion from the Catholic and Jewish points of view, was misdirected, according to Molnar, and it closed out of town.

The two theatrical newspapers had accolades for Sam Jaffe. *Variety*, on August 27, 1941, called his performance flawless and said that he invested the humble role with dignity. *The Billboard*, on September 6, reported that "... Sam Jaffe, as Rosenbaum, delivers one of the finest performances of his notable career. With little real meat in his lines, Jaffe yet manages to make real this strange little character who shakes off the beliefs in which he has been brought up and comes to feel the worth of another religion. Without Jaffe's beautifully paced performance which drives home the perplexity of the little peddler torn between two fires and struggling to retain his simple, quiet dignity, the play would fall apart."

The *Boston Daily Globe* had this salute: "... Sam Jaffe, well-known for his characterizations on both the stage and screen, plays the difficult role of Rosenbaum, the peddler, with a power and appeal that does much to overcome the wordiness of the heavier passages. Burdened with the bulk of the dialogue, he succeeds in shading the work with an acute awareness of the thought that is the author's message."

Jaffe's withdrawal had not diminished his abilities as an actor. However, even though Jaffe had tried his hand at acting again, he returned to his memories and his grief when the show closed. He might well have sunk deep into it again had it not been for a visit from writer Hy Kraft about his play *Cafe Crown*.

Though Jaffe's spirits had improved after long months of grieving and with the strong assist from Zero Mostel, he was still in no mood to talk about working on another play. He agreed rather reluctantly to read Kraft's script but he wouldn't commit himself.

Kraft brought Martin Gable and Elia Kazan to a meeting with Sam in his flat. The living conditions shocked Kraft who said that to call it a one-room would be an exaggeration. It was so bare: a cot, washstand, a couple of collapsible chairs, and a bridge table covered with assorted newspaper clippings. It was obvious that Jaffe still had no intention of fully recovering from Lillian's death.

The three men found Jaffe absorbed in his research for Lillian's memorial and his immersion subdued and awed them. They managed to divert him enough to talk briefly about the play, but Sam withheld any decision because of an appointment to attend a broadcast recital by some of Lillian's students. Kazan told Jaffe that rehearsals were to start immediately and Sam said he would make up his mind at the conclusion of the recital.

Kraft revealed that "the depth of Sam's despondency had a Chekhovian effect on Kazan." This was after Sam had emerged from the most severe time of the grief.

Sam did call as promised but he was still undecided. By this time, Hy Kraft was himself deeply moved by Jaffe's situation. He spoke from his heart: "For a moment I forgot my own stake in this affair. I'd had time to brood over the extent of Sam's surrender, the cold room, the picture of Sam pasting clippings, the utter loneliness and seclusion of one of the most gregarious of human beings, his indecision as well as his actions, dictated by a memory. I was desperate for myself and for him or I wouldn't have been moved to say, 'Sam, I think Lillian would want you to play this part. I think she'd like you to play a comedy part. You haven't played one in a hell of a long time. I'm sure Lillian would like you to enjoy yourself and give people enjoyment.' There was a pause; he agreed."

It was to be a turning point for Sam Jaffe, in his grief and in his career.

Aube Tzerko helped Sam find an apartment on Waverly Place and Sixth Avenue near what was then a women's prison. It was a step up from his cell. It had a very large living room, many books and oriental rugs, and his fabulous Steinway grand. Jaffe lived alone, but the place continued to be full of Lillian's pictures and recordings. He would play them for Tzerko who said, "It was like hearing a voice from another world. Her presence was reincarnated every time he would put those recordings on. We'd say what a beautiful singer she was and that was all it would take for him to put on her recordings."

The fire escape at the rear of the apartment faced the women's jail. Very often there were conversations across this courtyard. They could see Sam on his fire escape, which he called his terrace. It was a source of sun where he would sit and read. Eventually he requested some privacy and Tzerko rigged up a wire system about five feet high all around the fire escape where Jaffe grew morning glories. Jaffe lived in this small but comfortable place until he married Bettye and they moved to her place in Peter Cooper Village. The Waverly Street apartment had a quiet tone. It sat on the corner and its windows had eastern and southern views.

Actor Robert Brown visited Sam in his modest but tasteful village apartment. He confirmed what Aube Tzerko had said, that whenever Sam spoke of Lillian he remembered only how wonderful everything had been and how lucky he was. However, Brown saw the sadness in his eyes. He said, "You almost didn't want to hear it because you knew he was doing a stiff upper lip. He was like a zombie, almost. He kept finding reasons not to work, but was urged by his friends. He'd go to the library and the 4th Street book stores. He'd love to sit and have tea in the afternoon at the Jewish Cafeterias. He'd go to Gotham bookstore where the Joyce Society would meet, the New York intellectual meeting place. He'd sit in the back and read the great, expensive books. He was so gentlemanly and had such great dignity."

Following the production of *The King's Maid*, Jaffe developed a close friendship with Molnar. "I would meet him for lunch almost every day at a Bistro on 59th Street," Sam reported. "He wrote all his plays in a bistro. When he came home he said his wife greeted him with five fingers across his face saying that's because you have a lovely desk home and you do your plays in cafes."

Although Molnar was married, the great love of his life was a younger woman named Wanda. Sam knew her and was very fond her. According to Molnar, Sam treated her as if she had been his younger sister. In turn, Sam was the only one of Molnar's American friends for whom Wanda developed a real affection. Wanda died in 1947. Her loss was as great to Molnar as Lillian's had been to Jaffe.

In Molnar's book, *Companion in Exile: Notes for an Autobiography*, he talks extensively of his relationship with Jaffe and of the profound influence on his life of that friendship. Sam taught Molnar how to suffer the shock of Wanda's death.

Ben Raeburn, publisher of *Companion in Exile*, was certain Molnar might have gone under if Sam hadn't been there all the time: "He was left alone by the death; his life practically stopped."

The following extensive reflection from Molnar's book is a rare exposition of deep love between two men and how the mutuality of their life experience made both of their lives more tolerable. It also offers universal wisdom for dealing with grief:

"Sam's beautiful, young, gifted, and dearly beloved wife had died six years before. I never knew or saw Sam's wife. I only heard from others the story of this beautiful marriage, the young wife's tragic and untimely death, and the effect of her death on Sam. Sam had not been in the habit of talking to me about it. Now he called on me every day, and, you might say, tried to teach me how to stand up under the agony of bereavement.

"'There's no method in your suffering,' he said, 'that's not right. You loved Wanda like your child. You should sit down with Wanda's memory some day for a friendly discussion, and make a deal with her. Don't pay any attention to the people who tell you that time heals all wounds. It's not true. Either a person has loved somebody, or he hasn't. If he has loved her, there isn't enough time in all eternity to heal the wound. I've reached an agreement with myself to keep my wife's memory alive as best I can. There are enlarged photographs of her in my room. My wife was a singer. I have recordings of classical songs that she sang at her concerts. I don't usually get home until almost dawn. I sit down in an armchair under the floor lamp, and start the phonograph. And I listen to my wife's beautiful voice singing the world's loveliest songs to me.'

"He smiled as he spoke with his sweet, rapt smile, in which there seemed to be no sadness, merriment, nor irony, but only serene resignation.

"I took his advice. I reached an agreement with Wanda's memory and with myself that Wanda was to go on living for me. She would lead a faint, dim, and doubtful trance life, but she was to live . . .

"On the morning of my seventieth birthday, I went out to her in the cemetery. I took flowers for her grave, a snow-covered patch thirty inches square, the only real estate I had acquired in America, a bit of property that nobody can take from me by a manner of legal procedure. There is no more thoroughly protected private property in the world.

"Sam Jaffe came with me, although he had been run into by a car the day before, and hurt both his knees in falling so that he walked with a pronounced limp. Tramping about in the deep snow, we looked for Wanda among the graves under their heavy blanket of white. I was very much ashamed that I could not lead Sam straight to Wanda's grave without hunting around. Wanda was very fond indeed of Sam.

"We laid our flowers on her grave, and stood there in silence for a long time; in the vast, snowy serenity of the quiet cemetery.

"Among many thoughts that whirled through my head, sometimes Sam's dead wife, whom I never knew except from her pictures, would stand invisibly between us. Wanda would surely have been fond of her, too. It is out of the question for Sam not to have thought the same thing at the same time.

"We stood there for a long time; then at my suggestion we went into a little tavern near the cemetery, where we were the only customers. I drank a glass of wine, remembering how Wanda always celebrated my birthday by touching glasses and toasting me with the old Hungarian saying, 'God give you long life!'

"Again we were silent. We sat mutely at a table, staring out through the glass door at the snowflakes that were now falling gently, and behind them, as if through a veil, the dimly visible headstones and crosses of the cemetery. Then we went back to the grave in the cemetery to take our leave. All we did was stand without a word, gazing at her name carved in the stone, which will always be the most incomprehensible and inconceivable sight of my life, a sight that I had never imagined I should live to see: her name on a tombstone."

How true that must have been for Sam as well with Lillian.

As Mostel had been to Jaffe, so Jaffe had been to Molnar. Each reached a hand of help and love across the chasm of grief so that a friend might return from death's anteroom and reenter the light of life.

Molnar's most famous work was *Liliom*. When produced in Budapest it was a failure. Years later, it played in the United States as *Carousel*. Jaffe accompanied him to that opening night.

Sam was very close to Molnar during the last ten years of his life when he lived in room 939 at the Plaza Hotel. Sam recalled arriving one day to find Molnar at work: "He was changing some stories into plays for two characters. I said, 'Still writing?' He said, 'Habit. You always improve; you have to as you go along. Sometimes the genius springs spontaneously. Nobody knows how.'"

It is no wonder that Molnar and Jaffe became bosom friends. They had a great deal in common including similar humor, as evidenced in this vignette. Molnar and a friend went to see a play together. Molnar began to leave after the first act because he didn't like it. His friend was horrified: "We can't do that. We're here on passes." During the intermission Molnar went out, bought two tickets, took them to his friend and said, "Now we can go?"

Sam recounted other tales exemplifying Molnar's wit. "He was with a countess in Budapest and a man friend came along and said, 'Ferenc, I just read where the Jewish Encyclopedia has devoted almost an entire page to you. The countess said, 'Molnar, I didn't know that you were Jewish.' He replied, 'Madame La Countess, I had hoped you would learn that under more favorable circumstances."

Then there was the time Molnar was walking behind Puccini with a composer friend of his. Puccini had his hands behind his back and was moving his fingers and Molnar urged the composer to "Take it down."

One of Sam's treasures from Molnar was a picture of his cardiogram, saying, "To Sam, a picture of my old heart with love in it."

After Molnar's death, Jaffe translated one of his plays from the German. It was eventually *The Blue Danube*, written for Molnar's wife Lili Darvas. It played at the

Bucks County Playhouse in New Hope, Pennsylvania, under the direction of Ezra Stone. It had never been done in this country and was a typically frothy Molnar piece involving an elderly middle-aged innkeeper and his romance with a sexy young waitress in their inn. Lilli Darvas played the wife in this version, having been the sexy waitress when Molnar wrote it for her.

The cast included Sam Jaffe, Zero Mostel, Michael Strong and Barbara Baxley. Stone experienced Mostel as both a genius and incorrigible. He simply couldn't get him to do the same thing twice. Stone was grateful to have Sam in the cast as his professionalism was a big help.

Despite the length of Jaffe's grief process and the depth of his pain, speculation was present among those who knew him about when and even whom he might remarry.

There were those who thought that Sam and Emily Paley [following Lou's death] would be a perfect combination. Emily, on the other hand, spoke of a girl who was crazy about Sam. She sounded very much like a protective matchmaker as she described her: "She had a big backside. We weren't crazy about her. She went out to see Sam when he was living with the Robinsons. We were very upset. He used to go to her for blintzes. She made wonderful blintzes. She went to see him but she didn't even want to kiss him. She just wanted to be with him. Well, thank goodness it didn't go on for very long. She made good blintzes but she wasn't good enough for Sam. Then he met Bettye and that was that."

Sam's sister Annie believed that every person who came to visit Sam wanted to marry him. Merwyn speculated that the one Sam did want wouldn't marry him. She married Senator Jacob Javitz instead. Her name was Marian and she had appeared with Sam as Portia in *The Merchant of Venice*. In later conversation with Bettye,

Sam had few words on the subject. "I went out with her for a short time" is all he would say.

Margo also had interest in Sam. They had played together in film and on stage and knew each other well. Margo later told Bettye that she had come along too soon after Lillian had died. Bettye said that one night "we had a big party at our house and Margo and Ira Gershwin were seated next to each other. I came along to see if they wanted something and Margo was talking about me. She said to Ira, knowing I was there, that she was very interested in meeting me because she wondered if I might be good enough for Sam. Ira, in his gentleman-like fashion said, 'Gee, I was wondering if he was good enough for her.' He had a lot of style.

"We kept a wonderful relationship with Margo and Eddie [Albert] because we spent all the holidays with them, Christmas, Thanksgiving, New Years, 4th of July. We really have been a part of the family. And I was so glad to be accepted by them, too," Bettye mused.

Sam Jaffe had had many women interested in him. According to Bettye, Marilyn Monroe was crazy about him. While this may have been true, again, matters of the heart remained in Sam's private chambers.

Even though many women pursued Sam Jaffe, it wasn't until Bettye Ackerman that he decided to marry again.

In his early days, Sam Jaffe was a boxer. An injured fighter needs to stay down on the mat, lest more permanent damage result. Though his friends sought unabashedly to lure him from his grief, Sam had the wisdom to remain in his pain until it finished.

All too often, well-meaning comforters attempt to determine for another the time for the grieving process. It is a sign of great strength when individuals reserve that right for self. Mourning can't be rushed. The longer one stays with the time of bereavement, the better the chances of fully expending the energy and getting on with life.

It is only when a loss is completely experienced that the door can open to the possibility of a new union, on its own terms.

Sam Jaffe was a fine example of a man who grieved to the fullest. When he was ready, he picked himself up and went on.

****

ANNE MEARA, *Maedchen in Uniform*, 1955

"I had done some summer stock in Woodstock, N. Y. and one season of winter stock in Delaware.

"When I was cast at E.L.T., I was thrilled. It was great to work there because a lot of people in the industry would come to E.L.T. in those days, producers and agents. There was always an opportunity that your work would be validated and maybe lead to a paying job. We weren't focused on getting a job. We weren't auditioning. The play was the thing. It was a very close feeling we all had.

"It was wonderful artistically because we had many improvisations and rehearsal time. Barbara Barrie was in it. I drew on my own experience in a convent school that was an Eichmann-like environment.

"Doing the show contributed to my getting a soap opera live from Philadelphia. I played a nineteen-year-old unwed mother. Marty Balsam and Rosemary Murphy were on it.

"I think E.L.T. was one of the greatest things Sam did in his career. It gave actors opportunities.

"Jerry [Stiller] and I did a Love Boat, a charmingly shallow show, with Sam and Bettye. Sam was very sweet and kind. He had a great awareness of social problems and made us younger ones aware. He was quite wonderful."

****

Union Activities

Devoid of a love relationship, Sam Jaffe poured his energies into union activism and leadership. His decade-long tenure on the council of Actors' Equity was a turbulent time in the Association's history. Several irons stoked the raging fires simultaneously. Besides the struggle between the old and new orders, and the important issues of wages and working conditions, there was the nastiness of anti-Semitism and the poisonous fear of communism.

Actors' Equity suffered at the hands of a Republican from Kansas named Congressman William P. Lambertson. In July 1940, as a member of the sub-committee on appropriations, he fought to deny federal relief for actors because he said there were seven communists on the Equity Council.

Minutes of an Equity meeting list the seven accused as: Mr. Sam Jaffe, Mr. Philip Loeb, Miss Emily Marsh, Mr. Hiram Sherman, Mr. Leroy MacLean, Miss Edith Van Cleve and Mr. Alan Hewitt.

At the July 9 meeting, each of these seven members denied, either personally or in writing to the Council, membership in the Communist Party. Jaffe stated: "I was never a member of the Communist Party and never entertained any idea of joining it and have no affiliations, whatsoever, in any red organization."

In view of the denials, the Council called upon Mr. Lambertson to furnish proof of his charges or submit the source of his information. Lambertson was unable to satisfy the Council with proof and, instead, he requested that the entire matter, as represented by his considerable folder, be printed in the *Equity Magazine*. It would have taken an entire issue. A.E.A. considered this action but rejected it because of possible libel suits as the accused members did not consent to such publication.

At an Equity meeting on August 6, 1940, Sam Jaffe stated he would not consent to the publication of the statement in the *Equity Magazine*. He felt there should be an impartial investigation first and then have the results published.

One of Lambertson's complaints about Jaffe was that he signed his name to the so-called 'Golden Book' presented to Stalin upon the 20th anniversary of the U. S. S. R. Jaffe was appalled that Lambertson labeled this "a complete endorsement of the Soviet System." He said the signing simply called attention to the difference between fascism and communism. Besides, the so-called 'Golden Book' was compiled long before Russia had acted aggressively toward other nations.

A great struggle emerged within Actors' Equity. Members were in a financial bind and seemed more concerned with gaining federal relief funds than with protecting the integrity of the falsely accused. A large, demonstrative and at times turbulent Quarterly Meeting filled the North Ball Room of the Hotel Astor to overflowing. Members took an extremely strong stand against communism, its policies, practices and tactics. They adopted a resolution defending Equity's position regarding the charges brought by Representative Lambertson on this issue. They broadened the original resolution of condemnation with a recommendation to the Council that no communist, Nazi, or fascist, or a sympathizer with any or all of them, should hold elective office in the Association, or be employed by it.

The wording of the amendment read: "Whereas at a regular meeting of the members of the Association, held on September 27, 1940, the following resolution and amendment was adopted by an overwhelming majority:

1. This Council goes on record as declaring that it is unalterably opposed to communism, the Communist Party, the principles it advocates and the tactics it employs.

2. It repeats its definite denial that it is communistically controlled and earnestly requests that the claim that various members of the Council are communists or working hand in hand with them be investigated as promptly as possible by the Dies Committee ...

3. That no member of, or sympathizer with the Communist Party, the Nazi Bund or any fascist party may hold any office whatsoever or be employed by the Actors' Equity Association ..."

Although many members were in support of Equity's resolve, opposition to the amendment remained heated. The passage touched off fireworks with opposing sides heckling one another. The opposition called the amendment unconstitutional since the Communist Party was still a legal organization in the United States and appeared on ballots; and further, that there were no tests or grounds for determining who might be sympathizers with these groups or parties.

Philip Loeb attacked Congressman Lambertson for Congressional votes unfriendly to labor. Loeb had voted to denounce communism, Nazism and fascism. However, he would not vote to deny them the right to sit on the Equity Council. "If they are good enough to belong to Equity," he said, "they are good enough to represent the membership on the Council."

Actor Leon E. Janney described the amendment as reprehensible, pointing out Equity's seemingly small suppression of civil rights were similar to the methods used by the totalitarian governments they abhor. He said that they, too, started with restrictive actions for the good of the people, but once the precedent had been set, the cancer of the suppression grew until they had quelled all that was noble, free, and admirable.

Janney knew how Sam Jaffe and the others as victims of baiting tactics felt because when he rose to speak against the amendments, people called him a communist. Had his name been placed in nomination for Council membership, the unfounded accusation would have insured his defeat regardless of his complete innocence. The charge alone, because of the amendment, would have required an investigation. In spite of the subsequent proof of his innocence, the accusation and its stigma would have remained.

Janney's protest was all the more cogent when one considers that the Congressional Record, July 4, 1940, boldly states that "Seven communists are now on the governing board of the Actors' Equity Association. . . . Here is a situation where communists are occupying high places in a profession which Congress would undoubtedly be glad to help if we had the means of weeding them out. Innocent and deserving actors and actresses all over the country are thus being penalized and there will be no W.P.A. Theater Project as long as this condition is permitted to exist." The action had been taken without proof of charges or opportunity for challenge. Sam Jaffe, and the others accused, was condemned without benefit of investigation or defense.

As if this wasn't bad enough, in May 1941, Equity's Nominating Committee tucked its tail between its legs and added to the outrage caused by the Congressional accusations. In the "best interests" of the Association, they eliminated from nomination anyone, such as Alan Hewitt, whose political affiliations were questionable and could thus affect the obtaining of theater funds.

Florence Reed, Chairman of the Nominating Committee, along with Frank Wilcox, Ruth Gordon, and others, signed a statement that read: "The loss of governmental support to our theater has proved costly to our members. Under these circumstances the Nominating Committee felt it incumbent to consider solely the greatest good to the greatest number. In a word: the welfare of the membership as a whole, as opposed to the desire of one individual."

For a man like Sam Jaffe, this meant that it would be impossible to get a hearing — to publicly deny the charges; impossible even to discover the basis for the charges.

A storm of letters from performers such as the Lunts and Frederic March got Lambertson to modify his accusations against Hewitt, but this came in a personal note to Hewitt, not a public letter. Lambertson now called him a stooge of the communist front because he voted in council with someone "about whose affiliations and loyalties there can hardly remain any intelligent doubt."

The charge stood and was entered in The Congressional Record.

Equity Magazine reported " ... The Nominating Committee agreed that they thought the charge unjust and unfounded. But the Committee thought that Mr. Hewitt should not be nominated because the charge had been made."

In rejecting Mr. Hewitt's name, they were endorsing the absolutely unproven accusations, the slander, and the un-American procedure used against him.

Alan Hewitt decided to run as an Independent Candidate. The honor and integrity of Equity were at stake. He and others were being driven to defend the right of free speech and the right to a trial before conviction. The battle lines within the union were clearly drawn, with each side feeling as passionate about its stand as the other.

Again, Florence Reed, Chairman of the Nominating Committee, addressed the Association. "We are accused ... of having communistic infiltration in the membership and that seven of our governing board are communists. ... If I had been one of the seven what I would have done would have been to instantaneously resign from the

Council and clear myself. ... But that was not done ...

"This Nominating Committee wasn't working to vindicate Mr. Hewitt. It was working to vindicate the stain on the Actors' Equity Association and for the sake of the membership."

There was a basic flaw in this reasoning. There could be no "membership" without the individuals comprising it. Sam Jaffe knew this. By upholding the right of a single person, the honor of the group was defended. Reed functioned from the reverse perspective. Blinded to the primacy of the individual, she lobbied for members to stand up and fight for the Federal Theater Project funding by demanding that the Council's house be cleaned. She said they had accused her of bigotry and of being a reactionary. "I will never stop fighting to try to get rid of the malignant growth that is eating the vitals of this Association. ... I can't imagine any greater compliment in the world ... than to charge an American with the crime of fighting communism."

Passions flared; accusations flew. Tempers spilled over the rim of reason. Ben Lackland addressed the membership, saying that A.E.A. could represent Hewitt and others in contractual disputes between actor and manager but not in defense of his innocence. He also dismissed the charge that the Nominating Committee didn't nominate foreign-born like Mady Christians. He rushed to support his whitewash with a complete non-truth. He stated, "On our Council at the moment we have several naturalized citizens ... Mr. Sam Jaffe, born in Dublin, Ireland, believe it or not!"

Sam, born of Jewish parents on New York's Lower East Side, might have taken Lackland's updated version of his origins as cause for invoking "Saints preserve us!" to break the boil of the seriousness.

In the 1940's the struggle was between unity and uniformity. Alan Hewitt was eloquent in his differentiation. Unity was important but uniformity would lead to a dictatorship similar to those in Europe at the time.

Declaring that he had never been a communist, Hewitt proclaimed that he had done everything possible to refute Lambertson's charges. However, Lambertson's Congressional immunity kept Hewitt from taking action against him in the courts for libel and slander. Though he had begged for proof of the charges against him, none was forthcoming. He asked for a trial but was never tried. "What else could I do?" he lamented. "What else could any of you do? How else would you go about proving that you were not a communist?"

Sam Jaffe sat in the same sinking boat with Hewitt. Innocent and accused, the damage to them was irreparable. All it took was the naming of their names. Jaffe's career would be affected for years to come. Hewitt attempted to awaken union members to the unfair assault. He implored, "What has happened to me could happen to any one of you seated in this hall — don't you realize that?"

Lambertson based his withholding of funds on the presence of reds who he said would overrun the union. Even if the seven accused were communists, there were forty-three other council members. The seven hardly represented a powerful majority.

Those accused suspected that what was really behind the Lambertson attack was a movement to discredit unions. Red baiting was its most effective instrument. There was opposition to the progressive gain in working conditions for the actor.

Union activist Mady Christians pleaded with members to open their eyes before it was too late. She had experienced the witch hunters in full force in Hitler's Germany. Everyone suspected and labeled everyone else. Friends no longer trusted one another and persecution was general.

Christians had attended the meeting that forcibly dissolved the German Equity Association. It wasn't because it was overrun with communists. "That was a smoke screen that Hitler raised all over the world," she asserted. "Equity was dissolved because we didn't see the signs of alarm early enough and stand together. We didn't throw out distrust. We didn't watch."

Her strong statement to the union membership is as important to us today as it was in that specific context in the 1940's.

"... The German actors were not vigilant enough," she warned, "when the first alarm signs came of intolerance, witch hunt and reckless political slander. ... We did not stand up in time and strongly enough as a body and as an organization for those innocently accused. In times of great political tension, we did not think clearly. We did not realize that we could only fight as a body to keep our name clear. We did not fight enough. We did not force a showdown so that we could find the really guilty ones and throw them out and clean our house. ... We lost our heads in fear ...

"Let us not have that here. ... Let's not declare someone guilty without fair trial ... "

When the vote was taken, both Mady Christians and Alan Hewitt were elected to the Council for five year terms. However, the environment of fear continued in the union and in the Congress. Because of this fear, on March 21, 1942, the Equity membership, by a vote of 552 to 288 adopted a new section, numbered twelve, to Article II of the Equity Constitution: "Under the provisions of this section members of certain specified parties, groups and organizations (Communist Party of the Soviet Union, The National Socialist Party of Germany, the Fascist Party of Italy, the Communist Party of the United States or any subdivision thereof) whose activities are deemed inimical to the best interests of Actors' Equity Association and its members ... are barred from holding office in or being employed by Equity.

"Any person who publicly, knowingly or willfully advocates, advises, teaches or abets the doctrine, duty, necessity, desirability or propriety of overthrowing the Government of the United States or of any State or political subdivision thereof by force, violence or unlawful means" [is barred.]

The action, though designed to lay to rest the divisiveness within the Association, did not quell the draining factionalism. The prevailing issues found their way into critical matters for years to come. Jaffe's years on Council abounded in confrontation with the malicious matters of subversiveness and subtle religious divisions.

Despite the false assertion by Congressman Lambertson that Sam Jaffe was one of seven communists active in Actors' Equity, Jaffe's skills at mediation resulted in his being drafted into service within Actors' Equity in many areas. In December 1943, he was appointed Chairman of a committee to deal with increased living costs and the necessity for increased minimum wage. In February, he served as Chairman of the Committee *Re* New School Social Research to explore whether Equity members could be allowed to appear in productions there without pay. Sam was to examine possibilities of showcasing at the New School for Social Research.

It was very important that actors had outlets to play roles for which they might not be professionally hired because of typecasting. Casting of actors is generally by a combination of their physical structure and their personality qualities, and how this works together with the role as written. It is only in true repertory companies, of which there are sadly very few, that an actor has the opportunity to create a role significantly different from his appearance or essence.

Previously, The Black Friars, the Barbizon-Plaza,

the Hecksher, the Malin Studios, and other houses outside the regular theatrical district, provided actors with creative opportunities they desperately needed. Equity allowed these theaters to operate for a time. Too soon, members of other theatrical unions observed the selling of tickets and money paid out for production. They demanded that their members be employed at their regular rates and conditions, even though Equity members, by choice, weren't benefiting in this way. To support these sister unions, Equity removed permission for appearance by Association members.

In speaking of this situation, Sam observed that the experimental theaters had become "very important and so the Stagehands Society closed them down. They called it creeping professionalism. They knew they were robbing us."

The actors were being robbed of the opportunity to perform and develop, but the stagehands needed protection as much as the actors did.

Producers would encourage experimental theater to benefit from inexpensive tryouts. The actors would give their time and talent and end up not being hired when the show converted to full production.

Today, as in the yesterdays described, Actors' Equity puts forth great effort to protect its members. Yet actors still yearn to act wherever they can in order to give life to creativity.

With the collapse of experimental theater, a void remained. The bottom had fallen out on a temporary solution to a profound need and, as is the natural order of things, the "unseen overseers of the theatrical hierarchy" were rushing in with the planks necessary to put grounding beneath the projects that had fallen off their feet.

"Just by accident," Sam spoke excitedly, "there was a meeting of the three organizations: Screen Actors Guild, American Federation of Radio Artists, and Actors' Equity Association focused on what they could do for the war effort, how they could help. It was held right next door to the John Golden Theater, on 45th St. (at the Little Theater, the Winthrop Ames Theater)." Jaffe was sent by Equity to attend the meeting in recognition of his concern that actors work for decent wages and under creatively conducive conditions. He had a strong desire to establish outlets for practice of the art as well as showcasing the performer. Philip Loeb accompanied Jaffe at the meeting.

George Freedley, who was then the curator of the theater section of the New York Public Library, was in attendance. He informed those present that the libraries were helping the war effort by allowing soldiers to use rehearsal rooms to play musical instruments. As Jaffe listened to Freedley, he had a brainstorm. "Is there anything for actors?" he asked. Freedley replied affirmatively. They had thirteen little theaters in their libraries with spotlights. They were used by the neighborhood people. However, now, because of the war, they were idle.

Sam received permission to use the library theaters and brought that news to the attention of Actors' Equity. A committee, including Jaffe, Philip Loeb and Aline MacMahon, was appointed to look at the available theaters. They turned out to be wonderful and Equity gave the go ahead for their use.

Under Sam Jaffe's chairmanship the following guidelines for the new Equity Library Theatre program, as written up in the Equity Magazine program, were presented to the Council of Actor's Equity Association on November 16, 1943.

"I. A committee of six or seven Councilors to be elected or appointed as a 'Holding' or 'Control' Committee. This committee to control all production details, but to have no hand in casting. There should be a representative of the Library on this committee.

"II. Neither Equity, the Library, nor the committee shall assume any financial responsibility.

"III. Financial responsibility must be assumed by the individual groups presenting the plays and subject to the rules laid down by the committee.

    A. A fixed sum shall be set for all productions which no group shall be permitted to exceed.

    B. The production units must conform to the equipment on premises.

        1. No outside equipment can be brought in with the exception of hand props.

    C. In the event that any props need hauling, a union transfer company must be employed unless such props shall be donated.

"IV. There shall be no salaries.

"V. No admission charge. Admission by invitation only, except for neighborhood audiences.

"VI. The schedule of performance dates must be arranged and sanctioned by the control board in consultation with the branch Librarian.

    A. Provision shall be made for the number of rehearsals — which, in turn will depend upon the demand and availability of the library theaters.

"VII. Only revivals, or plays in the public domain shall be presented.

"VIII. When these theaters are used by Equity groups, the players must be members of Equity.

"IX. The number of performances shall be limited to three — not necessarily consecutive — but preferably within the period of a week.

"X. Distribution of seats — There shall be an arrangement with the Library where either a certain proportion of seats shall go to them or, say, two nights shall be allotted to the neighborhood audiences and one for the Equity group."

The report in *Equity Magazine* continued: "The Council accepted the report of the committee and authorized the committee to continue negotiations with the Library looking towards setting the plan in operation.

"And so members having in mind to do such presentations had better get in touch with Mr. Jaffe, through Equity, to learn what libraries may be available and when, and under just what conditions.

"This may not be the full-fledged experimental theater for which members have been seeking, but it is a reasonable and workable compromise with the exigencies of the situation and will have to do for the time being until further modifications seem necessary or desirable.

"The best way to demonstrate how far it goes in filling a very real need is to take hold of it and give it a try. It is, Equity believes, a long step in the right direction, and one for which both the Equity Committee and the New York Public Library deserve appreciation and applause."

The rules adopted were so successful and sustaining that E.L.T. was to continue uninterrupted for over four decades. It was when many of these principles were abandoned that E.L.T. went out of business.

So it was that in January 1944, actors began a creative, performing organization that was to flourish for over 45 years.

By April 1944, three excellent productions were completed. It took several months for many actors to comprehend the E.L.T. setup because their relationship to production in the past had always been to be hired by another party who was doing the producing and casting. It was hard to grasp that neither A.E.A. nor the libraries were producing or casting. E.L.T. was an opportunity for any member to form his or her own group.

By the end of the first season, six plays had been produced. Century Lighting provided free instruments and the actors themselves covered procuring of scenery and costuming. The response to the productions was so great that by the second season E.L.T. produced 104 plays.

The results delighted George Freedley. As dramatic critic of the *Telegraph*, he prevailed on other critics to review the plays. In addition, agents attended in search of new talent.

It was Sam Jaffe's baby. He reflected with pleasure, "It's something that I feel that I can look back to with a great deal of pride. Many an actor who was taken to Hollywood was taken from off one of those stages we had.

"In a sense we created employment because they could be seen in parts other than they would be cast for."

Sam Jaffe did theater a great service by starting the Equity Library Theatre. While no one ever disputed its value, one individual disputed its origins.

Terese Hayden, the originator of the much used *Player's Guide*, was a great contributor of time, energy and organizational skills to the project. E.L.T. gave her a start when she was young. She acted, directed, composed music, and produced for E.L.T.

Although she acknowledged that Sam made it possible for all those years, her view of how E.L.T. was birthed is somewhat different. She was very emotional as she talked of her memory of what transpired: "I wasn't a member of the council and therefore I had no official position. Sam wrote a beautiful article about me in *Equity Magazine* acknowledging what I was trying to do to help get E.L.T. going."

Then she blurted out, "I did start it. But they've always gotten the credit. So often I have been forgotten and since I'm still living, it hurts. So you have to forgive me for that. This has nothing to do with Sam. It's historical."

Her main connection with Sam Jaffe was through Philip Loeb, her teacher at the American Academy of

Dramatic Arts in 1939. During the war she had done shows for the Canteen in hospitals. She had wondered how they could continue doing these plays after the war. She asked Philip for help. He was living in a hotel and got a big hall for her so she could call a meeting to talk about this. Philip also spoke to Sam Jaffe about it.

"I cannot tell you what made Sam Jaffe talk to George Freedley of the Public Library but the two of them put their dear heads together and came up with the mechanics of making E.L.T. possible," Hayden said. "I didn't really have a working relationship with Sam but he turned it all over to me. Whatever I did in organizing he was making possible through the council."

Was E.L.T. Jaffe's or Hayden's idea? "The only thing that I remember about that," Bettye Jaffe said, "was when they were honoring Sam at the Lincoln Center Library. Sam was not well. He'd already had his stroke, but he spoke and he was just brilliant. But Terry Hayden spoke and she tried to take credit for having had the idea about the E.L.T., which was totally incorrect, and Sam flared up. He was ready to do battle.

"Sam never got any [advance] communication from Terry about 'her idea' — absolutely none," Bettye continued. "She came in later. Sam's recollections were really infallible, but of course we all have selective memories."

Following the Lincoln Center honoring, Jaffe wrote to Hayden:

"... In introducing me, you said that E.L.T. was your idea. It was a deliberate slap in the face to me. I had prepared to give you thanks for your help in getting a number of our members to clean the office allotted to us. But I became enraged and could only deny it and tell how E.L.T. came about ...

"If you can answer the following questions in the affirmative, I will write you a public apology.

"1. Was it you who knew of the 13 library theaters?

"2. Did you ask George Freedley whether they could be used by our members?

"3. Did he tell you that since the neighborhood groups that had used them, were drafted into the army, they were no longer functioning?

"4. Did you then ask him whether they would be available to Equity?

"5. Was it to you that he said, "He'd have to ask his board of directors?"

"6. Did he then tell you that he had the approval so that Equity could use them?

"7. Was it you who brought those glad tidings to the Council and made Equity and the library a fact?

"If you can, as I said above, answer yes to those questions, then I'm an impostor and all credit belongs to you. If you can't, then your claim in maintaining that it was your idea is absolutely unjust and morally indecent."

There is no reply to this letter, other than Miss Hayden's continued and expressed belief that she started E.L.T. and that Jaffe got the credit for it.

It is evident that both Hayden and Jaffe had strong feelings about the establishment of theaters where actors could warm up and exercise their talents. They each contributed in their own ways to making this happen. Hayden sought out Loeb's help and thought that what Jaffe created as E.L.T. was what she had instigated with her request and persistence. Loeb may have approached Jaffe, but clearly Jaffe was striving toward the same goal, and it was he who thought of exploring the matter with Freedley. The most important factor is that Equity Library Theatre became a reality.

As Terese Hayden observed, "George Freedley was

a gifted man and lover of the theater. How he and Sam got together is a mystery to me but it was a good thing because that union of the libraries with Actors' Equity Association was wonderful. Take the plays off the library shelf and put them on the stage."

****

Many famous names over the years supported the work of E.L.T. Among the donors were Harry Belafonte, Art Carney, Marge and Gower Champion, Katharine Cornell, Melvyn Douglas, Henry Fonda, Arthur Godfrey, Garson Kanin and Ruth Gordon, Jack Lemmon, Walter Matthau, William Morris Agency, Inc., Paul Newman and Joanne Woodward, Otto Preminger, Richard Rodgers, Eli Wallach and Anne Jackson. The Sponsors included Theodore Bikel, Russell Crouse, Arlene Francis, Elia Kazan, Harold Prince, Cornelia Otis Skinner, and Fritz Weaver.

Often specific patrons made possible particular productions and fund raisers. For example, some of the patrons for the preview benefit performance of *The Golden Apple*, performed in the 17th year of E.L.T. as its 376th production, were Julie Andrews, Richard Burton, Patty Duke, Maurice Evans, Angela Lansbury, Lore Noto, Sir Laurence Olivier, Anthony Perkins, Jerome Robbins, Dore Schary, Thornton Wilder, and Irene Worth.

****

". . . *Without E.L.T., where will the young actor practice his craft, and where will new audiences experience the magic of living theater?"*
— *Basil Rathbone*

****

"*E.L.T. is performing invaluable service. . . . E.L.T. is pointing the way.*"
— *Maurice Evans*

****

****

". . . This [E.L.T.] very worthwhile venture . . . gives the actors and directors invaluable experience. And for the audience . . . it provides one of the best theatrical bargains in town."

— *Clive Barnes,* New York Times.

****

The Actor's Benefactor

The acting profession often resembles the New York City subway system at rush hour. There are too many hopefuls striving toward the same goal in the same place at the same time. Only the lucky ones make it.

Given the gloomy statistics, namely, the minuscule percentage of union actors working at any given time, it is astounding that droves of newcomers continue to descend on the Big Apple seeking a bite of fame. From Amarillo, Bakersfield, and Charlottesville they come, hungry for the Broadway contract that will light up their names and bring them adulation. Some who come are talented. Others are experienced or well-educated. All are eager.

Alas, into the life of most actors comes all too quickly "the rub." To work, one must be known. To be known, one must be seen. To be seen, one must work.

Agents are a notorious part of this cycle. "Let me know when you're working," they say. "I'll come and see you." After hearing this many times, the actor leaves the office grumbling, "If I'm working, why do I need you?" The actors on this difficult journey-to-success endure the same shutouts as train passengers at rush hour. All too often, on the platform of hopes, the door to the immediate future closes in their faces.

Actors are survivors. Leaving the agent's domain behind them, they shift from grumbling to wondering how they can "get into something." They begin to hope, perhaps in excess, by falsely interpreting the agent's standard line, "Don't call us, we'll call you." They choose to hear it as, "Please, get a part so I can come and see you. I'm eager to. I want to." It's the actor's conversion of dismissal to impetus.

"Get into something" where? In previous days, actors sought small parts in anything, anywhere. Today the business is so overrun with those desiring to blush with pride in the face of rave reviews that established names gobble up minor roles that, for face-saving reasons, are called cameos. Beginning actors, desperate to be seen, now even pay to perform in organized showcases. These showcases have proliferated to the point of becoming their own business within show business. And actors resort to making videos of their performance pieces and submitting them as an audition or in the hopes of getting one.

This phenomenon is true in other creative arenas as well. I read recently with great chagrin of an event in Phoenix, AZ called Pitchapalooza where randomly selected writers are given one minute to present their best "elevator pitch" to a panel of book experts. One author would then be chosen to win an introduction to a literary agent in their genre. This approach is terribly degrading to writing and the creative process.

Getting into something, becoming known, being seen, becomes so all-consuming that creativity is often all but forgotten along the way. Actors should not have to be salespeople, selling self. Rather, they should concentrate on becoming artists who make characters come to life before an enthralled audience's eyes.

For some, like me, some of the joy of creating a role departs because of the need to depend on others to give us a chance. After 18 years of training and performing on stage, screen, television, and in commercials, I grew weary of the quest which no longer gave purpose to my life. A spiritual breakthrough led me to new ways to contribute to the world using my talents and creativity. I was glad to be freed from the striving and hoping. I replaced that with being and doing, with making a difference. Sam Jaffe was able to do both: continue as an actor and make a difference by how he lived his life. In this he was truly blessed.

Actors need to act, to practice their craft, not just to be seen in order to get other jobs. They need to be able to experiment, to succeed and fail, and to keep their instruments highly tuned.

Where? How? The questions are as old as the profession. Thus, the creation of Equity Library Theatre was a boon to actors, and even to audiences.

Following the actor's strike and the official establishment of Actors' Equity Association in 1919, one of the first general meetings considered the immediate creation of an experimental theater. Its design was to protect both actors and dramatists by ensuring that if they participated in a trial production, they would benefit should the play be produced commercially. Equity Players began in 1922. It was a vehicle for actors to present a trial production and to be seen. Those in the profession received it with enormous enthusiasm. Offers of money and services flooded in. While the opening was a glamorous success, weak audience support caused closure within six weeks.

Though Equity Players went under, the need it sought to fill remained as strong as ever, and continued into the 1940's with other attempts at experimental theaters.

It isn't easy to achieve real change. History resembles a long string of television reruns, played over and over until we so saturate ourselves with the way things are that we cannot help turning toward, and beginning to commit ourselves to, the way things might be.

Sam Jaffe, a working actor who didn't himself have the need to "get into something," hit upon a potent answer to the dilemma of the non-working actor with the launching of Equity Library Theatre.

On Saturday, June 10, 1944, Wilella Waldorf of the *New York Post* devoted her entire column, "Two on the Aisle," to a review of *Shadow and Substance* and the Equity-Library Theatre Project. She said in part:

"If the production . . . that we witnessed last Wednesday evening at the Hudson Park Library . . . is typical of what these groups are doing, we must say the agony seems worthwhile.

"Under the competent direction of Norman Fenster . . . a troupe of actors we had never seen before, or even heard of, held us interested through the four acts of Paul Vincent Carroll's by no means elementary play under pretty difficult conditions."

George Freedley's review in the *Morning Telegraph* praised the production and also stressed the talent potential of the Equity Library Theatre. He urged that it not go to waste and that producers, directors, authors and agents make a point of regularly attending performances at E.L.T.

Freedley and Jaffe made a great combination. They each wanted the best creative opportunities for actors. Sam's dear friend Karl Malden spoke of this with great feeling on February 7, 1985, at the anniversary celebration of the first E.L.T. production, when the entire season of plays was dedicated to Jaffe's memory.

"Sam was a beautiful human who helped more actors than any man I know . . . He hated to see actors out of work," Malden said. He told the story of a time when they sat together in a coffee shop near Actors' Equity when a young man and girl approached Jaffe in despair of running out of money for their E.L.T. production. Sam reached into his pocket, pulled out two $20 bills and said, "Here's $40. You'll get the rest." Malden knew that Jaffe had given them his last dollar because he had to pay for their tea!

Experiencing the generosity of Sam Jaffe, the true devotion to his chosen art form, and the kindness he expressed to humanity where and as he met it, one can see embodied a variation on the words John F. Kennedy spoke at his inauguration. Sam did not ask what the theater could do for him. It seemed his life was about what he could do for the theater and for actors. In all the years of his spearheading E.L.T., he never used it as a vehicle for himself.

"I didn't do any plays in E.L.T.," he said. "It wouldn't be fair, as if I created the project for myself." This was true even during the time he was blacklisted and unable to work.

It was Jaffe's greatest thrill to see others benefit. He remembered an E.L.T. production of *Faust* on 125th Street. Hans Sondheimer, a German refugee and well-known lighting designer, did such excellent projections of *Faust* that no scenery was needed. Sondheimer remained with E.L.T. as a technical supervisor who often took over entire productions himself. His donated work at E.L.T. led to his being hired by the City Center.

Sam was always alert for opportunities to enhance the creative process. He and George Freedley read that producer John Golden was ready to give help to the efforts of the young players who were starving. They went to see him and told him about E.L.T. He gave them $1,000. Out of that $1,000, each production got $20. The money was on deposit at the library and they handled distribution. Later, the amount was raised to $50 per show. Karl Malden joked that they could use the $50 in any way they wished: settings, costumes, make-up . . ."

Jaffe would write the advance notes of coming E.L.T. shows in the *Equity Magazine*. They never gave him a byline. He said, "They were afraid to give me any prominence." However, Jaffe wasn't seeking to draw attention to himself. He wanted actors to have the opportunity to choose a role for which they would never be typecast in commercial theater. "The actor's dream," [and surely Jaffe's dream since he was speaking of it,] "was always to do repertory so he could perform a variety of roles, giving him a chance to express himself."

In October 1944, *Equity Magazine* quoted Cyrus Staehle, an actor in E.L.T.'s *Shadow and Substance* who had clearly caught the fire Sam had ignited: "The vitality of the theater — its future worth to the public — depends largely upon the invention and imagination of our new young players — and of the enthusiasm and creative spirit they bring to the thing they protest they wish to do. Doing is much more important than the protest!"

Sam Jaffe was one of the greatest examples of this approach. Sam didn't sit on anything. He didn't sit for anything.

Terry Hayden remembered an event at the Lincoln Center honoring Sam. She was tired and had to sit down, but not Sam. He never sat down. He was always moving about. She described him as "standing there, imperially slim as he always was, and he had an incredible gift of energy, or stamina; something."

It was as if an inner light inspired him and kept him highly charged with life force all the time. He was excited about life, about theater, about making things happen, and about being one to make them happen. He put himself on the line. He put money, time, energy and heart behind making the dreams realities.

At Actors' Equity Association, "I got a telephone installed," he said. "An E.L.T. phone; separately installed. I paid the phone bills.

"A phrase used in those days," he recalled with a smile, "was that the E.L.T. office was in Sam Jaffe's hat." For about a year there wasn't any actual office. One was ultimately provided by A.E.A. on the fifth floor."

Sam remembered how Terry Hayden had cleaned that office and painted it. Cleaning the top floor, according to Hayden, was no small task. It was an event, more like a time-warp journey into the attic of one's beloved grandparents. It was a dusty archive of theater history: old photos and playbills, as well as data on Equity's attempts to create experimental theaters.

With the offices cleaned and functional, the work of E.L.T. continued under Sam's guidance. One of the wonderful advantages of E.L.T. was that it provided participating young actors with opportunities to develop their skills in the company of seasoned professionals. *Equity Magazine* reported an example of this in November 1944. "The Mary Stuart group has not yet chosen its library theater. Miss Blanche Yurka was approached for this group by Walter Greaza. She had just returned from Hollywood and had hardly been home an hour when he phoned and told her about the library theaters. Later a member of the group called and made an eloquent appeal for her to appear as Elizabeth in their production. They were successful. Miss Yurka begins rehearsals for a Broadway production next month, but will devote all of November to the library production ..."

The pleasure must have been warm on the face of Sam Jaffe as he reported on E.L.T.'s progress. "Golden became very much interested, and he gave us more money, enough to have a secretary whom we paid $50 a week. Imagine! This was pretty good, I should say. This was in 1944."

As the year ended, journalist Wilella Waldorf applauded E.L.T.'s vitality, praising the performers and performances. She said all of theater would benefit from the project, and she expressed the hope that someday Equity would establish an Equity Workshop in New York with a real little theater of its own. Her words turned out to be foresight rather than hope, and happily so for all concerned.

The ensuing years were good for E.L.T. As Sam had indicated, the structure of it provided actors with the opportunity to develop skills that spilled over into many disciplines, and contributors could bring their many talents to the aid of E.L.T. in return.

A report in *Equity Magazine* in January 1945, told of a meeting that was held "... for members of the Association who had manifested an interest in library productions but who had not yet taken part in any. These members were brought together in the hope that they would form their own groups to do library plays. However, the business of organization is a talent in itself, and the meeting might have failed in its purpose were it not for the miracle of Terese Hayden. Miss Hayden volunteered to help organize six groups from among those present. Moreover, she came prepared with a program of six plays and a list of well-known people whom she had already contacted as possible directors for four of them. ... Miss Hayden even undertook the job of getting the necessary royalty waivers. The committee and the members who attended the meeting are greatly in her debt."

Although there is no byline on this entry, it was surely written by Jaffe who acknowledged authoring all the early E.L.T. updates in *Equity Magazine*. Sam appreciated the ability to organize and follow through. It is a skill that is all too rare.

Requests for library productions had come pouring in at such a rate that by the middle of January 1945, a total of eighteen had been approved and more money was sought from the John Golden Fund to keep up with the creative desire being expressed.

The reviews in the major newspapers continued to be excellent; neighborhood interest in library plays was so high that over three-hundred theater-hungry people had been turned away from a production in Chelsea.

By the beginning of March, the top floor rooms at Equity were cleaned and ready as a meeting place and information center, and Wilella Waldorf proclaimed in a column that Equity Library Theatre was ready for Broadway because they not only had the actors, but the audience as well. By June of 1945, with the completion of E.L.T.'s second full season, 45 plays had been done in 66 weeks of the Library Theatre's existence.

Those who had worried about E.L.T. being able to draw agents could now surely be gratified by the great number of agents and scouts who made E.L.T. productions a must for recruitment. Sam's own assessment was that E.L.T. was fast becoming a steady, going concern and a "must" for the theater itself.

Help for E.L.T. came in all forms and directions. The Newspaper Guild provided free use of rehearsal halls. Eugene O'Neill gave his consent to perform his plays without royalty, as did Clifford Odets, Sydney Kingsley, Ferenc Molnar, and Maxwell Anderson. The following card of consent was sent to Lawrence Dobkin from G. Bernard Shaw dated February 22, 1946 in response to a request to do an E.L.T. production of one of his plays:

"You are making a fuss about nothing. If you read or perform any published play for your own entertainment and/or that of your private friends without charging them for admission or exploiting the occasion for profit, or for teaching, or for any other private use included in the price paid for the prompt copy acquired in the book shop, and not spoiling the novelty of a professional production or damaging the author legally, then you are presumably within your rights and so are E.L.T. and Mr. Golden.

"Why bother me about it? It is courteous of you to consult me; and I thank you; but courtesies cost time, and I have none to spare at 90."

As if Sam Jaffe wasn't already devotedly active in E.L.T. and on numerous time-consuming and important Equity committees, he lent his talents and energy to additional areas at A.E.A. while keeping up a healthy performance life. He served on the committee administering funds for the American Negro Theatre, and, in April 1945, he was elected to another five-year term along with Vera Allen, Matt Briggs, Russ Brown, Leo G. Carroll, Frank Fay, and others. While continuing with his other duties, he joined the Financial Committee in May. In that month, an issue involving his beloved friend, Philip Loeb, vied for his attention in the midst of all else he was doing.

The Nominating Committee, whose members included Augustin Duncan, did not put Philip Loeb's name up for re-election, in spite of a resolution passed by Council and in the face of instructions from the executive secretary that candidates be nominated solely based on their record of service to the organization.

Philip's accomplishments included: pay for rehearsals, elimination of the junior minimum so that all actors received equal pay, reduction of probationary period for joining the union, raising of minimum salaries twice, replacements in a cast to get the same pay as their predecessors, raising the pay of stage managers, birth of the American Federation of Radio Artists, and, first to suggest the Experimental Theatre.

Given this record, why did the Nominating Committee reject him? Few of the rejecters were present at the meeting and none rose to explain. Actress Ilka Chase raised the question, "Could it be that the rejection of Philip Loeb's name was due to blind prejudice, to the old bugaboo that maybe he was a communist and here comes the Kremlin? Could it be that when faced with the challenge of defending their behavior they hadn't the courage to reply because they knew they hadn't a leg to stand on?"

Loeb was unqualifiedly endorsed in speech after speech. The smear campaign against him was self-evidently baseless. It had begun with Lambertson who was now an ex-Congressman. Also, the Dies Congressional Committee, where smears originated, had been discredited.

The fight for Loeb was a struggle against limitations on the freedom of thought, expression and belief. Sam Jaffe appeared with a thick folder of names of those who had supported Mr. Loeb's independent nomination.

He proclaimed the sole issue to be Mr. Loeb's service to the Association, a criterion that was disregarded by the Nominating Committee. As soon as he learned that Philip had not been re-nominated, he instituted an independent candidacy and sent wires to all Councilors asking their position regarding it. He, and those working with him, wished to avoid a repetition of the maneuvers of the last election when marked ballots were circulated among companies with certain names, including Mr. Loeb's and his own, marked off in red. "All he and those associated with him were interested in was the welfare of the Association. If there were charges against Mr. Loeb," Jaffe challenged, "Let them be brought out here and now, or let the firing cease for all time."

Much heated discussion ensued. Actor Martin Blaine told the meeting that Mr. Loeb was called a red, not on what he had done, but on what he might be thinking. It was a sinister technique that indicated that the nation was ending the World War with no more understanding than when it had begun. Blaine declared the union must protect itself from having its leaders taken away by name calling.

Sam Jaffe defended the right of people to oppose any candidate, but he and others who supported Philip Loeb objected to the under-cover and smear campaign to which the opposition had resorted.

There was the simultaneous distasteful issue of anti-Semitism. Some union members accused the Jews on the Council of being trouble-makers. Both Jaffe and Loeb were Jewish.

In the election held July 16, 1945, Sam Jaffe, Philip Loeb, Frank Fay, Matt Briggs, Louis Calhern, Vera Allen, Leo G. Carroll were among those elected to full five-year terms.

Martin Blaine observed that "the breach in Equity between the conservatives and liberals had widened because actors are very vocal and passionate beings. For a lot of them, the general membership meetings of the union, where they got up to speak their minds, was the first chance they'd had of doing any self-expression for a year or two. So they made the most it. They'd stand up and carry on. I succumbed to the temptation myself on more than one occasion. This kind of thing, naturally, expands the flames of their differences. It's very emotional. The membership polarizes."

Ultimately, Jaffe, Loeb, Blaine and others, achieved their goals of improvements for actors, but the fight for them had been bitter.

I notice how much space I have devoted to Sam's friend Philip Loeb. I suspect it is because, like Sam, I am a champion of people's rights, of honor, and of justice. It is abhorrent to me that people can be proclaimed tainted in any way without proof. And it is even more repugnant that accusers can toss people aside and ruin their reputations because it benefits them financially or otherwise. Mady Christians made clear time and again, these witch hunts bore resemblance to Hitler's tactics. The world fought fascism for many bloody years; to have elements of it emerge in our nation must have been a horror for those afflicted by it. Sam stood up to it at every opportunity. For me, he set the example of how every one of us must stand when anyone's rights are trampled. It is never enough to say, "That's too bad." It is morally corrupt to allow others to suffer while we are safe. None of us is safe forever; better to stand up and be counted. This is how Sam Jaffe lived the whole of his life. I am honored to have been his friend.

John Golden continued his help to E.L.T. by doubling his original grant of $1,000. Sam Zolotow of the *New York Times* scooped the *Equity Magazine* story on September 9, 1945: "Yes. Mr. Golden met with Mr. George

Freedley and Mr. Sam Jaffe and promised his full support to the project, and a permanent secretary, and all this with the speed with which an unknown makes his way to a table at Sardi's, where the conference took place. Mr. Golden's tempo is decidedly modern. A year ago at our very first conference we had barely finished our request for a grant from him when he replied: 'Gentlemen, you have it.' This time he reversed the procedure; he said: 'Gentlemen, you have it. Now what is it that you need?'"

By the end of the year, Equity Library Theatre was deep into preparations for the establishment of an Equity Library Theatre of the Air, an expansion which would bring theater into a greater number of homes and bring participating actors into a greater arena of exposure.

By February, 1946, John Golden had moved from benefactor to chief patron, guardian and supporter of E.L.T. He became a prime mover in obtaining permission for a special showing of the E.L.T. production of *Tonight at 8:30*. To encourage a better all-around response from agents, scouts, and producers, he composed, printed, and sent invitations at his expense to all theater people who might be interested in finding talent. He also wrote Mayor O'Dwyer, requesting his presence and acquainting him with the project.

As a result of this production, six people got other jobs directly, not to mention the many more obtained through other productions, such as the success story of Mary James whose moving portrayal so impressed Jed Harris that he planned to cast her opposite Walter Huston on Broadway. John Randolph appeared in *The Silver Cord* and as a result was to get a screen test by Warner's, and Anne Jackson, seen in *This Property is Condemned*, was also approached by the West Coast.

Jackson, a young actress then, had no telephone. She lived in Greenwich Village in a one-room apartment and Sam Jaffe volunteered to come by and give her the information she needed to attend an audition. She remembered it as most extraordinary because Sam Jaffe was "a movie star from *Lost Horizon* and I thought that somebody was playing a joke.

"He always had the aura about him at that time, and from then on he was for me some kind of a saint, a fairy godfather; the little smile on his face and those twinkling eyes. Certainly there were the warnings that young actresses get: you have to watch out for this one or that one. There was never ever any sense of that kind of lechery on his part or anything. He was just so genuinely a kind man who greeted newcomers into the theater with benevolence and did very constructive things about it."

Sam Jaffe's joy increased with every E.L.T. accomplishment that benefited theater artists. "In one instance," he reminisced, "we did a play with a famous German actor, Basserman. He had gotten The King's Reindeer; that means the highest award as the greatest actor in Germany. He came to this country during the Nazi Holocaust and he did *The Wild Duck*. All the critics came. Naturally, he was a great actor. He appeared in E.L.T. That's the thing; the greatest actor of Germany of his time. I'll never forget that."

In March, Mr. Golden, already deeply into sponsoring E.L.T. productions, the John Golden Auditions, and the presentation of any prize play that might develop out of his scholarship arrangements with the dramatic departments of three New York colleges, appeared at an Equity Council meeting and spoke on the E.L.T. and the need of cooperation among the various groups in the theater. At his request a committee was formed with Raymond Massey, Mady Christians, Clarence Derwent, and Sam Jaffe, as chairman.

Jaffe's work as mediator on Council encompassed

a broad range of issues from serious affronts to personal freedom to small wrinkles of misunderstanding that required a simple smoothing. In March 1946, he became chairman of a committee to meet with the League of New York Theaters to discuss dissatisfaction with accommodations that had been available to actors on the road.

In addition, Jaffe was elected as an alternate to the Nominating Committee and continued with other prominent Equity members on a committee sponsoring the Equity Library Theatre.

Though Jaffe stood tall as a dedicated server on A.E.A. committees, the skunk of past communist accusations trailed him. In December 1946, 20 petitions signed by over 150 Equity members requested that the Council remove Sam Jaffe from the Committee on Criterion *re* Senior Membership qualifications. Eight reasons were set forth for the request, but top on the list was that the organizations to which he had subscribed were considered to be subversive by the Government of the United States. Therefore, the protesting members felt that it was not in the best interests of Equity for Sam Jaffe to serve on a committee to further the welfare of the newcomer to the theater.

Jaffe's response was that he was not a communist, was against communism, and that "if these persons thought he was not fit to serve on the committee for the reasons that they thought were valid, then they should proceed according to the Equity constitution to bring charges against him as a Council member."

As fear continued to reign at Actors' Equity, additional restrictions on liberty were introduced. At an A.E.A. meeting on January 9, 1947, the union obligated its members to sign a statement, under oath, that they did not belong to Communist or Fascist parties.

Sam Jaffe did not hesitate to speak out against this imposition. He announced that he was "ready to stand up and be counted as one who is disloyal to your resolution because of my loyalty to the only criterion of Americanism: the Constitution and the Bill of Rights."

In full, Jaffe's letter read:

"Dear Fellow Councilors,

"Like you, I have received Elliott Nugent's letter asking for support of his and Mr. Kennedy's resolution. This resolution purports 'to bring the whispers to the open' and asks the members of the Council 'to stand up and be counted as American constitutionalists or Stalinists or Francoites.' I for one, as an American constitutionalist, reject this yardstick or loyalty test because it is one that has grown out of hysteria which limits the very American constitutionalism that it is supposed to uphold.

"I have known and admired Mr. Kennedy and Mr. Nugent both as Councilors and men of integrity, and I know and believe that what Elliott Nugent says comes from 'a tired but fast-beating heart' — and so, though I believe implicitly in their sincerity, I challenge the truth of their criterion, for it is not a matter of a 'tired but fast-beating heart,' but a question of principle we must be concerned with. And on the question of principle I prefer to be bound by those of the Founding Fathers, as opposed to the hysterical symptoms of the times as reflected in the matter now before Council.

"For me the old criterion, namely the Constitution and the Bill of Rights, is the only criterion of Americanism, and I am not only willing to 'stand up and be counted' for the principles they embody, but to die for them if need be, and I repeat here as I have on many occasions in Council, that I have allegiance only to this country and no other country. Mine is yours, and I refuse to subscribe to any substitute test of Americanism no matter how well intentioned. I refuse to abandon the old criterion regardless of name-calling or consequences. I realize I have taken the harder course and that it would have been truthful as well as easier to swear that I am no Stalinist, communist, or Francoite, but I feel that if I had done so I would have betrayed a basic tenet of Americanism, namely that our democracy permits all climates of political opinion. Conversely, any limiting of political freedom, whether it manifests itself in keeping a person from being a Councilor or in keeping him from any job whatsoever, is contrary to the American ideal and borrows from and borders on totalitarianism, the very idea which the Messrs. Kennedy and Nugent abhor, I am sure.

"Compare their resolution with Justice Murphy's paraphrase of the late Justice Holmes' idea that we can meet any political idea in the open market in free competition because we feel that we have the best bill of goods to sell. Justice Murphy's statement has been used by the Civil Liberties Union in defense of the principles of the Bill of Rights wherever threatened. To desert this stand because of expediency or hysteria is to desert basic American principles. These are not times for less democracy but for more democracy.

"For instance, let us look at the casualties to democracy that this hysteria has brought us.

"1) Dismissal of liberal commentators. Apparently the networks also think that the people should not be interested in the competition of ideas.

"2) The Taft-Hartley Law.

"3) The decision of the high court extending the legality of searches without warrant.

"4) The President's order for 'dangerously vague' loyalty tests of Federal employees.

"5) The continued witch-hunting crusades of the House Committee on Un-American Activities.

"*The Best Years of Our Lives* and *Boomerang* are supposedly subversive. The effort to get at the records of the late President Franklin D. Roosevelt carries the implication that our great president himself was subversive. In last Sunday's *Times,* Mr. Atkinson reviewed the idea that *All My Sons* was considered subversive, and lamented the fact that a new yardstick was coming into art, an un-American and totalitarian one.

"6) Mr. Matthew Woll's blast against such outstanding men in our profession as James Cagney and Edward G. Robinson, and a demand for a boycott of their films because of so-called un-Americanism.

"I know and love both men, and would stake my life on their loyalty to this country and its democratic principles.

"7) The apparent disdain with which even the word 'democracy' was treated by Mr. Adamson, who was counsel for the Committee on Un-American Activities . . .

"For me personally this witch-hunting and hysteria is old hat by now. I have suffered, along with five others, two irresponsible Congressional outbursts, repeated smears in the press, and petitions circulated in Equity to undermine me. The 'Dillings' with their 'Red Network' include everyone, from our former Mayor La Guardia to our late, great President Roosevelt. The seditionists were most vocal and ardent in their witch-hunting. Haven't we learned our lesson yet — or is it true that we learn nothing from history?

"And now: why this resolution? What need of it? Haven't we reaffirmed the Cornelia Otis Skinner one to bar politics from our deliberations? Haven't we banned politics in a resolution passed by the membership asking us to return to our work and legislate for the benefit of actors and for our Association?

"And now to you, Elliott, I'd like to ask: Haven't the detractors done enough damage to our Association with the false charge of communism? Is there anything on our books that can remotely be called communist?

"Can it be, Elliott, that the Association's National Theatre stand has peeved you as a member of the committee who had other ideas of handling it? I refuse to believe that, for it was a stand of equity and justice, a stand against discrimination because of race, creed, or color, a stand against the phony argument of jobs and a principle of first- and second-class citizenship as opposed to the principles of Americanism.

"I oppose your resolution 'with all my beating heart.' It will not prevent any whispering and it only tends to emphasize strife. The tide of blindness, intolerance, and reactionary hatred is mounting. Your Resolution only adds to its force. The Actors' Equity Association is a microcosm that reflects apparently the hatreds in the world today. I have fought in the Association together with Philip Loeb against those hatreds. We have fought for principle and are fighting for that today. We are convinced from the European tragedy that as the unions desert the principles of democracy, fascism becomes more imminent. I prefer to stand by the principle of political tolerance, the principle of brotherhood, as opposed to hate. The great men you mention are on my side, and so I am ready to stand up and be counted as one who is disloyal to your resolution because of my loyalty to the only criterion of Americanism: the Constitution and the Bill of Rights. Sincerely . . ."

Mr. Nugent, in rebuttal to Mr. Jaffe's letter, said that it was an extremely clear and sensible argument but that he was suspicious of anyone inasmuch as the Communist Party rule was that any means justified the end and that it was all right, from its point of view, for its adherents to do anything so long as it was for the good of the party and its aim to dominate the world. He said that "you could not believe anybody and that you have to put them to a test."

He stated that the signing of an affidavit, under oath, was not a violation of anybody's civil rights, and that any organization can make its own rules for the members of its governing body or members of the organization and that Equity had a perfect right to rule what the requirements of a Councilor should be.

The issues of non-trust were not without humor. Ron Alexander sent Philip a post card of The Last Supper and said that these were a few of the guys he had dinner with one night. Loeb cabled back and said he should watch out for the one on the left.

In September, a large and representative meeting of the Council reaffirmed the six-year-old prohibition in the Constitution against communists, or fascists, holding office, serving on the Council or being employed in responsible positions.

To strengthen this renewed declaration of Equity's purpose, the Council imposed upon all officers, councilors and representatives, the further obligation of stating under oath that they are not members of either the Communist or Fascist parties.

This was passed, over the objections of many on constitutional grounds.

Until the end of the cold war, the struggles of the 1940's continued to tear at the national fabric. Given any opportunity, we raise fear of subversives and of the "devil." The questions we must ask ourselves today are the same Sam Jaffe dealt with in the 1940's. Do we function in fear or with initiation? Do we linger in self-protection or assert ourselves creatively? Do we arm against an "ever-present" enemy or do we reach from our abundance and give joyful birth to our potential?

Sam Jaffe had made an eloquent presentation to the Association. Yet it would seem that even reason cannot dissuade fear. People of principle and causes must stand for what they believe in spite of opposition. No one changes anyone else, even with truth. Jaffe devoted his life to the embodiment of what he held dear. Whether change would occur in others, in the Association, in the world, was a matter of time and circumstance.

After 35 years in place in Equity's constitution, Article II, Section 12, so previously hotly debated and born of the early stages of a witch-hunt period, was challenged on October 8, 1976, at an A.E.A. meeting following an inspiring presentation of the Paul Robeson Award to Lillian Hellman who had exhibited personal courage in the face of exclusionary and vicious thinking in this country.

The article, which states that no member of the Communist Party may be or become an officer, councilor or employee of the Association, and which led to the above mentioned loyalty oaths, was called unjustifiable hypocrisy.

On April 12, 1977, the Council voted to amend this section by deleting the language as written and replacing it with a new Section 12.

As reported in *Equity Magazine*, November 1977, the section's restrictions would now apply to anyone barred by law. At the meeting on October 7, 1977, Douglas Gordon had presented legal information that the changed amendment was an accurate statement of an already existing law and since all must comply, there was no reason for inclusion of such an amendment.

In a moment of triumphant redemption of those who had long suffered, Tony Kraber, whose name had been dragged before the House Committee on Un-American Activities by his "friend" Elia Kazan, was recognized and greeted with prolonged applause. He said that he had been one of the members who suffered during the era of the blacklist and "that of all the unions involved . . . Actors' Equity was the only one who tried to fight the blacklist." He suggested the Article in the Constitution be deleted entirely. Vincent Beck so moved. The motion to delete the section completely carried unanimously.

Change was a matter of time and circumstance.

Men like Jaffe laid the groundwork by taking stands in the face of all opposition. Eventually, hopefully, what is just, prevails. Men such as Jaffe opened the way so that in the future that which was hotly contested and delayed by fear could become reality.

Sam Jaffe in The Old Man Who Cried Wolf, 1970.

****

FRANCES STERNHAGEN, *Admirable Bashville*, 1955

"E.L.T. was invaluable. It really was what the union should have been doing all that time and in the beginning did do so well.

"I had had some success in Washington, D.C. at the Arena Stage. Because of that and a summer at the Olney Theater, I had decided to come to New York and plunge in. I came to study with Sandy Meisner in his professional class.

"In the spring of my first year in New York, Alan Schneider asked me to understudy Helen Hayes and Mary Martin in The Skin of Our Teeth. I went to Europe with it. After that I returned to study and couldn't find a job at all. I wondered, what do I do now?

"I heard that they were doing this little collection of Shaw one acts at E.L.T. I had never heard of E.L.T at the time. I went up. It was that lovely kind of casual atmosphere that used to exist in New York. The director, Chuck Olsen, said, 'My God, I saw you in Thieves Carnival. I had no idea you were this good.' I was cast. It was a wonderful cast. Later it was taken down to the Cherry Lane. It was that successful. I had no idea that E.L.T. was going to be such a stepping stone, or diving board, or whatever, to my career; a great stroke of luck.

"It does seem like luck because if they hadn't been doing that Shaw play at that time, I probably wouldn't have gone to audition and it wouldn't have happened.

"The quality of the people that E.L.T. managed to get stands out for me. It was quite high. Everyone pitched in to make it the best show possible. We all got along so well. There was this marvelous mixture of being able to work with the language and the style and still get the meat of the emotions that were going on by using this wonderful improvisational technique that I had just learned. It was very exciting to be able to do that in a Shaw play. The rehearsals were relaxed and stimulating at the same time. We used the emotions and the brain to serve the play.

"The crew took great pride in the play and they all would watch the rehearsals so that they felt very much a part of the production. It wasn't like now on Broadway where the crew hardly knows what production is coming into the theater. I have found that often off-Broadway is more sat-

isfying that way because the young crew is very eager to participate in the production itself.

"The amount of money we had to put a show on with was miniscule. It also shows how little you really need to put on a show.

"Sam was such a respected star at the time Equity Library Theatre originated. I thank Sam for following his instinct and his inspiration to do this. So many people have an idea, ("Wouldn't it be great if . . .") and they don't follow through. This man actually went through the struggle and the motions to do it. For that we've got to be eternally grateful.

"Even though it doesn't exist now, there are so many people who really did benefit from it that I can't believe that isn't going to rub off somehow. Even something like Steppenwolf Theater obliquely benefited from the principle behind E.L.T. And there are more companies like that.

"People say theater is dying because film is where the money is. It's like chamber music; it's somewhat esoteric. You simply cannot kill theater because right from the cradle up this is how people express themselves. They want to express themselves in front of live people with very little scenery or anything, the way children put on a play."

****

I was particularly delighted with Frances Sternhagen's take on E.L.T. and live theatre, especially off-Broadway. Frannie starred in *The Saintliness of Margery Kempe* off-Broadway at the York Playhouse in 1959. I had the privilege of appearing in that production as one of Kempe's many children. Gene Hackman (film superstar), in his second New York stage appearance, played my father. The fabulous actor-comedian, Charles Nelson Reilly appeared in a show-stopping role. (Coincidently, Charlie had made his stage debut in 1956 in an E.L.T. Lenox Hill Playhouse production of *Best Foot Forward*.) Among others in *Kempe* was George Maharis who became the star of the television series Route 66 the very next year. Famed designers Jules Fisher (lighting) and Theoni Aldredge (costumes) brought their magic to the show. One of the producers was Edward Hastings who went on to become one of the founders of the American Conservatory Theatre in San Francisco, CA. Even with all this talent, and more, to mount this production, the show ran only a night or two and was gone. Such is theatre!

Equity Library Theatre Excels

Praise and acknowledgment continued to surround Equity Library Theatre. *Theatre World*, a magazine which carried photographs of the promising new players of the season, devoted a page to E.L.T.

Newspaper reviewer Wilella Waldorf suggested that everyone would be crazy if they didn't realize that in the E.L.T. production family there was the nucleus of repertory. She hoped that by the next season it would be possible to find a real theater for E.L.T., with the branch libraries still used as rehearsal and tryout spots for productions.

With the completion of the third season in May 1946, E.L.T. was called the busiest managerial outfit on Broadway. *Equity Magazine*, May, 1946, elaborated: "... We may safely say that the major purposes for which the project was established have been achieved ... jobs, tests, and movie contracts ... amply justify the E.L.T. as a 'showcase' for our actors."

E.L.T. served as a training place by affording actors opportunities to appear in plays produced infrequently. Twenty percent of the participants were non-Equity in order that they have an opportunity to work with professionals. In addition, returning veterans had a chance to tune up and ready themselves for Broadway.

The aim to build a neighborhood theater audience succeeded to such an extent that the demand for *Othello* tickets was exhausted in three hours and the Hudson Park Branch received over 600 calls during the week of production requesting information and tickets.

Equity Library Theatre was the only experimental theater in New York in 1946 and it had every reason to take pride in its accomplishments.

By November of that year, over a thousand new applicants had registered to work with E.L.T.; the demand for E.L.T. productions easily exceeded the budgeted quota of forty; and, the Canadian government had sent a representative to observe the E.L.T. project in order to assist in the planning of a professional State Theater in Canada.

Although the 1947 budget called for 40 plays, the June 1947 *Equity Magazine* reported: "We did 56, almost half again as many as we had planned and budgeted for. It was no use telling that to the members or that we had a library booking problem even with forty, and that to increase that number meant paralleling playing dates of other productions, which was unwise. The urge to do an E.L.T. production was apparently greater than the arguments which could be brought forth against it. The added productions were therefore penciled in, in the hope that they might replace cancellations. There were no cancellations, however, and only through the great generosity of Mr. Golden and the endless patience of the librarians were we able to bear this added production burden."

On October 1, 1947, while Sam Jaffe was on leave, the E.L.T. Committee and John Golden met to formulate plans for the coming season. All was progressing beautifully until a letter was delivered from George Freedley withdrawing the use of all libraries, not only for performances but rehearsals as well. *Equity Magazine* indicated the reason was that the libraries are being renovated and the work would require the whole '47-'48 season to complete.

However, according to Sam there was another reason for the abruptness of the withdrawal of the use of the libraries. "Terry Hayden tried to take over," he grumbled. "She began using chairs and cutting up things that belonged to the library and George Freedley complained about it."

The problem arose when the actors got a little enthusiastic about carving up furniture for use in sets. Apparently there was no supervision over the company and the disregard of library property was the reason E.L.T. had been thrown out of the library, in spite of what *Equity Magazine* reported.

Sam put the blame on Hayden. "We got her out," Sam announced, "because she took over. Then John Golden got us a chance to play on 41st St and it was Golden who was able to get one of the E.L.T. shows on the USO circuit abroad."

It is hard to know if what Sam says about Hayden's library property destruction is true. He says that she tried to take over and was ousted. Yet, most of those who offered their reflections of the time, remember Hayden as a tireless contributor. Also, following E.L.T.'s eviction from the libraries, Hayden, according to *Equity Magazine* E.L.T. accounts, remained active and wrote the E.L.T. entries with a byline.

Whatever the real reason for the loss of the libraries, the fact remained that the work of E.L.T. needed to continue somewhere. The news was an unexpected, sudden blow. Instead of making plans, they were forced to spend their time discussing how and where they could continue.

Sam returned to offer his assistance. Given the crisis, he had reason to be grateful for Aline MacMahon who, he said, "started taking actors out to do little scenes for organizations. She knew somebody in the educational system who let them use a high school in the Bronx and she could charge admission so the actors were able to earn some money. That was Aline's project.

"We tried to get into the Board of Education with the help of John Golden and we didn't succeed."

Aline MacMahon, interviewed at age 88, presented refreshing responses to questions about the period. In her memory Sam Jaffe was remarkable "with all the kinky hair and the intense expression and the Russian charm; that tall, slender, intellectual, intense Sam was somebody that I enjoyed very much."

MacMahon had come to know Sam over the years, especially after appearing in a film with Sam's sidekick Edward G. Robinson. MacMahon attended parties at Robinson's and she remembered how his mother would make strudel and have strands of dough hanging from every chair.

Aline and Sam became closer as each of them had fine acting work in common. He valued her opinion and would call, knowing that she would tell him precisely what she thought.

It was easy to understand Jaffe's attraction to MacMahon. She was such a warm storyteller; she took the listener inside the corridor of her memories to walk there with her. She recalled Sam's marrying and how very happy that had made him. She remembered him as a quiet person whose hosts would plan small and select parties when he was invited because Sam didn't like big parties.

MacMahon had been genuinely happy for Sam because he was a man of quality and he was having a fine career.

MacMahon was a bit of a radical herself and so it pleased her tremendously that Jaffe and Loeb requested her help when E.L.T. was stymied. She made a survey of all the high schools in the City of New York that had large halls of 600 to 1000 seats. They would be ideal places to put on plays. Her dream was to have every one of over 600 schools simply filled with actors playing for a dollar a performance at most. The dream didn't work because if they were to pay everybody connected with the project even a nominal fee, they couldn't sell tickets for $1.00.

MacMahon reported that there was also another difficulty: "The real theater on Broadway was not in love with our idea of competing with it on a rainy night. You could take the whole family around the corner and see Shaw, Yeats, and Granville Barker."

They were able to obtain only two high schools during that 1948 season: Central High School of the Needle Trades and Joan of Arc Junior High School. *Hamlet* was performed at the latter and presented a new problem to E.L.T. The April 1948 issue of *Equity Magazine* reports, "The production was open to the high school students of the city of New York and they filled the balcony at three of the four performances. Many of the students had never seen a live production before and were not acquainted with proper theater behavior. They would march up and down the aisles during performance and chat with each other as though they were attending a movie. At times the noise in the house drowned the performance on stage and we are most pleased to report that the cast was able to work right through the noise and turn out a good performance." Later productions at the school were confined to adult audiences.

MacMahon's school project continued for a few years during which time other aspects of E.L.T. continued to develop.

During the transitions, Sam Jaffe made himself available to go to bat for E.L.T. whenever something was needed. He gave his support quietly, slipping into meetings, making a few pithy statements that brought necessary changes into being, and slipping out again.

In the early years, when E.L.T. needed a kick start, Sam had gathered all his friends and dragged them all over New York to the libraries to see the plays. He wanted the companies to know that they were supported and he went backstage after the show to congratulate everyone.

Despite adversity and difficulty, E.L.T. continued to produce both in abundance and in quality. John Golden summed up E.L.T.'s accomplishments in a piece entitled

"Equity Library Was the 'Mostest' Theater" in *Equity Magazine*, June 1948:

"... In its five years of existence more than 700 actors, directors, technicians and others have secured good jobs from the showing they made in these plays.

"It should be made a part of the record that, in the name of Equity, this project has undoubtedly set a world's record ...

"E.L.T. outdid all other theatrical organizations as a showcase.

"E.L.T. has done more than any organization to help unemployed actors play 'parts against type.'

"E.L.T. has gotten more jobs for actors, and made places for others in the various crafts of our profession than any other project previously known."

E.L.T. had outdone all organizations seeking to create an interest in legitimate theater. "It has played matinees for thousands of students and teen-age youngsters and evening performances for their parents and older friends, under the city's Adult Recreation System.

"E.L.T. has given a start to scores of new players through its twenty percent non-Equity plan."

E.L.T. "... has presented more revivals of standard and classic plays, from Sophocles to Shakespeare, from Shaw to Sherwood, than any other, and all of them free."

E.L.T. had outdone all in producing plays for neighborhood audiences: "... two-hundred free presentations all around the City of New York. In many instances these neighborhood audiences were seeing living actors for the first time."

Sam Jaffe had been a mover and shaker. He had struggled on many fronts simultaneously for actors' rights and for basic human dignity. Ironically, those very struggles resulted in his "removal" (technically, his resignation, at the urging of union President Ralph Bellamy) in 1949 from chairmanship of the E.L.T. committee. The shadow of communist issues was rudely and unjustly cast across the path of his light-filled activities.

In 1948, there had been a struggle to raise chorus salaries from $40 to $45 and the actor's salary from $45 to $50 a week. At the time junior members were earning only $25. As the senior members' salary rose, producers hired only the juniors. Sam had abhorred the unfairness. "Merit should be the criterion," he said. "So we made one minimum, $40, and when we did that they said that we were killing the theater. Every time you had to raise a salary you were killing the theater. It was going to go bankrupt and be out of business."

If Sam were alive today he would bristle to know that the same philosophy is at play in the current precarious US economy. The line proclaimed today is: If we were to raise taxes on businesses they would go out of business!

Business clearly stays in business when it watches out for itself and seeks to serve its best interests. This is understood as both wise and practical. Yet, when artists struggled to have their best interests met, and their rights upheld, they were seen as self-seeking and as killing the theater; moreover, the union organizers who fought, in the 1940's, on the side of the artists were seen as communist-inspired and destructive of the American Dream.

"... As the cost of living went up," Sam continued, "we felt it was necessary to increase the minimum to $50 but, oh, it was hard work. That was when The Forum first met. The Forum instituted all the reforms." The union had been willing to settle for unsatisfactory working conditions for its members, but the vanguard, the radicals and dreamers, were not. Those visionaries were accused of wanting to kill the union.

Sam's involvement with The Forum, as indicated

in Lee J. Cobb's later testimony before H.U.A.C., was a major cause of his troubles. According to Jaffe, Ralph Bellamy "insisted that I get off the committee of E.L.T. Otherwise he said it wouldn't function. He claimed that he wouldn't be able to get money for the project because of me. He said the same thing to Aline MacMahon. He asked us, wouldn't we resign? Aline refused. She was smarter; a wonderful woman, a good actress and a person of great integrity. But I didn't want the project to come to nothing. ... I didn't want the project to suffer ... so I resigned."

The incident remains as part of the history of E.L.T. The last Managing Director, George Wojtasik, spoke of it with deep feeling: "Sam spent his entire life regretting that he had to leave the E.L.T. committee at the request of Ralph Bellamy. He said, 'If I had had as much guts as that lady did I would have stayed and fought for my beliefs.' He had been asked to leave due to McCarthy and blacklisting. The impression I got was that Sam was pushed out of council. You probably won't hear that from councilors. He put his tail between his legs and went to California. He never forgave himself for that. Other than that, we have always revered the fact that he was our founder."

Bettye confirmed that Sam felt he had made a mistake in yielding to Bellamy, but rather than having his tail between his legs, she stressed his choosing to refrain from damaging Equity Library Theatre. "He regretted it," Bettye confirmed, "but I wouldn't say he never forgave himself. Sam didn't hold on to things. That was one of the extraordinary things about him. He could express how he felt. He felt absolutely dreadful at the time. He didn't hold grudges. He was not bitter, even with people who named names. That was the extraordinary thing. He felt sorry for them."

Though Bettye is emphatic in her assessment of Sam, it is also true that Jaffe refused to speak to people who had done things to harm others during the blacklist times. In that case perhaps the lack of honor was a motivating factor.

On January 7, 1949, Sam received the following letter from the E.L.T. committee: "Dear Mr. Jaffe: At the last E.L.T. meeting the news of your resignation came as a great shock to us all. Immediately there was an anxious discussion about how we might be able to persuade you to return on your former active basis. Then we realized that you already had given your whole heart to E.L.T. and it would be wrong to make any further demands on you, except that you accept an honorary chairmanship of E.L.T. Respectfully,"

Sam commented, with pathos, "Then the honorary disappeared. Many people went on to become stars: Charlton Heston, Kim Stanley ..." His voice trailed off. His woundedness could be felt. He went into retreat, but those who got their start from what he birthed, zoomed forward into professional excellence.

There was such bitter sweetness here. Grand accomplishment met with subsequent dismissal. "I was supposed to have brought on the root of evil," Sam lamented, "because I was a 'communist' they said."

Countless people were falsely accused of being communist. It is no comfort to know that those who would fiercely defend the United States from a 'red threat' mount their horses and indiscriminately and maliciously stomp on honest, patriotic, decent, creative and contributing citizens in the process. The blind vigilante in his zeal is as dangerous as other subversives. Sam was among those trampled.

With Jaffe gone from E.L.T., actress Lyn Ely, who had volunteered to help reorganize E.L.T., found herself thrust into the position of running the whole operation. Although she had never spoken in public before, she was now responsible for informing the Equity membership meetings about the progress of E.L.T. She felt she had been thrown to the wolves because the whole thing fell into her lap. In the first year Ely had 30 shows to produce in about 30 weeks. "It was absolutely wild," she recalled, "but we did very good shows."

Ely became executive director and was the only paid employee for four years. A membership committee was developed and five subcommittees which chose plays, sought new avenues of employment for actors, and ran the shows. Their goal was to have a democratic organization run solely by actors for actors.

As Jaffe had struggled with union reactionaries, Ely fought their efforts to control the types of plays E.L.T. put on, as well as the directors of those plays. There were constant battles against blacklisting.

By September, 1949, after six years of functioning in libraries, schools and community facilities, E.L.T. was given its first permanent home at the Lenox Hill Playhouse in the seventies. Seating increased from 75 at the library theaters to 250. When that building was torn down, E.L.T. moved to its final location on 103rd and Riverside Drive.

Equity Library Theatre had become an institution, and it continued successfully for decades. Those whose careers had benefited from an E.L.T. appearance were called upon to support its continuance in its new home. Among the 12,000 alumni were Tony Randall, Lee Marvin, Sidney Poitier, Jo Van Fleet, Jason Robards, Rod Steiger, Gene Saks, Marvin Hamlisch and 100 more stars.

Equity Library Theatre outlived Sam Jaffe. A year after his death in the winter of 1985, E.L.T. staged a tribute for its founder with a production of *The Comedy of Errors*, dedicated to Sam. Bettye spoke on that occasion, affirming Sam's abiding love of what had transpired and flourished since 1943:

"E.L.T. was Sam's pride and joy. I believe he was

more proud of the role he played in founding E.L.T. than anything. It seems particularly appropriate that tonight we're seeing and enjoying a Shakespearean play because some years ago when Sam was asked why, since his degree was in engineering and mathematics, he became an actor, he said, 'because of the great literature.'"

The tribute was a perfect blend of opening night subscribers, loyal supporters, and friends and family. Bettye thanked everyone for attending and making it easier for her to be "severed from my bliss," as she put it.

Equity's Council voted unanimously that as an additional tribute to the work and contributions of Mr. Jaffe, the union would forgive a loan in the amount of $5,000 that had been granted to E.L.T. in 1967.

Karl Malden presented the theater with a bust of Sam sculpted by Bettye Jaffe. The bust was to be prominently displayed in the theater lobby. Malden said, "Anytime an actor is out of work, he can just come and rub his shoulder. I'm sure a more appropriate home couldn't have been found for this statue than within these four walls of the E.L.T. because to me it will always be the Sam Jaffe Theater."

There was more than a statue of Sam Jaffe in the lobby. There was the essence of Sam and all he stood for. Lyn Ely put it well at the dedication: "My first impression of Sam was as a person with a mystical presence. He seemed to materialize out of the ether when E.L.T. was being challenged. His presence always gave a perspective to those of us who were caught up in the tangled web of organizing E.L.T. during the vicious days of the McCarthy era. Here, today, I have a strong feeling that Sam might materialize at any moment."

Over forty years before, Julia Johnson had written: "If the results of this season, 1944-5, are any criteria, Equity Library will play an important part in the future of our American theater." It did indeed.

By 1986, George Wojtasik, its director for over 20

years, reported that it was a $600,000 operation running in the black. It ran nine months a year, had a fine credit rating and track record, and needed to add 116 seats in the balcony because they were over-reserved on all weekends. This is certainly reminiscent of the earliest shows in the library theaters when the request for tickets completely overwhelmed the seating capacity.

Sam Jaffe had never had any children; no one to carry on his name or his influence. Here, surely, was Sam's legacy: born of caring and innovation, raised with devotion, E.L.T. had matured into a fine, upstanding contributor to art.

Actress Ruth Warrick labeled E.L.T. the major contribution of Sam's life. This, in spite of the fact that she also knew that anyone who has ever seen Sam's High Lama portrayal has been affected by it.

"E.L.T. has had a profound effect on theater, giving people a chance to do things of merit when they couldn't get a job in the commercial theater. He founded it and kept it alive against many difficulties."

Sam's "baby" had come through the usual adolescent growing pains. In the early days, clothing and furniture was scrounged up to create the illusion of the setting. In the end, they had mounted sets and full costumes. George Wojtasik had spoken with pride: "We have our own scene shop and our own costume shop. Rental of costumes and scenery is what costs a fortune."

In the 1980's, participating actors got paid a $5 a day expense reimbursement. They made a career investment of eight weeks to do a showcase, but they did get seen by people in casting positions. And they did get cast. About 60 percent of people who did an E.L.T. show got cast directly or indirectly from their exposure in E.L.T.

Surely this statistic would deeply warm the heart of the founder who cared so much for his fellow actors and their need to work, and to be seen.

It is sad to record the footnote that on October 22, 1989, the Equity Library Theatre went bankrupt. The demise was quiet.

At the end, the organization was $250,000 in the hole. Part of the problem may have been that management departed from the sole original intent to showcase actors. There was a strain on the budget because directors and designers were now also being showcased. Translated into financial terms, productions began to cost between $60,000 and $70,000 each. In the beginning, productions were mounted humbly for $50. The projects had focused on creativity, not elaborateness.

Another of the original principles to die was free admission. E.L.T. took on the burden of attracting paying audiences. The new thrusts could not be sustained. Famous alumni were approached for funding and many of them did not respond as generously as they might have.

Equity Library Theatre had been the longest running producing company in New York history: 48 continuous years.

****

PAT CARROL got her start as an actress-comedienne doing two plays for E.L.T. She said, "It was a place where you could go and work! We didn't have a beautiful theater in those days. I walked into the costume room and said, 'My lord, we have to go out to the Salvation Army to get our own costumes.' We didn't have any money. We'd have to play a tambourine on the streets. But the play got done. To be able to go to a place that had faith, hope and heart for the theater and continues to do theater is a heck of a wonderful thing. It helps you to keep going."

****

MARTIN ROSS, *Once Upon a Mattress*, 1966

"I had done nothing but summer stock before E.L.T. I was desperate to get seen in New York. It was a wonderful production. We all felt very grateful to be a part of it.

"The caliber of the production stands out, the costumes, sets, the talent. Everything about it was comparable to a terrific off-Broadway experience for an audience.

"God bless the foresight of Sam. There weren't that many other testing grounds at the time."

[Ross went on to two and a half years on Broadway in *Cabaret* and then replaced Joel Gray in the lead.]

****

House Un-American Activities Committee

Sam Jaffe had spent the decade of the forties championing actors' rights. He and fellow actor Philip Loeb were an incomparable team on the floor of Actors' Equity Association. They fought tirelessly for just working conditions and artistic dignity. A class act, they 'starred' in a full bill of accomplishments from which performers still benefit today.

With the entrance of the fifties, Jaffe and Loeb, though they never auditioned for or deserved the assignment, found themselves cast as players in a tragedy about communism in America. Each struggled in his own way with the difficult role and, as with all heart-brothers, each suffered for the other.

The period was best summed up in this statement in the liberal magazine, *The New Republic*: "Five years of witch-hunts have left their mark on America. A whole generation of adults has come to believe that a man charged by slander is guilty until proved innocent; a whole generation of adolescents has come to identify 'Americanism' with complete and unthinking conformism; a whole generation of children has been taught by heart the Pledge of Allegiance to the flag and has no notion of what is written in the Bill of Rights. We are committed to the death against dictatorship by the state. We are moving toward our own form of death — dictatorship by society. Both suppress the individual mind and conscience; both deify the collective prejudice and fear. Between the two there is no final contrast; the difference is one of degree."

I was one of the children subjected to blind allegiance and to the fear of communism. My teachers were terrified for their jobs; they never challenged the hearings on television, the shameful tactics, or the slander. I was eleven, in junior high school, and no one taught me to question what was transpiring. It wasn't until I was in my 20's that the subject came up again because, for the first time, I met up with new, older friends who had suffered blacklisting. I felt ignorant. I was distressed that I had been betrayed by my educators and by my country. My commitment to justice for all rose like a flag; that flag became my focus of allegiance. I came to see as heroes and champions, those who stood up to McCarthyism, to "dictatorship by society." So strongly did I come to feel about this, I might as well have suffered the horror personally. Coming to know of how Sam Jaffe responded to this dastardly time in our nation's history served to bond me ever more deeply to this man of conscience and honor.

Together and separately, Sam Jaffe and Philip Loeb fought the accusations that they were communists with all the means at their disposal. It would have been easier if there could have been a face to face confrontation with the adversary. In this case, the trampled were doing battle with the times in which they lived. These times included the aftermath of war, the glamour of patriotism, the birth of a brand new medium, network television, and its relationship to the all-important world of advertising.

It is hard, even for one who knew life-before-television, to conceive that big business was not sure of the future of the "new coaxial cable" in 1953. Nor was it sure of the safety of investing the large amounts necessary to use television for advertising. It was intolerable, therefore, to have any question raised about products, especially if their corporation was to be linked with anti-

Americanism. If big business sponsored a show, it was imperative that everyone connected with it be "clean."

Sam Jaffe and Philip Loeb carried the label "unclean." They joined the thousands of innocents whose careers were ruined and whose reputations were crushed by the anti-communist paranoia. Political vises entrapped them and shook them mercilessly until they would break, or break free.

From the very beginning of his acting career, Sam Jaffe's work was well received. One role led naturally to another, rewarding him with excellent personal reviews. In the 1930's he was held in esteem on the Broadway stage and in motion pictures as well. His career had momentum and he was on track toward becoming an important star.

No one lives in a vacuum. The times and circumstances in which we live affect us all. Alas for Jaffe, a destructive track in the nation ran parallel to the productive unfolding of his career.

At the end of World War II in 1945, President Truman sent word to Hollywood that it was to depict the United States favorably. The world was not to know of any internal difficulties on this shore, of any crises such as poverty, poor housing, or discrimination. The stars and stripes had survived a perilous fight. The White House wanted the "propaganda" to go forth that the land of the free and the home of the brave was unscathed. Fostering positive images of the United States seemed to be the President's way of combating the aggressive Soviet expansion in the world.

By 1945, Sam Jaffe had become a household name through *Gunga Din* and *Lost Horizon*. In addition, he had been a smash success as Kringelein and was appearing in *Cafe Crown* to superb personal reviews. Jaffe had endured the death of his beloved Lillian, suffered a year of profound grief, and had just re-entered his craft. As he was in the process of rebuilding his life, the nation itself was entering disintegrating political paranoia.

The Communist Party in the United States had dissolved in 1944. This did not appease those who believed reds had overrun Hollywood. They formed the Motion Picture Alliance for the Preservation of American Ideals. They felt Franklin Delano Roosevelt had been leading the country into communism because they assessed federal welfare programs were socialistic. They believed that unionism was an example of the left seeking to stir up the proletariat against the free enterprise system.

In the view of member-actors Gary Cooper, Robert Taylor, Adolphe Menjou, John Wayne and Ward Bond, and columnist Hedda Hopper, the red attack on Hollywood was real. They sought to defend its honor against those who were disloyal. To head their organization, they hired Martin Dies, investigator of red influences in Hollywood. They paid him $50,000, and they instigated a campaign by Washington conservatives to investigate communists in Hollywood.

Jaffe had thrown himself wholeheartedly into union activities. He and his best friend Philip Loeb were deeply involved in serving the humanitarian needs of their fellow actors. Little did they know that their spade work would be used to dirty their reputations.

By 1947, the situation intensified. The big studios needed financial assistance from major corporations and banks. They could not afford to offend. President Truman continued putting image-creation pressure on the Hollywood community, making patriotism all-important.

Following *Cafe Crown*, Sam appeared in the films *13 Rue Madeline* in 1946 and *Gentleman's Agreement* in 1947. He also continued his stage work in *The Greatest of These* and *This Time Tomorrow*. He was not yet being directly affected by the burgeoning witch hunt, but he was not unfamiliar with it either. The ambushers had already been after Philip Loeb for two years and Sam stood by his side and defended his honor at Actors' Equity meetings.

The successful prosecution of the Alger Hiss case in 1948 launched the House Un-American Activities Committee into national prominence. The committee was under the direction of Chairman J. Parnell Thomas. An ambitious young Congressman named Richard Nixon joined the staff. Attorney General Tom Clark and FBI Director J. Edgar Hoover supported the committee's power. The committee had access to the so-called Attorney General's List. It was a checklist of organizations that held supposed totalitarian, fascist, communist or "any other subversive views."

Originally compiled as an internal guide for use in screening Federal employees, the Attorney General's list later became the backbone of the witch hunts and a prime weapon of Senator Joseph McCarthy. McCarthy took over when J. Parnell Thomas was found guilty of payroll padding and taking kickbacks. Although he went to prison as a common felon, few people in the United States raised their voices in protest that this man had falsely accused people of principle and ruined their lives. When McCarthy replaced Thomas, things got even worse.

Sam Jaffe and Philip Loeb were among those who suffered as a result. Sam's emotions always flared when called upon to remember the forties and fifties. "[Ronald] Reagan fingered people for McCarthy when he was President of the Screen Actors Guild. That's a fact. I don't want to think of that period. Leave me alone."

The building of a career is a fragile process. Sam had begun his climb on Broadway in the late twenties. His successes led naturally to a string of profound performances in the thirties. It was in the forties that Sam Jaffe might have leapt from featured roles to character roles, and then to stardom. But he was grey-listed because of his union activities. Questions had been raised about his patriotism, and gray is a dulling color when applied to a budding career. It is hard to know how much his theatrical evolution was stifled by the whispers and edicts of the faceless powerful.

Sam Jaffe walked forward in his career, though he dragged the chains of accusation behind him. In his heart he preserved culture, goodness, and strength. Like the Grand Lama, he created a Shangri-La within the unyielding chambers of his soul. And, like Gunga Din, he continued with unwavering courage in the face of any onslaught.

The forties began a critical decade which tested the man. Were he not firm in his beliefs, he could easily have turned hopeless, if not bitter, and collapsed under the brutality of tyrants.

Sam Jaffe was not breakable. Each time he was decked by a dirty punch, he rose to his feet and stood in his integrity. He always went on, and forward. Hollywood made choices about when and whether to hire him, choices based on politics rather than talent and appropriate casting. Sam maintained his inner power by also making choices. He was careful and deliberate about the roles he selected. Whenever possible, Sam Jaffe made a statement with his work and his life.

Sam continued making movies, including *Rope of Sand* and *Under the Gun*, and reached the height of his career with his brilliant portrayal of a master criminal in *The Asphalt Jungle*. He won the Venice International Film Award as best actor of the year and the Academy Award nomination for best supporting actor. He didn't win the Oscar, perhaps because actor Ward Bond took an ad out in *Variety*, the show business trade paper, saying the Academy should not give Sam the award because he was a red. After years of development as an artist, Sam Jaffe had reached a pinnacle of his career only to fall victim to guilt by association.

An insidious publication, *Red Channels: The Report of Communist Influence in Radio and Television*, was compiled in June of 1950. It is hard to see how anyone could have taken *Red Channels* seriously since at one and the same time it served as detective agency, prosecuting attorney, judge, and jury. First it published allegations. Then it pressured viewers to write to sponsors to keep the accused off the air. Kenneth M. Bierly, a co-collaborator of *Red Channels*, admitted there had been no attempt to categorize whether the performers were reds, dupes of communists, or innocents who kept dubious company. Everyone was lumped together.

Many prominent commentators saw *Red Channels* for what it was and were not afraid to take a stance against it. John Crosby, in his Radio and Television column, *New York Herald Tribune*, November 19, 1952, in a piece entitled "Moral Cowardice," wrote:

"... This small booklet, which lists the names of the supposed Communist-front or leftist affiliation of 151 radio and TV performers, directors, writers and producers, has won the almost universal editorial condemnation of the United States press.

"No sponsor, no advertising agency man and no producer will come to the public defense of *Red Channels* and practically nobody will admit to using it as a blacklist. Its chief editor, Theodore Kirkpatrick (whose official title is secretary-treasurer of American Business Consultants, Inc. which published *Red Channels*) is on record as saying, 'We've never said the facts in *Red Channels* were correct or incorrect.' Many of the 'facts' were culled from the *Communist Daily Worker* or other bizarre sources — considering that the booklet is supposed to be violently anti-Communist in nature — and Mr. Kirkpatrick [a former member of the FBI whose name his organization freely uses for exploitation] has confessed that no attempt was made to check the allegations.

"... *Red Channels*, which almost nobody in the business approves of or trusts, is still in the secret library of all the ad agencies and is still at the elbow of casting directors for TV and radio, and has immeasurably damaged the reputations and careers of the people listed in it.

"The *Red Channels* blacklist is employed simply as a device to stay out of trouble with everybody as a matter of — in the most cynical use of the phrase — public relations.

"This is appalling moral cowardice. The livelihoods of a great many people are being destroyed by a cynical disregard for the most elemental standards of fair play ... without trial, without a hearing, without redress."

Red Channels listed Sam Jaffe and Philip Loeb because of organizations they supported. The listing was tantamount to their not working. Sam spoke heatedly about the unfairness: "There was also an association called Aware and they got the sponsors to back them. If you got a job, they'd call the sponsor and you'd be out. You'd be told the show has been changed. There was an axis between New York and Hollywood. When they condemned somebody in New York, the same was true in Hollywood.

"The various organizations I belonged to had marvelous names at the top, like The Honorable Charles Evans Hughes, Chief Justice of the Supreme Court [1930-1941] and Mrs. Eleanor Roosevelt. Look through *Red Channels* and you'll see some of the finest people in all the so-called communist-dominated groups."

Sam Jaffe had signed various petitions supporting humanitarian causes. The sponsoring organizations were labeled communist and Sam was kept from working.

After a 35-year career, begun at age 24 with the Washington Square Players, Jaffe was denied the fruits of his success. Sam spoke quietly of the period. "Once you were stained that way, people were afraid of you. There was a period during which people would look under the bed to see if there was a communist. I think it was one of our Secretaries of the United States who was so afraid that the communists were coming that he jumped out of a window and got killed.

"I had wanted to sue Ward Bond for calling me a communist and preventing me from winning the Academy Award for *Asphalt Jungle*. I was advised not to sue. There had been a previous suit that cost $20,000 and when they went to court all they got was a hung jury. The lawyer told him no jury would vindicate him. They'd be afraid that they would be attacked." Sam laughed as he continued. "What a crazy world this is. I often think that Shaw was right, that this planet is the lunatic asylum for the rest of the firmament."

During the 1950's, as the "red menace" stalked the nation, fear of a communist takeover led to an ironically un-American campaign to protect the American way. For example, on college campuses the Federal Bureau of Investigation employed the Nazi technique of recruiting student informers to expose radical utterances by professors. Simultaneously they enlisted the help of professors in identifying students who expressed subversive thoughts.

Supreme Court Justice William O. Douglas addressed this matter head-on in 1951. "Fear (in America) has mounted — fear of losing one's job, fear of being investigated, fear of being pilloried. This fear has driven many thoughtful people to despair. This fear has even entered our universities ... We have the spectacle of university officials lending themselves to one of the worst kinds of witch-hunts we have seen since our early days."

The fear of communism seemed to be a fear that democracy was not substantial enough to stand on its own and survive. The thrust of the anti-communist movement in the media, as well as in the esteemed Congress of the United States, was to inflict indiscriminate guilt. Smear tactics were used, such as labeling and name calling. One of the most basic of constitutional rights, namely, that one is innocent unless proven guilty, was eschewed.

Sam Jaffe, a great lover of the United States, lamented: "Blacklisting is a stain on America. It was like the witch hunts in Massachusetts. People had the theory that if they got someone out [of work] there would be room for them. This was their chance.

"The FBI would follow me home and ask me questions as if I was really a communist. They would never talk to you inside, only outside the building so that the neighbors could hear everything."

Sam realized that he was blacklisted when he couldn't get a job. Barred from television and films, he lamented, "They didn't hire anyone who was stained a little bit. Once you were stained you were finished. You were killed, so to speak."

The witch hunters used devious means to keep people from working. First Jaffe was signed for a role in *The Congressman* at MGM. Soon after, Jaffe lost the job because his name registered "unacceptable." The producers lied, saying script changes eliminated the need for Jaffe's services. They honored his former contract by paying him his agreed-upon fee. However, when Sam saw the completed film, the role he was to have played was there intact and unchanged. This technique was prevalent in television as well.

Jaffe had been fired without being fired; condemned without ground. He explained, "There was guilt by association. Not that they meant in any way to harm you, oh no. (He laughed sardonically.) But you suffered as a result of it.

"I was never a communist, but I did believe in free ideas. If you don't like the government, it's your business to change it, as long as you don't do anything overt."

Once the doors started to close, the process increased rapidly. The longer it continued the more desperate people were to work. Some were able to buy their way out. One congressman took money surreptitiously. There was another way out. The committee wanted the accused to name names. Names of communists were acceptable, even those previously named by others. Even the names of dead communists could serve as clearance! Sam didn't know any communists because he wasn't a communist. Even if he could have supplied names knowing that he would be able to work again, he would have refused.

He proclaimed, "I wouldn't go for it. I got poorer and poorer and I lived off my sisters. I stayed with them." It wasn't long before Jaffe was $7,000 in debt.

There were others like Jaffe who refused to name names, and a few would not remain silent in the face of the boot-stomping of character. Tom Paine reported in his newspaper column, "It took a playwright, Elmer Rice, to stage the first major rebellion against the radio and television industry's blacklist of suspected communists, former communists and present or former holders of liberal opinions.

"Rice quit the Celanese Theater program when the ad agency representing the sponsor refused to cast an actor (reported to be John Garfield, stage and screen star) in the leading role in Rice's *Counsellor-At-Law* because of his supposed political beliefs.

"'I don't care what the actor's political beliefs are, as long as he fits the part for which he is cast.' Rice declared." Each time a person took a stand such as this, it cost him work. To those of principle, justice was more important than money.

For the next five years, as a result of his staunch belief in democracy and his refusal to cooperate with the un-American activities of the house committee, Jaffe was an unemployed film actor. At the height of his career, character assassins obsessed with an omnipresent red enemy had pulled the plug on his follow spot. However, Sam, labeled a communist and a communist-sympathizer without proof, and denied work as a result, stood like David against a Goliath adorned in abusive patriotism. He was unshakable.

Sam loved Philip Loeb deeply. Sam loved deeply. When drawn to someone, he made lasting friendships, as if he had made a commitment. He was a champion and supporter of those he loved, giving of himself in all ways and with unwavering devotion.

Loeb's name in *Red Channels* represented the beginning of the end of his career. The listings appeared without verification. They came from organizational letterheads or mention in communist publications. Among other things, he was "accused" of sponsoring the baseball committee to end Jim Crow and of speaking at a Stop-Censorship Committee. They said he was a member of the Executive Board of the American Committee to Aid Spanish Democracy. The innocuous list goes on.

Loeb was in a particularly sensitive position because he was playing a leading role on television. Actors with even remotely questionable backgrounds were highly vulnerable because television was dependent on sponsors. Actors were at the mercy of a 63-year-old grocer from Syracuse, New York, named Lawrence A. Johnson who had assumed the role of inquisitor. It was difficult to fathom, but he could make or break the careers of anyone he chose.

Who was Johnson? What motivated him? How could he have risen from grocer to overlord, shackling the careers of hundreds he never knew and who were guilty of nothing?

Born on a farm in 1889 in Savannah, N. Y., Johnson was a high school dropout. He became a farm hand, then a grocer, and then founder of the second-earliest supermarket in the East and developer of a chain of four successful stores.

Johnson's story shows how time and circumstance can catapult an ordinary man from a minor urban center into a position of inordinate power. With no qualifications or credibility, one can become an authority. Fear, especially of financial loss, can lead to abandonment of the very democracy that is supposedly being defended.

The rise of a Lawrence Johnson occurs when the general population allows powerful people to say anything, to degrade anyone, to slur, without challenge, question, or outrage. It can happen when the term liberal is snidely maligned as "the L word." It can happen when a majority of the population replaces thoughtfulness with flag-waving. The nation becomes a football field where the highest value is placed on rooting for the home team rather than demanding fairness and honor in the game being played.

Johnson's ascent to a position from which he could trample persons and careers is the story of what happens when the people of a nation divide themselves into "we" and "they." It happens when people are beaten to the ground and the bystanders say it's a shame, but turn their heads because it is not happening to them.

Oliver Pilat wrote a revealing series of articles in *The New York Post*, beginning in January 1953, exposing Johnson's background and tactics:

"Johnson became entangled emotionally in radio-TV matters ... through his daughter, Eleanor Buchanan, wife of a lieutenant Marine in Korea.

"Early in 1951, Mrs. Buchanan began making speeches before Syracuse groups such as the Lions, the Kiwanis and the Sons of the American Revolution (of which her father was a member). She denounced the communists at home and their 'dupes' who were soliciting funds, she said, for eventual use against her husband in Korea.

"A pretty, dramatic woman with a suppressed dream of acting, Mrs. Buchanan made quite a hit. She was encouraged enough to try a mail campaign. One of her letters, issued June 8, 1951, began like this:

"'To the Lady of the House: Won't you join me? No money, no pledge signing, nor club membership is involved.

"'I am the wife of a marine fighting in far-off Korea ... Are you aware that some of your money is being paid to communist supporters operating behind his lines?'

"... After her husband got out she had one final fling at propaganda in an effort to force Hollywood to restrict movie hiring to members of her own 'white list' of actors and actresses guaranteed to be without political stain."

Johnson organized The Veterans Action Committee of Syracuse Supermarkets that sent a communication to "All Supermarket, Chain and Independent Operators, Buyers, Merchandisers and Everyone Concerned with the Retail Food Industry." It said, "Do you realize you are helping the communists? How? By pushing the products of certain manufacturers who employ those people in their radio and television advertising who have contributed to communism and communist front activities."

So it was that Lawrence A. Johnson, with no more than a tenth grade education, brought great talents, good persons, and fine minds to their knees. While they were down, he told them in his dialect, to "Go and be good Amur-ricans."

Johnson's major concern, in his own words, was how to keep "Stalin's little creatures from crawling over our supermarket products." This man was a determining factor in whether men such as Sam Jaffe, Philip Loeb, and hundreds of others were able to work in film and television.

Television writer Sy Gomberg, who spoke of himself as a spectator of the blacklist, said he didn't really know what was going on. "I'd come right out of the army and into the motion picture business. I didn't know why, but I saw people disappear, people who had been at the writer's table with me. But you were helpless in the face of what was going on in this country. We were living in hysteria, in a witch hunt period. When it finally faded it was something you didn't want to bring up anymore. Sam and I talked about people who had disappeared.

"Writers and producers, who were not visually recognized, could find some way to go on, under different names. Actors couldn't do it. Sam told me of some of the tragedies of people he'd known."

Gomberg remembered Jaffe as "a gentle man who had a firm belief in what this country was based on. He suffered because he believed in what the constitution said. He stood by his principles. Sam was a compassionate and decent man. We saw shocking things happen. One writer named 135 people. Can you imagine what he did to those lives? I had been fighting fascism for four years and we suddenly had it here."

A classic example of the tragedy descending on performers was John Henry Falk, a country singer. His daytime show was dropped suddenly when he ran on the anti-*Red Channels* slate in the Actor's Guild. Everyone who opposed the slate suffered. The Aware group reached the sponsors who canceled Falk. It came as a shock to him because he knew how popular his show was.

Falk investigated and took possession of a letter sent from Johnson the grocer to Falk's sponsors. The letter represented evidence of who was directing the blacklist against performers. Louis Nizer represented Falk in his suit. Nizer refused a fee. The case finally came to trial after many years, but by that time John Henry Falk had cancer. Nizer subpoenaed Johnson, but his lawyers presented documents saying he was too sick to appear. Falk had asked for a million and a half dollars in damages. The jury came in asking for much more than that.

As irony would have it, someone rushed into the court-
room with the news that Johnson had been found dead
only a few blocks from the court house. He had been in a
hotel directing the attorneys. Falk ended up with nothing
beyond the decision.

This was a period when flag-wavers grew gro-
tesquely large fingers of accusation. One such man was
Roy Cohn. Throughout his life, those who knew or met
him found him difficult, or arrogant, or self-centered and
very demanding. His way was the only way. Roy was
his mother's little prince. His parents had a miserable
marriage. His mother was extremely domineering and
neurotic. Early on, Roy learned to play his divided parents against each other. He would look to see which one
was on his side, and that was the one he would use.
His father was a judge. At 16, Roy would trade on his
father's name and influence by threatening anyone who
stood in his way. He always knew somebody who knew
something or someone, and manipulated that to his best
advantage.

Roy Cohen and HUAC called Loeb and Jaffe to cas-
tigation. Power reigned over intelligence, decency and
achievement. Loeb and Jaffe had backgrounds of scho-
lastic accomplishment and resumes of artistic contribution. Cohn hadn't distinguished himself at college. Columbia Law School rejected him until political pull by his
father got him admitted. That pull saved him from being
drafted in 1945, when others were shipped to France. He
served his own ends rather than his country, and then
later became a self-appointed judge of others' patriotism.

In 1951 Joseph McCarthy took up the issue of disloyalty in government. Using the by then well-recognized
anti-communist battle cry, he made himself the single
most powerful politician in the country. He and J. Edgar
Hoover determined whether one was a communist, a pa-

triot, or a subversive, as well as who deserved employment and the right of a passport.

Roy Cohn joined McCarthy in 1953 and together they used, indeed abused, the great power they had. They did this even though there was an almost embarrassing dearth of communists. The exposure of so-called reds had begun in 1946 and sensationalism had run its course. Nonetheless, they managed to arrange and conduct televised congressional marathons beginning in April of 1954. The objects of their witch hunt were usually persons whose political activity had peaked well over a decade before when humanitarian idealism, not subversion, was the focus. The past was artificially and inappropriately spotlighted in the present and made to seem conspiratorial and injurious in the now moment. Sam Jaffe was ensnared in precisely this way.

Those of like energy frequency fill the voids created by circumstances. Truman had initiated image-making. In Roy Cohn the government had an expert image-maker who invented and shaped the self he wanted the world to see. Furthermore, a major aim of HUAC was publicity-grabbing. Roy Cohn brought superb qualifications toward this end. As a lawyer, he was remembered much more for his publicity than for his convictions.

Nicholas von Hoffman states in *Citizen Cohn*, "Roy stole upward of a million dollars from the City of New York ..." He also says that Roy Cohn was not above fixing clerks or tampering with witnesses, that he acted as if he owned the courts, and that he was involved in skimming and cheating New York City out of parking lot moneys. This Roy Cohn was the very same man who later, in the 1980's, received the Americanism Award at a Washington reception and had President Reagan congratulate him through video.

Roy Cohn had friends in high places, powerful big shots who came to his aid later on when the legal committee considered disbarring him. A 59th birthday party was thrown for him by a New York real estate billion-aire; the guest list included Lee Iacocca, Donald Trump, and Helen Gurley Brown. When Cohn underwent surgery for liver cancer, he received a telegram saying: "I just learned that you are being sent home from the hospital. Nancy and I are keeping you in our thoughts and prayers. May our Lord bless you with courage and strength. Take care and know that you have our concern." The signature was "Ronald Reagan."

Sam Jaffe and Philip Loeb were not communists, but they were Jewish. Roy Cohn disliked all communists, but he hated Jewish communists most of all. He lived by the distorted belief that while all Jews were not communists, most communists were Jews. He spent his life trying to prove that whereas he was a Jew, he was one who was not a communist.

Roy Cohn was a prime example of the low quality of person who sought to discredit Sam Jaffe, Philip Loeb, and countless others who had graced the young television medium with their artistry. They were now replaced on the small but influential screen by the power-hungry who fed off their established careers.

Throughout these trials, Sam Jaffe retained his dignity. He continued to be the innovative man of integrity he always had been. His accomplishments could not be dimmed by false accusation; neither could his spirit.

Nonetheless, Sam Jaffe suffered. He suffered in his heart, in his career, and most all, for his friends.

****

JEAN STAPLETON, *The Corn Is Green*, 1946

"*E.L.T. was the prologue to my first big professional job [a national tour of* Harvey]. *It was a milestone for me because I was unknown. I was just a struggling actor in New York City seeking anything I could get.*

"*I had been doing stock in New Hampshire and got my Equity card, but I was totally unknown.*

"*I was cast in a very small part. Equity Library Theatre meant showcase and that was just perfect then. I knew the director, Ted Post, from some project I had done. I went down for it even though it was a very tiny role because I was so depressed about not working. I went in hopes of playing Mrs. Watty, the character role. I always did character roles, even as a very young woman. I was offered the smaller part of a Welsh woman. It wasn't a showcase role but I took it.*

"*The woman who was doing Mrs. Watty broke her leg. They asked me to fill in until they recast it. I was furious. I felt injustice reigned. I went to my room; I was living with my parents and sought direct help from the Bible which is what I normally turn to in distress. I found a verse from Jeremiah that says, 'The Lord is our judge, the Lord is our King, he will save us.' It was as if a light went on. This is where justice came from, not from any person. That was the source. It cured all my anger and, believe me, it was blind. What fell away was blind ambition.*

"*Then I was able to turn to the role of Mrs. Watty and be of some help, gladly. It was a week before we opened. It was eventually played by someone who was the right age for it. She was in it for a day or two and the producer, Diana Hunt, called me and asked me to do the role of Mrs. Watty. I had found my true sense of humility, the ability to be selfless about this whole thing.*

"*I went to the first rehearsal and the first thing Ted Post said to me was, 'Jean, you're not really right for this part.' It didn't bother me one bit. I said to myself, here is my proof where justice lies because I didn't have to change Ted Post's mind to have this great blessing. Without rancor I went on and did the part.*

"*Lots of people came to E.L.T. then. One of them was an agent named Sara Enright, one of the pillars of the agents in New York. Every agent's name was on a list when they attended and it was given to us. I went in to see her. She told me to go see Brock Pemberton who was casting the* road company of Harvey with Frank Fay. I did and I got the part of Myrtle Mae. That was a bonanza because I had never been west of New Jersey. We went all across the country, about 84 weeks of work, saw the whole country by train. We even went up to British Columbia.

"The tour was financially helpful to a very poor family struck by the depression. I sent money home. That whole experience in E.L.T. has fed me through the years. I'm very grateful."

****

The Worst of Times

Sam Jaffe felt strongly about the vile injustice being committed during the communist witch hunts, but no single emotion consumed him. What made him different from many was that he was usually able to see a larger picture. This helped him to keep from going under.

Jaffe took what work he could, principally in stage productions. He held his head above water despite rising levels of despair.

Florida Friebus, long-time actress and Actors' Equity Association Council member, recalled Sam in the midst of his suffering. Sam had been living in a beautiful Waverly Place apartment in Greenwich Village. The blacklist forced him to move to the Upper East Side, in the '90's, because he didn't have any money.

He asked Florida to help him with the relocation. "We were moving his possessions from this high-type home to a lesser one," Friebus recalled, "and he didn't rail or express his frustration or misery, which he must have felt. The thing he said was, and this was very typical, 'I think there will come a time when the American people are going to be ashamed of this period.' That was a type of overall look at the terrible situation, while moving little kitchen things. That was a very Sam Jaffe thing."

Jaffe did more than take philosophical stands on the blacklist. He was capable of expressing raging temper, and he did. During a council meeting at Actors' Equity, Frank Fay accused Jaffe of being a communist and it made Sam so angry that he began to throttle him. Sam, a former boxer, was very strong and powerful. Lunging at Fay, he laid him out on a desk and raised his hand in readiness to "slaughter him." Then Jaffe got hold of himself and stopped before smashing Fay. It was a frightening moment for those present; very untypical of Jaffe's normal behavior.

When Sam told the story, he laughed because of his great output of energy and expression. Perhaps he was laughing at himself for getting so riled up. Perhaps it was embarrassment. He remarked that Fay had been ready to kill him with the accusation. "He did kill me, actually, for a while," Sam said with seriousness.

During his years of being out of work he had lived on the money he had saved during his earlier successes. Being blacklisted caused him to use up all his resources and go into debt, but it did not change his generosity. He told his second wife Bettye the following story. At one point, Sam was down to $4,000.00 and he was going to a dentist who persuaded him that he could double the money in an investment. Sam had a friend, Herbert Rabinowitz, a brilliant lawyer who worked under Justice Felix Frankfurter. Jaffe loved Rabinowitz, who painted, played the piano, wrote, and read seven newspapers a day. Rabinowitz remembered everything he read, as did Jaffe.

Sam told Rabinowitz that he had turned over his $4,000.00 to his dentist, $2,000.00 in Zero's name and $2,000.00 in his own name, so that each would then have $4,000.00. What this story reveals about Sam is that even when he was down to his last $4,000.00, he was as concerned for his friend Zero's welfare as he was for his own.

Obviously, Rabinowitz knew something about the dentist that enabled him to caution Jaffe. He told Sam to go immediately and sit in that dentist's office until he got his money back. He scared them enough that Sam and Zero went right over carrying their lunches. Told the dentist wasn't in, they waited and ate their sandwiches and drank their milk. He finally came out and gave them a check for the $4,000.00. They hugged the check, ran to the bank and told them to pass it through this minute. The dentist went bankrupt two days later.

It was around this time that Sam began depending on his sisters for financial support. Simultaneously he held out hope that something would happen to enable him to work.

Bettye recalled that by the time she came along, "Sam was at his lowest ebb. He hadn't worked in about seven years. He was in debt to his sister Annie, and the FBI was following him home and harassing him."

Yet, 40 years later Sam would talk about friends and what they had suffered. He would never talk about himself and what he experienced. Some friends wondered if he avoided things that were personally painful by telling stories about others. He didn't readily reveal his personal life. Many people learned more about Sam from Bettye than from Sam.

Sam called the blacklist a blight on our country. However, he reminded people that worse than the blacklist and its repercussions would be to turn bitter and lose confidence. This could result in internal scarring. During the black days, he always advised others to work where they could because the plague couldn't last forever.

Sam believed that to carry anger toward those who were destroyers would be to become as filled with hate as they were. To see instead that this would one day be a cause for shame was to stay clear, and true to himself, even as the poison dart punctured his life and career.

Sam was indignant for the country, for himself, and for everyone who was in the same situation. However, he didn't succumb to acrimony and would invariably turn the subject to something lighter.

Hollywood writer Lou Garfinkle affirmed that Sam responded differently from others: "I never heard him lash out. He hated what happened to Phil Loeb. He told that story to me at least ten to fifteen times, always in a little different way to point out something to me. I never got the impression Sam had any political bias in favor of Russia or communism. I think he was improperly black-listed, if one can say that it was proper to blacklist any-one. He felt it was a terrible injustice to those who had a right to their own opinions."

Garfinkle called Sam a ridgepole of conscience, belief and knowledge who could handle any kind of attri-tion. People who were not as strong at the center couldn't handle such beating about the head.

While he was not acrid, Sam Jaffe's ability to hold a philosophical view did not lull him into acquiescence. Quoted in *Film Comments* in December 1987, Jaffe re-flected, "There were signs in the casting rooms that any-body who was on any of the lists need not apply. In mov-ies, agents were told not to present your name if you were on a list. It was an unfortunate period ... a witch-hunt period.

"You see, in our country a label changes every-thing. You take a bottle of champagne and instead put 'piss' on it, and people won't drink it. Labels are a ter-rible thing, and they tried to smear me with the label of 'communist,' which I never was. Not that I had anything against communism or communists. . . . I couldn't care what anybody else was. You did what you thought was the right thing. Some people were joiners and others weren't. I was not a joiner or a Jonah. I believed in doing what I felt would help the advancement of good in this world, and I hoped I did what was right."

Sam's brother-in-law, Robert Ackerman, had many talks with Sam about the subject. "He didn't ex-press personal bitterness, but it was bitterness, or dis-appointment, that it could happen. I think he never un-derstood it. He was puzzled by it. I don't think he liked to be puzzled. He wanted to understand it. I don't think he ever did."

Jaffe saw the witch hunts as a contradiction of

what he thought the United States ought to be about. It was important to him that his country filled a special mission of tolerance, an encouragement of creativity and freedom. The McCarthy era defied it. Jaffe wanted his country to encourage and permit a degree of freedom not enjoyed in the rest of the world.

Ackerman concluded, "He was never at peace with the fact that he considered himself to be that kind of patriot and that he was victimized by a movement that defied explanation. He was convinced, of course, that many people hid behind patriotism, that it allowed people to be mean, to be little. He was disturbed by that paradox, that patriotism, in a country with a strong commitment to freedom, allowed people to practice the reverse.

"I don't think he ever allowed himself to be disillusioned about America. Maybe that's the most remarkable thing. If he'd been disillusioned he wouldn't have been at all interested in voting. Sam couldn't understand persons who would not go and exercise their citizenship by voting."

Horrendous things happened during the blacklist times. Front page headlines declared Frederick March a communist and he spent over a quarter of a million dollars in legal costs to clear his name. The clearance appeared in the news as a tiny blurb on the back page.

Karl Malden recalled how Sam suffered and how miserable he was. "He couldn't get a job," Malden lamented, "and that is the most degrading thing you can do to a man who is healthy, strong, and vital."

There was nothing Malden could do to help his friend. "I was nobody," he said sadly. Malden was one of those unaffected by the blacklist. He was able to work, but he watched as people disappeared. One day Martin Ritt was directing at CBS. The next day they told him he couldn't work there anymore. No one knew to whom it would happen next.

Sam Jaffe said, a few years before his death, that he knew what dying was all about because he went through the blacklist. That's how terrible it was. And, when asked if he thought it could happen again, he remarked that what we really learn from history is that we learn nothing from history.

Karl Malden related that while Sam Jaffe had given up after Lillian's death, he did not give up during the blacklist. He chose to fight instead. Malden remembered, "Sam went to every goddamn Equity meeting. He was on the board and he got up on that platform. It wasn't easy to be there with the rest of the members knowing he was blacklisted."

While the networks blocked Jaffe from single television appearances, conditions were worse for Philip Loeb. He had created the role of Papa on *The Goldbergs*, sponsored by General Foods Corporation. It was a very successful show and they fired Loeb even though he vigorously denied any communist affiliation and demanded a hearing to refute the "charges."

The demand was not met because, as Oliver Pilat clearly painted the circumstantial predicament in The *New York Post*, "There is usually no way for a man to grapple with the blacklist. He can't face charges if there are no charges. Where there has been no formal accusation, formal clearance becomes impossible."

Loeb had been earning $20,000 in 1952, a big salary in its time. Over half of it went to the care of his son who had some years before become schizoid. Jaffe cared very much about Philip and his son and did everything he possibly could to help. Rather than pour his energy into recrimination, Jaffe sought to be constructive in the service of his friends.

Loeb appealed to Actors' Equity, which he himself had served tirelessly for 16 years, and to the Television Authority. Both vowed to support Loeb. Despite Loeb's popularity and the support of the show's producer and star, Gertrude Berg, he was offered a large buyout rather than an ongoing contract. NBC had demanded Loeb's removal from the cast because it was impossible to find a sponsor who would allow him to work. The reasons given were the 17 items listed beside Loeb's name in *Red Channels*. It was an open case of blacklisting, clearer than any that had appeared previously. Victims needed such proof to attack the vile practice.

Actors' Equity and the Television Authority had vowed to stand behind Loeb. However, actor Ezra Stone, a dear friend of Loeb's, said that what they initiated was too little, too late: "Perhaps it was because of organizational red (pardon the unintended pun) tape. Perhaps there was an undercurrent of reasoning that unemployment is a permanent risk of the profession. Loeb was a fine, experienced professional. If he lost one network job, surely another would soon turn up. But none did."

With each turn of the knife in Loeb's back, Sam Jaffe stood beside his friend while simultaneously seeking to cope with his own similar predicament. These two successful union "soldiers" were unable to confront the evasive enemy while it continued to attack.

When it came to taking any responsibility, disclaimers fell as fast as autumn leaves. One sponsor of *The Goldbergs*, Vitamin Corporation of America, said the show was offered to them without Loeb and they had nothing to do with dropping him. NBC had no comment.

The buyout on his contract amounted to an offer of $85,000. Though Loeb needed it desperately for his son's hospitalization in a private institution, he turned it down, telling Gertrude Berg, "No, I'm sorry. I have no price." He made a test case of his firing. He did what Sam Jaffe would have done. The two committed themselves to lofty standards.

Alas, time was not in Loeb's favor. His expenditures were great and his resources dwindling. Finally, he accepted the offer, but by then the show was much less popular and the payoff was less than half of the original offer. Asking for it, whatever the amount, was grievous to this man of high principle.

Journalist Murray Kempton chronicled Loeb's losing journey in a piece entitled "The Victim." "Sam Jaffe, who was his [Philip's] oldest friend, said ... that Loeb made the settlement and then wept.

"'It was,' says Sam Jaffe, 'the old question: if you are in a fire, do you save a baby or a priceless manuscript?' When Loeb gave in, he sacrificed his posture in the union and lost his will to go on in it."

What broke Loeb's heart was that he accepted the money for his son and then felt that he had betrayed the actors for whom he had worked for all those years. He was the one person who could have proven that he had been blacklisted.

"He had carried on for the last three years on the fringes of the theater," Kempton related. "He testified before a Senate committee investigating his past connections with communist fronts. He said he had never been a party member but intended to go on cooperating with anyone he thought was right. It was not a satisfactory performance.

"He was hired for the road company of *Time Out for Ginger* at a reduced rate for a star. 'Even though there is no blacklist in the theater.' says Sam Jaffe, 'they know they can get you a little cheaper.' When that was over, he spent a season off-Broadway at $87.50 a week.

"By then, he had used up his credit and was hopelessly in arrears for his son's maintenance. In the end, he gave up and transferred his son to a state institution in Massachusetts. Two months later, he got a letter from his son; it was a desperate, pathetic plea to get him back to a place where he might be cured."

Growing more hopeless, Loeb met with Ezra Stone

to remind him of his commitment to be the executor of his estate. He willed his money to Stone and allocated funds to repay several debts. During the last two weeks of his life, Loeb had been living with Zero and Kate Mostel. It was the last place anyone saw him alive.

On the night of Thursday, September 1, 1955, Loeb disappeared. A man can hide in New York City. He can vanish amidst the collars, cuffs, and sleeves of eight million clothed souls who crowd the sidewalks and form a bobbing, breathing wardrobe of humanity. A man can walk into the moving garment of endless people and be gone. Concealed in this way, he can break the thread that held him connected with the living.

Death stalked the society in the form of the blacklist. Death also stalked Philip Loeb. By that late summer night there was little spirit left to be broken.

Unable to reach Loeb that evening, Ezra Stone immediately called Sam Jaffe and Jack Gould at *The New York Times*. He felt there should be a public notice that Philip was missing. If he was still alive he would be recognized because he was very popular on *The Goldbergs* series. There might be a chance of interceding. After considerable deliberation, Sam didn't think it would be wise to make it publicly known that Philip was missing. Neither did Gould.

Jaffe, Zero Mostel, and others close to Philip engaged in an intense search to find their beloved friend. Frantic, knowing all too well that Philip had suicide on his mind, they called hotels all over the city to see if he might have registered. They needed to find him before it was too late.

Those individually and personally affected by the witch hunts were bonded to others in the same horrible circumstance. Each suffered the sufferings of the others. Telling the story of Philip Loeb is telling the story of a community of pain in which all the victims lived shunned, in year after year of unemployment.

While his friends frantically searched for him, Philip Loeb checked into a hotel to prepare for his final exit from this life-script.

For 36 sleepless, exhausting hours, Sam and his friends tracked every lead possible. Sam was already weary from his own struggles. Now he was pouring his remaining energy into this attempt to save Phil's life. Finally, the search ended.

On Friday, September 2, 1955, the following headline appeared in *The New York Times*:

PHILIP LOEB DEAD; PROMINENT ACTOR'S BODY
FOUND IN MIDTOWN HOTEL — OVERDOSE OF
SLEEPING PILLS APPARENT CAUSE

Sam and his companions heard it on the radio the night before. Sam went to the hotel to identify Loeb before he was taken to Bellevue Hospital. It was a devastating sight for Loeb's friends to see him stretched out in the morgue. The trials had been too much for Loeb; he simply couldn't go on.

As a brilliant man and an activist to the end, Loeb, even in the midst of his bottomless despair, had the presence of mind to make a statement through his death. He had chosen the Hotel Taft. He had hated Senator Taft and the Taft Hotel. He took his life on Labor Day Weekend. He registered under the name, Fred Lang, which in German means forever peace. Philip was of German-Jewish extraction.

Ezra Stone's wife, actress Sara Seegar, spoke of Jaffe's loss: "I will certainly never ever forget Sam at Phil's funeral. He insisted upon being there and speaking. Three spoke, Bill Ross, Sam, and Ezra. Everyone was opposed to Sam's going because they didn't know whether Sam would make it. But he did."

She had never seen a more tragic figure in her life than Sam Jaffe on the day of Loeb's funeral. He was extremely thin and had been very ill. Somehow, his ethereal-looking body stood up and spoke, and he got through it under his own power. Seegar called the event "a monumental tragedy ... this little figure remembering his friend."

She recalled that Jaffe had a mild seizure after he spoke: "He collapsed for a moment, but then he stood up and he walked out. The image of him that day remains. Everybody was really terrified that now this [Philip's death] was going to be the end of Sam."

Ezra Stone interjected a light touch into the tragic tale of the death of Loeb: "Philip and Sam at some time decided that they were going to deliver their own eulogy. The first line was 'Unaccustomed as I am ...'"

The curtain had come down. The life had ended. Weary and saddened, Sam held in his hands the last remains of a beloved friend: a newspaper column of words about a man and his career.

Sam did not condemn the executioners. He exhibited a different expression of grief. His focus was on Philip, not on those who destroyed him. In the harsh light of that unwanted September morning he said, "I cannot look back and think of anyone Philip ever harmed. In the same way, his enemies did not even hate him, and we can be sure that not one of them ever thought it would come to this."

A full page memorial appeared in *Variety*, Jan. 4, 1956, contributed to by Luther Adler, Joseph Anthony, Harold Clurman, Melvyn Douglas, Julie Harris, Sam Jaffe, Eli Wallach and others. It read: "During sixteen years as a councilor of the Actors' Equity Association, Philip Loeb compiled an extraordinary record of achievement on behalf of actors, creating a rich legacy in which all members of Equity, present and future, as well as others in the theater, share."

As for Sam Jaffe, he suffered a period of two-fold

grief. Not only had he lost his best friend but he also felt his country had fallen from grace.

Decades after the McCarthy period, the horror of the times has been revisited through the efforts of those who believe we must never forget what happened, and what could happen again. Actor Alan Miller is one of those. He chose the play *Are You Now Or Have You Ever Been* as a communication vehicle because it was incredibly compelling. In the 1980's in Los Angeles, it took Miller six months to gather enough actors with the courage to do the play. His agent desperately tried to stop him from doing it and it took four or five months to get a theater operator who was willing to have it in her space.

Miller revealed, "I knew a couple of hundred people [in Los Angeles] on good levels of directing and acting. I couldn't get one single one of them to participate in this production. I had two old dear close friends who I became totally alienated from when each of them said, 'Alan, I'd love to do something with you but not this.'"

Miller thought that the show would open, be blasted by the industry, and that none of them would ever work again. However, he said, most of them weren't working anyway, so they didn't give a damn.

The show's opening produced an opposite reaction. Telegrams came in thanking him for doing it. Miller remembered how many of the people who were personally hurt and were named in the play "would come back stage with tears brimming and just bow and say, thank you, thank you." He went on: "It was an amazing experience. It ran for 14 months. The revival ran another 12 months. Unfortunately, it needs to be done every once in a while."

Alan Miller referred to the blacklist time as "the worst period of censorship in any of our lives." He said most people didn't know that the House Un-American Activities Committee was empowered as early as 1933 and wasn't abolished as a standing committee until 1975. Its name had been changed to the House Internal Security Committee but it was exactly the same committee. Once McCarthy fell into disrepute, they changed the name.

Miller included that information as an epilogue to the play with the admonition: "Do not think that all of this has been taken care of because it had a new name. After 33 years, so many months and days, not one single indictment came out of the hearings. Over a hundred thousand names were tabulated and passed on from committee to committee. They are still there. Congress perpetuated the committee as a hatchet forum. It let that committee do anything that it wanted. It was awful. It goes on and on and on."

Sam and Bettye Jaffe attended a performance of *Are You Now* and while his friends sat weeping in remembrance, he remained the quietest among them. Because he had no apparent emotional reaction, Bettye asked him if seeing it didn't bother him at all? He responded simply, "You only die once."

****

WILLIAM HICKEY appeared in *White Wings* in 1953

"*My career was midstream at the time of* White Wings. *I started performing as a child. I'd been in vaudeville and musicals. In 1951 I was with Uta Hagen in* Saint Joan. *This was followed by* Tovarich, Marti Gras, *and then lots of live television in New York in-between.*

"White Wings *was directed by a dear friend of mine, Patricia Broderick, who is the mother of Matthew Broderick and the widow of James Broderick who was a wonderful actor. A lot of the actors couldn't take direction from her. They resented a woman. They'd say, "How can a young girl tell a man what to feel?" I'd say, "She's not telling you what to feel, she's just telling you where to move in a prayer that you might feel something." I automatically like any director just because they hired me.*

"*The show got me an agent and the reputation which I still have: 'He'll try anything.' So I've had a great assortment of parts.*"

****

No Exit

Sam Jaffe was a noble man of slender elegance, with a high glow of hair about his head. He held that head high, and didn't falter in his adherence to what he knew to be the truth. In April 1951, the House Un-American Activities Committee issued a subpoena to Jaffe. With that action, his film work ceased. There were no calls either to work or to testify. Sam had entered that horrendous world of suspension from meaningful activity while waiting at the mercy of others to see what course the future was to take. Though knocked to his career-canvas by the gloves of innuendo and thus deprived of his livelihood, Sam Jaffe endured. Though pummeled while he was down by repeated examples of friends being similarly ruined, Sam Jaffe struggled to his feet to speak on his own behalf. He would not waver from his knowing. He never employed counterattack.

The blacklist smashed Sam Jaffe at the height of his career. This is a tragedy in any line of work, but most especially so in the life of an actor. He had a vast playing range and had received excellent reviews. More than an interruption, the blacklist was like a bloody gash across his career.

Jaffe's lawyer, R. Lawrence Siegel, wrote Sam of his letter to Frank Tavenner, the counsel to the House Un-American Activities Committee on Aug. 30, 1951. "I ... told him ... that you are and always have been a loyal and patriotic American, that you are a liberal pro-democrat, and that you are not and never have been a communist or under Communist Party discipline. When this information [that Jaffe was not a communist] was first brought to Tavenner's attention, he expressed himself as surprised and astonished. I then went on to acquaint him with your character, activities and political views, trying to delineate for him the substantive difference between a communist and a liberal democrat. In doing so, I stressed that a liberal like you ran the danger of mistaken identification as a communist, but I hoped that he and the Committee would not make this tragic mistake. I added that I assumed that the subpoena had been served upon you because of the assumption that you were or are a communist or fellow traveler. Tavenner answered that he assumed you had been a communist until recent years. I told him about your position and activity on Finland, on aid to England and France before the invasion of Germany, and of my analysis of your views based on our many conversations. I concluded by asking him and the Committee to consider dismissing the subpoena without having you testify if they found that I was telling the truth and I offered to furnish documentary proof of my oral assertions to him. Tavenner promised to take the matter under advisement.

"Tavenner notified me that the Committee and he were satisfied with my statement regarding you and that the subpoena is being discharged and that you do not have to testify, upon the condition that I will send them a letter over my own signature concerning your past and present activities, affiliations and views. This letter will be for their files to show the basis for their clearing you.

"Tavenner advised against a public statement by us on the ground that it may be embarrassing and may cause somebody to complain to the Committee and thereby possibly cause them to call you again. I told Tavenner we will not issue a public statement but that I will discuss the situation with him at an appropriate time."

Because of Jaffe's past activities, he had received a subpoena on the assumption that he had been a communist. So much had the accusers predetermined Jaffe's status that they were surprised and astonished that he would disclaim communist affiliation. Only after the fact did they bother to check. The result was the discharge of the subpoena. Wouldn't it have been just as easy to have verified the facts before forming false conclusions and issuing a subpoena? The question is crucial. Once called, especially if innocent, the shadow of stigma remained cast across the reputation.

The accused, even when discharged, was advised, even threatened, against making a public statement. The Committee cornered the market on publicity. They did not want their power base diminished by announcements that someone had been cleared, or that his subpoena had been lifted. They preferred to have a dramatic advantage: namely, calling and coercing prominent personalities who were pressed to name names that the Committee already had. Getting the names took on less importance than getting the publicity from having "stars" help purify America.

In his autobiography *Timebends*, Arthur Miller captures the time period: "... We had all cheered the same heroes, the same mythic resisters ... from way back in the Spanish War to the German antifascists and the Italians, brave men and women who were the best of our identity, those who had been the sacrifices of our time.

"What we had now seemed a withering parody of what was being advertised as high drama. When the Committee knew all the names beforehand, there was hardly a conspiracy being unveiled but rather a symbolic display that would neither string anybody up on a gallows nor cause him to be cut down. No material thing had been moved one way or another by a single inch, only the air we all breathed had grown somewhat thinner and the destruction of meaning seemed total when the sundering of friendships was so often with people whom the witness had not ceased to love."

Two months after Jaffe's discharge by HUAC, Jaffe's lawyer, R. Lawrence Siegel, wrote to his agent, Philip Gersh. The letter concerned the difficulty Gersh was still having in securing work for Sam in consequence of his having been subpoenaed by the House Un-American Activities Committee.

Siegel explained that the House Committee did not issue "clearances." There were no such things: "You may then ask, what does 'clearance' mean ...? It means this. A person who is or who has been a communist, who testifies and discloses his past affiliations or activities as a communist, is considered to be 'cleared' by such testimony and therefore is able to work without fear of blacklisting, picketing, etc., in contrast to the man subpoenaed who does not appear or who appears and declines to answer questions relating to his affiliations on the ground of the Fifth and First Amendments or on other grounds . . .

"But remember ... [a clearance] applies to the communist, ex- or present. It does not apply, by the nature of the case, to the liberal or other person who has never been a communist, who is subpoenaed. He can never get such clearance; on the other hand, he runs the risk of great damage solely by the act of being subpoenaed. He is truly in a no-man's land."

This was the category Sam Jaffe occupied. His subpoena had been vacated and he was not required to testify. Yet, his name could never be cleared precisely because he was not, nor had he ever been, a communist.

Siegel continued. "Ideally, we would prefer a public announcement by the Committee, but it does not do that. . . . Where does this leave Sam? Right at this point: to the extent that he needed 'clearance,' he got the best possible clearance in the world when the subpoena was discharged without his having to submit to testifying at all. This was open proof and notice to the whole world that Sam was and is a loyal patriotic American. Anybody who has any question about this or the facts is free to check with the Committee or its counsel.

"It follows from all of this that it would be most unjust and unfair for anyone to deny or bar Sam Jaffe from employment in his profession. I do hope this will assist you toward that end."

Six months after the subpoena, Sam Jaffe was still not working. The loss of income was only a small part of the problem. Sam lacked outlets. This is slow death to an artist in the theater.

At the end of October, Sam's lawyer, Siegel, communicated again with HUAC counsel Frank Tavenner, pointing out the patent unfairness of Sam's situation: the subpoena had closed him out of all employment. He stressed that unless something was done in an open and public way to "clear" Jaffe of any taint, he might not work again.

Siegel wrote Sam: "Tavenner said he saw the indecent unfairness of the situation, expressed his interest and sympathy, promised to enlist the interest of the Committee in the problem, and asked me to write him at length about the situation and gave me carte blanche to make any remedial suggestions that came to mind. He has assured me he will do whatever he can to rectify the injury to you, which was caused by the issuance of the subpoena. And he is certain he will get the Committee to show enthusiasm for action which will right the wrong to you."

Months went by with no change in the situation. The Committee focused its enthusiasm on "getting communists," not on apologizing for its destructive errors or on resurrecting the lives of those they had hanged on the cross of un-Americanism.

To this day, I am shocked and suffer profound sorrow that this transpired in my country, a democracy that sees itself as setting an example of freedom and justice for the world. I was a child when all this happened, saluting the flag in school every day and being taught how pure we were as a nation and a people. Alas, over the years of my life I have witnessed other instances of cover-ups, ill-advised actions, mistreatment of citizens, and the horrendous ill-effects of the disease of blind patriotism that supports power-hungry usurpers of people's freedoms. I feel a deep sadness for Sam and all the others who suffered in this way.

A close friend of Bettye's and Sam's, actress Evelyn Scott, remembered how she and Sam were always talking about politics because they were very much involved. Sam felt passionately about injustice such as the blacklist. He wouldn't bring it up about himself. He would be more apt to talk of someone else's trials.

Scott said, "Sam was angry about what had happened in the blacklist. He wasn't above swearing if someone was an s.o.b. We didn't get over being angry. Sam didn't forgive anybody from those times. Neither did I. I was very glad that some of them came to bad ends, as a matter of fact."

No one ever admitted there was a blacklist. Scott continued, "The way they did it at the ad agencies was to send through a memo on the teletype asking 'Is Evelyn Scott available?' If yes, she wasn't blacklisted. If no, she was. But they didn't have a blacklist; they did it that way. My friend sent it through, 'Is Evelyn Scott available?' and it came back yes and I worked on the commercial on The Art Linkletter Show for 8 months. Sometimes I was blacklisted because I was married to a blacklisted writer. Anyone who knew of the connection — my name was Scott and his was Stone — I didn't work. He never worked a day after he was blacklisted."

When actor Marvin Kaplan was up for a role in

The Eddie Cantor Story, they asked him who could play his uncle. They needed a very wise, Jewish, philosophic man. "I said Sam Jaffe. At that moment it was like a boom descended on the room. This was about 1954. My interview was over. My agent looked at me in disbelief and later said, 'Why did you mention Sam's name? Didn't you know he was blacklisted?' I said, 'Yeah, but what difference does it make? He'd be great for the part.' He said, 'Marvin, not only can you forget about this part but all others with these fellows.'"

Kaplan remembered with distaste how actors had to clear themselves with Frank Nelson, President of the American Federation of Radio and Television Artists. As late as 1974 there was a section in the AFTRA constitution forbidding membership in the Communist party." Kaplan helped get rid of the ruling. He challenged the premise by pointing out that one could be a member of the Manson Family and join AFTRA but not a member of the Communist Party.

At first, Communist Party members were admitted but they couldn't serve on the Board unless they took loyalty oaths. AFTRA members remembered how blacklisting ruined careers and lives and they voted down the new restriction by 500 to 4.

The days of not working mounted for Jaffe. His lawyer wrote letters. His complaints on behalf of his client were acknowledged and agreed to. Yet, nothing changed. Sam held firm. He walked through the gales of fear and gusts of rhetoric until the storm died down. He knew that when the fear subsided and the opportunism was temporarily laid to rest, those who upheld and treasured the constitution would be there to give substance to those who merely waved flags and verbally proclaimed their patriotism.

It took great courage to continue in those grave days that dragged on into months and years. Jaffe had that courage, but he was not alone. When called before the Un-American Activities Committee, Zero Mostel gave them the Bronx cheer: "The villain is not the people you are after, the villain is you who takes our country away from us. Accuse a man but don't be cowardly and hide behind a committee."

The House Un-American Activities Committee was also challenged by people like Robert W. Kenny, President of the National Lawyers Guild. He argued that the Congress had no right to control hiring based on political beliefs, or to invade the freedom of speech of a medium of expression. It had no right to force motion picture content to coincide with conformity to the views of the Committee. Nor should the Committee exercise censorship, or investigate "propaganda." Kenny complained that the Committee had no business conducting an inquiry unrelated to legislation, or classifying speech as "good" or "bad," or as "American" or "un-American."

No matter how many statements such as this were made, the situation remained the same for far too long.

As mentioned previously, it was Sam Jaffe's signing of petitions and his union work that resulted in his blacklisting. His actions and motivations had been honorable but his associations, particularly in the break-away group called The Forum, were a mixture of advocates and communists.

In his autobiography, *A Life*, Elia Kazan described the situation from the communist perspective: "In 1934, when I was 'in the Party,' we helped start a left-wing movement [The Forum] in a very conservative Actors' Equity Association. Our prime goal was to secure rehearsal pay for the working actor and to limit the period when a producer could decide to replace an actor in rehearsal without further financial obligation." [This was also what Jaffe and Loeb fought for. They were known as the fiery petrols!]

Kazan said he was working on reforming Equity with "a fine man named Phil Loeb." Though their cause was just, "it wasn't an easy fight to win. We had to score with a majority vote at the annual meeting of Equity. We planned our tactics cleverly, scattering our forces (a decided minority) all over the ballroom of the Astor Hotel, where the meeting was held. This was so that when the reform motion was proposed, there would be actors speaking for the motion from every side, creating the impression that there were more of us than there were. We also planned who would say what, so there would be a swelling tide with no repeats until the vote was taken.

"Our other tactic was to wait until a time close to the end of the meeting, when 'new business' was called for from the 'chair,' because at that time all the working actors, those more affluent and because of this more conservative, had left for a quick meal before hustling into their dressing rooms to make up for the night's performance. Until that exodus, no hint was to be given of what we would be up to. Then, with the ballroom half empty, we went into action. Only the old professionals were present by then, and we Young Turks, waiting in ambush. At a signal, one of us jumped up and proposed our motion, reading a carefully prepared statement. Quickly it was seconded, and then came a fire storm of support from all sides of the ballroom. Our demands were heard and acceded to, and before long actors had their simple right, pay for rehearsal."

Kazan, Loeb and Jaffe championed the same issues but from very different political and philosophical bases. Kazan had been a communist seeking political leverage. Jaffe and Loeb had been union leaders devoted to benefits for members.

It was actor Lee J. Cobb who "incriminated" Sam Jaffe. Cobb had joined the Communist Party in 1940. Testifying before the House Committee in 1953, he reported that he had attended meetings of The Forum. He said that while The Forum was purportedly dedicated to liberal union issues, a communist faction played an important part in it. As a communist, he was instructed to vote in particular ways. The communist caucus hoped to gain control of the union by winning key issues and thus becoming powerful.

The House Committee asked Cobb who controlled The Forum. His response was reprinted in *Thirty Years of Treason*, under "Excerpts from Hearings before the House Un-American Activities Committee, 1938-1968": "Prominent in The Forum activities were, among others, Phil Loeb and Sam Jaffe, though I never knew them to be communists. And I don't mean by mentioning their names to suggest that they were. But in answer to your question, they were very active in The Forum ..."

This single paragraph, this non-accusative implication, this raising of question, was all that was needed in the 1950's in the United States of America, the land of the free and the home of the brave, to blacklist an individual and, in Sam's case, to keep him out of work for almost seven years.

As disturbing as this is, there is something even more shocking to remember. The Communist Party was a legal entity in the United States. No one was prohibited from belonging or attending Party or "front organization" meetings. This means that there was no basis for the hearings, no grounds for the badgering, no reason for the career destruction!

My research on the subject tells me that Congress passed the Communist Control Act in August 1954 in which the Communist Party was said to be an instrumentality of a conspiracy to overthrow our government, that it played a role as an agency of a hostile foreign power, and that it was danger to U.S. security. However, it did not say membership was sufficient cause for arrest or penalty. It said the Communist Party should be outlawed. However, it did not declare it outlawed. The Act did go a step further than the Internal Security Act of 1950, removing the rights, privileges, and immunities attendant upon legal bodies created under the jurisdiction of the laws of the United States from the Communist Party.

The Communist Party continues to exist to this day, but during the red scare days the U.S. Government used the Act's legislation to harass Communist Party members and other organizations that were deemed to have communist leanings such as the American Civil Liberties Union, labor unions and the NAACP. If there be such a thing as evil it resides comfortably in power-seekers who put self-interest above the common good.

J. Parnell Thomas, Chairman of the House Committee, said that the purpose of their investigation was to reveal subversive, communist, and un-American influence in motion pictures. They clearly presumed that influences such as that were already in films. They saw their task as formidable.

One has the sense that the committee felt the threat of communist takeover was so great that the country would need vast armed forces to contain the hordes of red gladiators swarming over the unions and mass media. Cobb's estimate of the actual number of people in his Communist Party group in New York City was that there were ten. Ten! In his group in Hollywood, there were 12.

Twenty-two persons is a surprisingly small number to be thought powerful enough to start an insurrection or overthrow the government. However, small numbers can be powerful, as witnessed by the very small number of witch-hunters who demonstrated astonishing power to destroy lives and careers, and who almost overthrew our constitutional freedoms.

The inquisitors revealed their mentality in this question asked of Cobb: "Was it possible that an actor can portray in any way the Communist Party line through the method of acting? Can he get over a political line or thought?" Cobb replied that he didn't think that was at all possible. Such a question, inferring that by a look, or delivery of a line, or assuming of a characterization, an actor could sway the population and eventually topple the nation, might be laughable except for how paranoid it is. Furthermore, it indicates very little regard for the American people and their intelligence.

There was a brief revealing exchange during those years between J. Parnell Thomas, Chairman of the House Un-American Activities Committee, and Ronald Reagan, President of the Screen Actors Guild. Referring to Thomas Jefferson, Reagan, then a liberal, offered his belief that the American people would not make the mistake of being taken in by the communist line. Thomas jumped on this as justification for HUAC. It was this very House Committee, he said, that was going to bring the facts to the American people. The Committee, he said, was going to hold the line and make America just as pure as possible.

Reagan, in a statement of trust that sounded very different from his rhetoric as President of United States in the 1980's, replied that he still thought that democracy could do it. The implication was that HUAC wasn't needed. Reagan later made a complete turnaround from liberal to conservative politics. In the opinion of many who surveyed the shift, it was a way of getting ahead. He followed the advice of those who saw which way the tide was turning and which position would best serve his political career.

Then as now, and perhaps forever, the challenge is: can we trust the principles we profess to believe? All too often we dare not take the risk. Instead, we recreate in ourselves the evil we battle against in others. We attempt to wipe out wickedness in them by implementing our own version of it. HUAC was a perfect example of that, proclaiming that communists sought to destroy our free society while diminishing basic constitutional guarantees through their investigative tactics.

The motion picture industry had a tremendous impact on the viewing public. This was even truer during the period of the early 1950's than it was at the film industry's inception. Movies such as *The Best Years of Our Lives* and *Gentlemen's Agreement* did more than move, talk and entertain. They caused viewers to think. They exposed them to problems in America such as unemployment, housing inadequacies, discrimination, and fascistic practices, and called into question the romantic notion that all in this nation was idyllic. Such expression of opinion was intolerable to those who feared for the stability of the United States if she was other than praised. It was intolerable to those in favored financial positions who were determined to remain there; those with racist beliefs; and those who simply believed there could never be anything wrong with the greatest nation on earth.

Sam Jaffe, and other thinking-feeling artists, were not afraid of, or alienated by, national shortcomings. Rather they saw them as opportunities to fulfill greater potential and extend our abundance to all among us. These artists, who walked full into the overpowering, foul wind of repressive tactics, stood up to those who abused power. As early as 1947, John Huston, Humphrey Bogart, William Wyler, Paul Henried, Danny Kaye, Gene Kelley, Lauren Bacall and Jane Wyatt presented a petition of redress of grievances to the House of Representatives. They demanded a reinstatement of faith in the democratic process and an elimination of criminal, trial-like proceedings in which the accused had no right to defend self. This Committee for the First Amendment later grew into the Committee of One Thousand, adding members like Helen Keller and Albert Einstein. It worked for the abolition of HUAC. Its members were in full agreement with Congressman Emmanuel Cellar of New York who was opposed to the use of even a little totalitarianism to preserve our Democracy.

There was a defense of battle lines and a demand for decency. However, the velocity of the wind intensified with statements by J. Parnell Thomas. He claimed that constitutional rights did not apply to those whom his committee had accused of being communists.

There was a clear drawing of sides. Sam Jaffe huddled with humanitarians in an unwavering stance against the witch-hunt, while HUAC drew hunters like Roy Cohn, a man capable of great cruelty.

Nicholas von Hoffman reports in *Citizen Cohn* that Roy Cohn "told a friend that at the beginning of the Nixon-McGovern campaign of 1972, it was he, Roy himself, who arranged for Senator Thomas Eagleton's medical history to be made public [after having been one of those who engineered his nomination because they knew of the skeleton in his closet]. The news that the Democratic candidate for Vice President had once been in a hospital getting shock treatments for depression forced him off the ticket." Hoffman reports that Cohn played a similar role in the wrecking of Geraldine Ferraro's campaign in 1984.

It is easy to see these as attempts to alter our fundamental premise. If that happened, we would end up with a government of a handful of people, for a handful of people, and by a handful of people. Meanwhile, the masses live under the illusion that their vote and voice are the determiners of our national fate.

Fourteen months after his subpoena and its subsequent dismissal, and numerous letters to the House Committee, Sam Jaffe remained blacklisted. He was still unable to work, still not cleared by those who agreed his treatment had been unfair.

On June 6, 1952, Lawrence Siegel wrote again, at

length, for Jaffe, this time to Edward Cheyfitz in Washington D. C.: "Sam's position is tragic. His inability to secure employment as an alleged communist or communist-fronter is indefensible. Sam appears to be unable to work in the motion picture industry solely because he was served with a subpoena ... [due to his having been] listed in *Red Channels* ...

"Sam's plight is especially sad because of his character, standing, and age. He is a truly noble guy, respected and revered by everybody who knows him. He is a liberal, an idealist, passionately devoted to the democratic way of life. He is a great actor and his sudden unemployability comes in the wake of his having attained international preeminence for his remarkable performance in *Asphalt Jungle*. Sam is at an age in life where he is much too old to carve out another career for himself, and if his status is not soon righted his case will be most desperate."

Siegel went on to restate the facts he had presented so often, to no avail. A person like Sam, he wrote, "... who is not and never has been a communist, is in a sad fix. He can never be 'cleared' in the popular sense. He is without a 'past' to disclose, no confederates to reveal, no anti-democratic philosophy to repudiate.

"Life to Jaffe is a continuous search for certainty, but he refuses to believe anyone has a stronghold on truth or right. [Jaffe's actual words were even stronger: "I fear anyone who has a strangle hold on truth."] Jaffe is trained as a scientist and mathematician. He thinks and experiments for himself. He could therefore never live in a totalitarian state, because freedom for this search is to him a paramount interest. He could therefore never be a Communist or a slave to any dogma ... (Note: Jaffe signed a non-communist oath in 1947.)

"As to the charges against Jaffe: *Red Channels* lists Jaffe as a supporter of several organizations with which he had nothing to do, and connects him with one organization, the National Council of the Arts, Sciences and Professions, which he says he positively refused to join."

Red Channels had two pages on Sam Jaffe. The following listings (condemnations) appeared. "Sam Jaffe, Actor pp.88-89.

Reported as: Supporter. Japan Boycott Conference. HUAC Appendix 9, p. 390, American League for Peace and Democracy.

Speaker. Carnegie Hall, 10/16/42. HUAC, appendix 9, p. 575, Artists' Front to Win the War.

Signer of declaration. HUAC, appendix 9, p.1531, Reichstag Frie Trial Anniversary Committee.

Signed letter to Governor Dewey asking pardon for Morris U. Schappes, HUAC, appendix 9, p.1560, Morris U. Schappes Defense Committee.

Cooperator, 1940, HUAC, appendix 9, p. 1786 Social Work Today.

Sponsor. HUAC, ap. 9, p. 1547 Theater Arts Committee.

Signer, HUAC, p. 1383, Open letter for Closer Cooperation with the Soviet Union.

Sponsor, Letterhead, 8/6/45, End Jim Crow in Baseball Committee.

Contributor, New Masses, 2/16/37, p. 21, New Masses.

Vice-chairman, Program, 3/5/47, Save the Voice of Freedom Committee.

Sponsor, Federal Arts Council, leaflet, 5/12/39, Workers Alliance.

American Sponsor, HUAC. Review of Scientific and Cultural Conference for World Peace, 4/19/49, p. 11, World Peace Congress, Paris.

Signer, Advertisement "We are for Wallace." NY Times, 10/20/48, National Council of the Arts, Sciences and Professions.

Attended and contributed $300. Rally at Madison Square Garden, 9/24/45, U. S. Senate Hearings on S1832, p. 539, Spanish Refugee "Appeal, Joint Anti-Fascist Refugee Committee."

Siegel went on to report Jaffe's active participation in a public chain letter to President Roosevelt supporting the sending of overage destroyers to Britain for her aid as "democracy's first line of defense" during the time of the Nazi-Soviet pact. This position was the exact opposite of the communist line at the time. The chain letter was sent out, on August 26, 1940, over Jaffe's signature, to a list of his friends and acquaintances, numbering many hundreds. It went through the New School for Social Research, which in its orientation is liberal-social democratic, anti-Russian and anti-communist. Jaffe had also opposed the Soviet invasion of Finland and supported aid to Finland, both privately and publicly.

Siegel continued point by point to discredit *Red Channels* false connections of Jaffe to organizations and publications. He then referred to Sam Jaffe's service in the United States Army during World War I. Although he was entitled to a government pension for such service after receiving his honorable discharge, he did not apply for the pension. In World War II he was awarded a citation by the United States Treasury Department for his efforts in promoting the sale of war bonds.

Lawrence Siegel concluded his letter with the appeal, "Please let me hear from you as to what you think should be or can be done to open the way to Sam's re-employment in the industry."

A year later, Sam Jaffe remained blacklisted and off the silver screen. It was not as if this were a boxing match where two equally endowed opponents went against each other one on one. The forces in conflict here were much larger than those on the Committee and those blacklisted. The real turmoil was taking place in the evolving American consciousness. It was a matter of time. How long would the American people dwell in the fear that allowed the unconstitutionality of the Committee's efforts to continue? There was a many-sided power struggle in process.

****

ANNE JACKSON, *This Property Is Condemned*

"E.L.T. was a godsend for young actors, for me. Eli [Wallach, her husband] and I met in an E.L.T. production.

"E.L.T. was and is terribly important for young people to have some support system that comes from that generation, the older generation, to bring you into the theater community. We had showcases and people saw us work and we got jobs. They did something practical. They didn't just talk about it."

****

Honor Among the Unemployed

Sam Jaffe had to wait until the power struggle was over. He had to search out off-screen means of performing as a creative artist. In the company of great talents like Geraldine Page, he did wonderful play-readings that expanded into performance readings at the New School for Social Research. It was a time for him to test his forbearance.

As a result of the blacklist, he had begun suffering from unpredictable heart fibrillation. He commented, "During fibrillation the heart does a dance and you don't know what's going to happen to you, really. Whether it will quit or it will be the finish of you, or whether you'll be able to carry on. It took some time to get over it."

He was often unable to attend theater because his heart would pound and he would have to leave immediately. There were times when he would faint. "I did *Noah* in Westport," he recalled, "and they had to close the curtain. I couldn't continue. I passed out. Alexander Kirkland directed that. I stayed with Joanna [Dublin]. They took care of me for about two weeks."

During a reading at the New School when he was playing Prospero, he had to hold on to the scenery to go on with the performance. He knew that if he gave in then, he could never act again. His friends Zero Mostel and Emily Paley were, fortunately, aware of his crisis and had a doctor waiting backstage when the performance was over. Sam knew it was then or never. He had to conquer his heart's response to the savage blacklisting; he had to surmount his emotional distress. The fibrillation continued into the first year of his marriage to Bettye [1956]. Then it ceased, until the last years of his life when he became desperately ill.

Sam was sure the blacklist couldn't last forever. He just had to find ways to outlive it while maintaining full integrity and reiterating who and what he was.

Karl Malden found it much easier to clear Sam's name in his own mind than the Committee did with extensive evidence. Malden felt a need to know conclusively about his friend.

Malden reported, "I talked with Sam. Mona and I had lunch with him one day and on the way there I told Mona, 'I'm gonna come right out and ask Sam.' And I did. I said, 'Sam, I'm going to ask you a question. You've been blacklisted. Maybe you made a bad choice, maybe you didn't. I don't know. Are you? Were you ever a communist?' He said, 'I am not. I never was a communist.' There you are. And I took him for his word. That was all I needed. Sam had always been a righteous man in whatever he felt. This delicate-looking kind of man had a strong will."

Others were not so strong-willed. Philip Loeb had collapsed under the pressure of the downpour. Jaffe hardly withstood the fall of that mighty tree. He witnessed other such deaths, both literal and figurative, of decent and courageous individuals. Mady Christians was an example. Jaffe knew her well. They had appeared together in *The Divine Drudge* by Vicki Baum and John Golden. The two had been praised for bringing their characters to sharp life. Sam's work was termed effortless. It seemed to have nothing to do with acting or technique. He simply became the scientist he was playing.

Mady Christians had played his wife in a radiant performance. She had power and sincerity in her emotional moments. A perfect pinup girl, she had been a big star in Germany at the time of Hitler. She wanted to leave Germany because she couldn't bear what was happening. When Hitler found out that she was leaving, he pleaded with her to stay. She declined and came to America, to the land of the free and the home of the brave.

Shortly after her arrival, the State Department asked her to appear at a luncheon in Washington for Russian and American friendship. The two countries were allies then. For this, Mady Christians later suffered persecution. She had survived Nazi Germany. She had come to this shore to serve on the board of Television Authority and on the council of Actors' Equity as a true fighter for civil liberties and justice. She was an informed, articulate anti-communist. However, like Sam Jaffe and Philip Loeb, she was labeled communist because of her fervent devotion to liberal causes within the union.

Christians tried to warn everyone that red baiting had been a chief weapon of Adolph Hitler; that it had eventually served as the downfall of their union and of artistic freedom. She had been the original star of *I Remember Mama* on Broadway but she "couldn't" be hired for the television series. Subsequent offers for two or three other TV shows were canceled at the last minute. Paid $1,250.00 for not appearing over video in one role for which she had been hired, she didn't have any further doubt about being blacklisted. She agreed to go on a tour in a revival of the play *Black Chiffon*, only to see it canceled, too, by pressure against theater managers.

Mady Christians then went to a hospital and died. Her death was a tremendous blow to Sam Jaffe. It was like living through a plague. He watched one friend after another fall and he suffered deeply with each one.

Television producer Stanley Kallis spoke of Sam's bout: "The blacklist hurt him very much. He was very angry. He was deprived of his profession for many years. I never saw Sam in the role of the revolutionary. He never talked as though he was going to go out and start a revolution, but he certainly was a humanitarian. He was dedicated, and any political cause that answered those things common to his spirit he was going to be involved in. He wouldn't flinch from stating his position."

There was another despair Sam lived through during this period. It was the death of integrity in those he respected and those who were his friends. For this death, Sam couldn't muster any compassion. When former communists made the choice to testify before the Committee and implicate others, Sam Jaffe became unforgiving and hardened in his heart toward those who could perform such a despicable act.

One such person was Elia Kazan. Kazan had chosen to name names.

Actor Marvin Kaplan spoke forcefully about his experience of Sam's relationship to Kazan: "He hated people who informed on others. He hated Kazan. He was very angry with him. He said he despised him because he acted out of self-interest to save his own skin. That was the only reason he acted as he did even if it meant sending other people to the guillotine."

Jaffe assessed Kazan's choice: "In a roundabout way, Kazan accused me of being a communist. He sang. He gave names. He took a one-column ad in which he accused indirectly all the people of The Forum, which is a terrible thing. He'd been a member of the [Communist] Party and he had a right to leave, but not to give names of others.

"I remember what Lillian [Hellman] said. It was very marvelous. She couldn't face herself in the mirror if she named names. What she did was her own. She didn't believe that democracy had changed its form, its garment, so to speak."

Sam would have nothing more to do with Kazan, even when it came to a choice between allegiances. Sam's good friend Karl Malden gave him a seat to the opening night of *The Desperate Hours*, a play in which he was starring. He wanted Sam to escort his wife, Mona. When Karl told Sam that he had also given a pair to Kazan and that he would be sitting in the same row, Sam refused to go.

This irreparable split occurred repeatedly in the world of theater. Creative loss surpassed even the loss of work. Malden lamented its effect as he reflected on the rift between Kazan and another great, Arthur Miller: "Two brilliant minds who had worked together for about five years. Because of the blacklist each one of these men took a different way to get out of their problem. One didn't say anything and one took the other way. Each one of these men ... went on, became more famous, made much money ... What suffered? The American theater suffered. If they had stayed together maybe another five years, God knows what would have happened. The theater suffered."

He spoke with increased passion. His volume rose: "You had to solve it. You solved it your way. I don't know whether I would have solved it that way, maybe I would have. I don't know. Who knows which way you would go when the time comes? But something suffered and I want to say the American theater suffered.

"And there was never any way for reconciliation. Never. That's over. It will never happen. That to me is the disheartening, heartbreaking thing about the whole thing. Because if you loved the theater the way Sam loved the theater, if you loved the theater, the art, the way Zero loved it, if you loved the theater the way Phil Loeb loved it, if you loved the theater the way Kazan loved it, who was on the other side, you see, then they must feel something. They must feel something. This thing that I love is being killed.

"It's not that each person had to do what he had to do. Each person was forced to do what he had to do. I say forced because of the circumstances. And it's true, choices were made. It was a big trauma in our industry."

Elia Kazan and Sam Jaffe: two artists, two choices. The juxtaposition of these two men of theatre is worth examining for character development.

In his autobiography, Elia Kazan describes himself as having been "... out of things, hostile, secretive, frightened, uncertain, adrift, a boy without confidence and with no direction, anxious about my future and living outside the course of the rest of humankind."

Kazan had had a yearning for meaning, for dignity, for security in life. His joining the Communist Party met those needs. Reflecting in his biography, he wrote: "I now felt proud, positive, busy, certain, confident, not only 'in' but in front, convinced of my worth, even a potential leader.

"My hostility was no longer an alienation. The Party had justified it, taught me that it was correct, even reasonable. I could be proud of it; it made me the comrade of angry millions all over the earth. I'd reacted correctly to my upbringing, to my social position, to the society around me, to the state of the world. I was a member of what was sure to be the victorious army of the future. I had comrades. I could believe in my hopes; they'd be realized."

Later, he had turned violently anti-communist because of their need for militancy, their conspiratorial nature, and their turning into an imperialist power.

Sam Jaffe grew up with a secure sense of his inner worth as a human being. He was always interested in liberal causes and helping others. He didn't need an organization or a philosophical dogma to guide his actions. He was an individual, aware of injustices and personally dedicated to influencing change for the better.

On May 14, 1953, two long years into his blacklisting and unemployment, in response to an outreach from Nate Spingold, Vice President of Columbia Pictures, Sam wrote of his convictions. The inquiry was in response to urging from Eddie Robinson, who was trying hard to get Sam working again. Sam wanted to work, but never at the expense of his dignity or values.

"Here is a brief statement of what I believe.

"I believe in 'Peace on Earth,' the 'Brotherhood of Man,' and the 'Abundant Life for All.'

"I believe that these can be realized only in a democracy where it is understood that disagreements will be settled through the competition of ideas in the market place, through the free and fearless use of reason without danger of reprisals from fellow-citizens, the government, or private organizations.

"I believe with Theodore Roosevelt that the Constitution of the United States 'should be treated as the greatest document ever devised by the wit of man to aid a people in exercising every power for its betterment and not as a straitjacket cunningly fashioned to strangle growth.'

"Moreover, as an actor and lover of the arts, I believe and I know that the theater and art in general cannot thrive except in an atmosphere of freedom and that in our constitution we have the best guarantee ever formulated.

"In lending my name to protest against injustice, or for minority groups, or toward the promotion of Soviet-American friendship at a time when that friendship was the official governmental policy, I feel that I acted in accordance with the foregoing principles.

"Reviewing these ideas after I left you Wednesday afternoon, I felt it would be useless for me to pursue my talk with you; for in spite of your generous offer to help me, first for myself as you said, and then because of the high regard in which you hold my friend Edward G. Robinson, whom I love, that help would have to come in a way that is inconsistent with a basic tenet of my belief, namely: that any group, private or governmental, that takes unto itself the right to examine a citizen's thinking and conscience, and sit in judgment on his right to express his thinking, is acting contrary to the principles which are the foundation of and reason for our existence as a nation."

In contrast, Kazan spoke this way: "What you watch is yourself, struggling against the fate you've made for yourself."

Kazan had resolved not to name names. He knew that to do so would put careers in jeopardy. He could also see, as countless others had seen, that Committee opportunists were conducting a ceremony of degradation. The information received wasn't nearly as important as getting others to inform. They already had the names they sought and were hungry for publicity.

Kazan bitterly resented their tactics, but he was a man with a character split. Two voices dialogued within him. One refused to toss people to the wolves; the other felt a need to expunge guilt over his having participated in communist tactics from which he now wanted to save his country.

Jaffe and Kazan had attended the same fervent meetings of Actors' Equity Association, as had Philip Loeb. Sam and Philip stayed up long into the nights devising strategies to forge ahead with reforms for performing artists. They focused on human beings, on achievement of necessary standards. Their motives were pure, as were their efforts. They were in the forefront of The Forum, as Lee J. Cobb had testified.

And, as he had testified, there were also members of the Communist Party in their midst, members focused on using the issues to attain powerful leverage. (Oddly, this was exactly the behavior visible in HUAC.) However, Jaffe and Loeb were not communists.

From Jaffe's point of view the difference between the union activists and the communists was that the former were earnest servers and the latter were self-serving.

Sam was outraged that Kazan would implicate him, along with Philip and others, in his testimony that the most active members of the Forum were communists. Kazan knew that Jaffe wasn't a communist, but the

Committee never asked witnesses to say who wasn't, only who was, or who might be by implication.

Kazan's motives as a communist at Equity had not been pure. Now, his other voice, from the split in self, shouted at him.

He recounts the inner battle: "Hadn't I played the same game of conspiracy in Actors' Equity meetings? The secret caucuses before, the clever tactics during, the calculated positioning of our 'comrades' in the meeting hall to create the effect of a majority when the fact was that we were a small minority?

"... Did I really want to change the social system I was living under? Apparently that was what I'd stood for at one time. But what shit! Everything I had of value I'd gained under that system."

Sam Jaffe, while not wanting to change our social system, did want to improve conditions for all, using the basic tenets of our system. Under no circumstances was he willing to compromise our basic rights, even if it meant turning down personal help for renewed employment. He could endure the horror of penalty-without-crime because he had unblemished beliefs and dignity. There were no debilitating divisions in his house of self.

Kazan, on the other hand, was a man consumed by the split in self. He raised questions within himself, and having no objective listener, he answered himself with his own previously drawn conclusions. Why shouldn't everyone name each other and be done with it? Why hadn't anyone else thought of it? Because they were adhering to Party discipline, he decided for them. Why were they stonewalling? Party protection, and self-protection, he decided. They were covering their pasts as he had done.

The voice of honor shouted at him again, reiterating that he couldn't give names. However, he wondered in response to himself why he should have to suffer alone and became angry enough to want to name everybody.

He was so upset with how the others responded to him (inside his own head) that he wanted to pull everyone down into the muck with him. It was an easy next step to talk himself into believing that if the situation were reversed, his former comrades would name him in an instant. So it was that he persuaded himself to implicate others.

There is a distinctively insular and false nature to circular thinking. One cannot answer for others, and say what their actions would be, from inside one's own head. In such cases one merely projects onto others one's own choices and then blames them for having made them. It is like the old story of the men of Chelm. Mendel decides in advance that, though his friend Goldberg had no justification whatever for refusing to lend him his sled, he probably would not lend it, ingrate that he was. Mendel goes on to Goldberg's house and instead of asking to borrow his sled, curses him for his refusal and punches him in the nose, leaving his friend in complete bewilderment over the one-sided transaction.

Kazan supported his own choices with unsubstantiated, though justifying, suppositions.

Jaffe did not engage in circular thinking, but then Jaffe had nothing to feel guilty about in this entire matter.

In *Timebends* Arthur Miller shares of the pain he suffered at Kazan's decision to name names: "Had I been of his generation, he would have had to sacrifice me as well. And finally that was all I could think of. I could not get past it.

"That all relationships had become relationships of advantage or disadvantage. That this was what it all came to anyway and there was nothing new here. That one stayed as long as it was useful to stay, believed as long as it was not too inconvenient, and that we were in a tank cruising with upslanted gaze for the descending crumbs that kept us alive. I could only say that I thought this would pass and that it had to pass because it would devour the glue that kept the country together if left to its own unobstructed course. I said that it was not the reds who were dispensing our fears now, but the other side, and it could not go on indefinitely, it would some-day wear down the national nerve. ... I felt a silence ris-ing around me, an impeding and invisible wash of dulled vibrations between us, like an endless moaning musical note through which we could not hear or speak anymore. It was sadness, purely mournful, deadening. And it had been done to us. It was not his duty to be stronger than he was; the government had no right to require any-one to be stronger than it had been given him to be. ... I was experiencing a bitterness with the country that I had never even imagined before, a hatred of its stupidity and its throwing away of its freedom. Who or what was now safer because this man in his human weakness had been forced to humiliate himself? What truth had been enhanced by all this anguish?"

Years later, after naming names, Kazan didn't want to apologize for his behavior. However, he felt that though the political aspect of his action may have been correct for him, all that mattered then was the human side of the thing. Speaking of his friend Tony Kraber, producer and folk-singer, and one whom he had named, he said "... I felt that no political cause was worth hurting any other human for. What good deeds were stimulated by what I'd done? What villains exposed? How is the world better for what I did? It had just been a game of power and influence, and I'd been taken in and twisted from my true self. I'd fallen for something I shouldn't have, no matter how hard the pressure and no matter how sound my reasons. ... I only wished that I could have been as generous and as decent as Tony had been with me."

Kraber, though deeply hurt by Kazan and his tes-timony, was nevertheless forgiving enough to express his sympathies to Kazan after his wife Molly's death. It touched Kazan deeply.

Sam Jaffe could not bring himself to forgive Kazan and others who named names. The action had been intolerable. Perhaps it was because of reports that Kazan "ratted" to protect his huge income from films. During questioning by Frank Tavenner, Tony Kraber was pressed into admitting that Kazan's testimony was true. Kraber had recruited Kazan into the Communist Party. In response, Kraber dramatically inquired, "Is that the same Kazan that signed the contract for $500,000.00 the day after he gave names to this Committee? Would you sell your brothers for $500,000.00?"

Freda Diamond, a New York industrial designer and long-time friend of Jaffe, remembered Sam as being one of the few celebrities who wasn't primarily interested in himself. "His acting was only a part of his life. He had so many more interests in life. That set him far apart. He had a sense of humanity. ... Sam was involved. Sam read everything."

Diamond remembers Jaffe having a strong reaction to Paula Strasberg [wife of Lee Strasberg] because she had ratted before the Committee: "I was in Sardi's with Sam and Paula came in. I forget the exact words. He said something to the effect ... There's a snake in the grass (!) which is the kind of thing you'd never expect Sam to say. I don't know what their relationship was before that but he certainly knew her well enough to know what she had done. He made his comment and then quickly cut off conversation about it. ... He did not say that he hated her; it's the way he said what he said. You could feel the depth of his derision. That had quite an impact on me." Because Jaffe urged others not to become bitter or hate-filled and not to waste precious energy in anger, this was a surprise to Diamond.

Jaffe had compassion for those who "broke" with themselves in front of HUAC, especially if that did not include naming others. Diamond recalled that she was very personally and privately disturbed that Sam still went on loving Eddie Robinson when, as she put it, he turned sour politically during the McCarthy days: "He did something to get out of it all that I thought, at the time, was reprehensible. I was amazed that Sam continued to be friendly and warm because a friend was a friend.

"Politically Sam would have had to agree with me about Eddie Robinson but would not like to have talked about it. I didn't discuss it with him. There's no point in making someone say something he doesn't like to say about a person he loves. And Sam was that kind of person. He would circumvent facing out loud the reality of unpleasant things about people."

The unpleasantness had to do with Robinson's giving in to the House Committee on Un-American Activities. They forced him into certain plays to show he wasn't a communist. Sam had refused, as he had refused to name people. He wouldn't bend. He wasn't sorry for anything he had done. "I didn't do anything wrong. I did only good," he reiterated often. His friend Eddie had made a different choice in relation to roles he accepted. In *All My Yesterdays: An Autobiography*, Robinson called himself "... a dupe, a sucker, a fool, an idiot." He admitted that he had been double-crossed ... that he had been a tool, "... an unsuspecting agent of the communist conspiracy."

Robinson hadn't really believed it to be true. Following his third appearance before HUAC in April of 1952, he was so beaten down and demoralized from the effects of being blacklisted that he verbalized the admission he had been a tool. To add salt to the wound, Francis Walter, Chairman of the Committee replied in response, "Well, actually this committee has never had any evidence presented to indicate that you were anything more than a very choice sucker. I think you are number one on the sucker list in the country."

According to Bettye Jaffe, "Eddie had tried to persuade Sam to do what he had done. He wanted him to appear before the committee, say that he was a dupe of the Communist Party and Sam wouldn't do it. He overlooked that totally in Eddie in their friendship. He protected Eddie in every way."

Jaffe could forgive falling apart and denigrating self, but he was immovable against those who abused others by naming them, particularly if the naming was for personal gain. This was true of many of his closest friends as well; they were people traveling the road of same values together. One such creative artist was like a son to him: the brilliantly, spontaneously original Zero Mostel. They shared the precept of honor among men. For them, that honor meant never to waver from truth.

Mostel was a favorite of Kazan, one of the most delightful and funniest companions Kazan had known. When Zero was blacklisted it was Kazan who came to his defense by hiring him. Several years later, after deciding to testify against those who had been communist supporters, Kazan ran into Zero on the street. By then he was hardened against disapproval of his Committee actions, but he found that he did care what Zero thought. He lamented in his autobiography, "He stopped me and put an arm around my neck — a little too tight — and said in one of the most dolorous voices I'd ever heard. 'Why did you do that? You shouldn't have done that.' He took me into a bar and we had a drink and then another, but he didn't say much and I didn't say much. All he did was look at me occasionally, and his eyes were saying what his lips were not: 'Why did you do that?' I never saw him again."

Zero's love and respect could not be there even though Kazan had once personally rescued him. What was there was his great pain over what his former friend had done to others. This was how Sam lived his life as well.

Sam would give up everything, and turn down all help, so that he remained integral. How could he forgive Kazan? In a confrontation with Lillian Hellman before going to testify, Kazan reportedly confessed, "All right, I earned over $400,000.00 last year from theater. But Skouras says I'll never make another movie. You've spent your money, haven't you? It's easy for you. But I've got a stake ..."

Stefan Kanfer, in *A Journal of the Plague Years*, quoted Hellman's reply. "I could never understand his terrible, twisted logic," she recalled with a special shudder; his feeling that he "had to compromise because he was rich."

More likely, Sam Jaffe would have related to the dialogue of John Proctor in Arthur Miller's *The Crucible*. Proctor offered to speak his own sins, such as they might be, but was unable to serve as a judge of others. Like Proctor, Jaffe had no tongue for it. He could not have faced himself if he had sold out his friends. Nor could he or would he relate to others who did.

Jaffe's friend Joanne Dublin thought that he couldn't forgive people who named names because there was no excuse in his mind that would make it possible to do that. "That was the core of his being: total loyalty," she said. "You might not always agree with Sam. He was very outspoken. But you knew there wasn't a thing in the world Sam wouldn't do for you."

Bettye Jaffe recalled that what was hurtful to Sam was that he knew that Kazan knew "that Sam and Philip were not communists because Kazan was a communist. Nonetheless, he tainted them with this brush and probably was one of the instigators in getting Sam blacklisted; he and Lee J. Cobb. Apparently Kazan had told Zero, 'I'll tell them,' and he went swaggering out. He did, he spilled his guts. When you read [his testimony], it's so sickening. I read Lee J. Cobb's. It's very heartbreaking because you see a man groveling, trying to hold onto his career, crumbling. Some writers could never write again.

"Sam did not want to be in the presence of Kazan. If Kazan came in, Sam simply got up and left. You don't live down a thing like that. Some people remember it more the more time goes on. It marinates. Sam was never bitter. He was just not going to say a word to that bastard. As we were leaving a friend said to us, 'Sam, Kazan has a lot of friends.' Sam said, 'Yes, all new.' He could say something that just said it all in a few words."

It may have been a flaw in Sam Jaffe that he could not forgive another his actions. Especially when, in this case, Kazan had later come to one great regret: namely, that he had hurt fellow human beings. This seems to be growth and change in the man, as well as insight. Jaffe had not changed.

While hardened toward those who sang, he remained bonded to those who chose to stand by a "betrayer," whatever his or her reason. Karl Malden was one such friend of Sam's. Malden thinks of himself as antipolitical: "I don't give a damn about politics. I'm against politics. I think they're all crooks. My basic thoughts on politics are: why does a man, a lawyer, a doctor, or a business man who is making maybe $150,000 or $200,000 a year want to join the Senate for $75,000 a year? That's my argument and I stop there. I didn't talk politics much with Sam. He knew that I was anti so he never brought it up, but we talked about a lot of other things. And I'm a dear friend of Kazan's. I still am. And we never talked about Kazan because I knew how he felt about Kazan and I didn't want to bring it up.

"He never forgave him. And yet, I can honestly say that I believe he loved me. We loved each other. It's like father and son feuding. It's that kind of a thing. 'I hate you because you like him' never existed with him."

In some ways Sam took a similar approach to Lillian Hellman's. Arthur Miller appropriately describes Hellman as one who saw her task in life as confronting people with what they already knew but didn't have the courage to live. She had little patience with unconsciousness as an excuse, or innocence either, for that matter.

Years after the hearings, she found herself in a social situation with "namers." Her visible disapproval provoked her hostess to implore her to forgive after all these years. Hellman poignantly replied, "And this is what it comes to. Nobody believed in anything."

Sam stuck to his beliefs. This was evident in his continuing exchange of letters with Nate Spingold, the President of Columbia Pictures, whose help he would not accept even though it would have meant reinstating his career.

Spingold pressed Jaffe: "It is alleged, and only you can testify to the contrary, that from 1942 to 1949 you participated in, advocated, or sponsored a number of organizations which have been cited as subversive by the Attorney General of the United States or by committees of the Congress. ...

"That is a record that you, and only you, created. I frankly don't think that 'lending my name to protest against injustice, or for minority groups' is a good answer; nor do I believe at this point in history with well over a hundred thousand casualties, American casualties in Korea, that forthright explanation of your position is, as you state, 'contrary to the principles which are the foundation of, and reason for our existence as a nation.'

"Please believe that I would like to be of help to you but I can only do that if you help me help you. Obviously, my thinking is sharply at variance from the viewpoint expressed by you. I cannot resist the time worn words of the immortal Holmes: 'Free speech does not envisage your right to call 'FIRE' in a crowded theater.'"

Sam's forthright reply, May 22, 1953, makes clear his position:

"I appreciate your personal friendliness, but I cannot submit myself to a process that is opposed to the principles that I believe in.

"The record of my public activities would, so far from constituting the basis of any charge of disloyalty or un-Americanism, be accepted, I believe, by any impartial tribunal as evidence of good citizenship and loyalty to the United States.

"I have never at any time been a communist. I have never at any time been under Communist Party discipline. I have at all times followed my own conscience and independent judgment and have repeatedly been in public opposition to the 'Communist Party line.' The principle that the end justifies the means, is one that I detest. The action by the Soviets suppressing Civil Liberties and interfering with individual freedom of conscience, art, science and religion, is abhorrent to my way of life and wholly to be condemned. So you see that I, as much as anyone, believe that 'Peace on Earth' must be attained, as you put it in your letter, 'with honor and dignity,' and I too do not wish the 'Brotherhood of Man' forced upon me 'under terms of communist propaganda' in destruction of our American heritage.

"As to these matters there is no issue between us. But I cannot subscribe to any means and methods which nullify freedom while purporting to make it safe. I believe that Justice Holmes would have approved of my viewpoint.

"Embedded in our thinking and practices is the doctrine that no man shall stand trial unless he has been legally and properly brought before a jury of his peers sworn to try him truly. The accuser may not be his judge or one of the jury. To abandon this doctrine is to adopt the tactics of the world forces we oppose.

"These are difficult times for liberals to live in, but there is a rising tide of protest that promises that our free institutions will endure. Men like Senator Lehman, Judge Youngdahl, William T. Gossett, vice-president and

chief counsel of the Ford Motor Co., Einstein, Dean Pike
and the Bishops Sayre and Sherill of the Protestant Epis-
copal Church, and Bishop Oxnam, keep alive our hopes
for the future. I share their viewpoint and hopes.

"'It is not a popular contest,' says William T. Gossett, 'but the preservation of liberty is not a contest for
popularity.'"

So it was that Sam Jaffe took his stand, jobless
but whole, unjustly victimized but undefeated. There
were clear lines drawn in the 1950's. Mercifully, the un-
American activities conducted by the House Committee
finally ended. Kanfer, in *A Journal of the Plague Years*,
sums up the ending of the period: "Of all the blacklisters,
not one was to remain in public view ... Aware, Inc. shut
down its files; they were no longer of interest even to
the FBI ... the blacklisters for the most part escaped with
dollars and reputation intact. As for those who cooper-
ated, who gave names and references, who helped the
inquisition continue — they had only the sentence of that
most overrated court, the personal conscience. None of
them was the type to wear sandwich boards reading Mea
Culpa. For a while they felt excruciating remorse, and
now and then, at some chance encounter, a cooperative
witness would receive a belt from [one] who had the te-
merity to remember."

The clock ticked. The months tumbled from the
calendar. Sam Jaffe waited in a creative void until the
fumes of the unconstitutional poisons passed and the
stigma no longer clung to his reputation. Many questions remained. What would his future be? How would
his present unfold? What was clear was how he got into
this mess to begin with. He had only to look over his
shoulder at his participation in union activities at the Actors' Equity Association to see how the red dye was cast
over his efforts and his expression of values.

Sam had struggled against inequities and though he suffered because of his commitment to change, he would have done it all over again. He was a man of unshakable principle, with tremendous respect for people's rights. The McCarthy times came and went, but as long as Communism reigned in the Soviet Union, red-baiting and the denigration of liberals continued in the United States. Watching the eternal dynamic, Sam commented: "It takes a long time for civilization to happen."

I have devoted a lot time to telling Sam's saga during this period of grave injustice. I was just into my teens when he suffered this blow to his life and career. During that time, because I didn't know any better and because my teachers were too frightened for their jobs to tell us any different, I thought that McCarthy and his gang were the true Americans and that they were protecting our nation. When I finally learned the truth all I could feel was sympathy for those whose lives had been ruined. However, when I became friends with Sam and then later decided to write a book about his life, I saw that I had a chance, belated though it was, to give him complete vindication by researching and telling the whole story of his trial by accusers. And so I have; this was a way for me to give Sam a gift. I hope that in small measure it equals the gift he gave the rest of us by standing firm in his principles and being an example of unshakable integrity.

****

TOM POSTON, *Richard III*, 1947 and *Belphegor, The Montebank*, 1950

"In 1947 I had just finished the American Academy of Dramatic Arts. The status of my career was getting any job that I possibly could, any place that I possibly could.

"I thought the production work at E.L.T. was top notch. I enjoyed the work, the rehearsal. It was marvelous to be able to hear those words and be a part of it, and to be familiar with that particular play from then on.

"In Richard III, I played one of the plotting lords of the court, but in 1950 I played the lead. Indeed, I had moved along quite far. For a man who hadn't made any mark in the business and was still scuffling and looking for work, I was still doing E.L.T.

"When I was in E.L.T., there was no off-Broadway. That came later.

"Words couldn't express the feeling that any sensitive, struggling artist would have for a platform for his work. There is no way to describe how important that is to a young person. That's all we ever wanted. If I could have settled, speaking of selling your birthright, for a steady 52-week-a-year job for Equity minimum at that time, I would still be working for $50 a week. That was how far away such a possibility was and how much I desired to just work, to just be seen performing. I wanted to be perfecting what I considered to be my art at the time and to have an opportunity to do that in any way, shape or form was precious."

****

Remarriage: Play It Again, Sam

Sam Jaffe was resilient. Concerning life, he was an undefeated champion. His childhood lacked stability and the abandonment by his father remained a scar on the wounded little boy within. He met the challenge of youth by making a choice for goodness and by becoming an academic achiever. Although he suffered great losses of mate, family and career, he never lost the will to continue to pursue the future. He never lost himself no matter how great the test or the struggle.

During my lifetime I too have learned this truth that was Sam's salvation: If you do not "lose yourself" you can weather any storm, surmount any difficulty. If you know who you are, honor that, and live that, you can move forward into the new.

When Sam suffered the death of his beloved Lillian, he was 50 years old and in such despair that his friends thought he would never recover. They watched his life-force diminish as he withdrew into hermitage and they were convinced that he too wanted to die. He had given up everything and sequestered himself. He didn't like going out because unexpected stimuli would re-ignite his despair. Late one night, as he was riding home on a city bus, he encountered a couple who were smooching. He looked at them longingly and told himself that that would never happen for him again. Scenes like that caused him to suffer tremendously.

It was hard for Sam's friends to keep him healthy during the grief period because he ate and slept very little. Yet, the austerity was not out of place with how Sam lived much of his life. As a vegetarian he had cut numerous foods from his diet. He never liked to see much food in front of him; it suppressed his appetite immediately.

He began only with a modest amount. If he wanted more he would have it. He didn't like foods mixed together, preferring to know precisely what he was eating. At the same time, he was also easy to please. If the cooking wasn't gourmet he didn't so much care. It was more important that he be served what he wanted and in the proper amounts.

He was a man who didn't need trappings. He lived a very simple life with little need for things. It was people he needed. He valued his friends above all else.

Sam did his grief fully and completely. Though his friends feared for his well-being, Sam never lost sight of his core self and when he had thoroughly suffered the loss of Lillian, he could lift himself up and begin again.

It is not uncommon for individuals to have second chances. What is unusual is when people come back from the depths and reach, not only toward recovery but toward greater heights. Sam Jaffe did this a few years later with his career by becoming the famed Dr. Zorba in the long running, highly successful *Ben Casey* television series. Before that, he did it with his love life.

In 1956, at the age of 65, when many men are retiring to the golf links and relegating their sex life to memory lane, Sam Jaffe began a brand new life with a bride almost 37 years his junior. The betrothal led to a 28-year union that was described by many as incomparable. There were others who questioned whether the bride, albeit willing, gave her life away when she said, "I do." The balance of devotion and dependency will be explored in this saga of their unfolding love affair.

Bettye Ackerman came to New York City from Cottageville, South Carolina, where she had been born in 1928, determined to have a career in acting. She was the granddaughter of a Methodist preacher and daughter of a Latin and math teacher who later became principal of the local high school, and then superintendent of

A young Bettye Ackerman.

schools in the district. Her father encouraged her to read and develop intellectually.

She served as an inspiration to her younger brother Robert, encouraging him not to be satisfied with the ordinary. After their father died, Robert had lost interest in many things, but Bettye encouraged him to read and to develop. Robert praised his sister for never losing the ability to get excited, to be enthusiastic. "She has innocence, a naiveté," he offered softly; "It's protection against the harshness around us. She's very bright. She was always intellectually interesting."

Robert thought that it was their mother, Mary Peoples, who encouraged Bettye to fulfill her desire to become an actress. Mary had an exciting quality about her, unlike their more straight-laced and intellectual father. He suffered chronic high blood pressure and died in his sleep in his late '40's. That was in the summer of 1948 while Bettye was in summer stock.

Bettye had been offered a job teaching English in a college. That had excited her father but she turned it down to be single-tracked about following her dream. She arrived in the big city, newly out of college, with $25 to pursue her goal. She sought acting jobs wherever she could find them and even played in children's theater.

Ackerman was to appear in a *Poetry Series* production of *Tartuffe*, at the Kaufman Auditorium of the well-known 92nd Street YM-YWHA, [Young Men's-Young Women's Hebrew Association] when the man who was to play the lead was hired out from under them with a paying job in a film. No one knew what to do when

Bettye suggested, "We should get the best Tartuffe anybody ever saw." Actor Lou Gilbert said, "Sam Jaffe is the greatest Tartuffe there is. Let's get him."

Others in the company didn't think it possible because Jaffe was such a big name. This was, however, when the blacklist web held Sam and he was taking any job he could to sustain his creative life force. The director told Bettye that if she would go with him, he knew a way to get to see Jaffe.

Bettye agreed. "Sam says I went as bait," she said. "I had no idea." When they arrived, Sam was leaving his comfortable Waverly Place apartment because he could no longer afford it. He was packing up his many books and he wore white gloves because the dust chapped his hands. When he and Bettye were introduced, they simply stared at each other. Clearly, destiny was playing its hand in this meeting.

Bettye had first seen Sam Jaffe in *Gunga Din*. That had been seven years earlier, in a movie house on 42nd St. Fleetingly, she had thought at the time: "That's the kind of man I want to marry. The hair wasn't showing then; he had that turban on. And he was covered up with chocolate. But he was lit up from within," she beamed.

"The minute I saw Sam in person I knew I was going to marry him," Bettye went on. "I knew it was an unlikely match and I didn't know he was looking for anybody. It's the kind of thing that hits you like a bolt of lightning. I had never gone out with an older man before."

When Sam saw Bettye he had a feeling of mystical betrothal. In later reflection he paraphrased Proust saying that he saw something when he looked into her eyes. It was a vision of growing together and it was something that he wanted, that he needed.

It was six months before they got married. "I was recalcitrant a little," Jaffe admitted. "My wife had been dead 15 years and I didn't think I'd be married again."

Sam found himself somewhat bound by convention, thinking that a young woman should marry a young man. However, other factors were at play. At their first meeting, he described feeling a strange spark that gradually went right through him like radiation. "At some point," he marveled, "the various rays come together and intersect. Like lightning [the very word Bettye had used]." He noted her bearing and forthrightness. He liked the assurance he saw. He responded deeply to her passion, her nobility.

Sam had had other chances to remarry before Bettye entered his life. Many women had been after him, but he had shown no interest whatever. When Bettye walked into his apartment, into a way of life the blacklist forced him to live, he was lifted into what would emerge as the next phase of his life.

After that fateful meeting, Sam and Bettye saw each other steadily and often. He wasn't the first man with whom she had been intimate. She had been with a writer whom she referred to as her dress rehearsal. What she felt for him was potent, but she knew it wasn't what she wanted for the long term. Bettye wanted Sam to know that she was experienced and she went so far as to introduce Sam to the writer. Sam handled the meeting well and never brought it up again. Years later, they attended a small dinner party and ran into Bettye's first lover. Sam didn't even recognize him. Bettye felt that represented great security in Sam, that he was mature and understood things in a way others didn't.

Jaffe took over the Tartuffe role and the performance was splendid. By the time the show opened, he and Bettye were in love. Zero Mostel told them that they just had to get married. When they found out that Bettye's birthday was February 28, as was Zero's, and that Lillian had died on February 28, they felt bound together. Zero told Sam: "Look, if any girl ever, under any circumstances, looked at me the way Bettye gazes at you, I wouldn't give it a second thought. I'd leap at the chance. She obviously adores you."

In an interview entitled "May-December Romances: Bettye Ackerman and Sam Jaffe," The *New York Post*, July 9, 1963, Bettye told Judy Michaelson, "I feel that the woman really makes the decision about marriage. I didn't ask Sam to marry me but I knew we would be married."

Sam truly didn't need much convincing. He volunteered that he realized they would get married the minute he saw her. When Bettye asked why it took so long for him to speak up, he replied that it took him six months to chase her!

Friends advised Bettye that if she was in love with Sam Jaffe she was going to have to make the first move because she was so much younger than he, and Sam was a very moral man. While she made the right moves, so did he. She said she chased him until he caught her!

Bettye didn't care that Sam was 33 years her senior. He was known for his energy and vigor. Bettye proclaimed forcefully, "I think Sam is more beautiful than the accepted matinee idol. I like his physiography. I like the way his hair goes zoom, too. I wouldn't call him a saint, but it's like a halo on a human being."

Sam's family wondered what such a beautiful young woman saw in an old man like Sam. However, his relatives were very proud that Sam found someone to cherish him. That was the way they put it and it revealed their values of how a wife was to be toward a husband. They did not say they were proud that the two found each other to cherish.

Cousin Irving Kahn agreed that Sam's life changed when he met Bettye. He too wondered what she saw in Sam: "I can see what he saw in her. Bettye not only turned out to be a good wife but a mother and nurse to him. Of course, Sam was an unusual guy. She wouldn't have found any other like him around the corner. He had great gentility and tenderness and affection."

Both before and after their marriage, the question of age came up repeatedly, particularly in others as they looked in on Sam and Bettye. Friends always asked director Fielder Cook what such a beautiful young woman was doing with an old man.

"It didn't occur to me that they didn't understand how lucky she was," was Cook's response. "They wondered how did he get her and I'm saying, how did she get him?" It's clearly all in the eye of the beholder.

Director Sidney Pollack was 26 years old and just starting his career in 1962 when he worked on *Ben Casey* and felt a little intimidated by Sam: "In those days, I was a very young man and I couldn't understand how a woman of Bettye's age could be married to such an old man. Now of course, I understand it perfectly, being an old man myself. In those days I thought, 'Gosh, how the hell do they make that work?'

Pollack went on: "She was awfully good with him. She adored him. They were terrific together."

While the age difference was great, many observed that they often seemed to be of the same age. He had a very young spirit and was, in the eyes of many, her teacher, father, and lover. Sometimes Bettye appeared to be the older one of the two, especially in the ways she took care of him.

While Sam was renewed in his relationship with Bettye, Bettye flowered as a human being and an artist in the presence of Sam. There was no question about their being meant for one another. What remained in doubt was whether they should marry. It was a serious question for Sam Jaffe and particularly at that critical juncture in his life when the scourge of blacklisting continued to stifle him.

He appeared to need encouragement and help with making a decision. Among others with whom he conferred was a friend from his radio days, Tony Leader. Jaffe asked Leader to join him at lunch with Bettye. During the meal, Jaffe hardly spoke. His face was almost riveted on Bettye Ackerman. At a subsequent lunch, Sam asked Tony what he thought. His question came out of the blue because they had been talking about something else.

Leader scrambled. "What do you mean, what do I think? What do I think about what?" Jaffe said, "About Bettye and me? Should we get married?"

Leader told Jaffe that he was a big boy who should be able to figure it out on his own, but Sam remained concerned about the difference in the age. His friend Tony offered this counsel: "You have less to lose than she does. If she wants to marry you she must have thought it out. She wants to live with you and share your life. And if you care about her enough, you're going to want to do the same. As to the disparity in years, when you sit with her today, you're happy to be there. It will be that way tomorrow too. Why not?"

With an almost boyish quality, Sam asked, "You really feel that way?" Leader replied firmly, "I do. I really feel that way. How do you feel?" Jaffe responded shyly, "I think I feel that way too."

Support from people he cared about enabled Sam Jaffe to have the courage to say yes. When he told Edward G. Robinson about his ambivalence, Eddie reminded him that Bettye certainly couldn't be after his money because he didn't have any. She couldn't be after his fame because though he was well-known, he wasn't very famous. He asked, "What could she want besides you?"

It was difficult for Sam to accept that such a remarkable and beautiful woman would want him. After their many long conversations, Eddie said, "What do you have to lose? The worst that will happen is that you'll get married and you'll be divinely happy for a while and if she changes her mind, you'll have had at least that many years of happiness. And if you don't marry her, you'll always wonder, did I miss it?"

One of the things Sam would have missed was Bettye's first words when she climbed into bed with him on their wedding night, "I gotcha," she said. "I gotcha." But that's getting ahead of the story.

As Sam struggled with whether or not to marry Bettye, the issue of his blacklisting weighed heavily upon him. He told Bettye he loved her, but that his future was behind him. Furthermore, he didn't want Bettye's career to suffer because of his predicament. This worry was dispelled as Bettye's career began to flow.

While Bettye was playing Antigone in a successful run of a Socrates trilogy off-Broadway, Sam's career took a positive turn and he moved immediately to propose to Bettye.

The incident occurred one afternoon when Bettye and Sam were having lunch at the Stanhope Hotel with Edward G. Robinson and Jane, whom he later married. Sam received word to contact producer Kermit Bloomgarden. Bloomgarden asked him if he would co-star with Julie Harris in a tour of *The Lark*. It wasn't the kind of role Jaffe liked and if he hadn't needed the work, he probably wouldn't have played it. Moreover, because Sam was blacklisted, they offered him only $500 a week, half of what he normally would have gotten. Worst of all, Bloomgarden was a friend of his. Sam complained, "That's what your friends did. They gave you a job and knew that you couldn't work anywhere else, so they bought you for pennies."

Later, Sam didn't refer to Bloomgarden as a friend. He said of him, "I knew him." To Sam, real friends were rare.

Leaving Bloomgarden hanging on the phone, Sam swallowed his pride. Returning to the table, Sam addressed Bettye in front of everyone, "I just got a job; will you marry me?" She said yes as quickly as was possible and he returned to the phone to say he would take the job.

Unbeknownst to Sam, Bettye had been offered the understudy to the lead but had turned it down because she didn't want to be gone all those months. Following Sam's announcement and proposal, she promptly called, expressed her interest and was hired.

Bill Ross, who directed *The Lark* on the road, remembered the story somewhat differently. Sam had called Bill to ask if he knew Bettye and what he thought of her. Bill knew and liked her. Bill asked Sam if it was important to him to have Bettye play the tiny role available and understudy others. Sam said that it was and Bill indicated that he would then fight with Lillian Hellman about it because she wanted someone else who was a friend. Through his efforts, Bill said that Bettye got the job.

A flurry of activity followed. Once Sam and Bettye decided to marry they didn't waste a minute, setting the date for the next weekend. By coincidence, Bettye's mother, Mary Peoples, was in New York City as a chaperone with a group of high school seniors. Bettye had arranged it so that she and her mother were going for a walk and the timing would be perfect for them to meet Sam along the way. Bettye said, "Mother, I want you to meet Sam Jaffe. We're going to get married." Before this, Bettye hadn't told her mother anything about Sam. They had dinner together, and the next morning Bettye and Sam drove off with Zero Mostel to tie the knot.

Mary had been open-minded about her daughter marrying an older man. She wanted for her whatever would make her happy. She couldn't get over the fact that Sam spoke seven languages. She proclaimed, "Good God, I don't even speak one well."

Bettye's mother had only one regret. "I didn't get to see her get married," she said. "I wanted her to have a wedding. I cried on the way home that she was getting married that morning and I couldn't be there."

Mary Peoples was still crying when she told the story to her son, Tom, after she returned from New York. She said Sam was older than Bettye's daddy would be if he was still living.

Sam and Bettye got married secretly on June 7, 1956, at East Haddam, Connecticut. Nobody was supposed to know, but almost immediately it came out in the papers. Sam had wanted to avoid the publicity because of his continuing concern that Bettye's career not be ruined as a result of marrying someone blacklisted.

Finally married, the Jaffes were unable to be together. Sam and Luther Adler were doing *The Reclining Figure* at the Roosevelt Theater in Miami. He got that job at the same time he was signed for *The Lark* and was able to fit it in before starting rehearsals. Bettye hadn't completed her run in the Socrates trilogy and couldn't go with Sam to Miami. She asked him what she should do. He said that the show must go on: "You can't put other actors out of work." So they got married and Sam loved laughing over the fact that he spent their honeymoon with Luther.

When Sam checked into his Miami hotel, he gave his 93rd Street address. When Bettye checked in three weeks later, she gave her Peter Cooper Village address. (They hadn't moved in together yet because of their show commitments.) The management couldn't figure out how that could be since they were married. [In those days, there was concern over whether people in hotels were married to one another. Sam had instructed Bettye to be sure to bring her marriage certificate with her.]

Bettye reported with a twinkle, "Usually in a hotel we'd ask for twin beds. The first time Sam said, 'You want twin beds?' I said, 'Yes, we'll both be in one twin bed. That was the idea.'"

When Bettye joined Sam in Miami, Luther Adler borrowed a broken-down jalopy from a friend and drove them around to see the sights. He took them out to dinner and the two young parking attendants were dumbstruck when they opened the doors to let them out. They kept staring at them, knowing they were well-known personalities. It was terribly incongruous to have them in such a vehicle. Finally one said, "Oh, it's a camouflage car!" They felt good having figured it out.

Bettye told how this was the first time they had ever tasted mangos. They were so juicy they had to stand over a sink to eat them, with juice running down their elbows. Then they both looked at each other and quit. They had had enough. They had eaten too many of them.

As with *The Lark*, neither Jaffe nor Adler was being paid very much since both of them were blacklisted. To make matters worse, Sam had trouble cashing his paycheck. He had already received the money and was holding it in his hand when a fan came up and requested an autograph. In the time it took him to sign, the teller had checked and discovered that the company account didn't have enough to cover Sam's paycheck. The teller retrieved the money saying he needed to recount it. Until Actors' Equity resolved the dispute, Sam was out the money.

When they were first married, Bettye questioned Sam about the ways he loved her. Sam mentioned the importance of her being a gifted actress. When she probed as to whether he would love her if she weren't gifted, he said, "No. Talent is a manifestation of a person; in talent you reveal yourself. You can tell on a stage. You can almost read a person."

His honest comment took Bettye back to a former

relationship with a very attractive young man. He was so sweet to her that she considered him a "maybe."

Bettye reported, "When you fall in love ... it hits you, you have no control, nothing. I think Socrates said that love was a serious disease of the brain. I heard this young man do *Hamlet* one night. I couldn't speak to him again it was so dreadful, and I had always felt guilty. Once I heard that Hamlet, he was out of the picture after the first speech. When I heard Sam's comment, there went all my guilt."

Bettye's mother visited Bettye and Sam soon after their marriage. Sam always introduced her as his mother-in-law, but she told him to cut it out because he was "a darn sight older" than she was. From then on he announced her as Bettye's mother.

Mary remembered Sam as one of the most generous people she had ever known. Mary declared, "I believe if Sam was walking down the street and he met a guy who was very raggedy and pitiful looking, he'd say, let me go get a barrel and I'll give you my clothes."

While making a movie in Japan, Bettye bought Sam beautiful shirts. When they came home, the man who was staying in their apartment admired the shirt Sam was wearing. Sam said, "I have several, I'll give you one." Bettye stopped him. "Oh no, you won't. I bought those shirts for you in Japan. You can go out in town and buy him a dozen shirts but you are not going to give him one of these." She had seen Sam wear shirts with frayed edges and give good shirts away. He was excessively generous.

When Bettye asked her mother how she felt about Sam being Jewish, Mary revealed that Bettye's great grandfather, Henry Metzelbaum, was a full-blooded Jew. Tracing the lineage, Mary told her daughter that she, herself, was one-fourth Jewish and that Bettye was one-sixteenth. Sam howled at the news.

Mary Peoples couldn't think of a better husband for Bettye. In the years to come, she spent many weeks with them in their home. During those times, she never heard a cross word. Instead, they called each other by endearing pet names. His was "my love" and she called him "Goki." Mary announced that if a third of the world got along as well as Sam and Bettye, divorce lawyers would be out of jobs.

Bettye's outspoken mother didn't see any change in Bettye after her marriage to Sam. She remembered Bettye could never be held on her lap when she was a child. She was always getting down because she had to be going places. When she was very little they put her in a walker outside. She would run the walker up to the root of a tree, turn it over and get out. She walked at nine months and refused to be put in her carriage.

Mary remembered the start of Bettye's acting career: "When she was two or three she exhibited her talent with little speeches. She'd start saying, 'Be kiet.' Then, 'Ittle Bo Peep had lost her sheep, leave alone, they come home bringin' tails behind 'em.' That's the beginning of her career.

"And, 'Here I stan on two ittle chips, come and kiss my sweet ittle ips.'"

It was after Sam married Bettye that the last leaves fell from his tree of grieving. Aube Tzerko (master pianist and head of the piano department at UCLA), who had walked through that tragic death of Lillian with him, was thrilled for his dear friend when Bettye entered the picture. "It was a total revitalization," he observed. "A new life opened for him. He would always tell me how beautiful she is, how attentive. She was always doing something for him.

"He was an entirely different person after their marriage. The whole past was gone. It was a new life. Revitalization doesn't adequately describe it. It was a renaissance of his life."

Tzerko had no doubt that Sam's marriage with Bettye prolonged his life. Had the sentiments that Sam bore continued, Tzerko had doubt that he could have existed as long as he did, and as beautifully as he did.

Karl Malden concurred wholeheartedly: "My impression on meeting her was like everyone else; my God, she's too young for him, but she wasn't. We were so wrong. She was the best thing that could have happened to him. She really was."

Bettye's career was just beginning. Although *Tartuffe* played for only one night, it was gloriously successful. Later, after their marriage, another producer formed a company of as many of the original as could come. Sam didn't want to do it but Bettye did and got wonderful reviews. Indicating her love for Sam, Bettye reported, "I left *Tartuffe*, much to the distress of everybody, when Sam got a picture with John Huston. I was so in love I couldn't stay."

Not surprisingly, Sam tried to help Bettye's career along. He made calls for her, setting up appointments with producers and directors. Some onlookers worried that Bettye was latching on to Sam because he was a star and could help her career. They worried only until they met her. Her gentility and love for Sam dispelled their concern. They could see the change for the better in Sam as a result of his relationship with Bettye.

Director Lenore DeKoven, who had known Sam since she was a child, saw a similarity between Bettye and Lillian: "As a child I always thought of Lillian as the epitome of the sophisticated artist. Bettye was solid oak American, and yet there was something similar. There was kindness; she was ladylike like Lillian; a kind of classic beauty that didn't need make-up. I've never seen caring such as she extended to him."

Sam thought that women had a practical grasp of

life. "Man is the more romantic element," he assessed. "He wants to give his wife the moon, the sun, the stars — and then he hesitates. But women see through. In Jewish families the woman takes care of the house; she takes care of the children; she is the one with a little money on the side. She knows how to manage with whatever ..."

Sam learned this view of women-in-marriage from his mother, his beloved aunt, and his siblings. His sister Anne thought it wonderful that Bettye would take care of his creature comforts and be a companion for him. Sam had watched the women in his life care for and cater to their men. The men ruled. Sam brought this view into his first marriage even though times were already changing and women were standing up for their rights. Lillian was far more than a housewife. She had a successful career of her own. Yet, she had yielded to Sam's wishes. She gave up musical comedy and she let go of her desire for children. Then she died. As the years tumbled by, women became clearer, stronger of will, and more determined to occupy their rightful place in the whole.

The Bettye whom Sam married was no wimp. She was determined to have a career and she was not one to settle for a lesser relationship. She chose Sam. She loved Sam. But, did she love him too much? Bettye was clear about many things in her relationship with Sam, not the least of which was that Sam's career came first: "I feel I love Sam better than I do myself."

Almost everyone who knew the Jaffes called their marriage the happiest they had ever seen. They agreed that Bettye's attention to Sam was unique. Rarely has there been such tremendously warm, unselfish, absolute devotion. Few had seen anything like it. Did he demand it of her? Did she give it because she was a new bride, head over heels in love? Did he reciprocate? More importantly, did he reciprocate equally?

Actress Ruth Warrick observed that the two of

them were never cloying in their love. An intellectual love accompanied the rest of it. They had tremendous respect for one another. "I think she just absolutely worshiped him," Warrick said. "And he, of course, adored her." There was mutuality but not necessarily equality of focus of attention.

Sam Jaffe didn't know what Bettye saw in him. The one thing he did know was that he was very happy with her. With her mix of independence and deep caring, Bettye was a perfect woman to fill the void in Sam Jaffe's life. They began in love and they remained in love, even long after Sam's death.

As soon as they got married the whole world opened up for them. In the strength of each other they could surmount anything. In the love of each other, their days were filled with joy. In the union of soul mates, the pall that hung over Sam Jaffe's life and career lifted and the light of new promise entered in.

Sam and Bettye Jaffe
at home in 1978.

****

MICHAEL LOMBARD, *Paths of Glory*, early 1960's.

"When I did the show I was just beginning. It may have been my first New York professional production. It was my first exposure and the first time I got to see agents who had come to see the play. It was a wonderful time for me, and for most of us in the cast. It was so hard to get to see anybody. E.L.T. was a really respected showcase for actors. It started my professional life in New York.

"It was not an ideal theater that we had at the time. It was an auditorium in a school. It was makeshift in many ways. It wasn't big budget. The actors were first rate and the production was quite exciting. It was very well directed. Tony LoBianco was in it. It was an opportunity for me to work with working professionals in a professional situation. I had a very good part and I was finally a professional actor. I had been in summer stock before as an apprentice but I was not on their level.

"E.L.T. put me in the mainstream. All I can say about E.L.T. is that I never had to work there again. It really set me on the road. I worked forever steadily ever since."

****

Mr. and Mrs. Jaffe

Once Sam finished his obligations in Florida, he and Bettye took to the road. Ironically, *The Lark* opened in Central City, Colorado, a mining town where Sam had done *The Doll's House* years before when Lillian had accompanied him.

Sam's life was on the move again. He had a partner and he had a job. He had seen his future as behind him. But he pushed the past behind him, and Bettye went forward with him. Life had been tough going for seven years. However, quoting the Bible Sam said, more solemnly than triumphantly, "Truth crushed to the ground will rise again."

One of his missions in doing *The Lark* was to be able to pay his sisters back the money he had borrowed. He took great satisfaction in being able to achieve this.

From the beginning of their love relationship, Bettye Jaffe was attuned to Sam in profound ways. Even when they were in performance together, no matter where Bettye was, it was as though she had a third eye for Sam. Bill Ross had noticed it during the tour of *The Lark*: "I've never been with them when I wasn't aware of Bettye reacting to Sam's slightest move."

This was a characteristic of Bettye's that lasted during their whole marriage. It wasn't that she hovered over Sam. Rather, she anticipated his needs and was there to meet them.

During the tour of *The Lark*, Jaffe got a call in the middle of the night from Henri-Georges Clouzot, the great French director. They conversed in French, since Sam was fluent, and also because Clouzot was testing Jaffe's ability. Clouzot had seen Sam's brilliant performance in *The Asphalt Jungle* seven times and he told him that he just had to have him in his new movie *Les Espions*. Sam wasn't sure he could even get a passport but Clouzot told him he would make sure that he got one because he had to have him.

Jaffe hired a lawyer, Sidney Cohn, to help him obtain a passport. When *The Lark* was playing in Washington, Sam had a hearing before the Passport Board in the afternoon, a performance that night, and a cast party after the show where, because it was Julie Harris' birthday, Sam presented Julie with a pewter plate. "Then he almost died when we came to the hotel," Bettye reported.

His exhaustion was a reaction to the hearing that had lasted three hours. He responded to all their questions, remembering every group he had ever supported. He reminded them that though he attended some socialist meetings, he had never been a communist. The socialists and the communists were bitterest enemies.

Jaffe's testimony and memory so impressed the Passport Board that they delivered a limited passport to him before he and Bettye could even board the elevator to leave the building.

Free to leave the country at the end of the tour of *The Lark*, Bettye and Sam continued to enjoy one of the richest aspects of their marriage, a shared creative life. They enjoyed being with each other while only one of them was working as much as they enjoyed working together. In addition, their work was to take them to different locations in the world where they could explore the new and build lasting memories together. Sam was given a new lease on his career and Bettye's began to flourish.

Sam's assignment in *Les Espions* allowed the Jaffes to spend four and a half months in Paris. Clouzot had helped Jaffe to break the barriers against him. After that, Sam was able to work in films again. Although the blacklist would always crop up, at least there was a crack in it. That crack opened the way for Jaffe to work for John Huston in the film *Barbarian and the Geisha* in Japan. Bettye and Sam lived there for 19 weeks and found it a heavenly experience.

In the same way the blacklist blockade had halted Sam's film career for over seven years, once the dam broke, the work flowed as if a mountain stream in the warmth of spring.

Sam's next role was Maimonides in the movie *Ben Hur*. It was a vast production and required significant preparation. Bettye remembered that it was very tedious for Charlton Heston who used to say that by Thursday it felt like Saturday! The company often worked until midnight and didn't even have Sunday off.

During the shooting of *Ben Hur*, Bettye left Sam for six weeks to do a film in Sweden called *Face of Fire*. [Sam was to have played the Judge, a wisdom figure. The part was written for him by veteran screenwriter Lou Garfinkle. But the timing conflicted with *Ben Hur*.]

Bettye's role in *Face of Fire* represented a turning point in their young marriage. She discovered that they couldn't be separated. It wasn't healthy for their relationship, even if it was beneficial for their careers. Bettye decided that from then on she would work when she could, but only if it didn't take her away from him. "It was from my point of view," she confided. "I didn't tell him. I just went and did what I wanted to do. I didn't want to be away from him. And he obviously didn't want to be away from me."

The way Bettye reports it here, it was all her decision and Sam in no way forced her to give up her career. He surely let her know that he needed her and wanted her with him. But she was the one who made the choice. She didn't want to be away from him. Was Bettye sacrificing herself for Sam's needs or was she fulfilling her own by her devotion to him? She says he didn't want to be away from her either. Yet, he did not turn down roles that would cause them to be apart. It was Bettye who made those career decisions. Sam's career came first with both of them. Sam came first, with both of them.

Bettye did continue working, co-starring with Steve Forrest in *Rascal* for Disney Studios, and then playing the executive secretary in *Bracken's World* and Nurse Marsh in *Medical Center*. Over the years, she appeared on *Mannix, Bonanza, Perry Mason, Hitchcock Presents, Chrysler Theatre, The F.B.I Story, Alcoa Presents*, and *The Waltons*.

Right after *Ben Hur* Sam played a wonderful part in the television series *Bonanza*, playing Emperor Norton, a fascinating figure in San Francisco who was a successful entrepreneur. He called himself the Emperor of the United States and the Protector of Mexico. Mark Twain and a number of others would write editorials and feature him. They were in love with him. He would act for any oppressed people.

When the show was run, the response to it was the largest made to any single episode of *Bonanza* and the producers asked Sam if he would do a series based on the character. The network took the decision out of his hands by deciding not to do a series based on a Jewish character.

Instead of a series, Sam continued to do one-shot television shows, such as his next role as a blind man on *Daniel Boone*. In every case, Sam received star-billing.

Bettye was delighted that Sam was working. On the other hand, the two of them were rarely alone. "That's why we'd run away for a wedding anniversary for two weeks," Bettye said. "One day we were going to spend the whole day together. We decided that that whole day, one would not speak to the other except in a cliché. I want you to know that you can say anything on earth; there's a cliché available for everything. We were hysterical. It was a game we played." That was a day they both cherished.

Sam and Bettye's relationship was probably one of the great love affairs of Hollywood. They not only adored each other, everyone could feel it. Their love was vibrant. It was a cultural experience for both of them, with on-going explorations and a spiritual dimension. It was a marriage of two artists who invested their daily time in what would enrich their careers. This, in turn, enriched their marriage. An example was when Bettye bought a recording of Horowitz playing at Carnegie Hall after an eight year hiatus. She set it up so that she and Sam would spend the afternoon lying on their Roman couch together, listening to Horowitz.

There was so much in life that interested them, including their friends and their problems, as well as their family. "We had a hell of a lot of fun," Bettye confessed. "We played a lot. When we went to Hawaii we each had a whole suitcase of books that we were going to read. A friend said, 'Sam Jaffe in Hawaii? There's no culture there,' which says more about the friend ..."

Their travel agent and friend Jimmy Rety`s response was, "Mr. Jaffe carries his culture with him."

Bettye and Sam spent their vacation days reading, and in the evenings they would go for walks and discuss what they had read. They used the dictionary and encyclopedia frequently as they were both interested in words, their different meanings, and how those meanings changed with time. Bettye marveled that Sam used words beautifully and in an unusual way. He could take a word and twist it, making it wonderful. After his death, she missed that terribly.

Bettye always addressed Sam as "My Darling," as if that were his first name. She had a unique talent for handling Sam and for smoothing things over when he dug in his heels or lost his temper.

On a typical occasion, the Jaffes were scheduled to go to Europe. When the time came for departure, Sam decided he wasn't going. Wheras Bettye was upset at first, she decided to let fate handle it rather than creating worry. She said very little to Sam, offering him no opposition. As if by some magic, the day before they were to leave, Sam announced that he was going.

While people often referred to Sam as a genius, Bettye's genius was in knowing how to handle Sam.

Right after their marriage, Bettye wanted Sam to go south with her but he didn't want to go. "You had the New York liberal prejudice against the south," she told him later. Sam said it was because of the hangings.

After going down for two weeks to visit family, Sam said, "There's more of the South in the North than there is in the South." Sam made this remark in 1956. Bettye indicated that he was clearly ahead of his time. When it came to integration, the North didn't do nearly as well.

Bettye reflected on the way they integrated in the North: "A lot of our friends, our liberal friends, were giving $150, $250, for bussing in the South and they had big rallies. Then when it came to talk about bussing where they were, it was a totally different story. Their children could not be bussed. And they did not want their children to be integrated with blacks. As soon as it meant that their children were to be integrated, they were totally against it whereas they had been so for it. It was because their children were different."

During the *Ben Casey* series, while the Jaffes were visiting in the South, Bettye's mother wanted her to come to see her nephew's new school that was a long way from his home. He had been bussed and when they arrived he was the only white boy playing on the basketball court. Bettye remembered how proud he was that they had come. "He came rushing over, introducing me to his friends," Bettye remembered. "I felt like crying. I was so emotional. Then the principal of the school, who was black, came out and he was very happy I was there. He asked me to come and speak to each room. I did, answering questions and talking to them. I didn't say anything to my mother because I suddenly realized that they were so much more advanced than our Beverly Hills friends. This was just a natural way of life." When Bettye's brother Robert came home later, she remarked that Mark's school was 75 to 80 percent black. He responded, "You're not going to believe this, but I never asked."

Bettye quoted the artist Charles White who said he trusted the southerner more than he trusted the northern liberal. When a southern loved you, you knew it was true. It was not a pretense.

Through Bettye, Sam developed affection for the South, though he had not changed his feelings altogether. Early impressions remained imprinted. Felix Bauer, who headed a college art department in South Carolina where Bettye eventually had several showings of her paintings, pointed this out in recalling a visit with Sam and Bettye and her family in Columbia, South Carolina: "Sam said with a kind of a smirking smile, 'What are we doing here? They are such lovely people but why am I sitting here in the kind of good southern society that fits in with *Gone with the Wind*?'"

The Jaffes career kept them so busy that Bettye's younger brother Tom and his wife Glenna didn't get to meet Sam until more than a year after their marriage. The Ackermans went up to New York City and Sam went out of his way to make sure that they had a good time. He joined them in tourist activities and they experienced him as very generous, sincere, and most eager to please.

Glenna remarked that while Sam never made fun of people, "He did find it fascinating that I, coming from rural Texas, didn't know what a bagel was and had never eaten pizza."

The Ackermans observed that Sam Jaffe had an ability to make anyone feel that they were very special. This was a remarkable trait of his that applied to interactions with strangers as well as family and friends. After an encounter, Jaffe knew the person because he listened with undivided attention to what he was saying. This was a unique quality. All too often people listen while simultaneously planning their response. Thus, they listen more to what they are about to say than to what is being said.

It wasn't long before Sam made a place for himself in the midst of Bettye's family. At first they were in awe of his intelligence and how unusual he was, but because he was loving and kind, they could quickly feel close to him. He was especially sweet to the children, making time for them and being gentle.

Because Bettye liked to go home for Christmas, she and Sam made the journey often. Sam, raised in Jewish traditions, was careful to ask questions about the customs in the Ackerman family. There were significant differences. In New York everyone just started eating without even waiting for everyone to sit down at the table. In contrast, Bettye's family would sit down and say a prayer. When Sam first joined them and immediately started eating, the children looked at him in amazement. Then Bettye intervened, explaining to Sam that they don't eat until the food is blessed.

When Tom instructed Sam about the holding of hands during the prayer, Sam wanted to know if that had anything to do with the blessing. "For us it's just the closeness of the family," Tom told him.

The next time the Jaffes came, Sam asked, "Do I wait now? Do I wait?" When he came down to eat his grits in the morning [he loved grits], he would put cream on it and then he would say, "Now what do I do about the blessing, Bettye?" Even when he was all alone, he wanted to do the right thing.

This was a piece of behavior modification Sam Jaffe was never to forget. The year before he died, Glenna and Tom invited Sam and Bettye to join several other guests to partake of fresh oysters they had brought from Savannah. Bettye called Sam to come in and get some oysters. He said, "Do you think it would be nice to eat before the guests come?" He had become southern in his manners.

On visiting with family, Sam practiced patience and endurance, but he also may well have developed an interest in family that was not there before. He was more willing to go to family functions in the later years of their marriage until he was ill and less able to travel. Wanting to make Bettye happy may have motivated his going. Family friend Paul Hardin thought, "It was one of his ways of thanking her, because he knew it was very important to her. In the process, he probably gained some appreciation of it himself."

Sam Jaffe was unique in Bettye's family. His young nephew, Mark, Robert and May's son, liked having an uncle from a big city. Sam brought qualities very different from what everyone was accustomed to in the little town of Due West, South Carolina.

Sam impressed his nephew and the rest of the family with his great memory. He was always reciting lines from plays he had been in. Mark said of his uncle, "Sam wasn't pretentious at all, but he was a special man and you realized that when you were around him. I was impressed with his perception of things. I remember when we lived in Madison, New Jersey, he and dad were arguing over the location of a particular college. Dad was a college president, so he knew. Uncle Sam swore it was not in that town. So they looked it up in an encyclopedia and Dad was right. Sam said, 'That must be an old encyclopedia.' His wit was incredible. He was very funny. He didn't crack a smile when he said it."

While reflective of his humor, the story also speaks

of Sam's stubbornness. Most people related to that stubbornness as endearing. It was reminiscent of the time at the Jaffes' Beverly Hills home when Sam was attempting to get out of their car. Unless Bettye parked it in a certain way, a tree was in the way of the door on Sam's right side. Jaffe was always hell-bent on getting in and out. Bettye would tell him to wait a moment while she backed up, but he wasn't going to wait. On one occasion he started to get in and suddenly caught his head in such a way that it could have been severed. Bettye rushed around to find his body in the car and his head trapped outside. She opened the door a little and turned his head so he could get in. His response was, "I told you I could do it."

Patience was certainly not a virtue of Jaffe's. Bettye once asked him about his never experiencing depression. His response was that he didn't have time for it.

Everything he did, he did whole-heartedly: his work, the way he loved, the way he went to a museum. Life was very exciting to him. Bettye recalled how he would run across the street to catch a taxi with cars blowing their horns all around him. "Once," she said, "a car struck him and he fell across the hood. The man was very concerned but Sam said, 'Go on. Go. Go. I'm in a hurry.'"

Just as Jaffe was humorous and lacking in patience, he was also very honest. If he didn't like a person, it was very quickly obvious. He was outspoken. Most people try to be polite. Sam was polite, but he said what he had to say without thinking about whether to say it. It was Bettye who taught him temperance. All his life he had too easily dismissed people he didn't like or respect. He wasn't nasty about it. Rather, he was often very humorous.

In one instance before Sam and Bettye were married they attended a yoga demonstration. The experience seemed pretentious to them and they started giggling to the point of causing their chairs to shake. During the intermission, Sam tasted the punch and called it piss. They could not cease laughing after that. The tears were rolling down their faces because they wanted to be polite and suppress their reaction but they couldn't.

Sam's New York upbringing groomed him to be outspoken. His friends were the same and they encouraged the practice in each other. They said and did outrageous things. One night in New York, at Lindy's, Sam Jaffe, Zero Mostel, and a very young comedian named Buddy Hackett, sat at a table near a man who was so volatile, loud, and obscene that it cast a pall at Jaffe's table. They pondered what to do about it. Suddenly Zero's rubbery face contorted and he was a Cyclops. He took a butter knife and a big piece of butter and he tapped the man on his shoulder. The man turned to Zero, terrified of his face because he really did look like a deranged Cyclops. Zero took the man's tie and smeared butter on it. He didn't say a word. Sam went into convulsions. The vulgarity at the table stopped.

Director Lamont Johnson remembered an experience in Beverly Hills with some of Jaffe's buddies. He went to Nate and Al's [restaurant] but it was too crowded for him to be seated. The lady maître d' looked around and told him that if he didn't mind sharing a table he could be seated immediately. At the table were Zero Mostel, Milton Berle and Sid Caesar. Johnson was awed. Zero took one look at Johnson and shouted gruffly, "Is this the one? He's a goy. Traif. Throw him out." The whole restaurant burst into laughter.

The Jaffes were not without spice in their relationship. They would argue with one another and neither of them would give in. Instead, they would go on to the next topic and have at it!

Bettye's brother Robert noted that the Jaffes maintained deep appreciation of each other. A strength of their marriage from the beginning was that they could argue and disagree without it becoming overwhelming. Each matched the other in stubbornness. Robert said Bettye "was an equal match for Sam, especially if something interested her. Many things that were deeply interesting to him were only of peripheral interest to her and she wouldn't argue with it. But if it came to something that was important to her, that she had studied herself, she could match him."

Questioned on the subject, Bettye confided, "We didn't have any real problems together. If we did, it was the tiniest thing. I remember once Sam got very angry about something. I don't even remember what it was. He shouted and went crazy. I started laughing. I laughed and laughed. It made him angrier and angrier and he said, 'What are you laughing at?' I said, 'Sam you're so silly.' There was a long pause. Then he threw himself into my arms and we laughed and laughed because he was so silly. He just looked like a jumping jack, that red hair and beard. One thing that was so lovely about him was that if he did get angry with me over some little something, we'd talk about it. He never brought it up again. That was it. It was never referred to again, as if it was totally forgotten. So many people I know bring up something again and again. He never did that. I consider that an enormous blessing. He'd bring something up and expend all the energy right then and there, and then it was finished. I learned that from Sam."

That was how Sam had emerged from the blacklist and still retained his patriotism. He fully expended his anger, despair, disappointment, and disillusionment. This enabled him to continue to love his country.

In the early years of their marriage, those who had long been friends of Sam wondered what it would be like to relate to the young wife he had chosen. They started out with apprehension, but from the moment they met Bettye they found her utterly delightful. Bettye was sweet, relaxed, and natural, and Sam's joy in having her was wonderful to watch. What had happened to him fascinated his friends.

People talked of the Jaffes' relationship as being on another plane. They were good for each other, each growing due to the influence of the other. Sam taught Bettye to have a deeper intellectual appreciation of theater and of Judaism. He added to her depth of being.

Bettye had a wonderful way with Sam. She felt that they were twins and that she knew what he wanted and needed even before he asked. She took care of him in a gentle, dignified way that was hard to describe. He not only let her, he asked her and wanted her to look after his needs. However, judgments on what the behavior meant would depend solely on the point of view of the observer.

Nanette Fabray described the dynamic as one in which Sam never had to do anything. She noted he "sat around and was the King Pasha." Fabray wondered who had set the arrangement. Was it Bettye's way of being a wife? Did she do so much so often that he came to expect it? Fabray thought it very old fashioned. "She happily was a geisha lady to him," she marveled. "She was extremely protective and watchful of him."

Fabray felt they were too good to be true. She wondered when it would all come crashing down because never once did she find anything about them that was less than perfect. It wasn't that they tried to be perfect, but rather that, as she put it, they were incredible people.

"Sam and Bettye were so bonded and yet they weren't closed off from the rest of the world," Fabray stated. "They shared themselves with everyone else. They were one and they let you in on it."

When Lillian died, Sam lost his center of gravity.

Zero had helped to steady him. The two were like mischievous little boys, playing all the time. When Bettye came along, she became his center of gravity and Sam's life took on new meaning.

Bettye did give Sam her constant attention and he did depend on her. Late in their marriage, during an interview when Sam was trying to recall his early theater career, he referred to Bettye as his memory. He called her into the room and asked her to help him. When she told him that she had much to do, he simply responded, "I know." Then she said of her own work, "I'll do it later," and she stayed there with him instead.

The role Bettye Jaffe enacted in the play of their marriage never disturbed her. It was as if it was her privilege to serve him rather than being expected to. The pattern lasted throughout their married life. One incident in their later years together is illustrative:

Being very knowledgeable in the area of art, Sam rallied to Bettye's support, encouraging her career as a painter around 1963. Her works have since been exhibited in many shows around the country. Sam would attend with pride and had a gracious way of stepping into the background, giving Bettye a chance to be the star for the evening.

During a show of Bettye's paintings in San Diego, she and Sam had spent a long day on their feet. The accolades Bettye received pleased Sam but toward the end of the day he grew very tired. Bettye, on the other hand, was in her glory. At one point he told her that he must go back to the motel. She was heard to say, "Yes, my sweetheart, of course you must." Then someone would interrupt to talk with her and Sam would call, "Bettye!" The people present saw him wanting her to pay attention to him, being demanding. Friends said of them, he wanted what he wanted and Bettye gave him what he wanted.

Situations like this, when he had physically gone past the point of being able to remain, must have been very trying for Sam. Yet he didn't pace himself, arrange for himself in advance, or call a cab when he had to leave. He didn't have to care for himself because Bettye did. Most of the women in his life did that for him.

There were areas in their relationship in which Bettye would not give an inch. An incident later in their marriage is a case in point. At the age of 76, Sam decided he wanted to buy a Honda motorcycle. This is the very same man who hated driving a car. Although he didn't drive, when he was out with Bettye he would want to tell her how to drive. He would want her to go the wrong way down a one-way street. He would insist that was where they wanted to go. They would argue and fuss. The few times he did drive would be at a snail's pace. When he would arrive at a corner, he would stop and wait. He would wait until another car began to cross and then he would dash across in front of it. He was very nervous and had no sense of judgment. He would wait until he felt safe. Perhaps it was more helpful to see another car and dart out than to anticipate a car coming out of nowhere and hitting him. Whenever he drove, it was like having a lethal weapon on the road. As previously mentioned, several in his family died after auto accidents.

Jaffe's fascination with motorcycles began when a fellow actor offered to take him to the bank on the back of his bike. Jaffe had the time of his life flying through the streets. He announced to Bettye that he was going to get one and she bellowed, "Over my dead body." She ranted and raved and refused to discuss the subject further. That night, they attended a party and a woman rushed over to Sam and told him she nearly ran into him that afternoon because she was so surprised to see him on a motorcycle. At that point, Jaffe gave up the idea.

Jaffe not only didn't drive, he had no sense of direction even when walking. He would step out of a hotel and Bettye would always have to grab him. He would be out the door and hell-bent on where he was going, but he would going in the wrong direction. He was confident he had turned correctly.

When they were out shopping one day, Sam disappeared after Bettye had turned away for a moment. He was nowhere to be found because he had a way of moving like lightning. Bettye found a policeman and asked if he had seen Sam Jaffe, the actor. The officer put his hand up high over his head to indicate Sam's hair and pointed in the direction of where he had seen him. When Bettye caught up with him she suggested that he try going left every time he thinks he should go right. Sam replied: "I could never fool myself that way."

While Sam Jaffe was intellectual and worldly, he was equally unsophisticated. One night, at a party, someone admired his shoes and asked where they came from. He said, "I don't know. Some little store there on Rodeo Drive." It was Gucci's. He had no idea who Gucci was.

Sam Jaffe was a mix of temper and tenderness. He was generous but also possessive and demanding. Yet together, Bettye and Sam Jaffe were an inspiration to everyone. They were living examples of goodness, honesty, and morality. They were people of substance in a marriage of mutual appreciation. The impression held by singer Stephanie Barber, who met them in the early 1970's was that they "weren't hugging and kissing every minute, but the love, affection, regard, and respect for each other what such that you could feel it. Sam was a happifying person. You'd prefer to be in his company than not to. Knowing Sam reinforced my own feelings that the most important thing in life is regard one for the other."

She said that she and others seemed to be better people for having spent time with him: "It was very potent. He gave forth an extraordinary kind of vibration."

My partner and I also met Sam and in the early 1970's. Sam was performing in a show in San Diego and a friend of theirs decided that the four of us just had to meet each other. Jerry was very right! After the performance he brought them over to our house. As I mentioned at the beginning of the book, it was love at first sight. We could have talked all night, but since it was past all of our bedtimes we decided to meet up again, at their house in Beverly Hills. Every meeting that followed was stimulating, enriching, fun, and mutually nourishing. We knew that Sam really liked us when, given a choice about where to go for Thanksgiving, Sam would choose to come with Bettye to San Diego to join the small gathering at our home.

As a couple, the Jaffes dealt with life-blows together. One of their strengths was that they never became bitter or hateful, or even mean. They didn't complain or feel sorry for themselves. Neither Sam nor Bettye ever seemed to want to take anything destructive on to themselves. At the same time, they did not avoid seeing. They made choices about how they would look at the world, and with what eyes they would look.

Bettye's brother, Robert, described them both as having "generosity of spirit." He meant a proclivity to see goodness in other people. He implied that seeing the good in others says something about the seer.

Robert knew that people often took advantage of Sam because of his generosity but he never heard him talk of it. On one occasion Sam did report to Bettye that he had seen that he had given too much of himself away. He said that he had reached down to help and that he had been pulled down in the process.

Both Sam and Bettye gave too much of themselves away. They were each distressed about what a spendthrift the other was with time, energy, and money.

Sam snapped at Bettye once for saying that someone had borrowed money from him that he never returned. Sam said, "Don't mention anything like that. I don't like it. When you give money, you give it. When a friend asks you to lend him some money," he said, "you don't ask what the problem is. You give it to him."

Throughout his marriage to Bettye, Sam was ever on the lookout for how he could be helpful in someone else's career. A job for Sam meant an opportunity for him to help another. For example, Sidney Pollack's first few directorial assignments were on *Ben Casey.* Sam told producer Sy Gomberg how much he appreciated Pollack. He told Gomberg, "Get this guy." Both Bettye and Sam recommended Pollack to him.

On the *Casey* show, it was difficult to find directors who could handle the fast pace and lack of rehearsal time. Sam would never knock anyone. Instead he said of Pollack, "It is such a relief to have a talented director. We have found one and we think you should know him. He makes you feel real."

Repeatedly this turned up in descriptions of Sam Jaffe. He refrained from giving voice to the negative. He looked for what he could praise and spent his energies in that way.

Both Sam and Bettye had an outward focus. They were always helping people and never taking credit. An example of this was the help given to their friend Charles Higham. When Higham was writing a biography of Ava Gardner, it was mandatory that he interview John Huston. He mentioned it to Sam and Bettye. Sam called Huston and said, "You will see Charles." He didn't ask, "Will you see him or would you like to see him?" He said, "You will see him." Huston said, "Yes."

When Virginia Bortin was writing a book about the great American patriot John Dickinson, Sam showed great interest because he loved that kind of personality.

She was trying to think of a saying to use at the beginning of this book to illustrate the man. Sam thought about it for a long time and much later on returned to Bortin with a phrase from Ibsen, having to do with the iconoclast always being 13th at table. It perfectly illustrated everything she wanted to say. She was very touched that he had spent time thinking about it. She had spent a year trying to find the right saying and Sam had just brought it out from the full place in his mind where he stored and remembered everything.

The Jaffes not only gave to others, they would give unasked if they saw a need. Their friend, actress Evie Scott worried about them. "Sometimes they got taken in by people," she remembered, "and in some instances they should have known better. There's such a thing as being too trusting with the wrong people. It means you haven't used your good sense."

Rather than be suspicious of anyone, Bettye would go overboard in the other direction. Whereas some people open their door to anyone, Bettye would take it off the hinges.

This helping of others, this commitment to making good things happen in the lives they touched, enabled them to allow their love to flow and expand instead of keeping it insulated and static.

Maxine Gomberg noted that when you walked into their house for a gathering, you could feel and see the pulse of the energy: "They had a beautiful relationship and made you want to have what they had; the way they looked at each other. They were so supportive of each other; so much so that they didn't have to talk about it."

Jaffe's generosity had another side to it. He didn't know how to receive from others and therefore denied them the privilege of being generous. When the Ackermans and the Jaffes dined at their favorite restaurant in

Hoboken, New Jersey, the Clambroth House, Robert considered it a major achievement when he could get the bill. Sam was aggressive about being generous. While Robert and others worried about Sam being taken advantage of, Sam was not only treating but closing them out. He was quick to insist because he determined that he had more money than the others present. Even when the other indicated he was on an expense account, Sam still insisted on paying.

It was a deficiency of Jaffe's that he wouldn't receive from others. When one is always on the giving end, he remains in control and in a superior position. While it is hard to know if this was important to Jaffe, his independence certainly was.

Robert told of an incident in Sam's later years when Jaffe had trouble walking on the way to the restroom at the Clambroth House. Robert didn't want him to go alone because of his unsteadiness, but he didn't want Sam to know that his motivation was fear for his safety. He stood with Sam, but felt very awkward because he knew it would insult Sam.

Jaffe was fiercely stubborn about such issues, sometimes foolishly so. He was a very difficult man to help in any way.

Robert never had an experience of Sam or Bettye needing anything from him. He said, somewhat poignantly, "I hope she would ask but I'm not sure that she would. Sam never asked."

Even in Sam's later years, when he was frail, he would carry the bags at the airport when he came to visit. He wouldn't let others carry them. He simply didn't know how to let others have the joy of giving to him.

He did, however, receive from Bettye, if not burden her. If someone offered to get him something, he would say, 'No, Bettye will do it.' He also allowed Bettye to take over other aspects of his life, such as deciding what foods he would eat when they went to restaurants together. She was aggressive about his health and he was very patient with her.

After the Jaffes moved to Beverly Hills, actor and director Ezra Stone often went with Sam to Nate and Al's for lunch. He remembered when Bettye gave Sam permission to eat something that he wasn't supposed to eat, and he was so grateful to her for letting him.

"He was happy as a lark, like a little boy with extra candy," Ezra chuckled. "It was always so wonderful to see them together and how well she took care of him; her pride in it and his colossal pride in her taking care of him. It was great fun to be with them. They were always like the little love birds outside their house." [This was a reference to a decorative wrought-iron piece that hung on the front of their house; a piece of Bettye's art work.]

When, in his last years, Sam met someone for the first time, he would say, "This is my beloved Bettye. She keeps me alive." It was perhaps his way of paying tribute to her. It seemed there was a clear recognition on his part of what Bettye was doing.

That was probably why Sam put up with her telling him what to eat. He put up with more from her than anyone. He also demanded more from her than anyone else.

When the Jaffes went to friends' for dinner, Bettye would often consult in advance about the menu, but if the food didn't fall into Sam's dietary choices, he simply wouldn't eat. He never made an issue of such an occurrence, but when the food was to his taste and liking, he was profuse in his admiration.

In the 1950's, vegetarians sometimes had difficulties with obtaining meatless dishes. They also took flak from their friends. Actor Lou Jacobi found Sam to be a tolerable vegetarian: "He never bored you with it. People who talk about vegetables and this and that, are the bores of the world."

Nanette Fabray confirmed that the Jaffes were low key about being vegetarians. At their own parties they always had different kinds of food for everybody. They never made an issue of it. When they went to visit Fabray she always had a supply of veggies for them. As others reported, no matter what they were served, they were very gracious.

When they visited us for Thanksgiving we always had a vegetarian meal; not just for them but because it was our preference as well.

There were times when the Jaffes drove their hosts crazy by arriving for dinner precisely at the appointed hour. Most guests, especially in Beverly Hills, had the courtesy to arrive at least a few minutes late to give the never-ready hosts a chance to pretend to be ready.

When Sam and Bettye worked together, they didn't try to influence each other. They would study separately and then come together later. When they did Shylock and Portia at Dickinson State College in North Dakota, Sam had done Shylock before. Bettye had done scenes but had never studied the character to do it. She stopped accepting work for three months and worked with someone on the iambic pentameter. She wanted to be sure she had that in her subconscious. Then she read the play almost every day for three months and listened to records to get her speech as good as she could. After the three months, the Jaffes went to Hawaii, spent two weeks working together, and immediately went to join the campus company that had been working together. They were both very thorough in their preparations for roles.

One of Bettye's great assets was her optimism. It permeated her life and was part of her essence. She was always sure that everything would be all right and that everything was all right. Sam took Bettye to task on one occasion for playing a role "too Christian." He explained that she was playing it with hope, that Christians have hope, and that this particular character was not supposed to have any.

It was a keen observation on his part because it was what was wrong with her playing of the role. The character was someone in despair. This was not something Bettye knew in her nature. Bettye came from a healthy, happy, loving family, from country folks.

Long after Sam's death, Bettye's optimism was alive and well. It was always a joy when we met in the Los Angeles area. We never ran out of things to share and being in her presence was akin to a bright sunny day; she was always filled with light and eagerness. Often she would drive a long way to meet us an airport. She never complained about making the trip; the time we shared together made the drive worthwhile. Whenever I think of Bettye, I simply fill with joy.

In their early years together, when they weren't elsewhere in the world making movies, the Jaffes based in New York, in Peter Cooper Village, a lovely place on the East River. It wasn't a formal environment. It was simple and gracious. Visitors would come and go often.

Bettye insisted that Sam take time to be alone with his friends. She didn't want to infringe on how his life had been before their marriage. Before long, Sam and his buddies wanted to join Bettye and her friends. Each felt free to make independent choices, but more often than not, they rejected separation.

Within five short years, Sam and Bettye were starring together in the *Ben Casey* television series and living in a house with a swimming pool in Beverly Hills. In the rear of that wonderful house, the bedroom is a few steps up from the dining area. Sam Jaffe always referred to it as their playroom. Despite their age differences, the Jaffes had an idyllic relationship, meeting each other on every level from the mind to the playroom.

Sam and Bettye Jaffe, love birds.

****

MICHAEL TOLAN, *Through a Glass Darkly*, 1949.

"It was the first thing I was in in New York. I was about 21 years old. I was struggling, just starting out. I had been in New York about three months. I will never forget it. It was a wonderful experience. It was the only real showcase for actors in New York at that time.

"I can remember how I felt on the day I was cast. I was thrilled. I had come from Detroit, Michigan. The Equity Library Theatre was the only place to be seen as a new actor in New York. I had a lot of experience in Detroit, but it was hard to be seen in New York anywhere.

"I remember very vividly. The director was a man named Ted Post who then went on to Hollywood and directed lots of television. My leading lady was Pat Carroll. There were three one-act plays. One of the others was The Triumph of the Egg with a young Earl Hyman, Frederick O'Neill (They had already been on Broadway in Anna Lucasta), and a beautiful black actress, Freddi Washington.

"The theater was on the east side, the Jan Haus. It was a wonderful, positive experience. I felt I was really in the company of artists. It was very professional, very high class.

"Soon after that I won artist-in-residence at Stanford, was 'discovered' by Warner Brothers, and was shot down to Hollywood under contract to do movies. I spent seven years playing a series of gangsters and Indians and came back to New York to really start my career."

Tolan was co-founder of American Place Theatre, the only off-Broadway theater then doing American plays exclusively.

****

Friendship Above All

Practically everyone who knew the Jaffes loved them. However, outsiders and mere acquaintances know only the exterior personality presented to the world. That exterior is often cultivated with care. For this reason, it was important to have Sam and Bettye described by insiders, by persons who were with them on a daily basis.

Carmen Canas began working in the Jaffe home in October of 1975, first as a day worker and then every day. She was very glowing in her opinions of her employers.

Jaffe had pushed Carmen to go to school so that she could learn English. Each day, when she would come to work, he would offer to help her with her homework. He served as a teacher to her, reviewing words and sentences, especially the grammar. Carmen thought him a better teacher than the one she studied with at school.

"I couldn't read much when I started," Carmen revealed. "Now I read plenty; books and papers. Thanks to him, I finished through sixth grade. I speak more English now. He was so so good. When I came he would prepare my breakfast; a half grapefruit, and toast, and the coffee pot. He'd say, 'Carmen you have to eat first before you do anything.' Every day. He was wonderful. That was when he was well. Sometimes I'd be running and he'd say, 'Carmen, stop. Nobody's waiting for you. You are doing very well. Don't run.' He was very considerate of me. He'd say to Bettye, 'Carmen needs rest.' "

In endearing terms, Carmen shared how she felt in his presence: "He always had a big respect for me. I called him Mr. Jaffe. He called me Mrs. Carmen, never just Carmen. Other rich people you work for don't treat you that way. He was excellent in his treatment of people. He was very special. Other people would push you to do more. He'd say, 'It's ten to four, time to go.'"

Carmen had worked many places but the Jaffes were the best employers, she felt, especially because of their kindness and their attention to her. They received her as part of the family. She felt free to bring her problems and discuss them in an atmosphere of heart. She felt very proud to work for them.

Sam Jaffe and Bettye Ackerman were celebrities, yet they gave equal time to everyone, no matter what their status.

Every day Carmen would arrive at the Beverly Hills home and find Sam Jaffe in good spirits. She marveled at his humor and how he would have his friends laughing all the time.

There were other times when Jaffe would become upset. This usually happened when the phone rang while they were eating. It bothered him that Bettye would run to the phone and he would say, "Please stop; eat first. Don't talk with anybody when you are eating because it's not good for your digestion."

Another person who worked inside the Jaffe home was Hal Cunningham who would tend bar at all their parties. Although he wasn't there on a daily basis, Cunningham worked enough Beverly Hills homes to be able to draw significant comparisons.

"Once you met Sam Jaffe," he proclaimed, "even the first time, you felt like you'd known him all your life. I'd love to go there because I'd love to hear him talk. I'd almost pay them to go. It was very pleasurable."

Cunningham loved every minute he spent at the Jaffes. After he would get set up, he and Sam would start talking. The guests would arrive and the two of them would still be talking. He didn't want to stop. It delighted Cunningham that "it didn't matter to him who you were. He never was one to blow his own horn. You'd think he was just an ordinary guy."

Hal continued, "If I could get out of another party to go there, I'd book someone on my party and go to the Jaffes. I loved to be there. You worked *with* those people, you didn't work *for* them. They didn't make any demands. They'd take my suggestions."

Cunningham worked for the Jaffes over a period of about nine years, three or four times a year. At the gatherings, conversation among friends was more prevalent than cocktails. Cunningham compared the Jaffe's events with others where the caterer "knocks himself out making beautiful food but the guests wouldn't know if it's chicken or veal because of so much drinking. At the Jaffes the food was always good and wholesome. There was a cocktail hour but there wasn't idle chatter."

The guests at the Jaffe home cared about each other. It wasn't ever just another Hollywood gathering. It was more like a galactic collection of extraordinary people. There could be as many as 40 guests at their great table with Bettye handling the staff and supervising the cooking. There were directors, actors, playwrights, and composers. It was the enlightened elite of the old Hollywood. They shared liberal attitudes and had great respect for traditional American values, for culture, learning, and the arts. Their viewpoint had grown up with them from their earliest days. Many of them had roots in the great days of New York theater and in Jewish theater.

The most spectacular personality to attend was Stella Adler, a grand dame who held in her carriage the genius passed on to her by her mother and father. Many of those present idolized Stella and she accepted her position as her due.

Ray Bradbury, the famed science fiction and screen writer, was first invited to the house after he and Bettye worked on a project for Hitchcock. After that, he became a regular at the Sunday get-togethers.

Bradbury mused, "On those Sundays, they introduced me to all kinds of people I would never have met otherwise. It was always very exciting to come there. There weren't many in this community who gave that kind of special Sunday for stage people to get together. There were more than just movie actors. There were people who could really act. Most good movie actors came from the theater. The theater people would be there by the dozens.

"The Sundays were a stunning experience. You wouldn't even have to be introduced to people. These famous people would be all around and I'd go up and introduce myself."

Bradbury singles out as one of the biggest events of his life going to the re-premier of *Lost Horizon* at Grauman's Chinese Theater. He accompanied Sam and Bettye, Frank Capra, and Jane Wyatt. "I was just bathed in emotion that night sitting with all of them," he gushed. "I'm an old fashioned autograph collector who luckily, later in life, was able to become a writer and do all the things I dreamt of doing. One of them was someday to be able to hang around people like the Jaffes because I've always loved and admired them." Bradbury was as unpretentious and childlike as the Jaffes he loved to visit.

When Sam was a guest at the homes of friends, he was not only entertaining and generous with his well-prepared thoughts on a wide variety of subjects, but he was also a good listener. He was a man who could sit silently because he wasn't trying in any way to impose his opinions. Because he knew so much and was articulate with his knowledge, it was his ability to be still that made him a unique participant. He was also a much appreciated raconteur, telling stories or expressing philosophy. One of his favorite subjects was friendship. It was very important to him. When someone would toast him at his birthday party, he would toast the group back and speak of the importance of friendship.

Jaffe had a remarkable memory. In his later years, he suffered a loss of hearing. His preference not to wear a hearing aid created some difficult situations but didn't dull his brilliance of mind or his extraordinary capacity to call up over 60 years of memories as though they had happened yesterday.

When he was on, he loved entertaining. At these times he was not only the center of attention, but people liked having him there because of his wit and intelligence. Once he had the floor, he knew how to hold the attention.

Filmmaker Robert Wise and his wife always delighted in visiting with Sam and Bettye: "I've never known anyone who had the endless stories and batch of new stories that he had. His particular strength was doing them in the Yiddish dialect. He was a consummate artist and great story teller."

Bettye had heard Sam's stories dozens of times, yet she listened as if each time was a new delight for her. It was not just because she loved him and wanted to please. Hearing the stories again truly thrilled her. She could never hear enough of him or see enough of him.

During the storytelling, Bettye never took her eyes off Sam. Actually, she watched him every second to see if he was comfortable and enjoying himself. However, she never made it obvious. Actress that she was, she had the capacity of doing it out of the corner of her eye, even when she was talking to someone else. Her eyes would move almost imperceptibly. Very few people knew it was happening. She could be fully involved in conversation, and sensitively participating, but her deepest ongoing focus was on Sam. Her attentiveness to him wasn't intrusive, embarrassing, or excessive. It was an expression of her profound spiritual union with Sam.

Although many who observed the Jaffes experienced their devotion to each other as equal, Bettye's devotion to Sam was the greater of the two. Karl Malden said, "He was such a special man that he deserved that in some way, I think. Maybe I'm wrong." While Malden's remark may seem like male chauvinism, he also devoted himself to Sam because of the special man he perceived Sam to be.

Malden felt that when Sam took advantage, it was a sign of his humanness. He seemed to excuse any of Jaffe's faults and he was glad that Sam had such human qualities, to balance his specialness. Malden's wife, Mona, a long time, close friend of Bettye, couldn't recall Bettye ever being angry with Sam, or Sam ever being angry with Bettye. She was sure that Sam's instances of taking advantage were "normal, as we all do. You know how marriages are, one time one person, one time another."

Bettye concurred, feeling there was an equality of relating between them, that each held the top position in their shared life. She saw this as a truly unique characteristic of their relationship.

There was mutual respect, sincerity, warmth, and unusual awareness between Sam and Bettye. According to Actor-Painter Peter Mark Richman, "Sam was very fatherly toward Bettye and her art." He would always talk about Bettye's work enthusiastically.

When Bettye would work on an acting scene for a class with Stella Adler, Sam was always helpful and supportive. He would watch it with a critical eye and offer fine suggestions. He was always very proud of her, as well as kind and loving to her, in anything that had to do with her art. Although Bettye looked upon all of this as mutuality, Sam was more in the role of teacher: one who offered praise and advice.

While Sam Jaffe wasn't ego-centered, he had a powerful sense of self that, in a social setting, could appear as the sun around which the planets revolved. When Sam attended a function, people in the room became aware that they had a brilliant figure in their midst.

Whereas Bettye's primary focus was on Sam, Sam distributed his attentions between everyone present.

People who knew the Jaffes often wondered what someone as young as Bettye saw in someone as old as Sam. More specifically, did they have a sex life and was it good. When asked directly, Bettye gave an answer without giving one. Her face lit up, her eyes sparkled, and her few non-revealing words implied it is for the questioner to find out and for her to know!

Director Fielder Cook was much more verbal on the subject: "Sam was one of the sexiest men who ever was on stage; the virility, the sensuality in his work. Look at *Asphalt Jungle*. That's the horniest, sexiest man that ever was on the screen. What's sexy is a true joy in one's manhood and adoring women. I would imagine that Sam Jaffe was one of the great lovers of the world and enormously attractive to women. I would imagine he could have as many women as he wanted. I would imagine he bedded every ingénue in every play that he was ever in. How can you have a great joy of life and sexuality without adoring women? It would be the dullest book in the world to deal with Sam only as a saint and leave out his sexuality."

This enthusiastic statement by Cook may merely be his projection onto Sam. After all, Sam had been inexperienced sexually until the age of 35, and doesn't seem to have had much contact with women in the years following Lillian's death.

Bettye doesn't reveal much by way of detail, but she is brimming with stories of women who were after Sam: "I happened to come in on the middle of a conversation when Marie Windsor was talking to Emily Paley. There was a moment of stopping and I thought, 'Oh, well, I'll move on.' Marie said, 'No. I want you to sit down. I want to tell you something.' She said, 'I don't know whether you knew this or not but I was always in love with Sam. I often wondered to myself if he would make any advances what I would do. I dreamt about him, but my dreams would always be that I was lying in his arms. I want to tell you that he was the sexiest man that I ever knew and I even went out with Clark Gable.' "

Marie Windsor used to visit the Jaffes and bring her vegetable sculptures. Bettye had always thought Windsor adored the two of them, but she realized, "It was Sam."

Sam Jaffe and Marilyn Monroe were in the film *The Asphalt Jungle* together. Jaffe had seen her silent test for the movie. He reported she didn't need words because her motion said everything! When he reflected on the test, he smiled appreciatively calling her motion, "Very nice."

Reporters once asked Bettye if she was jealous of

Marilyn Monroe. She asked if she should be, and they informed her that Sam used to go with her. Bettye replied in a fashion very typical of her quick wit: "Then I think she should be

Sam Jaffe with Marilyn Monroe in John Huston's film, The Asphalt Jungle.

jealous of me." After the interview, Bettye questioned Sam about his not telling her that he went out with Marilyn Monroe. He replied that it never came up in conversation. He was that casual about it.

Apparently Marilyn Monroe did pursue Jaffe. She even called after Sam and Bettye married. He thought she was lovely, beautiful, sweet and gifted. Since the fascination with Monroe is never-ending, Sam's possible involvement with her was a tantalizing subject. Edward G. Robinson's granddaughter, Francesca, and her husband, Ricardo, were with the Jaffes on a night when one of Monroe's movies was showing. Sam wasn't interested and didn't watch it with them. Following the movie, unable to squelch his curiosity, Ricardo asked Sam if he would tell him something. Sam toyed with him saying, "You can ask me."

Ricardo asked Sam if he ever kissed Marilyn Monroe. Sam said, no, but when asked if she ever kissed him, he replied, "I don't remember."

Monroe used to drive over to the Robinson house when Sam was staying with Eddie and Gladys. She would come in an open convertible and drive Sam around. It is reputed that, in response, he would try to explain books of philosophy to her to educate her. Sam wouldn't say where she drove him. He was silent about what they did together. He remained evasive to the end about whether he and Monroe had physical contact. The most he would say was there wasn't much to it.

Sam Jaffe had a very serious side to his nature, but he was anything but straight-laced. He had an ornery streak, told off-color jokes, and had a twinkle in his eye that many described as a pulsing light in his eyes.

Sam's humor was equal to that of his friends and he often confused people because of his very poker-faced delivery. During a dinner out on the West Coast at Perino's, Jaffe took one look at the prices on the menu and informed Bettye that he wasn't eating. Later, the violinist came by for requests and played "Someone to Watch Over Me" for Bettye. Jaffe wore a hearing aid and the playing was too loud for him. When the violinist asked Sam what he could play for him, Jaffe told him to play "silence." The violinist missed the humor. He asked Sam who wrote it and then went to the pianist in the bar to see if he knew it.

So often one reads of show business personalities who refuse to live in the Hollywood area because they can't live the wholesome kind of life they seek. The Jaffes created that wholesomeness within themselves and those they met with felt it instantly.

Television writer-producer Sy Gomberg saw Sam and Bettye as rare in this regard: "We work in a business that is so dog-eat-dog, so without morality, so full of greed, a business where most people hope that somebody in the competition fails. Writers look at a review and if the review is bad they feel better. Actors, directors feel the same way. Sam and Bettye didn't ever have that quality. There was an absence of malice."

As Sam's integrity was unshakable, so had he met his match in Bettye. Early in her career, she had gone to CBS for a job interview. When she left, the producer was in the elevator. He followed her down the street, making harassing remarks. Bettye kept walking, not paying attention even though he said he would get her a job. Finally he said, "Oh, you're a good girl, huh?" Bettye turned to him, replying, "I was under the impression that you were good if you resisted temptation. I'm not tempted." She walked away. About a block later, she turned and he was still standing there with his mouth hanging open.

Gomberg and his wife Maxine, as well as countless others, felt comfortable enough with the Jaffes to talk with them about everything. People could open themselves and laugh and cry with them. They were absolute human beings, menchen.

Gomberg's children loved the Jaffes instantly. They took it for granted that Sam and Bettye were the greatest people in the world. They never questioned or distrusted them. For many years the Jaffes showed up on Christmas morning with gifts for the kids. Their thoughtfulness was legendary in family after family.

Francesca Sanchez, the granddaughter of Edward G. Robinson, recalled her childhood and the importance of Sam Jaffe in her early life. Jaffe visited Robinson practically every day and since Francesca was often there, she had many firsthand contacts with his dearness: "He didn't play with me, but he would sit and listen to me, no matter what I was saying. I was seven, he was an adult, and he gave me his full and undivided attention. He listened, and responded."

In her later years she went to him as an adviser. She could go to him with a problem and he would listen, help her sort things out, and give her the best advice possible. Francesca's problems would look simple after discussing them with Sam because of the way he was able to show her the other side of the situation.

Sam had been a great friend to Eddie Robinson. When Eddie couldn't be a proper father to his son, Sam stepped in for him. He could understand his problems. Eddie asked Sam to keep an eye on Manny. Sam came to his rescue many times, on a human level, spiritually, and financially. While Sam didn't maintain good relations with his own nephews, he was very attendant toward Eddie's son. He even brought Manny, who was drunk, to a radio broadcast he was doing and held his hand while he was performing. Manny's father wouldn't have done that for his own son.

Sam was Eddie's best friend. There was great love between them. Francesca saw a difference between the two men: "My grandfather cared about people in a worldly way, but he also cared about his paintings and his clothes. None of this was ever important to Sam.

They had many of the same beliefs: love of humanity, doing good for others, giving of themselves, loving their craft and doing their best in their profession. But there was a spiritual side of Sam that I think my grandfather didn't have. The superficial things were more important to my grandfather than to Sam. My grandfather was too concentrated on his career and art and didn't know how to reach my father. Sam tried to reach him ever since he was a child."

Manny adored Sam. He depended on him. He would call the Jaffes in the middle of the night when he was in trouble. They would take him in and listen to him. They would give him money and never ask for it back. They gave him love and understanding he got from no one else.

Manny was unable to be a support system for his daughter Francesca. She also turned to the Jaffes, especially during her high school and college years. She described them as having "a great deal of strength. They'd never hold anything against you. You could tell them anything and they'd be honest about how they felt. And they understood, even if they didn't like particular people and you were still seeing them, they understood why. Sam would hold nothing back. He always said exactly what was on his mind. Sam was an original."

Jaffe didn't judge Robinson for not being able to father Manny. Instead he took on what he could to be of help in the difficult relationship. It was an expression of his love for Eddie Robinson.

When Eddie was dying, his wife Jane wouldn't allow anyone to see him. She proclaimed that he wasn't strong enough to have visitors. Those close to the situation, such as Nanette Fabray whose husband Randy was a friend to Robinson, said it was because Jane feared Eddie would change his will if his friends influenced him.

Sam sat in vigil outside Eddie's door for 23 hours, hoping to catch an opportunity to go in and see him before he died. It never happened and Eddie died alone, thinking no one wanted to see him. Sam was in such a state of shock and grief that he could hardly speak. He was very angry with Jane. Robinson's death represented a monumental loss in his life.

As time went on and Sam grew increasingly dependent on Bettye, he became very upset if she went off and didn't return at the prearranged time. Bettye described it this way: "He would have a little fit. But he was always so delighted when I came in that he could be angry for only a few minutes. Or I would laugh at him because he was funny when he got angry."

Although Bettye shrugged off events like this, the fact remains that Sam was excessively distressed when she was late. He did not treat her as an adult in this regard, and he was focused on his own needs for her to be there for him. He didn't like being at home alone without his wife. When she would call to check on him, he expressed upset that she wasn't home yet. He would be pacing, worrying about her, and wondering whether to call the police. Francesca had been with Bettye on one of those days and Sam's desire to have Bettye at home with him impressed her greatly. "Independent as he was, he was quite dependent on her," Francesca said. "Bettye gave up many outside excursions for him, but I don't think she regretted that in any way. It was a pleasure for her to be with him and to love him.

Francesca went on, "She had to go back east when her brother died and Sam wasn't too well at that time. He gave her a hard time about going back."

Evie Scott related a classical example of how Sam could be difficult. One Christmas Bettye was very eager to go home to visit her mother, in particular, who was getting on in years. Sam said he would go and Bettye got the tickets. At the last minute he decided he didn't want to go. "It's the night before," Evie stated with exasperation. "She told me he wouldn't go. I said, 'Of course he'll go. He'll go!'

"Bettye seldom if ever thought of herself; almost never," Evie continued. "This is too bad because it only backfires on you later on if you never think of yourself. It's not normal. Bettye adored Sam. She had been taught to always think of herself second. That's the way they were brought up."

Evie went on with the tale, revealing the drama as it built: "Early the next morning, the day of departure, Bettye called saying, 'Sam won't go.' I said, 'He won't go? I'll be there.' I called Urban [Evie's husband] at the office and said, 'Sam says he's not going. Meet me over at their house.' We met there in about 15 minutes. Sam said, 'I just don't want to go. I don't feel up to it.' He knew how badly Bettye wanted to see her mother. Who knows what his reasoning was at that time? We went back and forth. Urban, who is polite and well mannered, coaxed Sam, but he said no. Bettye was in the bedroom with a half-slip and bra on saying, 'Evie, he won't go.' I said, 'He will go.' I was so mad. I said, 'You get into your clothes.' Mind you, they had everything ready. All their bags were out, and the books they always take with them. I went in to talk to him. He was stubbornly not going to do it because he didn't feel up to it.

"Finally I let go. I said, 'Sam, you are behaving like a shit.' He looked at me. I said, 'That's right. You are going to go.' He said he'd be sick on the plane. I said, 'You won't be sick.' He said, 'I'll die on the plane.' I said, 'You won't die. You get into your clothes, you're going.' Like a director, I'm saying to Bettye, get your clothes on. Urban's standing there saying, 'Don't you think. . .' I said, 'No, get your clothes on. You're going.' I practically put his clothes on for him. 'You're going and we're going with you to the car.'

"All of sudden, dressed, Sam started walking to the car. Bettye came out trembling. Sam gets in the car and looks up at me out of the window and he said, 'You know, you're a very good friend to me, Evie.'

"Isn't that the topper of all time? I said, 'Yes, Sam, and sometimes good friends have to tell it like it is, don't they?'"

Sam not only went, they both had a wonderful time. This was a classic example of Jaffe not behaving very well. He could be very ornery and very stubborn. Evie Scott felt he could be very selfish. She proclaimed in no uncertain terms, "He was a human being. He was not God. With Bettye he was selfish because he did what he wanted and she did what he wanted to do. Always. There were times when she wanted to do something else, and it usually ended up with her taking second place."

On the other hand, even Scott affirmed that Sam was very supportive of Bettye in every way, with her painting and acting. As a good friend to Bettye, Evie talked with her often about allowing herself to live in Sam's domain. It bothered Evie, probably more than it bothered Bettye, that Bettye would let go of what she wanted because of opposition from Sam.

Worst of all, Evie hated it when Bettye went somewhere and Sam wanted her to be home exactly when she said she was going to. If she wasn't, he made it very difficult for her. Evie scolded, "He knew better. He's an actor. He knows that when you go on the set, you can't just say, 'I'm leaving because it's six o'clock and my husband is waiting for me.' He understood it, but he didn't accept it when it was Bettye who was late. He screamed at her. He yelled and carried on."

After his outburst, however, Jaffe would turn around and be so sweet that Bettye would immediately forget his poor behavior. It was her disposition. She would always tell Evie that she didn't mind. Evie would jump right back with, "Why not?" Evie thought Bettye should mind. When Sam would yell at Bettye, she would attribute his behavior to his being upset. It was his upset, not an attack on her. She would then go on to focus on the fact that he would get over it.

Bettye's position was difficult for Evie to understand. Somewhere deep inside, Bettye surely had to be angry about this, Evie thought. Anybody would. Bettye, however, was very unusual and would never harbor ill feeling.

Sam would be terrible about something but then he would forget it. It wasn't in his nature to hold on to anything. Then Bettye would say, "Isn't he adorable." Evie's response would be: "Sometimes, Bettye."

When ovarian cancer struck Bettye late in their marriage, Evie suggested that the cause was Bettye's having taken on more than she could handle and that it was eating away at her. She believed that when the body can't handle all the bottling up of feelings, it creates illness as a way of purging itself. Illness appeared to be the only way to get out of the situation, Evie suggested, even though Bettye was a healthy, youngish woman who never abused herself in any way. She didn't smoke. She drank very little, and she ate little.

Evie Scott didn't hold back in her feelings about what Bettye tolerated: "You don't take abuse from a person and say, 'It's all right. I love him.' I don't call that complete love. I call that martyrdom. I'm sure Bettye had enough of a wonderful life with Sam to feel that it was worth it."

When Bettye played the lead role in the television series *Return to Peyton Place*, she worked from 10:00 a.m. to 10:00 p.m. and rarely saw Sam. She gave it all up when she returned later than usual one night to find Sam standing in the middle of the road because he was so worried about her. It is hard to imagine that Bettye walked out on a leading role in a series rather than challenging Sam's overreaction. Given that *Peyton Place* followed her long and successful run in *Ben Casey*, she clearly wanted to pursue television work. She was in demand and was on her way to greater heights in her career. Sam's actions do not indicate respect for her career, or for Bettye as an independent person. Bettye quit rather than address that issue. She did it because she loved Sam, because she worshipped him. She valued him more than her career.

It was Sam who had the saintly reputation, but it was Bettye who relinquished all thought of herself in deference to Sam. Julie Harris was moved to poetic description when turning her attention to the Bettye: "Meeting her was like stumbling onto a very peaceful glade in the forest. You could sit down and just relax, she had such serenity about her. He seemed like the happiest man in the world. It was nice to be around the feeling that the two of them gave you together. It was as if he had put up a net and caught an angel."

Angels are often assigned as guardians. Bettye's assignment with Sam was unmistakable. No matter what he asked of her, she not only did it, she did it feeling ensconced in the most beautiful marriage in the world.

Every time I was around the two of them I felt their deep love for each other, an unshakable love. As Sam aged he needed more and Bettye was able to give him more; it was perfectly clear that she wanted to give him whatever he needed. She was devoted to him and embracing of him. If she saw that as her mission, I can say, from first hand observation, that she more than completed that mission. It was as if in fulfilling that purpose she gave herself the gift of meeting her own soul's desire. It is impossible to find fault with that or to reduce the focus to a relational issue. In my friendship with Bettye, I felt as many others did that she was an extraordinary individual who had been born with extra amounts of goodness, kindness, and utter dearness. To be in her presence was to be in soft light that never diminished. She enfolded everyone in the flow that emanated from her. Sam Jaffe had chosen well. He may have been demanding but it was also true that he was exceedingly blessed. He gave a lot to others; his beloved wife Bettye gave a lot to him.

Bettye's purity of spirit impressed numerous people. Biographer Charles Higham remarked: "I can name only four or five whom I've regarded as purely good. This can only be achieved by tremendous strength and will. Bettye's strength was even greater than Sam's because she had decided to make him the center of her life."

Bettye's good friend Evie Scott also singled her out as coming closest to being "the angel without the halo of anyone I've ever known. She has an inner beauty and goodness greater than anyone I can think of."

Bettye's friends reported that, by example, she taught them how to make a relationship a work of art. For example, Bettye knew how to play under Sam's lines. She gave him an elevated position while never lowering herself. Higham called it "an extraordinary duet for a fine and noble old cello and an exquisitely tuned piano.

****

HENDERSON FORSYTHE, *The Autumn Garden*, 1956.

"I came to New York in 1955. E.L.T. might have been one of the first things I did in the theater. It was a little bit above primitive. All the men were in one dressing room and all the women in another. That doesn't always happen. Sometimes we were all together with only a sheet between.

"It was a good showcase; quite a few people came to see it. I worked pretty steadily after that."

****

BILL MACY, *Room Service*, 1963

"I was just a struggling, fledgling actor in 1963. I had graduated from N.Y.U. nine years earlier and had done some summer stock and an off-Broadway show. Getting a job out of it wasn't the reason for doing an E.L.T. show. I made my living driving a taxi. I did theater because I was enamored with the profession. I was working on my craft."

****

An Actor's Actor

In a time of mounting divorces and of relational horror stories, the Jaffes loved one another and were a highly compatible couple. While they had their points of contention, they did know how to co-exist.

Several years into their marriage, Bettye, with Sam's encouragement, began expressing her artistic talents. Her career began as an appreciator. She spent endless hours at art museums and began seriously studying in 1961 after doing a sketch of Sam at dinner one night and not thinking much about it. A friend took it, framed it and brought it back.

Painter George De Groat explained how Sam was helpful to Bettye in the unfolding of her gift: "Sam had a good eye and excellent taste. He was very knowledgeable. I believe he had a lot to do with getting Edward G. Robinson started in his first collection. Robinson had been interested but had no expertise."

Jaffe could look at a painting and explain exactly why he liked it. His critique was always right on the mark. He had a good feeling for the subject matter and composition. He could pinpoint in technical terms if a work needed a more extensive range of values or an adjustment in composition. Although Jaffe had never been educated in art school, he was knowledgeable in music and the comparisons are exactly parallel. He applied his knowledge in music to the visual arts and the performing arts as well.

As was his practice with people, when a painting wasn't very good, he was kind enough not to say too much. He was a constructive critic, never cruel. Other gifted, intellectual people would likely be more impatient with artists and performers who were not at their level.

Sam always looked for what the artist had to bring out, rather than harp on what was missing.

Jaffe brought his skill as an art critic to the fore in his encouragement of Bettye in her career as an artist. Her talents flowered and by the time of Sam's death she had already had several gallery showings of her work.

Bettye's pen and ink drawing of Sam's head hung on the wall of their den. Bettye found it quite easy to do. "After all," she said, "I had the greatest model in the world."

At left is the drawing Bettye did of Sam on a napkin at a restaurant. It was later used for the sculpture that was placed at the Equity Library Theatre.

Rare as it was for a thespian, Sam talked very little about the roles he had played. Instead, he talked about other people's performances. He had done the same during the blacklist, talking about the tribulations of others but not about himself. In their relationship, Bettye talked about Sam and Sam talked about Bettye. Sam would praise her artistic endeavors and all that she did for him. Bettye would express delight in how gifted Sam was and in his intelligence. There was a mutual appreciation that kept them interested in each other's development.

Jaffe was not vain; he never bragged. Evie Scott, a close friend of the Jaffes, remembered attending a party where greater egos prevailed. She related, "We were walking around the pool of this fancy house and

Danny Thomas came up and said, 'Well hello, Sam, how are you?' Sam said, 'Fine,' and never got more out of his mouth. Thomas said, 'You know I'm going to be doing this show . . .' and he didn't stop for the next seven or eight minutes. I do this and I'm going to do that, my show this and my show that; never one other word about Sam. When Sam and I continued our walk I said, 'Gee that was a great conversation.' He just laughed."

Sam Jaffe was 74 years old when he completed his last show on the *Ben Casey* television series. He lived another very productive nineteen years. Those years included twenty feature films, numerous television shows, some stage appearances, and volunteer work on projects close to his heart.

One of the surprising twists of fate resulting from his long stint in the *Ben Casey* TV series was that Sam remained in California. This was partly because Bettye stayed with the show for another year, but it was also true that during their half decade on the West Coast, they had put down some roots. Sam became involved in activities in Hollywood that made use of his desire to bring goodness into the world. In addition, many of his friends were now also in California and he felt less like a visitor in a strange land.

Freed from the rigors of the series, Sam and Bettye spent a good part of their first year of mutual freedom vacationing in Mexico. Sam had taken the trouble to grow a beard to disguise himself but it made no difference in how identifiable he was. People simply "remembered" that he had the beard when he played Dr. Zorba. The time in Mexico turned out to be their real honeymoon in the seashore home of friends. Their first honeymoon had hardly been satisfactory with Bettye in New York and Sam in Miami with Luther Adler.

After their respite, Sam went to work on a two-part Tarzan film, much of which was shot in Mexico. Entitled *Bluestone of Heaven* and made as a feature film for Europe, it was later shown on television in the States.

Another film made while they were in Mexico was *Guns for San Sebastian*, with Anthony Quinn. Sam played a priest who granted amnesty to a rebel. The film was shot primarily in Durango, Mexico. When Sam spoke of the city, he recalled that someone said, if the earth needed an enema, Durango was the place to put in the tube. He called Durango the asshole of the world. It was a dreadful place that had no law or order of any kind. Sam said, "The monument there was a granite bottle of Pepsi Cola. They have no respect for life in the place. One man passed a car on the road with a commander in it and the commander shot him because he dared to pass him on the road. He killed him."

Given the environment, which was surely the antithesis of how Sam lived his life, it is not surprising that Sam became ill during the production.

They were in San Miguel de Allende when Sam suffered a bout with cystitis. Bettye called the company doctor and asked him to come to see Sam. The doctor wanted to play golf that Sunday and it was difficult to get him to come. When he finally showed up, he gave Sam a powerful medication that got rid of the symptoms. However, Sam got sicker and sicker. The doctor was not bona fide. Later, when they flew down to Durango, Sam got very ill. That night Bettye awakened to find Sam was climbing the walls. He couldn't urinate and blood was everywhere.

Bettye was desperate. The concierge of their little hotel called a doctor. The first two hospitals they tried were full and Sam was finally admitted to the third. Their doctor told Bettye he would do a great operation on Dr. Zorba and was thrilled to have him for a patient. Bettye knew then they were in trouble.

The doctor turned out to be a fraud who didn't even know how to use a catheter.

Bettye accompanied Sam into the operating room. He expressed concern that she wasn't sterilized but she put him at ease reminding him: "Neither is anything else here." The "doctor" was able to make an opening and use a tube to drain the urine. Bettye then immediately called Sam's urologist in the States, Dr. Peterfy. This was the beginning of Sam's later urological troubles.

The Mexican doctor got mileage out of the incident by calling a conference of the whole company and announcing that Sam had cancer of the prostate. Dr. Peterfy thought he was crazy and flew over eight hours by private plane to see Sam. Peterfy stayed for two weeks. He showed Bettye how to insert a catheter and he kept the original drain in the wound so it wouldn't heal over until Sam was able to get home to Cedar-Sinai where he stayed a week. The company didn't want to pay for Peterfy's coming, but they did.

Before Sam left Durango, he finished the movie. He almost fainted, but he held on with sheer grit until he finished the last scene.

Years later, Sam was to have additional prostate difficulties and problems with urinary control. He was not without a sense of humor about his condition. When told he had to re-train his penis, Sam's comment was, "How do you educate a head that's got no brain?" He joked about the long time he would spend standing at a urinal, assessing his troubles as "pission impossible."

Sam's friend, playwright John Tobias, sent Sam a verse paying tribute to his spirit while everyone was fooling around with his plumbing. He said that Sam and his electric hair would triumph over all adversity. In reply, Jaffe sent this verse, "Excuse it please. My hair electric and electronic rhymes with chronic. The hourly flow I have to undergo. The Latin Picator is fissure but the first syllable suggests pisher, which describes me to a tee. Wish it weren't so." Jaffe never lost his humor and spirit.

Lamont Johnson had the opportunity to direct Jaffe on television and what delighted and stimulated him was "that this brilliant, renowned, prize-winning actor still had the enthusiasm of a kid in first year drama school." He found him full of energy, excitement, and fun. Sam had a special generosity in sharing with younger people what he knew.

When Johnson worked with Jaffe, he thought Sam was in his early 40's but Sam was really in his late 50's. This happened again and again. Producer Stanley Kallis thought that Sam was too young to play the role of a man in his mid-60's who didn't want to retire and locked himself in his office, refusing to come out in *The Lawman and Mr. Jones*. Sam was in his mid-70's at the time! Sam was timeless, always looking both older and younger than his years.

Lamont Johnson commented on Jaffe's acting techniques. "He used schticklach [attention-getting devices]," he said, "and it was a little alarming, but I learned from that, too. I learned the good things about the tricks of the trade. Other old timers could leave you high and dry in a scene with the tricks they pulled. But Sam had basic goodness, gentleness. The charm and humanity of his character dominated his mischief."

Johnson went on: "In Sam's later years, when he was feebler, his enthusiasm was still great and so was the gleam in his eye with ladies. He was so gallant and so lovely. He was mad for Bettye and he had this old-fashioned courtesy and sexual eye for the ladies, still at almost 93."

Johnson mentioned Sam's departure from the New York speech patterns in which he had been raised: "He had the stage refinement of his basic speech which was a somewhat self-conscious use of the softened 'r' and the broader 'a' that you found among actors when they had their stage diction on. Very much like the famous story of Stella Adler. A young student of hers said, 'Miss Adler, it's so great to be working with a great British teacher.' She said, 'Oh no darling, I'm not British, I'm just affected!'

"The Adlers had a refined kind of stage diction, rotund voice and rolled speech," Johnson commented. "Sam had that. But in his excitement he would lapse into a lessening of the broadness making it sound more like New York."

Johnson did not ignore some of Sam's less attractive qualities as an actor. He called him "a ham" because he had a tendency to do some rather overly demonstrative things as an actor. These called attention to themselves. Johnson could forgive them because Jaffe was essentially a tremendous artist, with unique talent and personality. The excess seemed to be part of it. In a person of less charisma or dazzle than Sam's personality, the schtick would seem more offensive. His excesses were part of his eccentricities. "It was just Sam being Sam," Johnson concluded. "He was such an organic man."

The Jaffes contributed their time and energies to projects in the arts with the hope of bettering the Los Angeles area. They served together on the Board of Directors of the Hollywood Museum and Sam gave much of his energy to the Los Angeles Free Shakespeare Theater. An early reason for his becoming an actor was his great love of Shakespeare and fine language. Now, in his twilight years, he dedicated himself to bringing more of Shakespeare to Los Angeles. On the board with him were Peg Yorkin and actor Roscoe Lee Brown.

Brown remembered Sam as everybody's high lama: "In the '60's when people were going off to India to find spirituality, I told them they needn't make such a long journey. Just go to California and sit in Sam Jaffe's presence. There was an energy-giving serenity about him that flowed outward from deep inside. He helped us to know that we were there in that place called Shangri-La."

Sam was able, through the playing of a character, to create a sense of place through his presence. In *Ben Casey*, when Sam walked down the corridors, viewers knew they were in a hospital. They knew he was a doctor. They didn't think of him as an actor playing a doctor. It was a gift that Jaffe had.

Roscoe Lee Brown remembered how Jaffe would cut through all the brush and go directly to the heart of the matter at Free Shakespeare meetings. He used his mind in a disciplined way, as in mathematics. He bypassed logic and functioned with great calmness, knowing about every difficulty, "This too shall pass."

This quality enabled Sam to transcend many of the hardships in his life. It was visible in his work and in his relationships. He was in touch with self. He was himself.

The self that was Sam Jaffe was a very modest man, always interested in what everyone else had to say. It wasn't that he lacked for what to say. His mind and areas of investigation had an incredible range. There are endless avenues he could have pursued. When people are enormously gifted in one way, they are gifted in many.

Sam Jaffe was a consummate actor. When he worked on the set, people would stop to watch him because he was electrifying. Off the set, he was a great celebrity. Wherever he went people would walk up to him with great love and with light in their eyes. They weren't looking for an autograph but rather to compliment him. When the Jaffes would dine with friends at Beverly Hills restaurants, invariably someone would recognize Sam and come up to the table. He was always a polished gentleman and when people mistook him for someone else, he continued his early practice of never betraying that that was the case. Instead, he always said something charming and gracious.

Sam did not focus on himself, but others focused on him. It was simply the way it was.

Sam Jaffe wasn't in his profession for what he could get out of it. During his union days, and throughout his career, it was clear that he was concerned with what he could give to his profession. Hence, he didn't see that acting had helped his personal development but rather that the actor brings his personal development to acting.

"Your literature, your knowledge of art, your knowledge of music," he said, "all these are part of a reservoir from which you draw, depending on what you need for the particular role. It isn't that acting does it; it's you that do it in your acting. From novels that you read, characters that you find that are very well-developed, especially in the early novels, you learn a great deal. And your knowledge of the political scene, it's all a part of you. You take out of it all what you need for the particular character."

He used the image of starting with a blueprint of the role and filling it with walking, with thinking, with movement, with dress. The actor fills the blueprint with life in the same way musical notes are nothing until the musician plays them. He recalled that Tchaikovsky didn't realize how great his symphony was until he heard it played. Performing artists reproduce the character and make it come to life.

Throughout his later years in California, Sam had a fine relationship with his agent Sue Golden. She found him to be a joy to represent. He never pushed her for work and although he knew exactly what he wanted, he was willing to take her advice.

Because exposure was not Jaffe's goal, he turned down the chance to play the High Lama in the musical *Lost Horizon*. He had already done the role and there was no point to repeating it.

Golden wanted Jaffe to do more television because

he made good money when he did, but Sam didn't want to waste his time on television. She learned quickly that Sam Jaffe would never be a part of anything with foul language. The scripts would be returned to her almost immediately. It didn't matter to Jaffe if it was to be a successful film. What mattered were his principles. Given the language used in most films today, Jaffe would seldom work if he lived in these times.

Golden was amazed at how recognizable Sam was: "We were sitting in the hotel waiting to go out to dinner and a group of young people in their early 20's came in to go into the bar. They saw Sam sitting there and they absolutely freaked. Everyone had to come over and talk to him and get his autograph. They all knew who he was. They were literally at his feet."

When relating the story, Golden admitted that she shared the feelings of those young people. She had found herself thinking, "This isn't me handling this great man. It's just not possible. Suddenly, there on my couch was sitting a legend," she expressed with wonder. "It was unbelievable. I adored the man. As I do Bettye. You can't mention one without the other. She was his complete support system. I've never seen anyone with as much patience in my entire life as she had. He was the biggest part of her life for a long time and when he became sick she subjugated her career to him and to support him. He truly was one of the greats of the business. I don't understand to this day why the Academy hasn't so honored him. At the John Huston tribute years back, more time was spent on Sam than any other guest."

Golden felt sorry for people who didn't have a chance to know Sam Jaffe because it was her experience that he genuinely touched the lives and hearts of everyone who knew him. For those who didn't know him personally, there is the compensation that he left the world with a body of work that was truly exceptional and has been equaled by very few. Many of his films became classics and he played very different characters in each one. While Cary Grant was Cary Grant and John Wayne was John Wayne, Sam Jaffe covered a wide range of age spans and personalities.

What was even more impressive about this was that Sam was so unique in his appearance as to be identifiable as Jaffe. Yet he surmounted his own uniqueness in his different characterizations.

Sam Jaffe didn't talk much about his own fears or difficulties. At least, there were very few with whom he talked of this. It was not an area that he opened freely. He came closest to expressing his emotions when he played the piano. It is perhaps why he didn't like others to hear him play, because of how revealing of himself that was.

He was discriminating when it came to music; he could barely tolerate what he considered inappropriate. He expressed great exasperation with his brother-in-law, Tom, because his daughter's piano was out of tune. He made it clear that if she was to become a musician, the piano required tuning at least once a month and he left the room in a huff when Tom said he could just about afford a once-a-year tuning. The piano hurt Sam's ear and he warned Tom that it would affect his daughter's playing ability.

Jaffe was very particular in his musical tastes, enjoying what was classical and popular but detesting rock which he didn't classify as music at all. He rejected avant-garde music because it was arrived at intellectually and didn't touch the feeling level. He firmly believed that art must touch the heart as well as the mind.

I shared in these views and because I had so much respect for Sam I felt affirmed in my own tastes. I felt the same about art; modern art has little or no appeal for me, especially as compared with impressionism which embodies so much imagination. Once, Diane and I walked through an entire long, modern art floor of a museum without seeing a single painting that spoke to us. Then, a long way away we saw a painting that drew us; it was as if its energy called even though we could barely make out the content. It turned out to be a Monet!

As to art touching the heart as well as the mind, in my forty years of working with people on inner personal growth those who try to think their way to breakthroughs in consciousness are stuck on a treadmill of attempts. Those who awaken their feelings are the ones who are more easily able to move to new dimensions in self. Thoughts are more like little toy soldiers marching dutifully along a straight line; feelings awaken the blessing of chaos which disrupts the status quo and throws a palate of color across the path of perception.

Jaffe was a great teacher. He could clearly explain aspects of algebraic theorems and higher math so that practically anyone could understand. Teaching was part of his nature. He had so much inside to offer and he knew about every period of history. He taught by example. When he would expound on his knowledge, he often chose a very ancient way of expressing himself, that of using stories to illustrate rather than expressing his opinions. He would make a statement and illustrate with a story. Sam loved telling stories about ancient Jews and Jewish teachers.

Sam referred to G.B. Shaw as the greatest influence in his life. He also held Gandhi in high esteem. Following in Gandhi's footsteps, Sam named all religions when asked what his was.

His thought process was so minute and involved, and he was so interested in telling things through his stories, that he sometimes missed the overall message of the subject under scrutiny. He had more interest in the details than the synthesis. He didn't like coming to broad conclusions.

When he engaged with persons concerned with the broad meaning, he would elucidate with the specific knowledge the conversant didn't have. The result was that the two expanded each other. They stimulated each other's minds because they came by different approaches. Sam could engage with persons who brought him a large container that he could fill with all his knowledge. If the large container wasn't there, there would be no reason for him to bring up the specifics. Such meetings were acts of creativity in which something was birthed that neither had before, but both had afterwards as a result of the intercourse.

Poet Dorothy Parker told Bettye that she had married an angel and Bettye replied, "I sincerely hope not." Jaffe may not have been an angel but he did make a difference with his life. Those who knew him were better as a result.

By his example, he enabled others to be more aware of being good persons. Writer Virginia Bortin was one of many influenced by Sam. She confessed: "I'm aware of trying not to be unkind to people and trying to give more of whatever I have to others. When I do that, I always think of Sam and Bettye because they were always helping people, materially as well as every other way. Whatever they had, they gave. I think that that kind of love is the single most important thing we can ever have in our earthly life."

Stanley Kallis, television producer and writer, and his wife Lucetta, not only worked with the Jaffes but knew them socially. They marveled at how special their marriage was. Lucetta observed, "What was Sam was Bettye and what was Bettye was Sam. Neither smothered the other. They were unique but they were always on the same track even though they differed in certain key areas."

Bettye was very open to Eastern philosophy, to

karma, to things that are meant to be, such as her relationship with Sam. Sam didn't disagree but he tended
to have his two feet on the ground, in this world. His
spirituality was in the love of humanity. He didn't really
believe in an afterlife. If there was an afterlife he wasn't
going to concern himself with it because it wasn't something he could deal with in this life.

Sam believed in the spiritual nature, but he wasn't
religious or mystical. Bettye was. Sam would quote from
the philosophers or Shakespeare. Stanley Kallis spoke
of Jaffe liking pepper as much as salt, sour as much as
sweet. "He was very human," Kallis said. "He wasn't too
holy."

This honoring of their differences was a key to
their marital success. They made room in themselves
for perspectives that were important to the other and
this enabled them to stretch beyond their natural prefer-
ences.

They each had a way of sticking to their positions
but when it came time for one of them to give the pro-
verbial inch, each was capable of such concession. For
example, on the occasion of Jaffe's receiving the C.C.N.Y.
125th Anniversary Medal, he read Bettye a rewritten version of his acceptance speech. In it he sought to present a memorial to his friend Edward G. Robinson. Bettye
thought it was a terrible speech and wondered if she
should be honest with him. They were about to be picked
up and she didn't want to make him angry so close to
departure time. Bettye decided not to hold back and she
"let him have it." She told him it was a lousy speech;
it didn't have fire. She said, "It stinks." Sam didn't say
a single word in response. At the banquet, he stood at
the dais and reported to those assembled, "My wife says
that my speech stinks." He tore it up and gave a brilliant
speech in its place.

The Jaffes were two different people in temperament. Bettye, for example, was much more patient and

Sam, especially in his later years, could become cranky.

Though he had become a full-fledged West Coast resident, Jaffe was active in and concerned about the restoration, repair and saving of the Eldridge Street Synagogue in New York City. He was Vice-Chairman of the Board of Advisers. Members included Bettye Ackerman, Lou Jacobi, Jackie Mason, Molly Picon, and Henny Youngman. Dr. Eric Ray was Chairman.

The Synagogue was an impressive reminder of the Jewish immigrant experience on the Lower East Side. In Sam's lifetime that section of New York was one of the most densely populated regions on earth. People lived in crowded, uncomfortable, and unsanitary tenements. The synagogue was a spiritual counterpart for the harsh daily life. Completed in the late 1800's, it was the first great house of worship in the area, erected during the Jewish exodus by the Ashkenazic Jews from Eastern Europe.

Sam was very modest about his own work in the restoration and didn't want his name listed because he felt he had not been important enough in it. Though he was active in the preservation of the synagogue, he was not a religious Jew. When asked if he was an atheist, he said there was a mystery about the universe: "Call it life, call it nature, or the élan vital."

Director Fielder Cook valued Sam tremendously. He had no doubt about Sam or his abilities. "They can't make better actors," he said. "Sam is a true original. There are very few originals in the world. Ralph Richardson is a great original. Lawrence Olivier is not. Both are greatly, brilliantly talented.

"You can't do better than Sam Jaffe, and there's only one like him. Knowing him personally you know he's a divine man. It makes your life happy to get up in the morning and know he's there.

"If God has made you an original in this world, you'd

better know who you are, because the world doesn't take well to originals and you have to watch every step."

Cook was one who was significantly different for having known Sam: "You can't work with utter honesty and grace without being better. Sam makes everyone better when he's with you. He's an affirmation that something like that can exist in the world."

One can hardly have a finer legacy for one's life. It is imperative for all of us to know that a life of goodness and integrity is possible, that it does affect the whole, and it does make a difference. Sam Jaffe's life speaks of the evolutionary process. He was a man who stood a little straighter than most.

Albert Schweitzer encouraged people to set an example because other people may imitate us. Sam Jaffe took that advice to heart. Cook remarked that Jaffe had infinite compassion: "He saw beauty in the world and that's the way he walked in it. Because of this, he was protected in an ultimate sense. Nobody could really hurt him. They could blacklist him, but they couldn't touch him. He walked with beauty and no one could disturb that. That is the essence of innocence, because you're not giving anyone anything but the truth of who you are. All originals do that.

Cook went on: "Everything Sam Jaffe did for me [as an actor] was a triumph. When he finished there was nothing more to do. There are very few actors who can do that."

Jaffe played for Cook in *The Enemies*, a show on the Warsaw Ghetto. After that performance Cook came to the door late one night on his knees with a rose for Sam because his work had been so incredible.

Cook was one of those who worked hard to get Jaffe back into television work after the blacklist. He would submit his name for every show he could until eventually the "no" sayers wore out. He would submit Sam Jaffe's name even if he was casting a black Nigerian. He kept suggesting Sam Jaffe until the networks got used to it.

Sam Jaffe was original in his looks. His image made a lasting impression and he was easily recognizable. Through his very special persona he was able to create lasting portraits. His performances in *Gunga Din* and *Asphalt Jungle* were so distinctive that almost everywhere he went young actors were practicing recreating the key moments as Sam had originated them. It happened in Rome. Just after Bettye described the phenomenon to a friend, a young man stepped up and began playing out the juke box scene where Sam stood transfixed by a young woman jitterbugging.

Milton Berle spoke of the look on Sam's face in that scene. He said it would always be remembered: "Sam watching her while she was moving around. It was like, 'Oh boy, I want to jump in bed with her.' It was very sexy. You could tell the feeling underneath, the feelings of the man."

Berle loved Sam. Around 1961, Sam and Bettye went with Eddie Robinson to see Berle at the Sands in Las Vegas. This was during the stint in *Ben Casey*. Berle used to throw lines at Sam. Berle recounted: "He was playing Dr. Zorba and I'd say, my doctor is in the audience, I don't know if you know him; my friend, Dr. Zorba. Sam would get up, the spotlight would hit him. He was so recognizable."

One of the reasons Sam was so recognizable was his hairdo. His hair was often described as lightning bolts shooting out of his scalp. It was once called the eighth wonder of show business. It seemed to have a life of its own. "I've cut it, washed it, parted it, oiled it, starched it, pomaded it," Sam said with a sigh. "Still I lose combs in it. It has no respect for art."

A little old lady in a supermarket once stopped Sam and asked him if he was Rubinstein. When Sam said no, she asked if he was Harpo Marx. When he said no to that, she walked away saying, "I thought you were somebody."

Sam did have some resemblance to Rubinstein: the white halo of hair around a balding crown, the bright eyes and a friendly face that caught attention immediately.

Sam Jaffe's hair as a young man and in his last years.

People often told Sam Jaffe that his hair looked like a perpetual fright wig. It stood almost four inches high and made his head look like a wire brush that defied taming in any way.

Besides Rubinstein and Marx, people took him for Albert Einstein, Ezra Pound, and Ben-Gurion.

One of his favorite experiences was when a bird swooped down and plucked a beak-full of hair from his

head to feather the nest. He felt pride about the bird selecting him.

Another time, he was sitting in a theater and the woman sitting behind him leaned forward and asked, "Would you mind removing your hair, Mr. Jaffe?"

Sam inherited his hair from his father. He could

never do anything with it. Anything he attempted to tame it was useless. His hair would rise again in rebellion against any pomades or creams.

Sam Jaffe's hair as portrayed by Al Hirschfeld, the famous caricaturist best known for his black and white portraits of celebrities and Broadway stars.

Sam Jaffe never thought of himself as a star. He was a person like everyone else and he did things ordinary people do. He was one of Southern California's millions who rode the #83 bus down Wilshire's Miracle Mile. Sam loved the simple fact that he could call the bus company and be told how to get bus service to any destination at all! One of his favorite trips was to Farmer's Market.

Sam didn't ride the bus by default. He enjoyed it. One day, Nanette Fabray was driving to work and she saw Sam sitting in a bus stop. She pulled up and called to him: "Sam! I'm off to ABC. Can I give you a lift?" He said, "No, I like to ride the bus. Thank you." She couldn't believe it. He was on the same lot. He knew where she was going, and he chose the bus over a ride in a car.

Jaffe and his friend Ray Bradbury were experienced bus riders. Bradbury was amused that people would always say, "What are you doing on the bus?" Jaffe would say, "What are you doing on the bus?"

Bradbury had the highest regard for Jaffe. He thought of him as typecast for the high lama and delighted in being able to see him in Beverly Hills instead of having to make the long trek to Tibet. He admitted,

"That may be my romantic imagination. My wife says I cry at telephone books."

Bradbury admitted that if Jaffe had gotten up in front of a congregation he would have joined. It was his opinion that Sam "was brought into the world on a genetic level a little better than most of us. He saw that and he worked with it. He was closer to saintliness when he came in.

"With a performer like Sam," Bradbury continued, "when you look into his face, there's something going on there all the time. That's a great actor. They don't have to do much but there are shadows passing across the sun, the moon and stars, and their face. There's something in the eyes that holds you. There aren't many people like that. Or many who can do both stage and film. It's a mysterious quality."

Throughout his life Jaffe cared about people. He and Bettye attended the bicentennial of South Carolina and were part of a program with Bob Hope. They were invited to an event at the governor's mansion. They were staying with Bettye's brother, Tom, who had a Chinese exchange student living there. Sam told the exchange student that he could accompany them to the governor's mansion. He didn't have a ticket, but when they arrived, Sam announced, "He's my guest and he doesn't need a ticket." They let him in. It wasn't that Sam sought a special privilege for Sun Wa; it was that Sun Wa was his guest and he didn't want him excluded. He wanted to do this for Sun Wa. It wasn't that he wanted something special for himself.

The next day, Sam insisted that Sun Wa and Bettye's niece accompany him on the patrol car ride around town in the procession.

Years later Sun Wa and his family were living in Canoga Park and Sam kept up the connection. He even knew a little Chinese.

Sam Jaffe was part of the human race and saw himself as equal with others. He didn't set himself apart.

Terence Scammell, an actor who founded the Los Angeles Shakespeare Festival, met Sam in March of 1970 at the Center Theatre Group when they did *Idiot's Delight* together with Jack Lemmon and Rosemary Harris. Sam's gentleness impressed Scammell: "Ruth Gordon, Garson Kanin's wife, was a very rude woman. She was never even introduced to the company. One day Sam was sitting on stage discussing something with Kanin and suddenly Gordon yelled out from the audience 'Shut up, Sam. You don't know what you're talking about and get on with the play.' Sam had an incredible temper but only lost it when it really was deserved, and mostly at himself. I watched Sam handle that. He swallowed it and took it from this woman and he didn't pull rank. I looked at him and thought that man is considering the source because she was incredibly rude. It was wonderful the way he handled himself. He just ignored it."

Scammell remembered that the director of *Idiot's Delight*, Garson Kanin, was "a bit of snob." Every afternoon tea would be delivered to the 'stars' while the rest of the company had to stand waiting. Sam thought it was horrible. He said, "I find it embarrassing and unnecessary. It separates people and nobody's better than anyone else." As a contrast, during the run, Sam dropped in on Jack Lemmon's dressing room with a slice of his birthday cake wrapped in tinfoil.

Jaffe had a great surprise coming to him during rehearsals for *Idiot's Delight*. He got his paycheck and thought it was a mistake because it was more money than he expected. Yet, it represented the fruits of what he and Philip Loeb had fought for years earlier in Actors' Equity.

Jack Lemmon found Sam to be a total joy: "Sometimes you are fooled. Someone is totally different off stage. With Sam, there were no surprises."

Lemmon went on: "I always felt that he was a no-nonsense actor. There weren't a lot of frills. If anything, there was simplicity. There are truisms like 'less is better,' or 'simple, simple, simple.' These two would definitely apply to Sam's work, in my opinion. There was one thing going on and it was clear. I could see the line of where the character was going. As an audience, I felt I knew what the man was thinking. That has nothing to do with the words you say, necessarily. He listened to the other actor. He didn't just wait for a cue. I could listen to Sam. His work was clean and pure."

It was clear to Jack Lemmon that Jaffe was a total professional from the very beginning and that he had limitless energy in his work. Jaffe was direct and very strong. There was sureness about him; he was definite. Lemmon couldn't remember any time when he didn't just "walk on and bang, he was doing it, whereas Rosemary [Harris] and I were running around trying 18 different things. He did his homework, came in, and did it; same with the performance. He was like the rock of Gibraltar."

In the way Jaffe worked, he reminded Lemmon of Henry Fonda. When Jaffe worked in a scene with other actors, he made them all look good. There wasn't concern with what he could personally accomplish. The choice was rather, how do I play this character so that I carry out the author's intent? His focus was on what would make a scene work better.

Lemmon commented, "Better actors approach a scene as a director would, from the overall. Otherwise you get four actors in a scene with each one trying to be the maypole everyone else is dancing around. This was never the case with Sam or Fonda."

Lemmon found Sam to be both gentle and forceful. While he felt Sam could be anything, as an actor, he thought that Sam could work his butt off forever as a person and never cover up his human sweetness. He said that "Sam made acting look simple. He never rebelled against direction. It was his problem to work it out, not to make the director explain the whole damn thing."

Even more impressive to Lemmon was that Sam could play his role "the same damn way performance after performance. That is one of the biggest marks of a real pro . . . to be able to do it over and over and over again and give at least 85% of your best performance every time no matter what in your personal life is affecting your performance." Sam always kept his performance fresh and alive.

Lemmon commented on another quality in Sam that was significant to him. It was the energy in his eyes. That energy seemed to carry what he was saying on stage. The result was that it seemed this was the very first time he was saying the words, even if it was for the 100th time. "The words occurred to him and he said them now," Lemmon marveled. "Spencer Tracy and Robert Donat did that. That's the height of the craft. I always felt Sam was doing it for the first time. It's there, the original energy, and yet it seems natural. I try to do that. I try to let it happen each time."

Sam acted with other actors, not at them. He was present in the moment without any technique showing.

There were times in Sam's career when disquieting situations irritated him and he responded without his customary gentleness. During an episode of the television series *Streets of San Francisco*, Jaffe and Luther Adler were playing two Jewish cronies. In the story, they were looking for stolen money hidden in a shoe box and they found it under a manhole cover. The show was directed by Corey Allen whom series star Karl Malden described as a young boy who thought he knew a lot.

Malden related the following incident: "He had

two Jewish actors who between them had 100 years' experience, and this boy was trying to tell them how to
play the scene. Jaffe went down the hole and retrieved
the box. He brought it up, but Allen told him he wanted
him to stay below much longer. Sam went under again,
stayed down, and came up. Allen told him, 'No, Sam. Will
you stay down there for a count of eight? Count to eight
before you come up.' Sam said, 'All right,' went down,
stayed down and came up. Allen fussed, 'No, Sam. I said
count to eight.'"

Malden continued: "Sam took him on: 'I can count.
I can count in English. I can count in German. I can count
in Spanish. I can count in Yiddish. You want to hear me
count?' He counted in Yiddish and then in English; one,
two, three, four, five, six, seven, eight. He counted in
German: eins, zwei, drei ... Spanish: uno, dos, tres. Then
he said, 'I can count fast: one, two, three, four. ... I can
count slow: one, two, three, four. German: eins, zwei.'
He gave him a lesson in counting for at least an hour."

Malden said that he and Luther Adler ran away.
Malden laughed again as he remembered: "We couldn't
take it. We just ran away leaving Sam counting away,
telling this boy how he can count. I couldn't stand there
because I was laughing. I had to leave. He didn't do it to
be mean. He was just making the point, in different languages and different speeds. Everyone, the technicians
and the actors, everyone was just dying."

Jaffe and Allen had another unpleasant exchange
years later when Allen hired him for a show he was directing for Columbia. After signing Jaffe, they decided
they wanted him to shave his beard. Jaffe refused. Allen
reportedly told everyone that Jaffe would comply. There
was no possible way that Jaffe would shave his beard,
and eventually Columbia paid him off and had to hire
someone else.

These incidents of professional difficulty were few
and far between in Jaffe's total career. He was the kind

of actor most everyone enjoyed because he was disciplined, prepared, knowledgeable, and congenial.

It was Jaffe's realness, his simplicity, his kindness that drew people to him, and especially young people who were always on the lookout for the incarnation of their ideals. During the taping of the *SWAT* TV show, Sam was playing a professor leading students at a demonstration against a weapon's plant. Bettye had accompanied Sam, as she had throughout their marriage, to see to his needs and make sure he would be OK. One of the young girls, not yet 20, playing a student rushed up to Bettye during a break and gushed that she had fallen in love. Bettye told her she thought that was wonderful. The girl replied, "Yes, but it's with Sam." Bettye affirms that women were very attracted to Sam. She, herself, fell in love with him at first sight.

Bettye convinced Sam, something she seldom did, to do *The Dunwich Horror* film in 1970 in which he played a wizard. During that period, witchcraft was very popular in the colleges and universities. Bettye persuaded Sam that it would be interesting to play a character like that. It was the predecessor of *The Exorcist* and mystical pieces.

Sam wasn't too happy with the picture, but when actor Edward Albert took Bettye and Sam out to U.C.L.A. for a program, the young people surrounded Sam. Bettye thought it was for *Gunga Din* or *Lost Horizon* but it was for *Dunwich Horror*. Bettye could then ask Sam if she had been vindicated because the young people were crazy about the picture.

Sam had the unique reputation of turning down more scripts than other actors ever had a chance to play. He would never do a script that he felt would harm some part of the social theme, was violent or pornographic, or that slanted a certain group in the wrong way. He went into the business for inspiration, not degradation. He withheld himself from friends who broke this code and chose roles for money or exposure.

Ambition did not drive Jaffe. He wanted only to do the best he could. He never sought roles or favors for himself, only for others.

In these regards, Jaffe was almost too good to be true. For readers who derive pleasure from uncovering the dark nature of their movie idols, Sam Jaffe is a disappointing subject. Although there were faults and irritants, there were no hidden horror stories.

****

ALLAN MILLER, *Young Woodley*, 1955

"There was no status to my career when I did that production. I was not very well known. I had no agent.

"When I was cast, I was ecstatic, not only about getting
the part, because it was a very good part, but because ...
all the early rehearsals were improvised. We all felt like
real collaborators.

"The conditions at E.L.T. were homey ... you felt like
a member of the family. It was a very pleasant working
atmosphere. It was way the hell uptown, at 102nd St. or
something, so it was difficult. But it always had good audiences.

"I felt like a member of the Guild for the first time. This
was Actors' Equity; I was a part of the whole big thing.

"I believe I got an agent out of that show. I got excellent responses for the acting work that I did. Eventually it
did lead to some work.

"Sam: from all of us, from every young actor who has
looked for a place to be, thank you, thank you.

"E.L.T.'s demise represents a great loss. It's one of the
singular things that any one of our guilds was able to provide for its paid up members. It's a terrible loss."

****

The Sunset Years in Beverly Hills

Sam Jaffe had advice for young people just starting out in the acting profession. Referring to pitfalls and struggles, he urged "stick-to-it-iveness in order to go over these mountainous hurdles. Acting is something that has to come out of yourself. You must want to do it and you must stick with it."

Sam didn't agree with Stanislavski's statement that there are no small parts, only small actors. He believed that there were no small actors, only small parts. He added that there was as much truth to what he held as a point of view as there was to Stanislavski's.

Jaffe used a variety of techniques in the creation of different roles. One of his finest efforts had been in the film *The Asphalt Jungle* because he abstracted the character. He made up from bits and pieces of himself, a self that no one had ever seen before. It was a masterful creation.

All through his 80's, Jaffe continued working in his chosen profession. Where he worked was never as important as the role he played and how he played it. One of his passions was Shylock in *The Merchant of Venice*. It was one of Sam's life goals to vindicate him.

In September of 1971, as mentioned above, he and Bettye appeared together as Shylock and Portia at Dickinson State College in North Dakota. A cast of college students supported them and it was a rewarding engagement for everyone.

The process fascinated Bettye. She and Sam had worked on their roles in California while the students were working on their roles in North Dakota. Then they came together at the last few days. They had about nine rehearsals with the students.

"The first night when we started rehearsing," Bettye remembered, "Sam played the role for them. The young people were just stunned by the characterization that Sam had developed. We learned that some of the students had said after that, 'Well, I don't like the daughter now.' Their whole attitude changed with just the way he did the role. They began to think that she was a real louse to do that to her father." Sam's wish to clear Shylock's name enjoyed a measure of fulfillment.

All during his career, screenwriter Lou Garfinkle kept writing roles for Sam that he never got to play. Garfinkle said, "In *The Deer Hunter,* there was a croupier, whom I wrote as an old Dutchman to be played by Sam because I felt you could have this Caucasian god-figure in the orient running this worse kind of game but seeming to be moral and ethical in the way in which he did it. This was to underscore the corruption of the Caucasian in the way he deals with the Asiatic. The director used someone Chinese to play the role and we were roundly criticized from then on because we made it seem the Asians were the creators of their own difficulty without any help from us."

Garfinkle assessed Jaffe as one of the greatest actors ever to be on screen. "He would appear in small roles and overpower films suddenly," he remarked. "You knew that you could count on him to come up with the exact characterization. It wasn't Sam up there on the screen, it was this person. If you had a really difficult job to get done on a story, an actor of Sam's ability made it easy."

Before the blacklist, Sam was building toward greatness of characterization and playing very significant and different roles. Then he was knocked off his momentum. On his return, he played lesser roles and cameos. This was why Garfinkle kept trying to create roles for Sam that would underline his individuality and his capacity to symbolize. He saw him as capable of new characterizations.

Garfinkle wondered whether Jaffe lost his zest in his later years because he began turning down difficult material. Jaffe had been typecast as the old, wise man. He avoided doing controversy.

On the one hand, as mentioned earlier, Jaffe was firm about what he would and wouldn't play. He stuck to his integrity and wouldn't lend his name to film statements outside his beliefs. For example, he would never take a role in which an older Jewish man had negative attributes because he didn't want to portray any suggestion that Jews could be negative. The materials had to speak of the higher ideals of mankind. Garfinkle wondered if there was an element here of Jaffe slowing down in his response to new things. Whichever it was, and perhaps it was both, Jaffe by his choices significantly limited his film exposure.

Nonetheless, Sam Jaffe remained one of the great supporting actors. Instead of playing the same man all the time, he played individuals. He did this because he was an individual; it was how he lived. Garfinkle felt that his portrayals were as important, if not more so, as Paul Muni's, who had a good deal more screen time. "Sam registered," he said.

Knowing Sam Jaffe shaped a good part of Garfinkle's career. "I often tried to create characters that were worthy of him," he said. "I'm constantly trying to write protagonists that stand up tall, full of integrity and stick to their guns. It was always Sam who I knew was like that. I still think of it that way. It's hard to find people with that kind of strength. He was aware of the meaning of what he did, having a pervasive effect on civilization."

Jaffe had a very strong sense of self and felt good

about himself without turning it into ego fixation. He was able to take stands, in anti-Vietnam protests, for example, without caring whether they might endanger his career. What he felt and stood for was more important than what might happen to him. Bettye feared for him on occasion. One evening during the Vietnam conflict, Jaffe spoke at a doctor's home in Downey, a very conservative community. People milled outside with opposing posters, making it very clear that they didn't want the Jaffes there. Though fanatics might have harmed him, Sam went right on, speaking for what he believed. No one could make Sam Jaffe do anything and no one could stop him from doing what he felt was right.

On the night of Martin Luther King's death, the Jaffes were due at the grand opening of *2001 Space Odyssey* at the Pantages Theater. Bettye heard of the assassination on the television and told Sam. She suggested that they not attend the opening. There was a long silence and then Sam announced with great determination that they were going. Upon arrival, they were escorted to the interview platform were Sam announced: "Bettye and I welcome this opportunity in light of what has happened today. We're grateful to Stanley Kubrik, the producer of *2001*, for giving us the opportunity to leave this planet for at least four hours." Everyone was stunned. Jaffe was the only one to say anything about the tragedy.

Film director Steve Carver met Sam Jaffe through Eddie Robinson who invited Carver to a seder at his house in 1970. The Jewish community of Hollywood was made up of stars Carver had grown up on, and he found them to be warm and very human. They received him, a student, a Fellow at the American Film Institute, into their homes.

Carver did a film for AFI called *The Telltale Heart*. Sam Jaffe and Alex Cord played the roles for Carver for scale. Carver remembered: "Sam didn't mind that I couldn't pay him. He was interested in helping me, and in the piece as a good role. Sam had no dialogue. It was very graphic and suggestive and stylized. Sam himself was very sprightly and it was wonderful to see him play an old man. It gave me a lot of insight into actors and what they go through to become something real on film. Sam would say, 'let me try it this way.' He didn't treat me like a student or a kid, showing me how it's done. He was very gentle with me. In one scene Alex had to jump on Sam on the bed and throw his leg over him and I had to choreograph that carefully so Sam wouldn't get hurt. Sam was very trusting and encouraging."

Carver's film editor paid Sam the great compliment that he could be "easily cut." This meant that it was easy to match scenes in which Sam was shot at different angles. Sam could recreate easily and he could give a director what he wanted.

There was a scene in the film where Sam sits down to eat and has to shake because of his vast age. He created this as part of his character. In contrast, Sam was actually nimble and quick moving. The old man he created moved almost in slow motion. Carver said, "He was shockingly beautiful. He was something to look at. Without him in the film, the film wouldn't be anything. He made the film."

Carver spoke fondly of how Sam would often quote Yiddish expressions from his mother and explain them in English. "He may not have been religious, but that impression sticks in my mind. Maybe it was that he was very Jewish."

The Beverly Hills Library invited Carver to show *Telltale Heart* and he asked Jaffe to come. Sam did, and he swept the people off their feet, telling stories, answering questions. The auditorium was packed with over 300 people and Sam made the night.

Whether one-on-one or in front of a large audience Jaffe drew people in. He didn't create separations. He would look into people and they would know that he cared, that he was warm and real. For Steve Carver, Jaffe was the closest thing to a true rabbi. "There was a human touch to him," he said. "We'd talk about art and specific periods and he knew about everything. He was so well read. Knowing him at the beginning of my career gave me a more realistic, a more sane approach to actors. He portrayed authenticity in films. He had it in every picture I'd seen him in. In life, it was the same thing. It was a natural credibility. Sam contributes credibility to whatever he does. Few people have that or are consistent with it. He was."

This was one of the key factors about Sam Jaffe. He was authentic and credible in his roles because he was consistently authentic and credible in his life, and in his relationships.

In December of 1972, at age 81, Sam appeared at the Off-Broadway Theater in San Diego, in Rod Serling's, *A Storm in Summer* with Edd Byrnes and Patty McCormick. A review in the *Daily Californian*, on December 20, called Jaffe's performance outstanding: "Sometimes it is difficult to hear him above the rumble of a heating unit — and it can only be assumed that on those occasions gems are lost; every inflection, every jab of sarcastic humor that falls from Jaffe's lips seems appropriate for the moment. Even though he talks a lot to the picture of his dead son, he manages to make the monologue sound genuinely sincere when it would be easy to lapse into maudlin sentimentality."

Sam loved the play because of its universality and because it advanced the idea of loving one's neighbor.

Reviewer Jay Stanley called attention to Sam's creation of "a real human being, giving true emotions to Rod Serling's Abel Shaddick. It is a demanding role with much dialogue running the gambit of wisecracking lines intermingled with old world philosophy, to a final moving delivery of acting that in this role only Mr. Jaffe is capable of reaching the pinnacle causing the audience to be touched and each eye blurred with tears. ... The rapport between Rodney Bingley (playing the young black boy) and Sam Jaffe is like a love theme from a great symphony."

I tracked down the now grown Bingley and questioned him about Jaffe's impact on his life. Rodney, at age 13, had been struck by Jaffe's energy and electricity. Sam impressed Rodney with the importance of education and helped get him into Beverly Hills High School even though he was out of the district.

During the run of the play, Bettye and Sam would take Rodney out to dinner with them. They would walk down the street holding hands, with Rodney in the middle.

At night, after the show, Rodney would often get lonely for his parents. He remembered how Sam would embrace him and write poems for him. "I'd read them and feel a lot better," Rodney recalled. "He'd tell me stories and play the piano for me. To me he was like a giant with a heart like a mountain.

"One time we were on stage and Sam missed a cue. I was so

Sam Jaffe with Rodney Bingley during the production of A Storm in Summer *in 1972 in San Diego, CA.*

young then but so very alert. I used a couple of words to fill in and Sam used a few and we went right back on track and it made the audience clap. The director told us it was great that two people could have the energy and communication to know when one was lost and could bring the other one back in."

Sam Jaffe permanently imprinted Rodney's life with his warmth and his ability to see beyond color and bigotry. Rodney said: "This is a little inflated, but it's almost like having another Jesus; to be that gentle and understanding and loving. You could look at Sam's face and know he was real. He didn't have to rehearse being warm and loving. It was something natural. Human feelings and vibrations can't be faked. He never was too busy for me."

During the show, Rodney was always in Sam's dressing room. When he arrived, Sam would put aside the book he was reading and be present to him. Because of Sam, Rodney learned he could love anyone, no matter what their race or religion. Sam passed on to him the importance of friendship, and the two remained friends after the show.

Friendship was all important to Sam Jaffe. When his pal, artist Abe Birnbaum, was having a tough time, Jaffe arranged and paid for his first show and never told him. When Jaffe toured in *Cafe Crown* with Edward Franz, he announced that he would quit if Franz' salary was cut.

Whereas most people have a few friends and a multitude of acquaintances, Sam had a multitude of friends. The following story exemplifies how having Sam as a friend was used as a way of identifying self. During the shooting of the film *Roots of Heaven*, in the late 1950's in Africa, cast and crew suffered sunstroke because of the heat at the disastrous location. Eddie Albert was one of those stricken. His first recollection as he was coming to was that director John Huston was standing over him, lovingly offering him soup. In his quasi wakefulness, Albert asked Huston, "Are you the angel I see before me or the devil I've heard so much about?" Huston's response after a moment was, "Sam Jaffe is my best friend."

Many people, such as Edward G. Robinson, Zero Mostel, Ferenc Molnar, referred to Sam Jaffe as their best friend. When he was someone's friend, Jaffe was loyal and giving. He saw friendship as "life's sweetner."

James Rety met Sam and Bettye in 1963 when he served as their travel agent on a trip to Greece. As a result of the business transaction they became fast friends. "Sam was like my grandfather to me," Rety revealed. "I'm not a kissing man but I kissed Sam when I came to see him and kissed him when I left. I consider him part of my family. There was no one else I felt that way about. After you spent any time with him you always felt good."

Jimmy Rety spoke of Sam's devotion. "Even when he was not well, Sam knew that I was ill and if he didn't hear from me for a few days, he would call and say, 'Jimmy, this is Sam Jaffe. I haven't talked to you. Are you all right? Is there something that you need? If you need anything, I will tell Bettye to come to your home. She'll help you and she'll take care of you. Did you eat tonight?' This man was concerned about another human being."

Friends of Bettye's would see this offer by Sam as using Bettye. Jaffe didn't tell Rety that *he* would come over. He said that he would send Bettye and that she would take care of him. While Sam may have been in no condition to do that himself, he might at least have asked Bettye before offering.

It was when he was 81 that Sam Jaffe had his first stroke. It happened while he was in the audience at one of Stella Adler's classes. He was watching a scene that Evie and Bettye were doing. Bettye saw something happen to him but she didn't say anything. "My denial was so great that I went right on with the scene," she admitted. "The last night is always a big gala with lots of people invited. Sam attended the party afterward. But neither he nor I said anything about it and no one else noticed. A greater deterioration took place in a few days and then I knew I had to call a doctor."

She took Sam to Dr. Murray Cornfield who prescribed large doses of medication which Sam took for months. The medication affected him badly because he was allergic to it. Bettye and Sam returned to Cornfield. She told him, "I know that Sam is all there but I just get snatches of him. He's over-medicated." Cornfield asked her how she would know, proclaiming that as the physician he is the one who should know.

But Bettye did know. And so did others. Sam's sister-in-law, Glenna, had never seen Sam so depressed. It was the only time the family had ever seen him feeling sorry for himself. The family was very surprised to hear Sam talking about taking his life. That was the last straw for Bettye.

According to Bettye, it was really Jonas Salk who saved Sam's life at the time. He called Bettye one morning because he had noticed that Sam was acting strangely. Salk said he and Francoise were going away for a while and he wanted to know if Bettye needed him. Bettye said yes, because Sam was having a negative reaction to the medication. Salk said, any medication that is given to an artist should be cut in half. Bettye said, "I immediately cut his medication; the night before he had almost died. I didn't realize how desperately ill he was until I saw how the fluid was mounting up. If Jonas hadn't called me and I hadn't cut the medication in half, Sam would have drowned in his own fluid."

Sam was then taken to Dr. Corday. He told the doctor, 'I'm half the man I was,' and Corday said, 'Great, now we're all even.'

There was a transformation after Jaffe's medication was changed, and he made a comeback. His symptoms disappeared within ten days. While on the medication, his words had come out slurred and not in proper order. Bettye had asked him not to answer the phone. It was only when Sam got better that he realized he had been sick. Sam and Bettye never discussed the fact that he had had a stroke. She did everything she could for him, as she always did, but neither of them gave it a name. In the same way, it was unacceptable to Sam that Bettye be ill when she was later stricken with cancer.

At the time, Sam wrote to friends about the experience: "Now that the excruciating testing is over, I am beginning to feel a little better. The trouble with our medical profession is that it has become fragmented and that the specialist in each fragment is out to claim your ailment. Fortunately our doctor, Lloyd Corday, a most honorable member of the profession, vetoed some of the findings, took me off a great deal of medication, and I'm beginning to feel better. I now know I'm in good hands.

"I see that you too went through the blood-taking experience. Now the doctors have added drawing one's cash as well … how can a poor man ever hope to meet the astronomical bills?!" Under all circumstances, Jaffe was concerned about fellow-humanity.

Bettye knew that Sam had been over-drugged because of simple changes in him. Before the medication, Sam had always gotten up to fix the orange juice in the morning. He stopped doing that, along with other of his pleasurable routines, and started up again only after stopping the medication barrage.

After his recovery, Bettye found him standing in the kitchen one morning. He was just looking around. Focusing on his wife he said poignantly, "I know I wanted to die, but now I can't remember why." Bettye replied, "Welcome back, Sam." The experience with the over-medication had been horrible for both of them.

Sam fully recovered from the experience and in 1974 he appeared in *Next Year in Jerusalem*. It was a documentary sponsored by the Canadian Broadcasting Company and filmed in Jerusalem. Harry Rasky wrote and directed it. Sam had great appreciation for the material because it gave equal space to all the religions and focused on the lasting impact of the prophets' words. It was not surprise casting that Sam played Abraham. Marvin Kaplan observed that Sam got to play such roles of greatness because he was living out the greatness of his own being in many of the roles he played. It was clear he had great regard for Sam.

Two years later, in 1975 at the age of 85, Jaffe suffered a second stroke. Until that time, he could have been any age, no one could tell. One of the factors that had kept Sam in good health most of his life was his abstinence from meat-eating dating back to adolescence. He remained true to this diet through all his years on the road. In earlier days it was not always easy to obtain vegetarian cuisine. A basic staple for him was raisins, nuts, and dry cereals.

A typical breakfast included half a grapefruit, followed by wheat germ, a tablespoon of lecithin, a tablespoon of yeast, kelp, and some K cereal over that with milk.

He would enjoy pot cheese with strawberries for lunch, and often ate fish for dinner.

He balanced the eating with a short callisthenic drill upon awakening, followed by a long walk during the day.

After the second stroke, Jaffe began to age. Yet even during the decline, he remained quite healthy because his body had benefited from the years of good eating and exercising. Sam lived his life to the fullest. He was game for adventure even after entering his ninth decade of life.

His friend Urban Hirsch mentioned that he was going to take his 34-foot boat to Catalina. He never dreamed
that the Jaffes would agree to make the journey with him
at Sam's age. To his surprise Sam and Bettye decided to
go. Bettye thought it would be very good for him.

Urban remembered that they left on a Friday
morning: "We had a nice breeze going over. I showed
Sam how to use the head; it's mechanical on a boat. I
told him it wouldn't be on a level, and it would be best
for him to sit down because it would be hard to aim with
all the movement. Sam can be pretty stubborn. The end
result was that I spent a fair part of my time cleaning
up."

They started back on Sunday. At about three in
the afternoon they had a 35 knot wind. Sam was down
below the whole time, not at all bothered by seasickness.
It amazed Urban that a man of Sam's age could stand
that kind of motion.

Urban's wife, Evie Scott, didn't accompany them
on the trip. She agreed with whoever it was who said,
having a boat is the most expensive way to be uncomfortable there is.

Working was what kept Sam alive. Tom Ewell once
stood up at Actors' Equity and said there's nothing wrong
with any one of us that a job wouldn't cure. Bettye made
sure that Sam remained active and working into his last
years.

Bettye forcefully defended her strategy against
all comers: "Some people just love to tell you what to
do. They thought I was just dragging Sam around." One
of Sam's doctors thought that Jaffe shouldn't be doing
Meeting by the River, a play by Christopher Isherwood,
because he was too old. This was in the early part of
1979, five years before his death. It was his last engagement on the New York stage. During this time Sam wasn't
at all well. According to director Albert Marre, Sam had

concentration problems. He would forget things. It was also true that he couldn't have tried harder.

Sam played the role of an old guru. The company was nervous for him because he had a difficult entrance from under the stage and they hoped he would find his way up the stairs in the dim light. Two boys were assigned to guide him. During the performance at the University in Knoxville, Sam lost his balance and fell backwards. The students caught and held him until he could regain his balance. The audience gasped for him. The director changed his entrance after that.

During one of the previews in New York, at the Palace, Sam went up on his lines and left a hole in the scene big enough to drive army trucks through. He was doing the scene with Simon Ward who later lamented, "Oh God, I'd rather do 12 rounds with Mohammed Ali."

On opening night in New York, however, Jaffe was absolutely perfect. Everything came together without a moment's problem. Jaffe retained his stage presence and remained unique in manner. Jaffe exuded spirituality, other-worldliness. It was something inside that he could call on. He could produce ineffable sweetness. There was a sense of interior wisdom that he could turn on at will.

The show opened and closed the same night with a big opening night dinner at Trader Vic's. Everybody who was anybody was there, including Tennessee Williams. Williams was thrilled to see Sam. He told him that his performance was the one shining moment of truth. He hugged and kissed Sam. Playwright Christopher Isherwood was on one side of Sam and Williams on the other in a picture that was in every paper and magazine. Unpretentious as Sam was, he asked Bettye who the little guy beside him was. It was Williams and he didn't even know it.

Robert Wise and his wife saw Sam in the play during previews and felt very differently about Sam's work. When they got back to Los Angeles, she called Mona

Malden and told her to tell Bettye to get Sam out of that play because he was very ill. Mona got so angry with her that she broke up the friendship. Mona said if anyone knows what to do for Sam and with Sam, it was Bettye and she wouldn't dare interfere.

Bettye reinforced Mona's position: "Sam played a guy who died on stage. What did they expect? Sam must have done it so convincingly! People should mind their own business. I guess they want us to sit home on our asses and do nothing. Well, we're going to do something." Bettye's strong reaction, tinged with defensiveness, may well have been a reflection of her enormous investment in keeping Sam alive.

Bettye's brother Robert thought that Sam and Bettye had developed a pact of some kind, maybe never articulated, that Sam would die with his boots on: "I think she decided this when he was doing *Meeting by the River*. He was very frail at the time. They had to actually stop one time and get a pacemaker. She just kept pushing him to keep on. That did, in fact, extend his life; without any question. If she had let him become an invalid, he would have died. I have no doubt. It was obvious during the rehearsals.

"Sam looked ghastly. We were at a party afterwards and someone said, 'Does Bettye have any idea how frail Sam is?' And my wife said, 'Of course, she does.' That's when the idea came about the pact that he would go right along until his last breath. They weren't so much testing fate as not yielding to it."

Sam had his 88th birthday during the show in Knoxville. They had a surprise party and two big cakes. It so surprised him he practically staggered into the room.

The production was eventful in other ways. Bettye and Sam flew to New York for the opening on a flight hijacked by a woman on the plane who threatened to blow up the craft with a bottle of nitroglycerin. She demanded that the President of the United States appear on television on behalf of a religious cause and held the passengers' hostage and in fear for almost nine hours. It wasn't until daybreak that the police snatched the vile she carried, which proved harmless. The Jaffes and the other passengers sat on the runway during all that time. When released, it was to a barrage of lights and television cameras. Sam complained that everyone was pushing a microphone in your mouth asking you how you felt.

Following this incident, Sam had fainting spells due to a blocked artery.

As a result of the whole experience, Sam became aware of how absolutely useless it would have been had all these uninvolved, innocent people been killed. It was the blindness of the potential tragedy that struck him, not so much a fear for himself. The experience moved terrorism beyond the normal pale of justice for Jaffe. He began to entertain the possibility of capital punishment for terrorism.

The closing of the play was not the closing of Sam's active life. In 1982, two years before his death, Sam and Bettye did a working cruise together for the Princess Lines. This one included Dorothy McGuire, Virginia Mayo and Sam and Bettye. It went from San Juan, through the canal, to Saint Thomas, Curacao, and then Caracas. Sam absolutely charmed the people on ship board. The cruise featured a star of the day, highlighting one of their films or television shows. In the late afternoon, the stars were interviewed. Jaffe was a fascinating guest star. He had a fund of stories, and a marvelous human touch when he presented them.

People simply and naturally loved Sam Jaffe. At dinner one evening, one of the young waiters ran up to Sam and asked if he was Leopold Stokowski. When told it was the actor Sam Jaffe, the waiter said, "Oh wow, that's even better."

Ann and Arthur Knight had vivid memories of the cruise. In their taxi in Caracas, when everyone was grumbling about the heat and demanding limousines, Jaffe was the only one without complaint. He started telling stories and jokes. Soon he had everyone laughing and forgetting the heat. It helped the others to see things through his eyes. By this time in Sam's life he was blind in one eye, wore two hearing aids, and had a heart condition.

Ann Knight remembered that when they arrived at the airport in San Juan, it was hot and crowded. Sam was over 90 and looking frail. Arthur had gone to get him a wheelchair because the airport was dreadful. Bettye had their luggage and was trying to manage that. Arthur came with the wheelchair and Sam stood up, tall and dignified, and in a loud voice said, "Arthur, if I'm going to see the world, I'm going to see it on my own two feet."

Jaffe had done the same thing in his television work. Young crew members would hold cue cards up for him because they thought at his age he wouldn't remember his lines. He waved them away saying he didn't need those idiot cards.

Jaffe was not a quitter, nor would he allow himself to lean on crutches. The night he came out of the hospital following surgery on his eye, Bettye woke at about three and missed him in the bedroom. She went about the house looking for him. She found him sitting under a lamp reading Greek philosophy. He hadn't been able to read for so long that he couldn't wait another minute.

Arthur Knight made a keen observation of Sam Jaffe: "He was so bright that he could see people's weaknesses, but he chose to wear a blindfold. He looked only at the good side of people. He had courage and tolerance and patience with people. He made you feel good and that you were a worthwhile, beautiful human being. He had dignity."

This is the face Jaffe wore in the world. It is no wonder that so many remarked about these qualities in him. Very few saw his darker side, the side he vented most in Bettye's presence. He didn't want others to know of his weaknesses, but he did allow himself to know them because he exposed them to Bettye.

In the later years of their relationship, there were more instances of Sam's stubbornness and his demanding nature. Bettye wasn't run by Sam but she continued to do what he wanted, not because she was governed by him but because, as pointed out earlier, she wanted to. Nor did she make her choices automatically. As time went on, and as Sam became more insistent, Bettye also began to care for herself.

During a show of her paintings in San Diego, Sam was insistent that he was going to take everyone to dinner. Bettye kept refusing the plan because she was working on a television series the next day and she needed to go over her script and have some rest. While everyone else understood that, Sam wouldn't let it go. Finally Bettye prevailed, but he made it very difficult.

Another time, Bettye and Sam attended the gala showing of the long version of *Lost Horizon*. The theater was jammed to the rafters and Frank Capra was on stage speaking. Jane Wyatt, one the film's stars, heard a commotion going on behind her and turned to discover it was Sam Jaffe arriving. The Jaffes had made reservations at Scandia restaurant for after the film and Sam didn't want to be late. He insisted it was time for them to go. He thought nothing of leaving in the middle of something. Bettye marveled: "He never thought anyone knew who he was!" Bettye calmed Sam down and told him she thought they could be a few minutes late.

In May 1983, Paul Hardin, the President of Drew University in Madison, New Jersey, featured the Jaffes at commencement and gave them a pair of honorary degrees. Hardin remembered that "Sam was physically feeble by this time. After we read this long list of Sam's accomplishments he spoke into the mike saying, 'What about my modesty?'"

Sam Jaffe and Bettye Ackerman at Drew University in May of 1983. Both were given honorary degrees. With them is Bettye's brother Robert Ackerman who was at the time Dean of the College of Liberal Arts at Drew.

One of the television shows Sam did in his last years was *Love Boat*. Some wondered why anyone with his capacity would do that show. Bettye advocated Sam's taking the job, in keeping with her knowing that it was important for Sam to work to keep his sense of self alive. They did the *Love Boat* together. The script was written for the two of them.

Love Boat producer Henry Colman hired the Jaffes because a casting preference on the show was to use actors from successful TV series or movie stars. In Sam's case, Colman had concern because of his age and whether he would be able to remember his lines.

"Time is money," he said, "and you can't sit and wait for someone to remember the lines. Nor can you insult an actor saying, shall we get you a teleprompter. I very tactfully discussed it with Bettye and she said, 'Just have them there and if he needs to use them he'll use them.' Instantly, he was quite expert with the cue cards. We positioned the man with the cards so that Sam could look at Bettye and look past her to the cards when he needed them. But as I recall, he didn't need them that much. And this was when he 91."

Colman had never met anyone like Sam. They became fast friends and Colman did a video interview of him that led to a series of taped interviews designed to inspire older people. During the interview Colman learned a lot about how to live. Sam was very clear about who he was and what his ideals were for the world and for himself.

"His humility ran deep," Colman said. "I would tell him how fabulous he was in *Lost Horizon* and he would give some offhanded humorous remark, trying to simplify what he did."

Henry Colman noted that Sam was not swayed by anyone or anything: "He had his own ideas and philosophy. He had opportunities to make a lot of money but didn't make his choices on that basis. He was a very good person and believed that people were here to give to other people."

Jaffe inspired Colman to pursue his interests right up to the very end of his life. Sam consumed life and, above all, he remained true to himself. It was Jaffe's integrity that impressed Colman more than anything. It was remarkable to him that in spite of the blacklisting and other major disappointments there was no bitterness or cynicism. "If there was cynicism," Colman remarked, "it was at such a high level that it was humorous cynicism."

An example Colman gave was Sam's blistering

comment about famed Broadway producer Jed Harris, detested by many. Sam said Harris couldn't possibly have fathered an out-of-wedlock child ascribed to him. He suspected instead that the actress "got it from a toilet seat."

This humor was rather crass and seems to have its roots in a New York street upbringing. Sam reserved his coarse observations for those he viewed with disapproval. It was as if Sam got caught up in negativity in trying to take a deserved swipe at a despicable individual. His crude-sounding comments were a jarring aspect of his personality because of the very different aura he projected most of the time. However, the unrefined part of Sam Jaffe was an equal part of who he was even though many overlooked it or called it cute.

Sam Jaffe was vital and alive as he moved into the ninth decade of his life. He remained involved in his community and profession and he continued to educate himself. In an interview with Jordan R. Young in the *Los Angeles Times*, on March 14, 1981, Jaffe reiterated his penchant for being highly selective about the roles he plays.

"'I only want to do a part that means something, that has something to say. ... First of all, pornography is out. Recently a script was sent to me; it was interesting, but there was one scene I couldn't be associated with. I feel a responsibility to people who see it.

"'You can still watch *Lost Horizon* today, because it has something to tell you. I did other films that weren't so great, but they had something to say.'"

Jaffe was sympathetic with others who couldn't afford to be as choosy as he: "'Maybe sometimes an actor, to save his soul, has to pawn his body. It's very tough to get started. You must be convinced that that's what you want to do, and so you make sacrifices for it — something takes you by the scruff of the neck and says, this is it, and you stick to it. An actor is a man against the world.'"

Jaffe never wavered in the matter of individual responsibility. He would never support, even indirectly, anything that went against his principles, not for money, not for so-called defense of freedom of speech. To allow harmful words to be spoken by him would be the equivalent of advocating them. Artistic freedom is appropriately guaranteed by the constitution, but choice of participation is something each must guarantee for self. When we give something voice, it contributes to the reality created in the world, and for that we bear responsibility.

At 90, Jaffe remained a voracious reader. He believed an actor had to be aware of what was happening in the world and that one could never know enough. He quoted Socrates: "Knowledge is power." Sam Jaffe knew that his power grew as his knowledge grew. "When you stop growing," he said, "you're dead."

Sam Jaffe, in his nineties, still standing tall, eyes open to the world around him.

****

JERRY STILLER, *Men in White*, 1954, and *The World We Make*

"When I did E.L.T., I wasn't thinking about career. You went down and you tried out and it was always a great feat if you got a job. I was told this would be a great opportunity to be seen by producers and get further work, and it usually did get you work.

"In The World We Make, I worked with a dog. The dog became the star, naturally. Not only that, but it got me work with other dogs. Years later I worked with a dog in Shakespeare in the Park. I kept him with me for years until he died. I couldn't just turn the dog out after he got all those laughs. I called him a Shakespearean retriever. He got all the laughs that I missed.

"It was a very unpressured environment at E.L.T. Who knows, maybe I was untalented so I didn't know any different.

"They took chances with me, giving me character work. In The World We Make I certainly wasn't old enough to play the role, but they made some adjustment. It showed great courage on somebody's part.

"We rehearsed all the way up around Third Avenue and 125th St. I said, 'My God, you really are going off, off-Broadway.'

"I was completely unknown. The director, Ray Boyle, said, 'I was going to give it to some actor that I worked with who I thought was wonderful, but your reading was so great that I had to use you.' I was swept away by that. Later, he was the casting person for John Houseman at the Phoenix. He cast me and Jack Klugman and Gene Sax. The contact of just meeting Ray Boyle helped me get in.

"In those days, Anne [Meara] and I were married only a couple of months and it was an amazing piece of luck to find yourself playing in a theater with stars like Robert Ryan and Mildred Natwick. There was a feeling of, God, what a nice business we're in. People were very friendly and warm.

"Anne and I did a Love Boat with Sam and Bettye. It was a thrill. He was so sweet. He was a great storyteller. I didn't know he had started E.L.T. As kids we would idolize these people.

"During the shooting, Sam fell down some stairs and

the whole set went berserk. He immediately got up and brushed himself off and went on. He had no awareness that he had gone down a whole flight of stairs. It was very frightening for all of us. He picked himself like the trooper that he was and he went up there and did it again.

"Sam, do you know that you got me a lot of work in this business? You got me started."

****

IRENE DAILEY, *Idiot's Delight*, 1949

"Idiot's Delight led to Jeff Hunter becoming my agent. The status of my career was nowhere at the time of E.L.T. I was working at night as a waitress and was studying in the day. I had no money at all. The character had to look glamorous. You supplied your own clothes, wigs, make-up, everything, in those days. Mitch [Erickson] came to one of the early dress run-throughs. He went to Klein's [department store] and he bought three outfits. The store's rule was you could keep it for five days and if you didn't detach the sales ticket you could return it.

"For our final dress rehearsal I wore those three outfits one after the other and they picked which one they liked and Mitch took the other two back. I couldn't have gone or worried about it. I was in rehearsal and I was working. I'll never forget what he did as long as I live. I have a picture of me as a blonde in that. [The picture of Dailey as a blonde in E.L.T.'s Idiot's Delight got her the starring role in a play in London a decade later.]

"It was a very professional environment. The theater was on 77th Street between First and Second Avenues. They normally had long rehearsal periods. We're going back now to when there was no off-Broadway. People had jobs and we worked around schedules for about four or five weeks. The stage was small as I remember, but it was certainly adequate. The play was very well received.

"It was a great role for me at that time. I was in my late twenties. Until then, I had played wisecracking people, athletes, and whores. It was the first New York leading woman I had ever played. I wasn't nervous about being in a lead. And it's a wonderful role for a woman. She's extremely funny.

"I think E.L.T. started a million people. Part of what was great about it was the smallness of it, the camaraderie, and it was run very democratically. It was open to professional actors who wished to read and audition. You didn't have to be sent by anybody. I think it should be there again. But of course there are no actors who care for the theater anymore. They just want to get a television serial. I think E.L.T. should exist. It was a great idea when it was started and it would flourish today.

"In its primary years you'd have very well-known people who were playing poetic parts, things they weren't hired for. That's the marvelous thing that would still be the same. It's still the reason one would want to do an E.L.T. show."

****

The Dwindling Days

In his ninth decade, Sam Jaffe was asked to single out the best years of his life. His response was typical of the way he lived. "I have nothing against any of the years," he replied. "If things didn't go well ... Life, I feel, takes after the dumbwaiter. It's up and down."

At 91, his hair still looked like "an explosion in a mattress factory," to quote his friend George Burns. He laughed about his impossible hair and thoroughly agreed with the pronouncement that it was a "hairdon't" rather than a hairdo. He wore hearing aids and a thick wooden cane steadied his walking. As with many people of advanced age, the skin on his face had become translucent. The look bespeaks the ebbing of the temporal connection and the soul's uniting with its lucid nature. Although his face depicted the approaching transition, Jaffe retained his alertness, presence of mind, and continued involvement in life.

He lived with awareness of the élan vital — the life force that carries on, that remains. Jaffe sustained that with the conviction that one could always improve on what he had done. This practice kept him engaged with life in a dynamic way.

It was the improvement dimension that had continually drawn Jaffe back to the theater. He knew that there he had a better chance to develop a role because he had four weeks of rehearsal in which to create a character. He would often say that the movies took the cream off the top: "Movies are catch as catch can. Television is movies in a pressure cooker."

He compared actors to painters. As they needed to be familiar with oils, charcoal and engraving, an actor must be familiar with all mediums. On stage he could release a measure of creative force. In film work, he had to be economical, to hold back.

For years he had done this in his life as well. Compared with his friend Zero Mostel, Jaffe knew how to conserve. Zero was always performing, making it impossible to have a conversation with him. In contrast, Sam was personable and present. If he was talking to a shoemaker, he would start a conversation about shoes. He was interested in the other person and it enabled him to expand and grow.

In the winter of his life, Jaffe sustained his interest in learning and research, as well as his practice of studying languages. Sam could still dazzle visitors with his mastery of German, French, Italian, and Yiddish. Then he would evoke a laugh by indicating that he also knew "a little English." Years earlier he had also known some Japanese, Polish and Russian, but these had faded because of lack of use. Conscious of this, Jaffe used all his faculties as best he could, for he knew that life also faded, if and as it was unused.

He would spend his days writing letters and reading. He knew the direct correlation between keeping busy and remaining vitally alive.

Sam Jaffe didn't stop working, or thinking, or investing his energy in being a force for good in the world. In both his life and his career, his motion was always forward into the new and the more.

Sam Jaffe at his piano in his earlier days.

It took him ten years to get around to viewing his performance in *Gunga Din*. This came about only because friends of his wanted see it and Bettye showed it at their house! When he finished something, his interest in it ended. It was completed and he moved on. Once a film was in the can, there was nothing anyone could do about it. He never wanted to be like an old general showing his medals.

This was a trait that extended to other areas of his life. He did what there was for him to do without any desire to call attention to himself. Often Bettye would fill in with praise where Sam chose to be matter-of-fact. A typical interaction with a visitor would have Sam stating: "I read some." Bettye would jump in with the correction, "You read a lot." Inevitably, Sam would dismiss the compliment with, "Nothing to boast about." In truth, until the end of his life, Sam was a voracious reader. He used his stored knowledge to help others.

When a friend couldn't remember something in a William Safire column that they had both read, Sam promised that he would look it up. Pat Tobias thought it was just party talk and never expected to hear any more from him. In a few days, she received a copy of the column in the mail. Sam had looked it up, xeroxed it, and sent it, marking the passage they had discussed. Sam took conversations seriously. If he said he would do something then he would follow through on it. It kept his mind young.

Bettye's brother, Robert Ackerman, was impressed that Sam was always a student. He never failed to bring a book when he visited and would even study calculus or language. He gave Robert many books by Bertrand Russell, whom he appreciated.

Robert saw a similarity between Jaffe and Russell. "There's nothing more beautiful than a radical who grows old," he said. "Most of us tend to become more conservative as the years go by. There was some of that in Sam, too. He became so sickened by terrorism that he became a bit more tolerant of capital punishment. He was heated in his discussion of that."

When Sam wasn't steeped in heated points of view, he was a font of anecdotes. They were all richly observant and penetrating. Jaffe was a man of immense knowledge and history who looked at things in a wise, detached way.

At age 91 Sam appeared in the film *Nothing Lasts Forever*. The young director, in his 30's (Tom Schiller), said that Sam was one of the youngest people he had ever met.

Jaffe's focus was always on what his next project would be and especially on lending his acting talents to works that stood for decent standards of living. Even at his advanced age, the calls kept coming with offers of roles. In one month, he was offered parts in three features. However, he remained selective, choosing what was in harmony with his basic nature. He looked for solid characters that were real and worthy of his effort.

Sam firmly quoted Job: "To my integrity I hold fast. Though he slay me, yet will I maintain my ways before him."

Sam's approach not only didn't limit his career but may well have added to its excellence. Of his numerous films, many are considered classics.

As he chose roles that spoke to him, so he continued to support causes in which he believed. "An actor can't be an actor unless he's involved in the times in which he lives," he said. "He must understand the community and the world.

In his later years, particularly when he was ill, Sam became more irritable. He expressed it with his wife while bringing his more social side into view in public. This dimension increased the longer they were together and the older Sam got. Bettye's nephew, Mark Ackerman, accompanied them on a trip to New York City. The effort tired Sam and he began to complain. Jaffe was forthright, calling the trip a bad idea. Mark noted that Bettye was quite adept at easing Sam into the situation. Once they had arrived, everything fell into place and Jaffe did a complete turnaround because most of the people present had come to see the two of them.

When Sam was impatient with Bettye, she continued to let it move right through her and remained focused on her own objectives in relation to him. Once, during one of his hospital stays, she wanted him to get up and walk because she thought he needed exercise. He said no, he wanted to sleep. She kept after him and he barked at her to leave him alone. She persisted, and he responded harshly, causing concern in observers. Bettye stuck to her position, insisting in spite of his protestations. In a little while, he was up and walking. She didn't quit then either. Instead, she started in on how he was walking and ordered him to pick up his knees. Friends thought it a wonder he didn't tell her to go to hell. However, they were quick to realize that Bettye sustained his life in this way. He complained that he felt like a soldier, and that he didn't want to march. But he did it anyway.

Charles Higham was among many who were thoroughly impressed with the way Bettye functioned in her primary love relationship. "Her joy was in Sam," Higham revealed. "I had only seen that kind of love in the pure sense once before. Bettye was a saint. She would literally take him by the hand and will her life into him. And it took a terrific toll. She sustained the spirit of Sam Jaffe in all of our lives. It's the noblest thing I've ever seen.

"I don't think that Sam is a saint," Higham went on, "but Bettye is. There's no question. She has a purity of vision and is not in any way corrupted. She can't be bought or sold. She is incapable of lying or deceit. She has a single-minded unselfishness."

Bettye's family felt that she was walking a tight-rope in those last few years. She did push Sam to doing things so that he would live longer, but it took a physical and emotional toll on her. Her nephew Mark remembered the last Christmas they came to visit. During dinner, Sam set down his glass but it didn't quite make it into the coaster. Bettye watched the tilted glass. Mark knew that she was trying to decide whether to tell Sam or whether to reach over and make him feel embarrassed or angry and put that glass in the coaster, or what to do. Finally, she didn't do anything. He picked it up and drank, setting it down correctly the next time.

Mark remembered: "The most pathetic thing I ever saw him do was put his wine glass down next to the candle and next time he went to get the wine he picked up the candle. We felt sad about it."

The family had been concerned that Bettye pushed Sam too hard in bringing him home for the holidays. Yet, humor also accompanied the pressured time. On one occasion, Sam said he was turning his hearing aid up but he turned it off instead.

According to agent Sue Golden: "After Sam's death, all the people, the so-called friends, who came to the house after the funeral said: 'We'll see what we can do for you [meaning helping Bettye to get jobs].' I've made a number of phone calls and most of them have done absolutely nothing. For a while she wasn't ready to work because she was too devastated by his loss. Then when she was ready to work, it wasn't easy. I'm really amazed at how many people don't really know who Bettye is. It's because she dropped out."

Bettye's friend, actress Tamar Cooper, defended

Bettye's commitment to Sam, reiterating that it was what Bettye wanted. It fulfilled her needs and his. Bettye may have given up parts of her career, but there was a trade-off. Cooper said: "Sam was her pleasure, not her burden. Sam was more than an actor working up to the very end; he was a mensch standing up for human rights. But you need a Bettye to be able to work to the very end. Everyone should have one."

On one occasion when Bettye was ill with the flu, she had to rush Sam to the U.C.L.A. Medical Center. She directed his care from her sick bed, sending friends and nurses in to be at his bedside. When she was able to be beside him after a few days, she was horrified to find that he was "not the man" she had left. Two doctors had been standing at Sam's bedside and Bettye threw them out of his room. With the help of one of Sam's private nurses, Bettye pulled Sam out of the bed and into a chair. He was dying. He was on his way out.

Bettye didn't know what she was going to do, nor did she have time to think it out. "I was just reacting," she said, remembering the desperation. "I must have known that I couldn't speak down to him. I had to get him on a level. I put him in the chair and I got another chair. I went right up to him and began screaming, 'Look at me.' I kept yelling, 'Sam, look at me.' I went on and on in that vein, really screaming. 'I love you too much to let you go this way.'"

His eyes began to focus and he said, "I love you too." Later, a dean of medicine told Bettye that she had interrupted Sam's wandering toward death. She called him back, and he came.

In several instances, if it hadn't been for what she had done, not the doctors, he would not have lived. Bettye would intervene, not allowing doctors to do what she felt to be disharmonious. She would use her intuition. She seemed to be in sync with a greater plan. She did the right thing at the right time. She loved Sam in a way few people ever experience. She practically breathed for him. There isn't a moment in the 24 hours that she wasn't thinking about his welfare above all else. No matter what it was, he came first. He always did.

Person after person who knew the Jaffes reinforced this view. Terence Scammell expressed disbelief that some people thought Bettye married Sam because he was famous. It was the only way they could fathom her marrying such an older man. He countered, "It's ludicrous because the love between the two of them is something I've never seen before and I don't think I'll ever see again. Her cancer was her body manifesting the agony she went through over Sam. I wondered how much longer she could stay healthy seeing this man in the state he was, what his anguish was. He was such a powerful man, and yet such a quiet man, such strength and depth in him. And I believe that the higher you go on the spiritual plane, the deeper the agonies."

In July of 1983, during a U.C.L.A. Hospital visit with Emily Paley, Sam admitted that his life continued thanks to Bettye: "It's pretty tough. She's taken care of me before my allotted three score and ten and for 22 years after my allotted three score and ten. I've been a terrific burden to her. She may say no but I know what I am."

Bettye asked Sam if he would do the same thing for her. He said of course, but he insisted that Bettye deserved more credit for what she had done. "Mine is just talk," he said. "Bettye took care of me, answered every one of my demands." Sam had not missed the fact that he was demanding and that Bettye had met his demands.

He called her a ministering angel. "She's everything that's good," he declared. "Bettye is exceptional in many ways. Not only in her care for me but in her talent in general, for her spiritual qualities, for herself. She deserves the highest praise. The fact that I'm here is all thanks to her."

Sam would occasionally express exasperation with his illness. He would talk about living too long with his frailties. This was especially true during the time he was having trouble controlling his urine and it was embarrassing for him. He was a man of great pride.

Robert Ackerman had a picture in his mind that stuck with him with great pathos: "They took us to U.C. Santa Cruz and Sam was having great trouble with his kidneys at the time and he went behind a bush. When he came out, he was wet. I thought, 'Oh, how pathetic,' because he was a man of great pride. And I thought then, 'Cruel fate.'"

Jaffe's serious difficulties had begun in August of 1981 when prostate cancer resurfaced. It had already spread to the bone. The doctors organized a program of protection for Sam because he also had cardiac problems. It was not a program of aggressive attack.

The doctors wanted to allow Sam as much freedom as possible and make his life pleasurable. They didn't do chemotherapy or radiation. He did have a catheter for a brief time to allow for the urinary flow. Bettye administered the catheter, cared for Sam, and consulted with the doctors.

Sam didn't complain to the doctors about having a urine bag attached to the side of his leg or about the discomfort of the catheter. They saw Sam as a very brave and courageous patient who was beset with multiple system difficulties. The painful bone disease caused everything to hurt when he moved. The doctors could treat with sedation and then go to narcotics and stronger narcotics, all of which cost the patient because of dulling nerves. But they didn't want the patient to be a vegetable; they wanted to leave some of the light on. They needed to judge the degree of pain that can be handled in order for patient not to be 'out.'

One of Sam's concerns was he wanted to die with dignity. He wanted to preserve his sense of self.

Jaffe's urologist, Dr. Peterfy, said that Sam was not alarmed by the prostate cancer. He experienced Jaffe as a good patient who didn't complain. Instead, Jaffe was always anxious to talk with his doctor about human problems and he remained keenly aware of events transpiring in the world. Peterfy benefited greatly from having Sam as his patient. "Treating him made me a better doctor," he proclaimed. "Sam was so patient and so appreciative. If he could be patient with himself and with me, then I should be able to be patient with others."

While Jaffe was patient in the presence of his physician, he expressed his distress to his wife. It was as if Sam had public and private sides. He impressed his doctors with his ability to take things in his stride and instead to be concerned with world problems. But once at home with his confidante with whom he felt safe to rage, he revealed his frailties. He hated having a catheter. For him it was like being a baby again. He was often very vocal about it. He wanted to live but not with indignities. His anger often spilled over onto Bettye. Bettye remained unruffled.

Mona and Karl Malden observed the Jaffes during this difficult period. Mona said that in spite of Sam's outbursts, he was devoted to Bettye. "And if he ever took advantage of her," she hastened to add, "he didn't do it out of meanness or out of being able to take advantage. It was just part of what was happening to him physically."

Karl jumped in: "Maybe the last five years, when he was sick, he took advantage. She had to handle him like a child and she did. And maybe he hated her because she had to do that and he knew it."

By September, 1983, Sam's urine was again clear. But the beginning of the end was nearing.

The Maldens thought that Bettye suffered for those ten years of being patient. She never said an angry word to or about Sam, before or after his death. Everyone who knew her was concerned for Bettye's health.

Bettye's only concern about her own diagnosis of cancer was that she might die before Sam. She gave her brother Robert the name of the attorney he should call and she made provision for Sam to go into the actor's home.

In the end, she clearly wasn't satisfied with any of her preparatory arrangements and just decided to get well instead. Robert agreed that she no doubt got well "out of cussedness."

Robert didn't think Sam could conceive of surviving Bettye. That might be why Sam never dealt with her having cancer, or if he did, he never shared it. As a former boxer, Sam probably would have liked the opportunity to spar with some of life's unfairness.

It is no wonder that Bettye and Sam struggled with the potential loss of one another, given the profoundness of the love they shared. They always found ways to meet each other. There were times when Sam would say he was too tired to go out to dinner. However, Bettye would get made up and dressed, and she would look so beautiful that Sam would extend him himself and consent to go.

Sam wanted to get out of his deteriorating body, but he felt he couldn't leave Bettye. He told Terence Scammell that he would drown himself in the pool but he felt that the moment she found him she would follow him.

Sam suffered the agony of being encased. His body closed down while his mind stayed brilliant. The physical deterioration of illness took its toll emotionally and mentally as well. Bettye asked Terence to take Sam to the doctor in Beverly Hills. They set out in his car and drove around. At the back of the building there was a one-way alley. They arrived and Sam looked up and said, "No, this isn't it. It's going the wrong way."

They drove around and Terence could see Sam was starting to get agitated because he was so punctual. He said, "Sam, why don't we park the car? It's obviously in this area, and let's walk."

He pulled the car in and as they walked, Sam looked up and said, "This is it but it's wrong. The arrow is going one way; it's going the other way." He started getting mad at himself. "Damn it!" he fussed. "You know what it's like? Now the brain's going, the body's going."

He became somewhat hysterical in the street. Naturally, people were recognizing him. Terence tried to quiet him, telling him everything was all right. But Sam lamented that Terence didn't understand.

"I can't find my way around the street," Sam proclaimed angrily. "God damn it, you don't know what it's like."

Terence took him into the building to find a phone. Once inside, Sam looked around and said, "This is it. This is my building." For some reason, the city had changed the one way street around. Terence spoke with distress: "This poor man went through all this agony thinking he was going absolutely mad and thinking now the brain is going, and all it was, was they had turned the street sign the other way. It was so agonizing. His feelings were so deep. Sam hated so much to be a burden on anybody because he was always giving and giving."

Living in doubt was not something with which Jaffe had much experience. He had always been sure of himself, had always met life full on and sparred with it. He enjoyed a good battle.

During their whole marriage Bettye and Sam had argumentative exchanges. Bettye's brothers expressed surprise because Southerners didn't behave that way. The Jaffes didn't think anything about it.

My partner, author Diane Kennedy Pike experienced them both as very strong willed. Many times those two wills would come up against each other. She reflected, "The words that passed back and forth didn't go very far because they were both standing their ground. I wonder if that wasn't one of the strengths of their marriage."

Their marriage certainly grew as a result of their differences, and they respected each other's opinions. Bettye would get most angry with Sam when he didn't take good care of himself, or when he sacrificed himself. Not surprisingly, these qualities were prevalent in Bettye.

Tom Ackerman didn't worry about his sister when she and Sam argued because he knew that she was powerful. He said that their salvation was that they were both always right! Tom smiled: "Bettye could always maneuver Sam and he wouldn't know he was being had. She would say, 'We're coming home for Christmas. Sam doesn't know but I'll work it out; don't worry.'" She always did work it out somehow.

The love Sam and Bettye had between them, they shared generously with friends and family. They were particularly giving to other people's children. Delia Gottlieb remembered how every Christmas they would send the most expensive and elaborate presents until finally she told them they had to stop. Children had a very special meaning for Sam. He loved and cared about them.

Bettye's brother Robert said Sam would occasionally be impatient in other parts of his conversation but he never saw any impatience with the children. When Sam grew a beard after *Ben Casey*, Robert's daughter Roxanne, who was four years old, wanted to know what he had on his chin. She told him she didn't like it and began tugging at it. She urged him to take it off immediately. Sam was absolutely patient with her. She harassed him about it and he not only endured it, he enjoyed it.

The children would tell Sam stories about what was going on in their lives and he was always interested in what they were doing. He was a good audience and very encouraging of their projects and talents.

On one occasion in California, the Malden's 18-month-old grandchild went all around the social scene that was taking place, getting a reading on every guest. Finally she made her selection. She pulled her little chair up beside Sam and started talking to him as though she had met a kindred spirit.

Sam was at his sweetest with children. He would talk with them for a long time, listening to them. He could hold undivided interest in others, and he carried this trait over to children as well.

Sam and Bettye's fascination with others was genuine and deeply felt by the recipients. Nanette Fabray remembered how the Jaffes were among the few who rallied to her side when she was widowed. "There are people who can't handle death and they drop you," she confided. "They love you and care about you but they can't deal with the situation. Some who I thought were dear friends drifted away and the ones I felt were just social acquaintances turned supportive. Sam and Bettye were two who rallied and who tried to never let me be by myself. They were warm and loving. They would call and show up at odd hours of the day and night, in the early evening or in the early morning when they know those are very difficult times. They always seemed to know."

After Stella Adler's husband died, she was in seclusion except for her teaching. Sam broke through that and brought her back. Stella invited the Jaffes to her home for dinner but they never did get to eat. Stella and Sam talked and laughed and cried for hours. The cook finally just left. Bettye wasn't even there as far as they were concerned. Sam told Stella all about his grief over Lillian. It was a great experience of commiseration and a turning point for Stella.

Jaffe's reaching out to others was related to one of his life's desires: to lessen man's burden.

Though ailing, Sam still loved to go out to eat with his friends. Norman Lloyd, a frequent restaurant companion, remembered that what Sam loved best was noodle kugle. Lloyd reported: "Sam found that the best place to get noodle kugle was in Beverly Hills at the Hamburger Hamlet, of all places. The thing was, he wasn't supposed to be eating this stuff. So he would corral me and then we would get in the car. Supposedly we were going to some innocuous place, and he would say, 'Noodle kugle.' I would protest, 'But Bettye ...' And he would say, 'Shhh ... noodle kugle.' We would go and promise never to tell Bettye, but I did."

Sam Jaffe loved restaurants and he was loved in restaurants. Lloyd said that when they went to Nate and Al's, "it was like the Chief Rabbi of America walking in. There would be a line out the door but Sam would come in and they would say, 'Mr. Jaffe, we'll have a table right away.' They would rush somebody out and in no time Sam had his table and he hadn't done anything about it."

On one occasion Sam told Norman about Nate and Al's great potato latkes. They made a special batter for Jaffe that had no salt. They both placed orders.

In a few minutes the potato latkes arrived and they each had three. Lloyd finished his but Sam was eating very slowly. When Jaffe had gotten half way through, Lloyd realized he needed to put money in the meter. When he returned, Sam announced that they were bringing more potato latkes. It seems that while Lloyd was out, Jaffe went to the men's room. The server thought that the two men had left and removed Sam's remaining one and a half latkes. When Sam returned to the table he asked his waitress what had happened. New people were already seated in his booth. A scurry ensued. The wait-

ress quickly forced the people out of their seats while as-
suring Jaffe that everything would be all right. The management insisted that he would have three more potato
latkes. Sam said it wasn't necessary, but he didn't put up
too much of a protest.

When the additional latkes came, Sam told Norman he would have to help him. Norman told him, "I'm
not helping you, Sam. You're going to have to eat every
one of them. You can't go out of here leaving a shred of
a latke." Sam worked his way through the order. About
half way through he asked again if Lloyd was sure he
didn't want any. Jaffe did his duty, eating every one. He
would not let them feel bad after they had gone to all
that trouble.

Lloyd's face softened with endearing memories as
he recalled how Sam loved to go out for lunch and how
he loved restaurants.

Jaffe's condition worsened with time. Lenore DeK-
oven realized how ill
Sam was when she
saw him at an art
show Bettye gave at
Drew University. Sam
stood through the en-
tire cocktail reception.
"He never sat down,"
she remembered. "I
asked him if he didn't
want to sit down and

*Sam Jaffe in "his" chair
in his nineties, still
full of light and en-
thusiasm for life.*

he said 'If I sit down, I'll never get up.' That's when he started looking fragile and frail."

As the months dwindled by and Sam entered his final winter, his inner spirit became increasingly visible as his fragile body sat all bundled up in his favorite chair. There was almost a glow about his head. His eyes remained wide with the wonder of life and his look retained its childlike quality. His mind was as sharp as ever and he often felt anger that his body was failing him. He would lament, "There's just this mind in this ruined body."

Sam had great distaste for his infirmity. He was angry at not being able to function, so he found ways to continue to live usefully. When DeKoven would visit, he would tell her stories. She told him she was looking for a play to direct and he would dredge out obscure plays as suggestions. She would have to go to the library to find them and she wondered, how could he remember? He was 93 and dying and still he was DeKoven's "high priest." He sat in his special chair near the door and she sat at his feet.

Relative Peter Keane didn't sit at Sam's feet, but he vividly remembered the chair in which Sam spent much of his remaining time. Bettye had given Sam a special chair for Christmas. He loved it so much that he preferred it to his bed. He called it his heaven. He felt comfortable there. He slept there. He held court in his chair. With Peter he would talk about old times and family.

Peter remembered: "He was very upset about his illness which he felt stemmed in part from an incompetent Mexican doctor when he was working on a picture and had a prostate problem. Whatever the doctor did had made it worse and he never really got over that. He said he was incompetent and that he wrecked him."

On one of Peter's last visits, Sam told him that if it weren't for Bettye being around and Bettye being ill, he would find a pill and just get rid of himself because of the burden that he was putting on Bettye. He asked Peter not to talk about Bettye's illness or to recognize it. Peter said: "Even if he hadn't mentioned that, I wouldn't have recognized it in Bettye's behavior because she carried herself so completely free of the fret and worry that one normally has."

It was degrading to be old and to have to live as Jaffe was living, and he allowed himself to be discouraged. However, when he began talking with others and engaging his mind, he would perk up.

During these occasions, Bettye would sit beside him, always leaning toward him. It was as if she was giving him her energy, holding him there with her life force. He would say something and she would leap right in with another statement that would move him on to yet another thought. Pure love pulled her forward and motivated her.

Sam's closest friend Aube Tzerko spoke of the ambivalence in Sam at the end of his life: "When he became very seriously ill he was very sensitive about the fact that the problems Bettye had were compounded. She had to take care of all details and she had to leave the house. This would annoy him no end. He would be really mad, angry that she had left him for so long. She was dealing with the necessities of their life, but he just couldn't bear the thought that she wasn't there."

Sam felt security with Bettye. When she wasn't beside him, he would yield to his pain and illness. He would say things like: "I don't know what I am. I'm lost." Bettye was his connection to consciousness. He couldn't sustain that connection when she was not with him. In her absence he would wonder: "Do you want to kill me?"

Sam loved Bettye's mentally handicapped brother Ricky. They had a special connection, communicating heart to heart. Ricky would always throw his arms around him and say, "That's my Sam." Ricky died during Sam's rapid decline and Sam couldn't bear it when Bettye left him to go to the funeral. He couldn't understand how far away she was and why she wasn't at home with him. It was evidence of how very ill he was.

Sam's tremendous dependence on Bettye had another side to it. It was a healing of his former inability to receive from others. He allowed himself to need Bettye, to know how much he needed her, and to say so. It was a way he expressed his affection.

He sometimes expressed his needs with ill-temper and crankiness. When he was impatient and angry, it was not with Bettye. Rather, it was with what was happening to him.

Sam and Bettye Jaffe toward the end of his life.

Jaffe balanced his demands on Bettye by complimenting her on everything she did. She would make a flower arrangement and Sam would tell everyone how beautiful it was. He couldn't wait to show off her newest painting. Even when he couldn't walk, he insisted that friends go out to the studio to look at it. He was very proud of her painting and acting work and wanted her to pursue her life fully, but he needed care and she was the only one he would allow to fill that role.

Evie Scott described Bettye as selfless and good. "You see it shining out in her face," she marveled. "There's nothing in her face that isn't beautiful. She is the best person I know. She never thinks of herself." Scott reported that rather than be suspicious of anyone, Bettye went overboard in the other direction. "Whereas some people open their door to anyone," she said shaking her head, "Bettye takes it off the hinges."

Bettye Jaffe had a good, sweet nature, but she never lacked strength. She had always been able to hold her own in conversations and gave herself equal time with Sam. She was quick to attack injustice and, like Sam, she would be angrier about an injustice to a friend than to herself.

The goodness that Evie describes as shining out of Bettye's face was there for everyone, not just for Sam. Diane and I experienced it whenever we spent time with her. She was a being of goodness; she was radiant. It wasn't something she put on; rather, it emanated from her core. I count my blessings that Bettye was my friend.

In her supreme effort of caring for Sam, Bettye was drawing on a greater power. While she was able to sustain her outpouring, her body experienced a toll of its own. She was diagnosed with ovarian cancer. Although the disease is most often fatal, Bettye rose above it, announcing to her friends that she was fine. She stated without question that she was not going to die because she refused to leave Sam all alone. Bettye repeated her resolve every time she spoke with someone.

By this time, Sam Jaffe was not only quite old, but not far from his own death. To have his beloved Bettye deal with a women's reproductive cancer similar to the one that took the life of his first wife Lillian was probably more than he could bear. It would have sent Sam careening into an endless tunnel of pain had he allowed it to enter his consciousness. It would appear Sam was in denial. Meanwhile, Bettye's doctor sent her off to radiation.

An uncanny reversal had occurred. In the first instance, Lillian had protected Sam from knowledge of her fatal cancer by forbidding her doctors from telling Sam. In the second instance, Jaffe protected himself from awareness of Bettye's similar illness by refusing to allow it into his consciousness. Evie Scott believed that Sam didn't have what was needed to be supportive of Bettye. She felt that because he wasn't capable of it, he pretended the cancer didn't exist rather than admit that he couldn't cope.

Although Bettye could understand Sam's denial, she was taken aback when Sam's nephew Peter Keane said angrily, forgetting his promise to Sam not to mention Bettye's illness, "How could you do that to Sam?" It was an especially ironic comment because Bettye had said of her own cancer, "I won't do this to Sam." She remembered the moment the thought came. It was etched in her mind.

After Bettye's surgical removal of her ovaries, she was deathly ill, but she was still taking care of Sam. She never would think of herself at all. She would forget her appointment with the radiologist because she had to take Sam somewhere.

Bettye remembered that she went on sleeping with Sam and taking care of him, but that she was deteriorating. "Radiation is like dropping a small atomic bomb on someone," she said. "I just got sicker and sicker. Then I got chicken pox. The doctors didn't think I would survive the cancer, but I knew I would and didn't accept it when they told me I had microscopic cancers all over, in addition to the ovarian cancer. I remember, just slightly, a flash of light."

Bettye went on. "After the radiation treatment the doctor asked me if I realized what I had been through. I said, 'Yes, but I hardly ever think about it.' I made my mind up that it was not acceptable to me. I had scars from the radiation, but Sam never said a word about it, never asked me about it or what it was. I kept it covered as much as I could."

The cancer continued to drain Bettye until Evie Scott insisted that things had to change. She demanded that Bettye hire nurses and that Bettye sleep out in her studio so that she could get rest. Sam was furious and he rejected the first nurse brought to care for him.

As for Bettye, she willed herself to live and became a medical miracle, enjoying a complete recovery. Years later, a researcher from the hospital called to find out when Mrs. Jaffe had died, certain she could not have lived more than five years. She was very surprised to find a very alive Mrs. Jaffe on the other end of the line.

Toward the end, Sam had pneumonia and congestive heart failure. He would be in and out of the hospital. Sometimes he and Bettye would be home only one night and then back again, or even the same night. On one occasion, Sam awoke from his pain and asked Bettye: "Have I been in an automobile accident? I'm all broken up."

The cancer was extensive in Sam's extremities. While he had pain, he didn't complain. He got up every day, until the last day, and went for a walk.

He had been known throughout Beverly Hills for his strolls. If he missed a day, the police would stop and ask Bettye, "Where's Sam? Is he all right? We didn't see him walking today."

In his later days, when he grew weaker and had less command of his body, he was ashamed to be seen in the neighborhood. Sam and Bettye tried a nearby park, but the moment they stepped out of the car, admiring people gathered around him.

There was something natural about the way death came to call on Sam. Little by little his resistance wore down until he was ready to give up his last breath.

****

STEVE FRANKEN, *Comedy of Errors*, 1958

"I was thrilled when I was cast. At the closing night, I became affiliated with Terry Hayden. I think of her as my true mentor. She came backstage and said, 'You were so wonderful.' I felt so insignificant that I turned around to see if she was talking to the person behind me. She said, 'No. You were wonderful.'

"She was working for Herman Shumlin and she got me a job in Inherit the Wind *as a $2.00 a night supernumerary* with Paul Muni. Watching him every night was an education. Eventually I got a one-line real part in the National Company with Melvin Douglas. When I got the part, it was a Saturday morning, I ran out the door and ran up the alley to 41st Street, then over to Broadway and didn't stop running until I got to the 60's. I was so excited. I had a wonderful formative year touring the country. I understudied five parts and played one. Subsequently I became the second assistant stage manager. That led to Say Darling and to Dobie Gillis *on TV in Los Angeles.*

"I also did Comedy of Errors *for E.L.T. in 1958. I owe my* whole career to the opportunity that Sam Jaffe gave me to appear in E.L.T."

****

ELLA GERBER, directed *Dark of the Moon*, 1949.

"It was unusual to run into the kind of quality and sensitivity Sam had.

"E.L.T. was of tremendous value. It provided me with an avenue to get in as a director. Sam was helpful in every way to everyone. And he was such a brilliant actor. His presence was felt everywhere that he went. He exuded caring. He reached out to everyone. Sam Jaffe needs to be lauded to the skies. He was a rare human being and exemplary of where the human race can move and especially people in the theater."

****

Exit in the Light

During his last decade, Sam lost his beloved friend, Zero Mostel. Zero was only 62 and his death was such a tremendous blow to Sam that he wasn't able to go to the funeral. He simply couldn't deal with it. Jaffe's friends knew that he was suffering profoundly, but not because he expressed that suffering publicly. His friend Karl Malden reported, "He would never give out his inner feelings. Cry and you cry alone. Laugh and the world laughs with you. That was Sam. When you came, it was, 'How about a little tea? How about a little social?' And that was it."

By the winter of 1983, Beth Cagan arrived as the first nurse to work with Sam in the home. She was there for almost a year. She took the night shift from 11 p.m. to 7 a.m. It wasn't until much later that the day shifts began.

When Beth came for her first interview, Bettye introduced her to Sam who sat ensconced in his favorite chair. Beth noted that he was pleasant, cordial and smiling. She thought, "This is going to be very nice." They chatted for a while. Bettye showed Beth around. Soon it was time for Sam to go to bed. Bettye told Sam that she was going to use the studio so his constant waking wouldn't bother her. She needed to get her sleep. She told Sam that Beth would be with him and that she would call her if he wanted her.

Serenity hit the fan when Sam realized that Beth was to be his nurse. He had thought that Bettye was going to have a nurse for herself. He knew that her months of taking care of him had exhausted her. His mood changed quickly and his stubbornness took center stage. Very insulted, he denied needing a nurse. Sam went to bed and Bettye went out to the studio, leaving Beth to handle the awkward scene. Sam didn't talk to Beth that night. He ignored her though she saw to his needs. He wanted Bettye; that was all there was to it.

When Bettye had spent the nights with Sam, he was up and down all night. That first night with Beth, he didn't get up very much because he didn't want to have anything to do with her. Surprisingly, he slept quite well.

Beth told Bettye about it in the morning and Bettye knew it was because Sam was angry. He was angry for several days. Then the situation eased. Even though he still didn't think he needed nurses, Sam accepted it after a while. After five days, he got used to Beth's being there at night and he accepted a drink of water from her. However, Jaffe remained in charge of his life and his house.

In the early morning, Bettye would come in at about 6:00 a.m. to crawl into bed with Sam, and Beth would retreat to the kitchen. That morning time was their special time alone together.

Bettye wanted to make sure that Sam didn't feel that she had deserted him. She recalled, "I whispered to him, 'Would you move over, I want to get in bed with you.' He would always say, 'Wonderful.' We managed very well in that hospital bed.

Bettye remembered: "He got up every morning and we took a walk to exercise his legs. We walked around the pool and then he rested on the chaise lounge almost every day of those last eight months. Our azaleas were never so luxuriantly beautiful. Sam commented on their beauty almost every day. He always kept telling me how much he loved our home, which made me happy. He would say with joy, 'I'm home.' The rabbi said that in the Talmud home and wife have the same connotation and that he was talking about me, really."

Bettye went on: "During that period, the birds built a nest. You could have reached out and touched the nest. They were not disturbed at all by his being there. We watched the whole process as they brought the sticks from larger to smaller to finer to down. They were never afraid of Sam."

In the evening, before going to sleep, Sam would sit at the bar area in the kitchen and he would have a little snack. Once he warmed to Beth, they would have discussions during his repast. "He was so brilliant," she said. "He knew about everything. He would go into detail about things. Even Bettye would say, 'I didn't know you knew about that.' He was like a walking encyclopedia," Beth related.

When Sam was restless, he would go to his favorite chair in the living room and read. He continued to read avidly until the very end of his life. He never failed to read the first page of the newspaper. He often fell asleep in his chair and Beth would cover him.

Sam was very polite to Beth, and very considerate. Although he would become gruff at times, Beth's interpretation was that he was mad at himself, and angry because Bettye was sick.

Once Sam got used to having help around, his humor returned. He had a cane to help him with his walking. One day, his nurse fell against him and hit him with the cane. She said, "I'm so sorry, Mr. Jaffe, I didn't mean to hit you with the cane." Sam inquired, "What did you want to hit me with?"

After a time, as Sam required more care, two other nurses joined to round out the shifts. The day nurse, Suzie Jamgotchan, came on around 6:45 a.m., and she was followed by Joyce Knudson. There had been another day nurse whom Sam didn't like at all because she was more domineering. Suzie replaced the irritating nurse. Sam greeted Suzie as he had greeted Beth. He raised his voice and opened his eyes wide, looking to Bettye and shaking his finger. He furiously insisted that he didn't want anybody to come to work for him. Suzie was shocked: "This was my first experience of someone telling me right to my face that he didn't need me or want my help. And that was even though he already had a nurse working for him.

"The shock I was in must have reflected on my face. He looked at me and this time, in a lower voice he said, 'I don't have anything against you. You may be the kindest person or an excellent nurse, but I don't need you. I don't need anybody. This I keep saying to my wife and she won't understand.'"

By now Suzie understood that she was facing an un-ordinary man of very strong character, who had complete control of himself and didn't care what people thought about him.

Suzie went to work the next day, but it was only at the very end of her stay that he acknowledged that he needed help. Before that, he never asked for anything. He always wanted to get up and help himself.

Another quality of Jaffe's that remained to the end was that he spoke his mind. It didn't matter if he was in the presence of a friend or a dignitary. What he thought, he said. It surprised his nurses. They were also taken aback by his temper that he exposed freely.

While Sam was still able to travel, he and Bettye had gone to Texas for a documentary narration he was to do. As they descended the hotel stairs, they met up with a crowd. Bettye tried to walk next to Sam and to hold his hand. In front of everyone, he lost his temper, exclaiming, "Leave me alone. Don't hold me up, I'm capable." He was very independent. On these occasions when he expressed irritation with Bettye, it is easy to see that his diminishing abilities caused his great upset.

Sometimes he refused his medication. When he refused, no one could make him take it. During his last days he enjoyed back rubs, saying, "It makes it a little less painful, helps me bear the pain." However, he never complained.

Jaffe had his greatest surge of energy in the early morning. This could well have been the result of the infusion of life force from Bettye. He would walk, exercise, and have a bath. Around noon he started getting tired. He would enjoy soaking his feet in warm water.

During the last few months, several trips were made to U.C.L.A. and Cedar Sinai hospitals. He never wanted to go to the hospital. Bettye told him he had to go because they needed the help. He would improve slightly after each visit until the last time.

Bettye's brother Robert saw Sam at the hospital about a month before his death. He and his wife May understood that Sam would not live. "Bettye and May went for a walk and I stayed with him for a while," Robert remembered. "When he was awake, he was awake. There was no senility. The intellectual side of his vigor remained. His last comment to me was, 'Thank you, Robert, for minimizing the banalities of this occasion.'"

The nurses were unanimous in their assessment of Jaffe as a very special, intelligent, likable person. They also observed that Sam didn't want Bettye to go out of his sight. He wanted her to be there all the time and she was there almost all the time. They had to force her to go out once in a while, so great was her devotion.

Bettye became great friends with the nurses and maintained her relationship with them after Sam's passing. She told them they would all be friends until the end of their lives.

Knowing that the end of Jaffe's life was approaching, Bill Ross flew out to see Sam the day after his 93rd birthday. It was two weeks before Sam's death. He came bearing three helium-filled balloons that gave Sam a big kick. Ross noted that Sam was very tan. Bettye had him out around the pool every morning. Ross told Jaffe he looked like Joe College with a sunburn. Jaffe responded immediately with a joke. "Did I ever tell you the story of the actor who went away to summer stock and he came back at the end of the summer as brown as a mahogany board. His friends remarked about his wonderful tan and wondered how he managed to get it. The actor replied that he had a lousy agent!"

Ross returned to New York with the feeling that he would never see Sam again.

Even during his last days, Sam always wanted to do something to help people. If anyone questioned Sam, he would rush to give them the answer. At 93, he was ill but remained very alert. Until the day before his death, Sam went to the bathroom on his own. Even at the end, he insisted on being put on a chair and pulled to the toilet. Until the last minute of his life, he always wanted to get up.

During Jaffe's last days, Norman Lloyd went to see him every day. He and Karl Malden sat with Sam and lifted his spirits a little in the hour they spent. Malden observed, "Sam was a smart man and I have a feeling he knew he was dying. It's a terrible thing to say, but I think he was just waiting out the time. His heart wouldn't give out and that was it."

It was a poignant observation of the suffering of his friend. Would that Sam Jaffe could have made use of the wisdom of advanced Native Americans who know how to release the soul from the body and just go on. Instead, he waited out the time.

Toward the end, Jaffe was in increasing pain. At first, he wouldn't say so. Before the nurses began giving him injections for pain, he had suffered more than anybody knew because he didn't express it. He had such a powerful will that he gave the appearance of being stronger than he probably was. He seemed to be fighting to live, to live for Bettye. He worried about her. He lived for her and she lived for him. As each protected the other from losing, each was bound in a no-win situation.

Sam would continue to get up and walk and do things. It wasn't until the very end that he was bedridden and the recipient of shots of morphine prescribed by his doctor.

During the last week Sam couldn't eat. Bettye tried to get him to eat. However, Sam would say, "If I wanted to eat I would eat. You don't have to tell me." His friends were still coming and he never failed to be happy to see them. George DeGroat drove down to say good-bye to him the week before he died. "It was obvious that he was very worn out and ready to go," he said. "He expressed no fear or morbidity."

Jaffe showed little interest in things such as heaven. He saw everything as being "down here, in this world."

During the last three days, Jaffe was extremely weak. Norman Lloyd remembered Sam's great pain in his last days and how he objected to the indignity of it all: "He couldn't walk well in the last year or so. He had to stay on the chaise lounge in the living room. Food had to be brought to him. It was almost like being a baby again and that wasn't Sam."

Lloyd affirmed that Sam was a proud man. His physical disintegration deeply affected him. This was an integral part of his illness.

Lloyd carried the oriflamme of his dear friend's pride: "It's unfair to fasten on the last years of man's life when a man is not himself, when a man is dying. It was difficult for Sam to lie there all those hours and not be able to walk. They would want him to eat more and he didn't want to. These were all things the illness produced that had nothing to do with Sam."

Norman Lloyd, a man of eloquence and discrimination, distinguished Sam as among the most uncorrupted persons he ever knew. Lloyd and actor Martin Blaine were with Sam on the Thursday before he died.

"He was in pain," Lloyd recalled. "But I must say he carried it off. He saw us; we talked. We stayed about an hour at most. He was in pain and yet he was trying to carry on a conversation. Morphine apparently had no effect on the pain. He insisted that Carmen bring some cake and coffee. She set up a little table. He was always feeding me. As soon as you come in, 'Have a cup of coffee. Carmen bring him. . . . Oh, somebody brought me some cheese cake. You gotta try this cheesecake.' Always."

Lloyd felt fortunate to have known Sam Jaffe: "I've been very lucky in some friends and Sam was one of the pieces of luck. You could sit down with Sam and you could talk about things in the world. Most people are idiots."

Sam's last days were a nightmare. The doctors didn't want to prescribe morphine because of the community uproar around over-medication. Ironically, Sam had had his own previous bout with over-medication and it was Bettye who had fought for and won a reduction in the dosage.

Jaffe's pain was excruciating. Occasionally he would say, "I can't stand it." He was very restless.

The nurses would hold his hand. It was their great pleasure. In a sweet little plaintive voice he would whisper that nobody's arms were around him. It startled everyone. They didn't know he wanted touching that much.

He wanted somebody to be rubbing him or some human touch to comfort him because he knew he was dying. This was especially true on the last day, the Friday. Everyone knew that the end was not far.

On Thursday morning, two days before he died,

Sam let Bettye know that having her in bed with him hurt him. The cancer had spread extensively into the extremities. When Joyce and Bettye were trying to take care of him, he was in so much pain that they had to adjust the bed to take the weight off his arms and legs to give him some relief. They propped up his head and knees so that he was practically in a sitting position. Bettye was very concerned and was trying to feed him something. "We were each on one side of him," she reported. "He said, in very strong, oracular tones, very strong, turning to both of us, 'Don't think about me. Think about you!' That was not long before he died." He wanted Bettye to concentrate on herself; he wanted them to stop focusing on him. "Both of his fingers were pointing out to each of us," Bettye related. "We were stunned with the amount of energy he was putting out. He was definitely telling us that he was going."

Bettye went on: "He whispered to Suzie, 'Bettye and I are twins you know.' Suzie said she didn't know that. Sam whispered to her, 'Shhhh, neither does she.' To him that meant that we were bound, that we were truly one. It was the last time I got in the bed with him, in that tiny little hospital bed. That morning I realized I had hurt him. So I knew that it was the end."

By Thursday evening, the pain had become unbearable. Bettye kept trying to reach Dr. Corday to get morphine. He told her he couldn't get it, that she should call Dr. Bierman because that was his department. Bettye couldn't reach him because he was speaking somewhere. She kept begging for him to call her. Until that last night, Sam had remained alert. By now, his hearing had grown very acute. Suzie Jamgotchan recalled how everyone had to whisper because "if you talked in a normal voice it hurt his ears. In his case it was more pronounced than in most patients. This happens with terminal patients. They become more sensitive to touch, hearing." Sam began thrashing about in his bed as his condition worsened. It was a dreadful night for Bettye — an unmitigated night-mare. She was so desperate to get drugs for Sam that she was ready to buy them on the street.

They were saved by Ricardo Sanchez who came in from Port's Head, about an hour's drive, bringing some Demerol prescribed for Francesca's mother who had died of cancer five months before. That brought Sam relief and he had begun to dose off when Dr. Bierman called a little after 11:00 p.m., six hours after the acute pain began. Bettye arranged to go by his office early the next morning to get a prescription for morphine.

Friday, the day before Jaffe's death, Francesca went to be beside Bettye. Sam was in terrible pain and was moaning almost constantly.

Aube Tzerko, one of Sam's closest friends, had been with Sam almost every day for weeks, on his way to school or on the way back. He recalled, "I spent many hours into the night just prior to his demise." As Aube continued, he could barely speak. He was choked with tears and despair:

"The only time — that's probably one of the most touching moments in my life," his voice quivered and broke — "the only time he ever asked for anything, he was in terrible agony. The last couple of weeks, particularly the last few days of his life, and one time about one o'clock in the morning, he cried out, 'Aube, you're my dearest friend and even you can't help me.' It was dreadful ..." Aube broke into sobs.

Tzerko's wife, Saida, interrupted with her own pain: "Why they ever allowed him to suffer like that, I will never figure out. Why didn't they have enough stuff to just kill that pain? It was an experience I won't ever forget. It was an impossible situation."

Aube continued weeping quietly as Saida contin-ued: "I can never forgive whoever was in charge for not providing for that man." Recovering somewhat, Aube tried to quiet Saida. He elaborated on what she sought to communicate. "Sam was begging Bettye, 'Can't you please put an end to this? It's just beyond my capacity to bear.' She was always comforting him, not allowing him to think that he was actually dying."

Sam surely knew he was dying. It was a frantic time. Saida was furious with the doctor because he never gave Sam what he really needed. Saida's real fury might better have been laid on merciless death and its relentless agent, pain.

Perhaps no drug could have relieved Sam in those last few days. His pain was beyond human capacity to alleviate.

Death has been called an act of finality. This is a questionable definition when one sees how alive the process of death is in the memories of surviving loved ones. To touch the pain in Aube and Saida Tzerko was to touch the pain of death as it had visited Sam Jaffe.

That last day, Friday, when Suzie was giving the report to the doctor, Sam said, "Are you not finished yet? A dying man needs you."

All day Friday Bettye sat and held Sam's hand. She and Joyce sat on either side of him giving him Demerol from a syringe with the needle removed. This was along with the morphine. The cancer was everywhere and causing Sam agony.

Carmen, their trusted and beloved housekeeper, suffered Sam's pain along with him: "In the last few days the pain was terrible. He would moan, and I would pray to my God to take him. I felt terrible when he would yell about the pain. I felt very painful when he was yelling about his pain."

The last night, the nurses, based on long experience, knew that Sam would go before daybreak. His pulse and blood pressure were very low and his color had changed. Bettye was sleeping out in the studio and

Joyce informed her that she might have to get up early and that Beth would wake her when the end came.

Sam was on oxygen and had the labored breathing of the dying when the throat tightens and the noise of trapped fluid is heard. His pain medication continued every four hours. He remained alert and was very weak.

During his last hours, Sam found it more difficult to communicate his wishes. He kept trying to ask for something, but each time the nurse put it into words, it was not what he was signaling. It was at that point that they called Bettye. They barely had to touch her and she was up on her feet and on her way to Sam. Once she was at his bedside, Sam went very quickly. It was as if he had been hanging on until Bettye came.

It is often true that patients die toward the early morning, after they are sponged, cleaned, and given energy by their loved ones. Bettye touched Sam and gave him the energy to go.

The main water line burst the night Sam was dying. The place was a mess. It was one of those symbolic touches of the life fluids leaving Sam Jaffe's home and physical body.

Bettye reported that when Beth had come to get her, they entered the room from a different point of view. She said, "I had never experienced a death before. We walked into the dining room and looked up into the hospital bed and there was a light around his entire body which was about an inch wide. It was very bright, not glaring but very strong; an off-white with other colors in it. It was so definite. It was so there. It went right around the whole body. We just stood there. Sam was already in the death rattle so he couldn't talk. I just stood and talked to him while she did what there was for her to do. He couldn't give me any communication. It was the death struggle.

"Then he was gone. I'm amazed that I just turned and walked away. I didn't want to see him. I went from there into the living room just to get away. Beth followed me and she said, 'Bettye, I've never known people like you and Sam.'

"That same day I called Beth at her house and I said, 'Beth, I have to know if I saw what I saw.' She said, 'I have to have you tell me that you saw what you saw, so I'll know that I saw what I saw.'"

Bettye asked if she had ever seen the light before. The nurse replied, "Not all over." It seemed to Bettye that the bed was slightly elevated. The light illumined the whole room. The only actual light was small and turned against the wall. The whole room had the glow Bettye was witnessing. She said that if she had stayed in the room, she wouldn't have had that perspective and might not have seen it.

Once there were no vital signs, the nurses removed the oxygen and summoned the doctor. Bettye's friends, the Maldens, Francesca, and Evie came immediately and stayed with her while Sam's body was removed. Bettye was weeping and in shock.

A quiet settled over everyone. There was no high emotion. The house remained quiet for a long time after Sam's death.

Karl's repeated sense was, "Thank God." He had seen Sam about two days before he died, and he described him as already gone: "When he couldn't get up to go to the bathroom anymore, everything fell apart." It was a period of humiliating occurrences and it was time for change. Mona and Karl were happy for Bettye, and for Sam. It was time, truly time.

Sam died on the Sabbath. For a Jew this represents a special blessing, a holy passing.

Sam's death had been a terrible struggle, a severance through a process of great pain. The survivors spent the day planning his funeral and arranging for the cremation Sam had requested. Bettye was at the forefront of making the arrangements. Francesca, Edward G. Robinson's granddaughter, stayed with Bettye for next few nights.

Following Sam's death two radio stations in Los Angeles gave Sam the top of the 20 minutes for 48-hours. They told vignettes about him.

On the day of the memorial service, Bettye had gotten up at about 5:00 a.m. and felt that she was not going to be able to get through the day. She lay down again. She didn't go to sleep. "I was just lying on my right side," she said, "and suddenly Sam appeared and I got a good three-quarter view of him looking past me and upward. He had the most beautiful healthy color. He had a little smile. I thought, 'I'm going to open my eyes. I've got to see what this is, if I'm asleep.' I opened my eyes and there was nothing there. I closed my eyes and he came again. I said, 'OK darling, I got the message.'"

Francesca said that when she slept over at the Jaffe house immediately following Sam's death, she noted that though it wasn't raining or windy, she definitely felt a presence in the house, and felt that it was Sam. She felt that Sam had touched her and said "Everything's going to be all right." She was perfectly awake. "I wasn't dreaming," she insisted. "I waited for a while to tell Bettye because I didn't want her to think me 'off.' Sam was in the house!" [Not long after, Bettye was in New York City with her friend, Barbara Barlow. They were on a bus and a voice said, 'Hi.' They both heard it and looked around. No one was there. Bettye knew it was Sam's voice. It was as if he was saying, "Have fun." Coincidentally, Barbara had been there when Sam and Bettye had first met.]

Sam Jaffe played to standing room only at his funeral. Karl Malden was dumbfounded by the overflow of people: "This town is what I call 'here today, gone tomorrow.' It's fast turnover. The memorial service was packed. People stood outside. I didn't expect that. I've been to these things where you would be lucky if you would see 50 people. And you must remember, Sam was no big star. Sam was Zorba in a TV show. No one remembers him from *Gunga Din*. That was way back. I honestly felt that we were going to be there and it was going to be family and friends and that would amount to about 75 people. But when I saw that group who couldn't get in, I think there were at least 100 people outside who couldn't get in, I said, 'You see, it pays to be a human being like he was.' He had a kind word for everybody, I don't care who it was."

The turnout did not surprise Bill Ross. Anyone who had ever walked down any street with Sam would understand. People came up and would ask his advice about acting or anything, and Sam would stand there for 20 minutes and talk to this person. In those 20 minutes they would become friends. It was an extraordinary quality.

A year before his death, Jaffe was asked how he would like to be remembered. He threw his head back and laughed off the question with the reply: "When you're gone, you're gone. If what you've done is worthwhile, you will be remembered."

Sam Jaffe's ashes were scattered at sea off Urban Hirsch's sailboat. Karl, Bettye, Urban, Aube and Carmen went. They sailed out a few miles from shore. Karl took charge: "The time came to scatter the ashes. They were in a little container. Urban couldn't open the container. I looked at it. I asked for a screwdriver. Bettye was standing there. I tried prying it. I said, 'Just a minute.' I put it down and punched it with the screwdriver. It popped. I said, 'Here, Bettye.' She didn't want to do it. I leaned over the boat as far as I could, and scattered the ashes. And the wind changed and some of the ashes got up on the sleeve of my blue windbreaker. I rubbed but the ashes are still there. I can't get it out. I washed it. But they are still there." Karl's wife Mona believes that Karl doesn't really want them to come out.

Following Sam Jaffe's death a plethora of sympathy letters was sent to Bettye. Included among them were these:

From Monty Hall, March 29, 1984: "A legend has left us, but what beautiful memories remain. You were so lucky to have Sam for so many years, and I am sure that this Renaissance man brought so much to your life. He was lucky to have you. You brought him so much happiness. Together you gave Hollywood a certain beauty. While part of it is now gone, I am sure you will continue to grace the profession and the city, with Love, Monty."

From Ray Bradbury on March 29, 1984: "Dearest Bettye: One of the greatest nights in my life was the night I was able to sit in the same audience with you and Sam when they re-premiered *Lost Horizon*, and we were able to watch the High Lama inspire us to tears all over again, just as it was in the year, just out of high school, when I first saw the film, and thought that Sam Jaffe was one of the most beautiful men I had ever seen perform on the screen. What a fire there was in his eyes. This week, that fire still burns in my heart. I shall never forget him. God bless you, Bettye, Yours, Ray."

From Richard Widmark on March 26, 1984: "Dear Bettye, We are so sorry. Sam was such a rare man. Love, Jean and Dick"

From Max Warner on June 27, 1984: "... Sam's humor, the twinkle in his eyes, his fun with mathematics, all made the *Casey* experience a moving one. Of all the happenings there, the final take of the long *Ben Casey* 'you know everything about medicine and nothing about living' speech late one night during the shooting of the pilot, after which the entire cast and crew gave Sam a standing ovation, still gives me goose bumps. THAT was a professional performance equal to anything I've seen in the operating room or anywhere else!"

From Robert Wise on April 3, 1984: "... We were very, very saddened by the news. He was such a very unique and special and talented person in so many ways that those of us who knew him and had worked with him will have such strong and lasting and warm memories of Sam Jaffe. He was unforgettable. Millicent joins me in sending our most heartfelt condolences and much love, Bob."

From Michael Feinstein on April 26, 1984: "... my memory is still vivid with the remembrance of your visit to Ira Gershwin's home when Emily was in town and Sam told the most wonderful anecdotes about George and Ira and ... very funny stories and jokes ... I hope that by this time you have begun, perhaps, to find a little more comfortable place in your heart for your loss. All best always ..."

From Ambassador John Gavin on April 4, 1984: "Dear Bettye, My sympathy and condolences on Sam's death. What a remarkable man and what a remarkable life. Affectionate regards, Jack."

From Ezra Stone on March 24, 1984: "Dearest Bettye, In those dark days after Lillian's death, you brought new light and life to our beloved Sam. You not only married him, but all of his friends too. You shared your love with all of us. You kept him productive, alert and alive for the world and for all of us to enjoy.

"You and Sam were the ... example of true husband and wife bliss. I never say, 'my darling' to Sara without hearing the echo of your sweet soft voice. Sam was a saint on earth — and so are you, Forever, Ezra."

From Martin Manulus on April 3, 1984: "... It is always a sadness, but what a long and wonderful life he had, and how happy-making that you were able to share so much of it together. I'll always remember how his face would light up, looking at you across a room. Love is the greatest of blessings, Martin."

From Stella Adler on March 24, 1984: "Dearest Beloved Bettye: If I could give you my heart to help you I would. The nobility of your lives will remain a symbol for us all, Stella."

From Paul Hardin, President, Drew University on March 24, 1984: "Dearest Bettye: Sam was indeed, 'fantastic.' And there are myriad other suitable superlatives. What I liked especially was the unique mix of mischief and majesty, the boyish persona who inhabited that ancient body, with the matchless head and hands. And we think of you at this moment too. You are such a magnificent person in your own right, but strong enough to put his interests and well-being ahead of your own — time and time again."

From Frances Laurence, March 31, 1984: "... I knew about the both of you that you were kind, fair, honest, manly, womanly, and seldom if ever cruel or unconsidered in your expressions to people. I also know neither of you were, or are, saints. But because Sam looked like one, I suppose I found it confusing that he dealt so well with today's world. It has always taken me a moment to adjust to the innate virtue you both gave off in a positive emanation. It is what has fascinated me, this goodness that has no goody-goodyness to it, this quality without preachment, without affectation. How do they do that? I would ask myself each time we had the pleasure of your company. I have an answer now, right or wrong. I think it is because neither of you were 'self-conscious' in the way most of us are who aren't sure of our core and protect our small egos constantly from possible hurt. How did you manage it? I think it comes from having much good intent sans ulterior motive and great striving to understand and excel, unadulterated by smaller considerations. By golly, I want to be like that before I depart this world, if I can. ... It's an amazingly wonderful gift, to make people feel better about themselves."

From Harry Rasky, March 26, 1984: "... The image of Sam is the image of Jerusalem which is the image of eternity. There is a moment in the film [*Next Year In Jerusalem*] which I look for each time I have seen it over the years, when Sam is in the middle of the wilderness between Jericho and Jerusalem, being Abraham, the camera pans up to the sky and the colors dissolve to blue and gold and then through again to the Chagall windows, and I have always thought that Sam had been there always, will be there always; so naturally full of the joys and juices of our people forever and ever ... the spirit of timelessness. Sam is all these things.

"I have been lucky to know some of the great people of our century. Each of them has become a part of my work and my life. Perhaps there has been a handful that are with me daily. Sam is one of these. For our family, he was brother, and father and grandfather. ... If it is true as Chagall said that God is Love, then Sam is part of God. Even though it's said that no man can see the face of God, I agree with Whitman who said, 'In the faces of men and women I see God.' I always felt that with Sam. The humor and his life force even now bring joy and comfort."

Not long before his death, Jaffe was asked what he would do if he could live his life all over again. He responded with his customary humor: "If I had my life to live over ... what would be fresh about it? Once you do it, it's done."

At a tribute for Sam in New York, Bettye worried about whether she would get through it. Looking absolutely beautiful, Bettye accepted the award with utter grace. Everyone held their breath because it was highly emotional for her. Everything she said was perfect. Then Karl Malden got up and told a story about Sam. As he began to speak, Jimmy Rety leaned over and asked Francesca Sanchez, "Didn't he tell that story at the funeral?" They began laughing, an appropriate expression in honor of Sam Jaffe.

Here is Karl Malden's story:

"When I first went to New York, I had a couple of very good years. I thought: how easy this is, being an actor in New York, the big time!

"Then suddenly the bottom fell out. I could not get a job. I couldn't get past the secretary in the outer office. They didn't know me.

"On this particular day, I was making the rounds, looking for work, knocking on doors, trying to get in. I saw Sam coming toward me, right in front of Radio City Music Hall. I had done a play the year before with Sam called *The Gentle People.*

"He asked me how I was. I said, 'Not too well. The two years working here doesn't mean a thing. No one knows me.' We kept talking for a short while when suddenly he took me by the hand and we walked to the next block. We went up a flight of stairs, right past the secretary in the outer office. He opened the door to the office and there I was facing Eva Le Gallienne, Joseph Schildkraut, Howard Bay [the scenic designer], and Lem Ward, the director. Without any introductions, Sam said, 'Here's the man who should play the druggist.'

"Lem Ward said, 'But Sam, he's too young' Sam came back with, 'Let him be the son of the druggist.'

"There was a long pause. Finally, Eva Le Gallienne said, 'Do you mind reading?' I said that I didn't, if I could look at it for a moment.

"They gave me a script. I stepped out to the outer office. In about five minutes Sam left saying, 'Don't worry about a thing.' I went in and read and they asked me to come back the next day to sign the contract. The play was *Uncle Harry* and it ran for over a year.

"What I didn't know for years was that Sam had just come from that office having refused to play the druggist. That's my Sam Jaffe story. You could multiply that by hundreds. Sam helped."

Bettye got through the proceedings beautifully. Then, as now, with Sam present or gone, one truth remained for her: she and Sam were twin souls.

A Note from the Author: How Blessed I Am to Have Known Them

It is said that there are only six degrees of separation between people, no matter who they are or where they are in the world. That is how having known Sam and Bettye feels to me. In my wildest dreams I could never have imagined that they would be my friends. Perhaps it was our mutual commitment to integrity, compassion, honor and justice that enabled us to bond.

Having known and loved the two of them, and been loved by them, I am richer in spirit and in heart. Walt Whitman saw God in the faces of men and women. It is a true statement. I think Sam and Bettye would agree with me that one doesn't have to be famous, successful, ultra good, saintly, or anything else for God to be there in your face. By virtue of the fact that we are, God is in our faces. We are of God; we are the manifestations of God. Some of us know that and allow that light to shine through so that others can see it. That's what Sam and Bettye did. I seek to emulate that every day. It is more than a tribute to the two of them; it is the way all of us should live.

I want to thank all those who gave me interviews for this book. Special gratitude goes to Bettye Ackerman, of course, her brother Robert Ackerman for his encouragement, and Diane Kennedy Pike for her help in editing and in preparation for publication.

— *Arleen Lorrance*

Awards:

Equity Paul Robeson Award
> 1978

C.C.N.Y. 125th Anniversary Medal, 1973

Primetime Emmy Awards, USA
> 1962 Nominated for Outstanding Performance in a Supporting Role by an Actor
> for:"Ben Casey" (1961) (ABC)

The Townsend Harris Medal
> **for distinguished post-graduate achievement,**
> December of 1962

Venice Film Festival
> 1950 Won Volpi Cup for Best Actor
> for: The Asphalt Jungle (1950).

Academy Awards, USA
> 1951 Nominated for Oscar for Best Actor in a Supporting Role
> for: The Asphalt Jungle (1950).

Box Office Blue Ribbon Award, 1939

Stage Credits:

A Meeting by the River, Mar. 28, 1979 - Mar. 28, 1979 Tarun
> Maharaj (Original Performer)

Mademoiselle Colombe, Jan. 6, 1954 - Feb. 27, 1954   Gourette
> (Original Performer)

This Time Tomorrow, Nov. 3, 1947 - Nov. 29, 1947 Wouterson
> (Original Performer)

Thank You, Svoboda, Mar. 1, 1944 - Mar. 4, 1944 Svoboda
> (Original Performer)

Cafe Crown, Jan. 23, 1942 - May 23, 1942 Hymie
> (Original Performer)

The Gentle People, Jan. 5, 1939 - May 6, 1939 Jonah Goodman
> (Original Performer)

A Doll's House, Dec. 27, 1937 - Apr. 30, 1938 Nils Krogstad
 (*Original Performer*)

The Eternal Road, Jan. 7, 1937 - May 15, 1937 The Adversary
 (*Original Performer*)

The Bride of Torozko, Sep. 13, 1934 - Sep. 22, 1934   Herschkowitz
 (*Original Performer*)

Grand Hotel, Nov. 13, 1930 - Dec. 5, 1931   Kringelein
 (*Original Performer*)

Poppa, Dec. 24, 1928 - Mar. 1, 1929   Pincus Schwitzky
 (*Original Performer*)

The Jazz Singer, Apr. 18, 1927 - May 1, 1927 Yudelson
 (*Original Performer*)

The Jazz Singer, Sep. 14, 1925 - Jun. 1, 1926 Yudelson
 (*Original Performer*)

Ruint, Apr. 7, 1925 - May 1, 1925 Lum Crowder
 (*Original Performer*)

Izzy, Sep. 16, 1924 - Nov. 1, 1924 Eli Iskovitch (*Original Performer*)

The Main Line, Mar. 25, 1924 - Apr. 1, 1924   Izzy Goldstein
 (*Original Performer*)

The God of Vengeance, Dec. 20, 1922 - Apr. 14, 1923 Reb Ali
 (*Original Performer*)

The Idle Inn, Dec. 20, 1921 - Jan. 7, 1922   Leibush
 (*Original Performer*)

Samson and Delilah, Nov. 17, 1920 - Mar. 1, 1921   Kristensen
 (*Original Performer*)

Film and Television Credits:

1984, Downstream, El Gabacho

1984, Nothing Lasts Forever, Father Knickerbocker

1981, Foul Play (TV Show), Barbary Bob Norwood

1980, Battle Beyond the Stars, Dr. Hephaestus

1979, Buck Rogers in the 25th Century (TV Show), Council Leader

1978, Flying High (TV Show), Dr. Alsdorf

1977, The Love Boat (TV Show), Professor Roscoe Weber

1976, The Bionic Woman (TV Show), Admiral Richter

1976, The Sad and Lonely Sundays (TV Movie), Dr. Sweeny

1975, S.W.A.T. (TV Show), Dr. Brunner

1975, Medical Story (TV Show), Dr. Gershowitz

1974, QB VII (TV Show), Dr. Tessler

1973, Harry O (TV Show), Dr. Howard Cambridge

1973, Kojak (TV Show), Papa

1973, Saga of Sonora (TV Movie), Old Sam

1972, Circle of Fear (TV Show), De Witt

1972, The Snoop Sisters (TV Show), Issac Waldersack

1972
The Streets of San Francisco (TV Show), Alex Zubatuk

1971, Bedknobs and Broomsticks, Bookman

1971, Alias Smith and Jones (TV Show), Soapy Saunders

1971, Owen Marshall: Counselor at Law (TV Show), Henry Noll

1971, The Tell-Tale Heart (Short Film), The Old Man

1971, Enemies (TV Movie)

1971, Sam Hill: Who Killed Mr. Foster? (TV Movie), Toby

1971, Columbo (TV Show), Dr. Henry Willis

1970, The Dunwich Horror, Old Whateley

1970, The Old Man Who Cried Wolf (TV Movie), Abe Stillman

1970, Nanny and the Professor (TV Show), Dr. Lazko

1970, Quarantined (TV Movie), Mr. Berryman

1969, The Great Bank Robbery, Brother Lilac Bailey

1969, Love, American Style (TV Show), Mr. Palvecko

1969, Rod Serling's Night Gallery (TV Show), Bleum

1968, Guns for San Sebastian, Father Joseph

1967, A Guide for the Married Man, Technical Adviser

1966, Batman (TV Show), Zoltan Zorba

1966, Tarzan (TV Show), Dr. Singleton

1964, Daniel Boone (TV Show), Jed Tolson

1961, Ben Casey (TV Show), Dr. David Zorba

1961, Cain's Hundred (TV Show), Louis Speckter

1961, The Defenders (TV Show), Dr. Graham

1960, The Westerner (TV Show), Old Man McKeen

1960, The Islanders (TV Show), Papa Mathews

1960, The Law and Mr. Jones (TV Show), Martin Berger

1960, The Robert Herridge Theater (TV Show), Mr. Bates

1959, Ben-Hur, Simonides

1959, Bonanza (TV Show), Joshua Norton

1959, Play of the Week (TV Show)

1959, The Untouchables (TV Show), Luigi Valcone

1958, The Barbarian and the Geisha, Henry Heusken

1958, Naked City (TV Show), Lazslo Lubasz

1958, Shirley Temple Theatre (TV Show), Zacharias

1958, The Donna Reed Show (TV Show)

1958, Westinghouse Desilu Playhouse (TV Show), Younkers

1957, Les Espions, Sam Cooper

1956, Playhouse 90 (TV Show), Carpenter, Grandy, Schiller

1955, Alfred Hitchcock Presents (TV Show), Hal Ballew, The Abbot

1951, I Can Get It for You Wholesale, Sam Cooper

1951, The Day the Earth Stood Still, Professor Jacob Barnhardt

1951, Under the Gun, Samuel Gower

1950, The Asphalt Jungle, Doc Erwin Riedenschneider

1949, Rope of Sand, Dr. Francis Hunter

1949, The Accused, Dr. Romley

1949, The Big Story (TV Show), Hal Studer

1947, 13 Rue Madeleine, Mayor Galimard

1947, Gentleman's Agreement, Professor Fred Lieberman

1939, Gunga Din, Gunga Din

1937, Lost Horizon, High Lama

1934, The Scarlet Empress, Grand Duke Peter

1934, We Live Again, Gregory Simonson

CPSIA information can be obtained
at www.ICGtesting.com
Printed in the USA
FFOW04n1537070214
3485FF